Sentences, Paragraphs, and Beyond

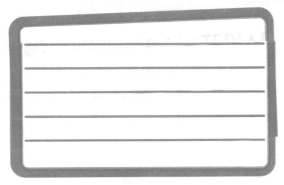

Sentences, Paragraphs, and Beyond

A Worktext with Readings

Third Edition

Lee Brandon

Mt. San Antonio College

Kelly Brandon

Santa Ana College

Houghton Mifflin Company   Boston   New York

To Shane, Lauren, Jarrett, and Matthew

Senior Sponsoring Editor: Mary Jo Southern
Associate Editor: Kellie Cardone
Editorial Associate: Danielle Richardson
Project Editor: Tracy Patruno
Senior Manufacturing Coordinator: Marie Barnes
Senior Marketing Manager: Nancy Lyman

Cover image: © Jacqui Morgan/SIS

Text credits appear on page 445, which constitutes an extension of the copyright page.

Printed in the U.S.A.

Library of Congress Catalog Card Number: 00-133891

Student Text ISBN: 0-618-04262-8
Instructor's Annotated Edition ISBN: 0-618-04263-6

456789-WEB-04   03   02   01

Contents

Chapter 21 Comparison and Contrast: Showing Similarities and Differences 347

Preface

Working on another edition of this textbook has given us yet another opportunity to improve our material through the evaluations of those who use it, as well as through observing what works in our own classes. We believe that a good textbook should cover the field broadly but with direction, serve instructors with differing pedagogies and personalities, present instruction pertinent to the needs of society, and energize students to learn with enthusiasm. Such a vision must address an audience of both instructors and students, and we believe that *Sentences, Paragraphs, and Beyond*, Third Edition, will serve this two-part audience well. We have worked to produce a book that is comprehensive, adaptable, relevant, and stimulating.

Principal Features

Comprehensiveness

The text's three parts and the appendixes cover the full array of topics needed for developmental writing.

Part One: Writing Sentences includes parts of sentence structure, phrases and clauses, kinds of sentences, sentence combining, sentence problems, pronoun use, modifiers, punctuation, and spelling.

Part Two: Writing Paragraphs and Beyond covers the writing process with instructions, examples, demonstrations, and exercises in freewriting, brainstorming, clustering, topic sentence writing, outlining, revising, and editing.

Part Three: Connecting Reading and Writing provides guidance in reading critically and writing summaries; practicing reading-related responses; and recognizing patterns such as process, cause and effect, and exemplification. Reading selections by students and professional writers are dually grouped by pattern and theme.

Appendixes cover parts of speech, taking tests, writing a letter of application and a résumé, and a guide for ESL students.

Adaptability

The first two parts, "Writing Sentences" and "Writing Paragraphs and Beyond," move from short to long units of discourse. The third part, "Connecting Reading and Writing," adds reading selections and suggestions for written responses. The instructor can move easily within and between the parts according to his or her pedagogy and students' needs.

These are some of the basic course needs that *Sentences, Paragraphs, and Beyond* can serve:

- a course dealing almost exclusively with paragraph writing

- a course beginning with paragraph writing and ending with short-essay writing

- a course mixing paragraph and essay writing with assignments of different patterns of writing (paragraphs for simpler forms such as description and exemplification, for example, and essays for more complicated forms such as cause and effect, comparison and contrast, and argument)

- a course mixing paragraph and essay writing with assignments that vary from student to student, depending on students' abilities and student-instructor contract or other agreement
- a course (a one-unit design) dealing almost exclusively with grammar and the sentence

Relevance and Stimulation

Each requires the other. Relevance minus stimulation equals dullness. Stimulation minus relevance equals emptiness. Presented at the developmental level without condescension, the text has been successfully class-tested with college students. The examples and reading passages reflect a wide range of current and enduring concerns, as these section titles show: "Growing Pains and Pleasures," "Prized and Despised Possessions," "Living in the Age of Irritations," "The Joy and Grief of Work," "Compulsions and Addictions," "Cultural Blends and Clashes," and "To Regulate or Not."

Changes in and Enhancements to the Third Edition

The third edition emphasizes writing the sentence, paragraph, and short essay. It includes

- more than 60 percent new reading selections
- computer-related writing tips incorporated into the text
- many exercises that require the writing of sentences
- more emphasis on organization and revision
- new content for many exercises
- a comprehensive chapter on argumentation and critical thinking, with special consideration of logic and examples of persuasive paragraphs and essays
- more activities pertaining to reading-related writing with a separate chapter (discussion, examples, and exercises) on types: summary, reaction, and two-part responses
- examples of work by students who have completed writing assignments in stages (shown with seven forms of discourse)
- career-related writing topics added to reading-related topics and general topics
- a Self-Evaluation Chart to help students track their needs and goals and to promote self-reliance
- a Writing Process Worksheet suitable for photocopying and designed to provide guidance for students and to conserve time and effort for instructors
- culturally diverse anthology materials grouped according to topic and pattern of writing
- cartoons that irreverently and hilariously make instructional points

Computer-Related Writing

In serving a wide range of students, including both those who do and those who do not yet have easy access to computers, this edition incorporates computer-assisted writing in several ways:

- Discusses the basic functions of features on word processors, such as spell checker, style checker, and thesaurus, pointing out the advantages of electronic devices, while cautioning against their infallibility.

- Includes numerous references to word processing, alternative assignments involving the Internet, two exercises with computer-related narratives ("Exploding Cyborg" and "Cyberella"), and an article that allows students to combine interests, computer skills, and writing strategies for discussion and assignments ("Are Kids Too Tangled in the Web?" Chapter 23).

Support Material for Instructors

The Instructor's Annotated Edition contains immediate answers for excercises and activities, along with the following support:

- The Instructors Guide (all parts included in IAE)

- Reproducible quizzes for sentence writing and many professional essays

- Suggestions for effective and time-saving approaches to instruction

- A sample syllabus

Software resources include

- *English Microlab* for PC and Macintosh. Teaches and reinforces the basics of grammar, punctuation, and mechanics. An accompanying data disk allows instructors to manage and record group results.

- *Expressways,* Second Edition, for PC, Macintosh, and Windows. Interactive software that guides students as they write and revise paragraphs and essays.

Acknowledgments

We are grateful to the following instructors who have reviewed this textbook: Marilyn Black, Middlesex Community College; Kathryn Beckwith, Arizona State University; John Bell, New York City Technical College; Christena T. Biggs, DePauw University; Wendy Bishop, Florida State University; Betty Bluman, Community College of Allegheny; Marlene Bosanko, Tacoma Community College; Elizabeth Breen, Pierce College; Deborah Burson-Smith, Southern University–A&M; Janet Cutshall, Sussex County Community College; Eddye Gallagher, Tarrant County Junior College; Nicole Greene, University of Southwestern Louisiana; Roslyn J. Harper, Trident Technical College; Carolyn G. Hartnett, College of the Mainland; Bradley S. Hayden, Western Michigan University; Grady Hinton, Jr., St. Louis Community College at Forest Park; Wayne P. Hubert, Chaffey Community College; Anna Jo Johnson, Community College of Western Kentucky University; James C. McDonald, University of Southwestern Louisiana; James Rice, Quinsigamond Community College; Athene Sallee, Forsyth Technical Community College; Susan Schiller, University of California–Davis; Ann Shackleford, Bacone College; and David White, Walters State Community College. Thanks also go to the faculty members at Mt. San Antonio College (with special appreciation to the Basic Courses Review Committee) and Santa Ana College for their suggestions.

We deeply appreciate the work of freelance editors Marilyn Weissman and Margaret Roll, Nancy Benjamin of Books By Design, Inc., as well as our colleagues at Houghton Mifflin: Mary Jo Southern, Kellie Cardone, Danielle Richardson, Nancy Lyman, and Tracy Patruno.

We are grateful to our families for their cheerful, enduring support, especially Sharon, Erin, Jeanne, Michael, Shane, Lauren, Jarrett, and Matthew.

Student Overview

"As you work with writing skills, don't compare yourself with others. Compare yourself then with yourself now."

Writing effectively is not as difficult as you may think. You can learn to be a good writer if you practice effective techniques. The operative words are the last three: "practice effective techniques." A good piece of written material includes clear organization, solid content, and good use of language skills. You should have something to say, present it in appropriate order, and write correctly. All of those points will be covered in the three main parts of this book: Writing Sentences, Writing Paragraphs and Beyond, and Connecting Reading and Writing.

Part One: Writing Sentences

The first part, Writing Sentences, concentrates on effectiveness. Beginning with the simplest aspects of sentences, namely subjects and verbs, the text moves to the larger word units of clauses and sentences, with their numerous patterns. It shows you the difference between complete sentences and incomplete sentences, between sound and unsound arrangements of words, and between correct and incorrect punctuation. While giving you the opportunity to experiment and develop your own style, it leads you through the problem areas of verbs, pronouns, and modifiers. If you are not sure when to use *lie* and when to use *lay,* when to use *who* and when to use *whom,* or when to use *good* and when to use *well,* this book

1

can help you. If you're not sure whether the standard expression is *between you and I* or *between you and me,* or if you're not sure about the difference between a colon and a semicolon, you will find the answers here. That line of *if* statements could be applied to almost every page in this book. Perhaps you are not sure of the correct answer to most of these questions. The good news is that by the end of the course, you will be sure—and if your "sure" is still a bit shaky, then you will know where to find the rules, examples, and discussion in this book.

The text in Part One follows a pattern: rules, examples, exercises, and writing activity. Again, you learn by practicing sound principles. As you complete assignments, you can check your answers to selected exercises in the Answer Key in the back of the book so that you can monitor your understanding.

Part Two: Writing Paragraphs and Beyond

The second part, Writing Paragraphs and Beyond, presents writing as a process, not as something that is supposed to emerge complete on demand. Writing begins with a topic, either generated or provided, and moves through stages of exploration, organization, development, revision, and editing. If you have suffered, at least at times, from writer's block, this book is for you. If you have sometimes produced material that was organized poorly so that you did not receive full credit for what you knew, then this book is for you. If you have sometimes had ideas, but you did not fully develop them, so that your work was judged as "sketchy" or "lacking in content," then this book is for you.

Part Three: Connecting Reading and Writing

The third part, Connecting Reading and Writing, gives you models of good writing and lively ideas for discussion and writing. The selections are presented with observations and exercises to help you develop effective reading techniques. In working with these assignments, you may discover that you can learn a great deal from other writers—if you can read perceptively, understanding both what the writers say and how they say it.

Some reading selections are paragraphs and others are essays. They are rich in invention, style, and cultural perspective. Several are written by celebrated authors such as Maya Angelou, Gary Soto, and N. Scott Momaday. Some are written by students, individuals like you who entered college, worked on language skills, and learned. Well-written and fresh in thought, these models are especially useful because they were done as college English assignments. Each of the students whose writing is included in this book learned writing skills in a developmental program before taking freshman composition. Several of them also studied in English as a Second Language (ESL) programs.

The selections are grouped in two ways: according to theme and according to form of writing. For example, the writings in "Prized and Despised Possessions" are all descriptions. Of course, no one selection is entirely in a single form, although one may predominate. Many forms are presented—narration, description, exemplification, process analysis, cause and effect, comparison and contrast, and argument—because you will need to use many of these forms in your college work. Topics such as "Discuss causes of (*a war, depression, a disease*)" and "compare and contrast (*two theories, two leaders, two programs*)" abound across the curriculum. Studying the principles for these forms and reading good examples of pieces that demonstrate the effective use of these forms will help you get full credit for what you know, in your college classes and elsewhere.

Appendixes

This book also has four appendixes, a collection of support materials that were too valuable to be omitted from a college book on writing: Parts of Speech, Taking Tests, Writing a Letter of Application and a Résumé, and Brief Guide for ESL Students.

Strategies for Self-Improvement

Here are some strategies you can follow to make the best use of this book and to jump-start the improvement in your writing skills

1. *Be active and systematic in learning.* Take advantage of your instructor's expertise by being an active class member—one who takes notes, asks questions, and contributes to discussion. Become dedicated to systematic learning: Determine your needs, decide what to do, and do it. Make learning a part of your everyday thinking and behavior.

2. *Read widely.* Samuel Johnson, a great English scholar, once said he didn't want to read anything by people who had written more than they had read. William Faulkner, a Nobel Prize winner in literature, said, "Read, read, read. Read everything—trash, classics, good and bad, and see how writers do it." Read to learn technique, to acquire ideas, and to be stimulated to write. Especially read to satisfy your curiosity and to receive pleasure. If reading is a main component of your course, approach it as systematically as you do writing.

3. *Keep a journal.* Keep a journal even though it may not be required in your particular class. It is a good practice to jot down your observations in a notebook. Here are some topics for daily, or almost daily, journal writing:

   • Summarize, evaluate, or react to reading assignments.

   • Summarize, evaluate, or react to what you see on television and in movies and what you read in newspapers and in magazines.

   • Describe and narrate situations or events you experience.

   • Write about career-related matters you encounter in other courses or on the job.

     Your journal entries may read like an intellectual diary, a record of what you are thinking about at certain times. Keeping a journal will help you to understand reading material better, to develop more language skills, and to think more clearly—as well as to become more confident and to write more easily so that writing becomes a comfortable, everyday activity. Your entries may also provide subject material for longer, more carefully crafted pieces. The most important thing is to get into the habit of writing something each day.

4. *Evaluate your writing skills.* Use the Self-Evaluation Chart inside the front cover of this book to assess your writing skills by listing problem areas you need to work on. You may be adding to these lists throughout the entire term. Drawing on your instructor's comments, make notes on matters such as organization, development, content, spelling, vocabulary, diction, grammar, sentence structure, punctuation, and capitalization. Use this chart for self-motivated study assignments and as a checklist in all stages of writing. As you master each problem area, you can erase it or cross it out. Most of the elements you record in your Self-Evaluation Chart probably are covered in *Sentences, Paragraphs, and Beyond.* The table of contents, the index, and the Correction Chart on the inside back cover of the book will direct you to the additional instruction you decide you need.

- *Organization/Development/Content:* List aspects of your writing, including the techniques of all stages of the writing process, such as freewriting, brainstorming, and clustering; the phrasing of a good topic sentence or thesis; and the design, growth, and refinement of your ideas.

- *Spelling/Vocabulary/Diction:* List common spelling words marked as incorrect on your college assignments. Here, *common* means words that you use often. If you are misspelling these words now, you may have been doing so for years. Look at your list. Is there a pattern to your misspellings? Consult the Spelling section in the Handbook for a set of useful rules. Whatever it takes, master the words on your list. Continue to add troublesome words as you accumulate assignments. If your vocabulary is imprecise or your diction is inappropriate (if you use slang, trite expressions, or words that are too informal), note those problems as well.

- *Grammar/Sentence Structure:* List recurring problems in your grammar or sentence structure. Use the symbols and page references listed on the Correction Chart (inside back cover of this book) or look up the problem in the index.

- *Punctuation/Capitalization:* Treat these problems the same way you treat grammar problems. Note that the Punctuation and Capitalization section in the Handbook numbers some rules; therefore, you can often give exact locations of the remedies for your problems.

  Here is an example of how your chart might be used.

Self-Evaluation Chart

Organization/ Development/ Content	Spelling/ Vocabulary/ Diction	Grammar/ Sentence Structure	Punctuation/ Capitalization
needs more specific support such as examples, 299	avoid slang, 231	fragments, 55	difference between semicolons and commas, 172
refine outline, 224	avoid clichés such as "be there for me," 231	subject-verb agreement, 93	comma after long introductory modifier, 164, #2
use clear topic sentence, 221	it's, its, 201	comma splice, 68	
	you're, your, 203	vary sentence patterns, 22	comma in compound sentence, 164, #1
	rec<u>e</u>ive, rule on, 198		

5. *Use the Writing Process Worksheet.* Record details about each of your assignments, such as the due date, topic, length, and form. The worksheet will also remind you of the stages of the writing process: explore, organize, and write. A blank Writing Process Worksheet for you to photocopy for assignments appears on page 6. Discussed in Chapter 1, it illustrates student work in almost every chapter. Your instructor may ask you to complete the form and submit it with your assignments.

6. *Take full advantage of technology.* Although using a word processor will not by itself make you a better writer, it will enable you to write and revise more swiftly as you move, alter, and delete material with a few keystrokes. Devices such as the thesaurus, spell checker, grammar checker, and style checker will help you

revise and edit. Many colleges have writing labs with good instruction and facilities for networking and researching complicated topics. The Internet, used wisely, can provide resource material for compositions.

7. *Be positive.* To improve your English skills, write with freedom, but revise and edit with rigor. Work with your instructor to set attainable goals, and proceed at a reasonable pace. Soon, seeing what you have mastered and checked off your list will give you a sense of accomplishment.

Finally, don't compare yourself with others. Compare yourself then with yourself now and, as you improve, consider yourself what you are—a student on the path toward effective writing, a student on the path toward success.

Writing Process Worksheet

TITLE _____

NAME _____ DUE DATE _____

ASSIGNMENT In the space below, write whatever you need to know about your assignment, including information about the topic, audience, pattern of writing, length, whether to include a rough draft or revised drafts, and whether your paper must be typed.

STAGE ONE **Explore** Freewrite, brainstorm (list), cluster, or take notes as directed by your instructor. Use the back of this page or separate paper if you need more space.

STAGE TWO **Organize** Write a topic sentence or thesis; label the subject and the treatment parts.

Write an outline or an outline alternative.

STAGE THREE **Write** On separate paper, write and then revise your paper as many times as necessary for coherence, language (usage, tone, and diction), unity, emphasis, support, and sentences (CLUESS). Read your paper aloud to hear and correct any grammatical errors or awkward-sounding sentences.

Edit any problems in fundamentals, such as capitalization, omissions, punctuation, and spelling (COPS).

PART **One**

Writing
Sentences

1

Subjects and Verbs

"Look carefully and you will see that each sentence has a skeleton and that the skeleton's two indispensable bones are the subject and the verb."

The two most important parts of any sentence are the subject and the verb. The **subject** is who or what causes the action or expresses a state of being. The **verb** indicates what the subject is doing or is being. Many times the subject and verb taken together carry the meaning of the sentence. Consider this example:

> The <u>woman</u> <u>left</u> for work.
>   subject   verb

The subject *woman* and the verb *left* indicate the basic content of the sentence while providing structure.

Subjects

The **simple subject** of a sentence is usually a single noun or pronoun.

> The judge's <u>reputation</u> for order in the courtroom is well known.
>   simple subject

The **complete subject** is the simple subject with all its modifiers—that is, with all the words that describe or qualify it.

<u>The judge's reputation for order in the courtroom</u> is well known.
                    complete subject

To more easily understand and identify simple subjects of sentences, you may want to review the following information about nouns and pronouns. See Appendix A, p. 396, for more information about all eight parts of speech.

Nouns

Nouns are naming words. Nouns may name persons, animals, plants, places, things, substances, qualities, or ideas—for example, *Bart, armadillo, Mayberry, tree, rock, cloud, love, ghost, music, virtue.*

Pronouns

A pronoun is a word that is used in place of a noun.

- Pronouns that can be used as subjects of sentences may represent specific persons or things and are called personal pronouns:

I	*we*
you	*you*
he, she, it	*they*

  Example: <u>They</u> recommended my sister for the coaching position.
                 subject

- Indefinite pronouns refer to nouns (persons, place, things) in a general way:

  each   everyone   nobody   somebody

  Example: <u>Everyone</u> wants a copy of that photograph.
                 subject

- Other pronouns point out particular things:

  Singular: *this, that*   Plural: *these, those*

  This is my treasure.   *These* are my jewels.

  That is your junk.   *Those* are your trinkets.

- Still other pronouns introduce questions:

  Which is the best CD player?

  What are the main ingredients in a Twinkie?

  Who understands this computer command?

Caution: To be the subject of a sentence, a pronoun must stand alone.

  This is a treasure. (Subject is *this;* pronoun stands alone.)

  This *treasure* is mine. (Subject is *treasure. This* is an adjective—a word that describes a noun; *this* describes *treasure.*)

Compound Subjects

A subject may be **compound.** That is, it may consist of two or more subjects, usually joined by *and* or *or,* that function together.

The *prosecutor* and the *attorney* for the defense made opening statements.

He and his *friends* listened carefully.

Steven, Juan, and *Alicia* attended the seminar. (Note the placement of commas for three or more subjects.)

Implied Subjects

A subject may be **implied,** or understood. An imperative sentence—a sentence that gives a command—has *you* as the implied subject.

(You) Sit in that chair, please.

(You) Now take the oath.

(You) Please read the notes carefully.

Trouble Spot: Prepositional Phrases

A **prepositional phrase** is made up of a preposition (a word such as *at, in, of, to, with*) and one or more nouns or pronouns with their modifiers: *at the time, by the jury, in the courtroom, to the judge and the media, with controlled anger.* Be careful not to confuse the subject of a sentence with the noun or pronoun (known as the object of the preposition) in a prepositional phrase. The object of a preposition cannot be the subject of a sentence.

The <u>car</u> <u>with the dents</u> is mine.
   subject   prepositional
   phrase

The subject of the sentence is *car.* The word *dents* is the object of the preposition *with* and cannot be the subject of the sentence.

<u>Most</u> <u>of the pie</u> has been eaten.
subject prepositional
   phrase

The <u>person</u> <u>in the middle</u> <u>of the crowd</u> has disappeared.
   subject   prepositional   prepositional
   phrase   phrase

Trouble Spot: The Words *Here* and *There*

The words *here* and *there* are adverbs (used as filler words) and cannot be subjects.

There is no <u>problem</u>.
   subject

Here is the <u>issue</u>.
   subject

| Exercise 1 | **FINDING SUBJECTS** |

Circle the subjects in the following sentences. You will have to supply the subject of one sentence. (See Answer Key for answers.)

1. Mahatma Gandhi gave his life for India and for peace.

2. Through a practice of nonviolent resistance, he led his people to freedom from the British.

3. Ponder his preference for behavior rather than accomplishment.

4. There was only good in his behavior and in his accomplishments.

5. His fasts, writings, and speeches inspired the people of India.

6. He taught his people self-sufficiency in weaving cloth and making salt for themselves against British law.

7. Gandhi urged the tolerance of all religions.

8. Finally, the British granted freedom to India.

9. Some leaders in India and a few foreign agitators questioned the freedom of religion.

10. Gandhi, the Indian prince of peace, was killed by an intolerant religious leader.

| Exercise 2 | **FINDING SUBJECTS** |

Circle the subjects in the following sentences. You will have to supply the subject of one sentence.

1. More than two hundred years ago, some tractors were powered by steam.

2. They could travel at about three miles per hour for about ten minutes.

3. Consider that information in relation to the following material.

4. There was a great future ahead for these self-powered vehicles.

5. About a hundred years later, in 1897, Freelan O. Stanley and his associates produced the Stanley steamer, the best-known steam automobile.

6. Around the same time, William Morrison built an electric car.

7. Without polluting the atmosphere, it could go twenty miles an hour.

8. After traveling for about fifty miles, its batteries had to be recharged.

9. Meanwhile in Germany, Gottlieb Daimler, Karl Benz, and their engineers were developing the internal-combustion engine.

10. In the 1890s, the first successful gasoline-powered automobiles took to the roads.

Verbs

Verbs show action or express being in relation to the subject of a sentence.

Types of Verbs

Action verbs indicate movement or accomplishment in idea or deed. Someone can "consider the statement" or "hit the ball." Here are other examples:

> She *sees* the arena.
>
> He *bought* the book.
>
> They *adopted* the child.
>
> He *understood* her main theories.

Being verbs indicate existence. Few in number, they include *is, was, were, am,* and *are*.

> The movie *is* sad.
>
> The book *was* comprehensive.
>
> They *were* responsible.
>
> I *am* concerned.
>
> We *are* organized.

Verb Phrases

Verbs may occur as single words or as phrases. A **verb phrase** is made up of a main verb and one or more helping verbs such as the following:

is	*was*	*can*	*have*	*do*	*may*	*shall*
are	*were*	*could*	*had*	*does*	*might*	*should*
am		*will*	*has*	*did*	*must*	
		would				

Here are some sentences that contain verb phrases:

> The judge *has presided* over many capital cases.
>
> His rulings seldom *are overturned* on appeal.

Trouble Spot: Words Such As *Never, Not,* and *Hardly*

Never, not, hardly, seldom, and so on, are modifiers, not verbs.

> The attorney could *not* win the case without key witnesses.
>
> (*Not* is an adverb. The verb phrase is *could win*.)

> The jury could *hardly* hear the witness. (*Hardly* is an adverb; *could hear* is the verb phrase.)

Compound Verbs

Verbs that are joined by a word such as *and* or *or* are called **compound verbs.**

> As a district attorney, Barbara *had presented* and *had won* famous cases.

> She *prepared* carefully and *presented* her ideas with clarity.

> We *will go* out for dinner or *skip* it entirely.

Trouble Spot: Verbals

Do not confuse verbs with verbals. **Verbals** are verblike words in certain respects, but they do not function as verbs. They function as other parts of speech. There are three kinds of verbals.

An *infinitive* is made up of the word *to* and a verb. An infinitive provides information, but, unlike the true verb, it is not tied to the subject of the sentence. It acts as a noun or describing unit.

> He wanted *to get* a bachelor's degree.

> *To get* a bachelor's degree was his main objective.

In the first example, the word *wanted* is the verb for the subject *He.* The word *get* follows *to; to get* is an infinitive.

A *gerund* is a verblike word ending in *-ing* that acts as a noun.

> *Retrieving* her e-mail was her main objective.

> She thought about *retrieving* her e-mail.

Retrieving in each sentence acts as a noun.

A *participle* is a verblike word that usually has an *-ing* or an *-ed* ending.

> *Walking* to town in the dark, he lost his way.

> *Wanted* by the FBI, she was on the run.

> The *starved* dog barked for food.

In the first example, the word *walking* answers the question *when.* In the second example, the word *wanted* answers the question *which one.* In the third example, *starved* describes the dog. *Walking, wanted,* and *starved* are describing words; they are not the true verbs in the sentences.

Exercise 3	FINDING VERBS

Underline the verb(s) in each sentence. (See Answer Key for answers.)

1. Chimpanzees live and travel in social groups.

2. The composition of these groups varies in age and gender.

3. The habitat of the chimpanzees is mainly forests.

4. They spend more time in the trees than on the ground.

5. Each night they make a nest of branches and leaves in trees.

6. Sometimes a proud male will beat on his chest.

7. Chimpanzees are violent at times but usually live peacefully.

8. After finding food, a chimp hoots and shakes branches.

9. Other chimps hear the commotion and go to the food source.

10. Chimp tools, such as leaf sponges and sticks, are primitive.

Exercise 4	FINDING VERBS

Underline the verb(s) in each sentence.

1. Chimpanzees share many features with human beings.

2. More than 90 percent of basic genetic make-up is shared.

3. Both human beings and chimps can use reason.

4. Chimps have a remarkable talent for communication.

5. Chimps do not have the capacity for human speech.

6. However, chimps can use other symbols.

7. In one experiment, chimps learned American Sign Language.

8. Chimps can learn a complex system of language.

9. Chimp scholar Washoe has learned more than 160 signs and can ask questions.

10. Another chimp, Lana, uses a computer.

Location of Subjects and Verbs

Although the subject usually appears before the verb, it may follow the verb instead:

Into the court <u>stumbled</u> the <u>defendant</u>.
            verb   subject

From tiny acorns <u>grow</u> mighty <u>oaks</u>.
          verb   subject

There <u>was</u> little <u>support</u> for him in the audience.
    verb   subject

Here <u>are</u> your <u>books</u> and your <u>papers</u>.
       verb   **subject**   **subject**

Verb phrases are often broken up in a question. Do not overlook a part of the verb that is separated from another in a question such as "Where had the defendant gone on that fateful night?" If you have trouble finding the verb phrase, recast the question, making it into a statement form: "The defendant *had gone* where on that fateful night." The result will not necessarily be a smooth or complete statement, but you will be able to see the basic elements more easily.

Can the defense lawyer *control* the direction of the trial?

Change the question to a statement to find the verb phrase:

The defense lawyer *can control* the direction of the trial.

As you will see in Chapter 2, a sentence may have more than one set of subjects and verbs. In the following passage, the subjects are circled; the verbs are underlined.

(We) <u>should be</u> careful to get out of an experience only the wisdom

(that) <u>is</u> in it—and <u>stop</u> there; lest (we) <u>be</u> like the cat (that) <u>sits</u> down on

a hot stove lid. (She) <u>will</u> never <u>sit</u> down on a hot stove lid again—and

(that) <u>is</u> well; but also (she) <u>will</u> never <u>sit</u> down on a cold one any more.

Mark Twain, *Epitaph for His Daughter*

| Exercise 5 | **FINDING SUBJECTS AND VERBS** |

Circle the subject(s) and underline the verb(s) in the following sentences. You will have to supply the subject for one sentence. (See Answer Key for answers.)

1. Read this exercise and learn about the Aztec empire in Mexico.

2. Aztec cities were as large as those in Europe at that time.

3. Government and religion were important concerns.

4. There was little difference between the two institutions.

5. They built huge temples to their gods and sacrificed human beings.

6. The religious ceremonies related mainly to their concerns about plentiful harvests.

7. Aztec society had nobles, commoners, serfs, and slaves.

8. The family included a husband, a wife, children, and some relatives of the husband.

9. At the age of ten, boys went to school, and girls either went to school or learned domestic skills at home.

10. The Aztecs wore loose-fitting garments, they lived in adobe houses, and they ate tortillas.

11. Scholars in this culture developed a calendar of 365 days.

12. Huge Aztec calendars of stone are now in museums.

13. The Aztec language was similar to that of the Comanche and Pima Indians.

14. The Aztec written language was pictographic and represented ideas and sounds.

15. Both religion and government required young men to pursue warfare.

16. By pursuing warfare, the soldiers could capture others for slaves and sacrifice, and enlarge the Aztec empire.

17. In 1519, Hernando Cortez landed in Mexico.

18. He was joined by Indians other than Aztecs.

19. After first welcoming Cortez and his army, the Aztecs then rebelled.

20. The Spaniards killed Emperor Montezuma II, and then they defeated the Aztecs.

Exercise 6	**FINDING SUBJECTS AND VERBS**

Circle the subject(s) and underline the verb(s) in the following sentences.

1. Who are the Eskimos?

2. Where did they come from?

3. How do they live?

4. How has their way of life changed in the last century?

5. These questions are all important.

6. There may be different views on some of the answers.

7. They live in the Arctic from Russia east to Greenland.

8. Their ancestors came from Siberia in Northern Asia

9. They have learned to live in a land of perpetual snow.

10. The word *Eskimo* means *eaters of raw meat* in a Native American language.

11. Their own name for themselves is *Inuit* or *Yuit,* meaning *people.*

12. For hundreds of years, their homes during hunting and fishing excursions were made of blocks of ice or packed snow called *igloos.*

13. They ate the raw flesh of caribou, seals, whales, and fish.

14. During the 1800s, the whalers enlisted the Eskimos as helpers.

15. Later the traders came and bought furs from the Eskimos.

16. The traders and whalers brought guns, tools, technology, and disease to the Eskimos.

17. The Eskimos used their new harpoons and guns, and killed more game.

18. Their simple, traditional way of life changed.

19. Now most Eskimos live in settlements.

20. Despite the many changes, Eskimos still treasure their ancient ways.

Chapter Review: Subjects and Verbs

The **subject** carries out the action or expresses the state of being in a sentence. The **verb** indicates what the subject is doing or is being.

Subjects

You can recognize the **simple subject** by asking who or what causes the action or expresses the state of being found in the verb.

1. The **simple subject** can be single or compound.

>My *friend* and *I* have much in common. (compound subject)

>My *friend* brought a present. (single subject)

2. The command, or **imperative,** sentence has a "you" as the implied subject and no stated subject.

>(*You* understood) Read the notes.

3. Although the subject usually appears before the verb, it may follow the verb.

>There was *justice* in the verdict.

4. The object of a preposition cannot be a subject.

>The *chairperson* (subject) of the department (object of the preposition) directs the discussion.

Verbs

Verbs show action or express being in relation to the subject.

1. **Action verbs** suggest movement or accomplishment in idea or deed.

>He *dropped* the book. (movement)

>He *read* the book. (accomplishment)

2. **Being verbs** indicate existence.

> They *were* concerned.

3. Verbs may occur as single words or phrases.

> He *led* the charge. (single word)
>
> She *is leading* the charge. (phrase)

4. A **verb phrase** may be separated in a question.

> Where *had* the defendant *gone* on that fateful night?

5. Compound verbs are joined by a word such as *and* or *or.*

> She *worked* for twenty-five years and *retired.*

6. Words such as *never, not,* and *hardly* are not verbs; they modify verbs.

7. Verbals are not verbs; **verbals** are verblike words that function as other parts of speech.

> *Singing* (gerund acting as a noun subject) is fun.
>
> I want *to sing.* (infinitive acting as a noun object)
>
> *Singing* (participle acting as a modifier), he walked in the rain.

Chapter Review Exercises

Review 1	FINDING SUBJECTS AND VERBS

Circle the subject(s) and underline the verb(s) in the following sentences. You will have to supply the subject for one sentence. (See Answer Key for answers.)

1. Read this exercise carefully.

2. What causes earthquakes?

3. How much damage can they do?

4. Earthquakes shake the earth.

5. There is no simple answer to the question of cause.

6. The earth is covered by rock plates.

7. Instead of merely covering, they are in constant motion.

8. These plates bump into each other and then pass over each other.

9. The rocks are squeezed and stretched.

10. They pull apart or pile up and cause breaks in the earth's surface.

11. These breaks are called *faults.*

12. The formation of a fault is an earthquake.

13. During the breaking or shifting, a seismic wave travels across the earth's surface.

14. These quaking vibrations are especially destructive near the point of the breaking or shifting.

15. Their force is equal to as much as ten thousand times that of an atomic bomb.

16. For many years, scientists have tried to predict earthquakes.

17. There has been little success in their endeavors.

18. Earthquakes are identified only after the fact.

19. Some states, such as California, experience many earthquakes.

20. Somewhere in the earth, a quake of some magnitude is almost certainly occurring now.

Review 2	FINDING SUBJECTS AND VERBS

Circle the subject(s) and underline the verb(s) in the following sentences. You will have to supply the subject for one sentence.

1. Consider this information about Puerto Rico.

2. Just where is Puerto Rico?

3. What do the words *Puerto Rico* mean?

4. Are Puerto Ricans citizens?

5. How is Puerto Rico different from our states?

6. Will it ever become a state?

7. The Commonwealth of Puerto Rico is located southeast of Florida.

8. *Puerto Rico* means "rich port."

9. Puerto Rico became a U.S. territory in 1898 after the Spanish-American War.

10. It became a commonwealth with its own constitution in 1952.

11. Puerto Ricans are citizens of the United States.

12. They cannot vote in presidential elections and do not pay federal income taxes.

13. On several occasions, they have voted not to become a state.

14. However, there are many in favor of statehood.

15. The majority of the citizens speak Spanish.

16. Their economy is based on manufacturing, fishing, and agriculture.

17. The Caribbean National Forest is treasured by Puerto Ricans and visitors.

18. There in this tropical rain forest parrots and orchids can be seen.

19. Tourists by the thousands visit the Phosphorescent Bay at La Parguera.

20. On moonless nights, the phosphorescent plankton light the water.

Review 3	**WRITING SENTENCES WITH SUBJECTS AND VERBS**

Using the topic of work, *write five sentences. For variety, include one sentence with a compound subject, one with a compound verb, one with the verb before the subject, and one with the subject followed by a prepositional phrase. Circle the subjects and underline the verbs.*

1. _____

_____

2. _____

_____

3. _____

_____

4. _____

_____

5. _____

_____

2

Kinds of Sentences

"Is it not curious that though the English language has about two million words, we writers have only four ways of arranging them in basic sentence patterns?"

There are four kinds of basic sentences in English. They are called simple, compound, complex, and compound-complex. The terms may be new to you, but if you can recognize subjects and verbs, with a little instruction and practice you should be able to identify and write any of the four kinds of sentences. The only new idea to master is the concept of the *clause.*

Clauses

A **clause** is a group of words with a subject and a verb that functions as a part or all of a complete sentence. There are two kinds of clauses: independent (main) and dependent (subordinate).

    Independent Clause: I have the money.

    Dependent Clause: When I have the money

Independent Clauses

An *independent (main) clause* is a group of words with a subject and verb that can stand alone and make sense. An independent clause expresses a complete thought by itself and can be written as a separate sentence.

Sabrina plays the bass guitar.

The manager is not at fault.

Dependent Clauses

A *dependent clause* is a group of words with a subject and verb that depends on the main clause to give it meaning.

since Carlotta came home (no meaning alone)

Since Carlotta came home, her mother has been happy. (has meaning)
   dependent clause   independent clause

because she was needed (no meaning alone)

Kachina stayed in the game because she was needed. (has meaning)
   independent clause   dependent clause

Relative Clauses

One type of dependent clause is called a *relative clause*. A relative clause begins with a relative pronoun, a pronoun such as *that, which,* or *who.* Relative pronouns *relate* the clause to another word in the sentence.

that fell last night (no meaning alone)

The snow that fell last night is nearly gone. (has meaning)
        dependent clause

In the sentence above, the relative pronoun *that* relates the dependent clause to the subject of the sentence, *snow.*

who stayed in the game (no meaning alone)

Kachina was the only one who stayed in the game.
   independent clause   dependent clause

In the sentence above, the relative pronoun *who* relates the dependent clause to the word *one.*

Trouble Spot: Phrases

A **phrase** is a group of words that go together. It differs from a clause in that a phrase does not have a subject and a verb. In Chapter 1, we discussed prepositional phrases (*in the house, beyond the horizon*) and saw some verbal phrases (infinitive phrase: *to go home;* participial phrase: *disconnected from the printer;* and gerund phrase: *running the computer*).

| Exercise 1 | IDENTIFYING CLAUSES AND PHRASES |

Identify the following groups of words as an independent, or main, clause (has a subject and verb and can stand alone); a dependent clause (has a subject and verb but cannot stand alone); or a phrase (a group of words that go together but do not have a subject and verb). Use these abbreviations: IC (independent clause), DC (dependent clause), or P (phrase).

_____   1. Under the table

_____   2. After I scanned the document

_____ 3. I scanned the document.

_____ 4. To find a fossil

_____ 5. Mr. Darwin found a fossil.

_____ 6. Over the bridge and through the woods

_____ 7. We chased the wind over the bridge and through the woods.

_____ 8. Which is on the floor

_____ 9. Find your new socks.

_____ 10. Because of the new guidelines

_____ 11. Standing on the corner

_____ 12. Why are we standing on the corner?

Types of Sentences

This section covers sentence types according to this principle: On the basis of the number and kinds of clauses it contains, a sentence may be classified as simple, compound, complex, or compound-complex. In the examples in the following table, the dependent clauses are italicized, and the independent clauses are underlined.

Type	Definition	Example
Simple	One independent clause	<u>She did the work well</u>.
Compound	Two or more independent clauses	<u>She did the work well</u>, and <u>she was paid well</u>.
Complex	One independent clause and one or more dependent clauses	*Because she did the work well,* <u>she was paid well</u>.
Compound-Complex	Two or more independent clauses and one or more dependent clauses	*Because she did the work well,* <u>she was paid well</u>, and <u>she was satisfied</u>.

Simple Sentences

A simple sentence consists of one independent clause and no dependent clauses. It may contain phrases and have more than one subject or verb.

The *lake looks* beautiful in the moonlight. (one subject and one verb)

The *Army, Navy,* and *Marines sent* troops to the disaster area. (three subjects and one verb)

We sang the old songs and *danced* happily at their wedding. (one subject and two verbs)

My *father, mother,* and *sister came* to the school play, *applauded* the performers, and *attended* the party afterwards. (three subjects and three verbs)

Exercise 2	**WRITING SIMPLE SENTENCES**

Write six simple sentences. The first five have been started for you.

1. This school _____

   _____

2. My desk _____

   _____

3. My friend _____

   _____

4. In the evening, I _____

   _____

5. Last night the _____

   _____

6. _____

   _____

Compound Sentences

A compound sentence consists of two or more independent clauses with no dependent clauses. Take, for example, the following two dependent clauses:

> He opened the drawer. He found his missing disk.

Here are two ways to join the independent clauses to form a compound sentence.

1. The two independent clauses can be connected by a connecting word called a coordinating conjunction. The coordinating conjunctions are *for, and, nor, but, or, yet, so.* (An easy way to remember them is to think of the acronym FANBOYS, which is made up of the first letter of each conjunction.)

   > He opened the drawer, *and* he found his missing disk.

   > He opened the drawer, *so* he found his missing disk.

   Use a comma before the coordinating conjunction (FANBOYS) between two independent clauses (unless the clauses are extremely short).

2. Another way to join independent clauses to form a compound sentence is to put a semicolon between the clauses.

   > He opened the drawer; he found his missing disk.

Exercise 3   **WRITING COMPOUND SENTENCES**

Write five compound sentences using coordinating conjunctions. The sentences have been started for you. Then write the same five compound sentences without the coordinating conjunctions. Use a semicolon to join the independent clauses.

1. He played well in the first quarter, but he _____

   _____

   _____

2. She was happy for a while, and then _____

   _____

   _____

3. The dog is our best friend, for _____

   _____

   _____

4. She is not the best player, nor is _____

   _____

   _____

5. I will try to help, but _____

   _____

   _____

6. _____

   _____

   _____

7. _____

   _____

   _____

8. _____

   _____

   _____

9. _____

_____

_____

10. _____

_____

_____

Complex Sentences

A complex sentence consists of one independent clause and one or more dependent clauses. In the following sentences, the dependent clauses are italicized.

> *When lilacs are in bloom,* we love to visit friends in the country. (one dependent clause and one independent clause)

> *Although it rained last night,* we decided to take the path *that led through the woods.* (one independent clause and two dependent clauses)

Punctuation tip: Use a comma after a dependent clause that appears before the main clause.

> *When the bus arrived,* we quickly boarded.

A relative clause (see page 23) can be the dependent clause in a complex sentence.

> I knew the actress *who played that part in the 1980s.*

Exercise 4	**WRITING COMPLEX SENTENCES**

Write six complex sentences. The first five have been started for you.

1. Although he did the work quickly, _____

_____

2. _____
because we got caught in a storm.

3. After you go to the party, _____

_____

4. Because you are smart, _____

_____

5. _____

_____ when he turned to leave.

6. _____

_____

Compound-Complex Sentences

A compound-complex sentence consists of two or more independent clauses and one or more dependent clauses.

Compound-Complex Sentence:	Albert enlisted in the Army, and Robert, who was his older brother, joined him a day later.
Independent Clauses:	Albert enlisted in the Army Robert joined him a day later
Dependent Clause:	who was his older brother
Compound-Complex Sentence:	Because Mr. Yamamoto was a talented teacher, he was voted teacher of the year, and his students prospered.
Independent Clauses:	he was voted teacher of the year his students prospered
Dependent Clause:	Because Mr. Yamamoto was a talented teacher

Exercise 5	**WRITING COMPOUND-COMPLEX SENTENCES**

Write six compound-complex sentences. The first five have been started for you.

1. Because he was my friend, I had to defend him, and I _____

_____

2. Although he started late, he finished rapidly, and he _____

_____

3. She had not eaten since the clock struck twelve, and she _____

_____

4. The man who was sick tried to rise, but _____

_____

5. If you want to leave, _____

_____

6. _____

_____

Procedure for Sentence Analysis

1. Underline all the verbs and circle all the subjects in the sentence.

2. Draw a box around each clause.

3. Label each box as either IC (independent clause) or DC (dependent clause).

4. Add up the number of each kind of clause and apply the following formula. (See the chart on p. 24 for a more detailed explanation and examples.)

   One IC = Simple

   Two or more ICs = Compound

   One IC and one or more DCs = Complex

   Two or more ICs and one or more DCs = Compound-Complex

   Example:

   DC

   | Although (he) <u>played</u> well all season, |

   IC

   | his (team) <u>lost</u> ten games and <u>finished</u> in last place. |

   1 DC + 1 IC = Complex

Exercise 6   **IDENTIFYING TYPES OF SENTENCES**

Indicate the kind of sentence by writing the appropriate letter(s) in the blank.

   S   *simple*
   CP   *compound*
   CX   *complex*
   CC   *compound-complex*

Underline the verbs and circle the subjects. Consider using labeled boxes as shown above. (See Answer Key for answers.)

_____ 1. The most popular sport in the world is soccer.

_____ 2. People in ancient China and Japan had a form of soccer, and even Rome had a game that resembled soccer.

_____ 3. The game as it is played today got its start in England.

_____ 4. In the Middle Ages, whole towns played soccer on Shrove Tuesday.

_____ 5. Goals were built at opposite ends of town, and hundreds of people who lived in those towns would play on each side.

_____ 6. Such games resembled full-scale brawls.

_____ 7. The first side to score a goal won and was declared village champion.

_____ 8. Then both sides tended to the wounded, and they didn't play again for a whole year.

_____ 9. The rules of the game were written in the late 1800s at British boarding schools.

_____ 10. Now nearly every European country has a national soccer team, and the teams participate in international tournaments.

Exercise 7	IDENTIFYING TYPES OF SENTENCES

Indicate the kind of sentence by writing the appropriate letter(s) in the blank.

S   *simple*
CP   *compound*
CX   *complex*
CC   *compound-complex*

Underline the verbs and circle the subjects. Consider using labeled boxes as shown on page 29.

_____ 1. For both rich and poor in Rome, public baths were a daily pleasure.

_____ 2. The baths were somewhat similar to modern health clubs, although they had little equipment for exercising.

_____ 3. Rome alone had 856 baths; most of them were private.

_____ 4. Citizens who became rich were expected to build baths for their fellow citizens, and many generously built huge marble facilities.

_____ 5. For the equivalent of about a quarter-penny, any Roman could be massaged, scrubbed, and soaked in a public bath.

_____ 6. First bathers might exercise, and then they went to a hot, dry room to sweat.

_____ 7. Next came a visit to a hot, steamy room, and the final stage was a plunge into ice-cold water.

_____ 8. After the citizens finished their baths, they would wrap themselves in towels and visit with friends or walk about the grounds.

_____ 9. The serious-minded could browse through the bath's library.

_____ 10. They also sat around and played chess and checkers in game rooms.

Exercise 8	**IDENTIFYING TYPES OF SENTENCES**

Indicate the kind of sentence by writing the appropriate letter(s) in the blank.

S	*simple*
CP	*compound*
CX	*complex*
CC	*compound-complex*

Underline the verbs and circle the subjects. Consider using labeled boxes as shown on page 29. (See Answer Key for answers.)

_____ 1. In ancient Egypt 3,000 years ago, both men and women used cosmetics.

_____ 2. One concern was the matter of using beauty aids, but another was protection against the brilliant desert sun.

_____ 3. The three main colors of their makeup were green, black, and red.

_____ 4. These colors came from crushed rocks that were mixed with water or oil.

_____ 5. Lipstick was made from crushed iron ore and oil; it was applied with a brush that was made of animal hair and bristles.

_____ 6. They applied dark green and black makeup around their eyes by using small sticks.

_____ 7. They made perfume by crushing flowers and fragrant woods and by mixing that substance with oil.

_____ 8. They put cones of this perfume into their hair, where it melted slowly and gave off a fragrance.

_____ 9. Although they were apparently concerned about making themselves attractive to others, they quite effectively protected their skin, lips, and hair from the dry desert air.

_____ 10. Many containers of these cosmetics have been preserved in the pyramids.

Exercise 9	**IDENTIFYING TYPES OF SENTENCES**

Indicate the kind of sentence by writing the appropriate letter(s) in the blank.

S	*simple*
CP	*compound*
CX	*complex*
CC	*compound-complex*

Underline the verbs and circle the subjects. Consider using labeled boxes as shown on page 29.

_____ 1. Around 500 B.C., the Mayans began to create their civilization in the southern Gulf Coast region and present-day Guatemala.

_____ 2. The result was remarkable for its brilliant achievements.

_____ 3. Although they had no wheeled vehicles and no beasts of burden such as horses or oxen, they moved great pieces of stone to build their temples.

_____ 4. They had no iron tools; however, because they shaped their stone blocks so skillfully, their pyramids still stand.

_____ 5. The pyramids were the center of Mayan religious ceremonies.

_____ 6. The Mayans built many city-states, and the ruins of at least eighty have been found.

_____ 7. The tallest pyramid was as high as a twenty-story building.

_____ 8. A small temple was constructed at the top, where priests conducted ceremonies.

_____ 9. These pyramids were surrounded by plazas and avenues.

_____ 10. The Mayans were able to build complex structures and to invent an accurate calendar because they knew mathematics well.

Chapter Review: Kinds of Sentences

On the basis of number and kinds of clauses, sentences may be classified as simple, compound, complex, and compound-complex.

Clauses

1. A **clause** is a group of words with a subject and a verb that functions as a part or all of a complete sentence. There are two kinds of clauses: independent (main) and dependent (subordinate).

2. An **independent (main) clause** is a group of words with a subject and verb that can stand alone and make sense. An independent clause expresses a complete thought by itself and can be written as a separate sentence.

> I have the money.

3. A **dependent clause** is a group of words with a subject and verb that depends on a main clause to give it meaning.

> When you are ready

Types of Sentences

Type	Definition	Example
Simple	One independent clause	Susan was having trouble with her spelling.
Compound	Two or more independent clauses	Susan was having trouble with her spelling, and she purchased a computer with a spell checker.

Type	Definition	Example
Complex	One independent clause and one or more dependent clauses	Because Susan was having trouble with her spelling, she purchased a computer with a spell checker.
Compound-Complex	Two or more independent clauses and one or more dependent clauses	Because Susan was having trouble with her spelling, she purchased a computer with a spell checker, and the results made her expenditure worthwhile.

Punctuation

1. Use a comma before a coordinating conjunction (FANBOYS) between two independent clauses.

     The movie was good, but the tickets were expensive.

2. Use a comma after a dependent clause that appears before the main clause.

     When the bus arrived, we quickly boarded.

3. Use a semicolon between two independent clauses in one sentence if there is no coordinating conjunction.

     The bus arrived; we quickly boarded.

Chapter Review Exercises

Review 1   **IDENTIFYING TYPES OF SENTENCES**

Indicate the kind of sentence by writing the appropriate letter(s) in the blank.

     S   *simple*
     CP   *compound*
     CX   *complex*
     CC   *compound-complex*

Underline the verbs and circle the subjects. Consider using labeled boxes as shown on page 29. (See Answer Key for answers.)

_____ 1. Bastille Day is a holiday in France, for the French love freedom.

_____ 2. The Bastille was a famous prison in Paris, and the French people know its history.

_____ 3. The Bastille will not be forgotten as a symbol in France and in other French-speaking countries.

_____ 4. For hundreds of years, the Bastille was used to imprison those who offended the royalty, but on July 14, 1789, the common people stormed the gates.

_____ 5. The police guarding the Bastille decided to surrender; if they did not, they would lose their lives.

_____ 6. During the French Revolution that followed, the common people became fierce fighters for freedom.

_____ 7. After the war, some of the common people showed that they too were capable of cruelty.

_____ 8. Nevertheless, the French remember the Bastille as a symbol of political repression.

_____ 9. On July 14 of each year, businesses in France close, and people gather in the cities.

_____ 10. Bastille Day is among the most famous of all national holidays anywhere.

Review 2	IDENTIFYING TYPES OF SENTENCES

Indicate the kind of sentence by writing the appropriate letter(s) in the blank.

S   *simple*
CP   *compound*
CX   *complex*
CC   *compound-complex*

Underline the verbs and circle the subjects. Consider using labeled boxes as shown on page 29.

_____ 1. El Salvador's leading crop is coffee.

_____ 2. El Salvador has problems, because it has a large population and a relatively small area.

_____ 3. Because of reports that communists were trying to take over El Salvador, America increased its foreign aid to that country.

_____ 4. In recent decades, people moved to the cities, and later many emigrated.

_____ 5. Although El Salvador is a very poor country, a few landowners are quite wealthy.

_____ 6. The favorite food of El Salvador is called *pupusas*, which is a pocket sandwich stuffed with beans and meat.

_____ 7. A national law supports compulsory education; therefore, almost 70 percent of the citizens can read and write.

_____ 8. The volcanoes of El Salvador produce rich soil, which is excellent for agriculture, but there is not enough of it to serve the large population.

_____ 9. After the rainy season begins, the people expect floods in the low areas, and they take precautions.

_____ 10. A stable political future for El Salvador is much more likely now.

Before practicing writing sentences of different types, review the discussion of sentence types in the Chapter Review. Remember when and how to use the coordinating conjunctions (FANBOYS) and the common subordinating words. Keep in mind these main points of punctuation:

- Use a comma before a coordinating conjunction between independent clauses.

- Use a semicolon between independent clauses if there is no coordinating conjunction.

- Use a comma after a dependent clause that appears before the main clause.

Review 3	WRITING TYPES OF SENTENCES

Write a paragraph or two (a total of about ten sentences) on the topic of food (eating or preparing). Then examine your sentences and mark at least one example of each kind: simple (S), compound (CP), complex (CX), and compound-complex (CC). If any kinds are not represented, do some simple sentence revision.

3

Combining Sentences

"$\mathcal{A}$* piece of writing made up of a long series of choppy sentences probably suffers from a bad case of the monotony blues. The remedy may be found in a judicious dose of sentence combining."*

The simple sentence, the most basic sentence in the English language, can be exceptionally useful and powerful. Some of the greatest statements in literature have been presented in the simple sentence. Its strength is in its singleness of purpose. However, a piece of writing made up of a long series of short simple sentences is likely to be monotonous. Moreover, the form may suggest a separateness of ideas that does not serve your purpose well. If your ideas are closely associated and some are equal in importance and some not, you may be able to combine sentences to show a clearer relationship among those ideas.

Coordination: The Compound Sentence

If you intend to communicate two equally important and closely related ideas, you certainly will want to place them close together, probably in a **compound sentence.** Suppose we take two simple sentences that we want to combine:

> I am very tired.

> I worked very hard today.

We have already looked at coordinating conjunctions as a way of joining independent clauses to create compound sentences. Depending on which coordinating conjunction you use, you can show different kinds of relationships. (The following list is arranged according to the FANBOYS acronym discussed in Chapter 2. Only the first conjunction joins the original two sentences.)

For shows a reason:

> I am very tired, *for* I worked very hard today.

And shows equal ideas:

> I am very tired, *and* I want to rest for a few minutes.

Nor indicates a negative choice or alternative:

> I am not tired, *nor* am I hungry right now.

But shows contrast:

> I am very tired, *but* I have no time to rest now.

Or indicates a choice or an alternative:

> I will take a nap, *or* I will go out jogging.

Yet indicates contrast:

> I am tired, *yet* I am unable to relax.

So points to a result:

> I am tired, *so* I will take a nap.

Punctuation with Coordinating Conjunctions

When you combine two sentences by using a coordinating conjunction, drop the first period, change the capital letter that begins the second sentence to a small letter, and insert a comma before the coordinating conjunction.

$$\text{Independent clause} \left\{ \begin{array}{l} \textit{, for} \\ \textit{, and} \\ \textit{, nor} \\ \textit{, but} \\ \textit{, or} \\ \textit{, yet} \\ \textit{, so} \end{array} \right\} \text{independent clause.}$$

Exercise 1   **COMBINING SENTENCES: COMPOUND**

Combine the following pairs of sentences by deleting the first period, changing the capital letter that begins the second sentence to a small letter, and inserting a comma and an appropriate coordinating conjunction from the FANBOYS list. Feel free to reword the sentences as necessary. (See Answer Key for answers.)

1. James Francis "Jim" Thorpe, a Sac and Fox Indian, was born in 1888 near Prague, Oklahoma. At the age of sixteen, he left home to enroll in the Carlisle Indian School in Pennsylvania.

2. He had had little experience playing football. He led his small college to victories against championship teams.

3. He had scarcely heard of other sports. He golfed in the 70s, bowled above 200, and played varsity basketball and lacrosse.

4. In the 1912 Olympic Games for amateur athletes at Stockholm, Jim Thorpe entered the two most rigorous events, the decathlon and the pentathlon. He won both.

5. King Gustav V of Sweden told him, "You, Sir, are the greatest athlete in the world." Jim Thorpe said, "Thanks, King."

6. Later it was said he had once been paid fifteen dollars a week to play baseball, making him a professional athlete. The Olympic medals were taken from him.

7. Soon a Major League baseball scout did offer Thorpe a respectable contract. He played in the National League for six seasons.

8. Not content to play only one sport, he also earned a good salary for that time in professional football. After competing for fifteen years, he said he had never played for the money.

9. Many regard Jim Thorpe as the greatest athlete of the twentieth century. He excelled in many sports at the highest levels of athletic competition.

10. Off the playing fields, he was known by his friends as a modest, quiet man. On the fields, he was a person of joyful combat.

| Exercise 2 | **COMBINING SENTENCES: COMPOUND** |

Combine the following pairs of sentences by deleting the first period, changing the capital letter that begins the second sentence to a small letter, and inserting a comma and an appropriate coordinating conjunction from the FANBOYS list. Feel free to reword the sentences as necessary.

1. Sailing on its maiden voyage, the *Titanic* was considered unsinkable. On April 14, 1912, it struck an iceberg.

2. The ship sank 1,600 miles northeast of New York City. About 1,500 lives were lost.

3. The *Titanic* had been designed with great care. Its structure included sixteen watertight compartments.

4. Four of the compartments could be flooded without the ship's sinking. On that night five of the compartments flooded.

5. There were not enough lifeboats for the passengers. Lifeboats were considered unnecessary.

6. The management of the *Titanic* was supremely confident about the safety of the passengers. No lifeboat drills were required.

7. The killer iceberg was spotted just before the crash. It was too late.

8. At the time of the collision, another ship, the *Californian,* was only twenty miles away. The radio operator aboard the *Californian* was not on duty.

9. Some people behaved heroically. Others thought only of saving themselves.

10. Most of the survivors were women and children. The victims included the rich and famous.

Semicolons and Conjunctive Adverbs

In Chapter 2 we saw that a semicolon can join independent clauses to make a compound sentence. Here are two more simple sentences to combine:

> We were late. We missed the first act.

We can make one compound sentence out of them by joining the two clauses with a semicolon:

> We were late; we missed the first act.

We can also use words called conjunctive adverbs after semicolons to make the relationship between the two clauses clearer. Look at how the conjunctive adverb *therefore* adds the idea of "as a result."

> We were late; *therefore,* we missed the first act.

Conjunctive adverbs include the following words and phrases: *also, consequently, furthermore, hence, however, in fact, moreover, nevertheless, now, on the other hand, otherwise, soon, therefore, similarly, then, thus.*

Consider the meaning you want when you use a conjunctive adverb to coordinate ideas.

As a result of: *therefore, consequently, hence, thus, then*

To the contrary or with reservation: *however, nevertheless, otherwise, on the other hand*

In addition to: *moreover, also*

To emphasize or specify: *in fact, for example*

To compare: *similarly*

Punctuation with Semicolons and Conjunctive Adverbs

When you combine two sentences by using a semicolon, replace the first period with a semicolon and change the capital letter that begins the second sentence to a small letter. If you wish to use a conjunctive adverb, insert it after the semicolon and put a comma after it. (However, no comma follows *then, now, thus,* and *soon.*) The first letters of ten common conjunctive adverbs make up the acronym HOTSHOT CAT.

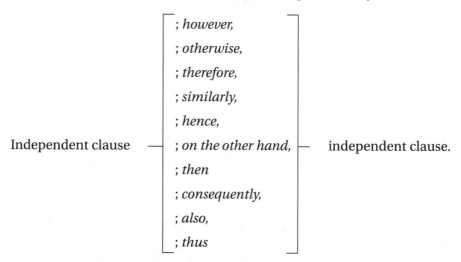

Independent clause

; however,
; otherwise,
; therefore,
; similarly,
; hence,
; on the other hand,
; then
; consequently,
; also,
; thus

independent clause.

| Exercise 3 | COMBINING SENTENCES: COMPOUND |

Combine the following pairs of sentences by replacing the first period with a semicolon, changing the capital letter that begins the second sentence to a small letter, and inserting a conjunctive adverb if appropriate. Consider the list of conjunctive adverbs (HOTSHOT CAT and others). Do not use a conjunctive adverb in every sentence. (See Answer Key for answers.)

1. The legendary island of Atlantis has fascinated people for centuries. It probably never existed.

2. According to the Greek writer Plato, the people of Atlantis were very ambitious and warlike. They planned to conquer all of the Mediterranean.

3. Initially, they were successful in subduing areas to the west. They became wealthy.

4. Then the people of Atlantis became proud. They became corrupt and wicked.

5. They were confident and attacked Athens. Athens and its allies defeated the invaders.

6. The story of Atlantis is probably just a tale. Many people have believed it.

7. Some writers have tried to link the legend with such real places as America and the Canary Islands. No link has been found.

8. The Minoan civilization on Crete was destroyed by tidal waves. A similar fate may have befallen Atlantis.

9. Some people speculate about a volcanic explosion on Atlantis. A volcanic erup-
    tion did destroy part of the island Thira in the Eastern Mediterranean in 1500 B.C.

10. Some writers have conjectured that American Indians migrated to the New
    World by way of Atlantis. Archaeologists dispute that idea.

Exercise 4   **COMBINING SENTENCES: COMPOUND**

*Combine the following pairs of sentences by replacing the first period with a semi-
colon, changing the capital letter that begins the second sentence to a small letter,
and inserting a conjunctive adverb if appropriate. Consider the list of conjunctive
adverbs (HOTSHOT CAT and others). Do not use a conjunctive adverb in every sentence.*

1. Camels can cover much distance in heat with little or no water. They are well
    adapted to the desert.

2. They can walk easily on soft sand and carry heavy loads. They are useful pack
    animals for human beings traveling in the desert.

3. The typical desert offers little vegetation. That circumstance does not affect the
    camel.

4. A camel stores food in one or two humps of fat on its back. When food is scarce,
    the camel uses that fat for energy.

5. The Arabian camel has one hump. The Bactrian has two.

6. Camels are known for their bad temper. Most people are not surprised when
    camels bite, kick, and spit.

7. Camels grunt and groan when mounted. Once under way, they carry their
    loads patiently.

8. Camels have mouth linings as tough as leather. They can eat a thorny cactus
    without injuring themselves.

9. In the 1850s the U.S. Army imported camels for desert transportation. The
    development of the railroads made camels unnecessary.

10. Working camels in Africa live for as long as fifty years. In circuses and zoos they
    die by the age of thirty.

Subordination: The Complex Sentence

Whereas a compound sentence contains independent clauses that are equally important and closely related, a **complex sentence** combines ideas of unequal value. The following two sentences can be combined as either a compound sentence or a complex sentence, depending on whether the writer thinks the ideas are of equal value.

> My neighbors are considerate.
>
> They never play loud music.

Combined as a compound sentence, suggesting that the ideas are of equal value, the new sentence looks like this:

> My neighbors are considerate, and they never play loud music.
> independent clause   independent clause
> (main idea)   (main idea)

Here are the same two ideas combined as a complex sentence, suggesting that the ideas are of unequal value:

> Because my neighbors are considerate, they never play loud music.
> dependent clause   independent clause
> (less important idea)   (main idea)

Although both the compound and complex forms are correct, the complex form conveys the ideas more precisely in this sentence because one idea does seem to be more important—one idea depends on the other.

Thus if you have two sentences with closely related ideas and one is clearly more important than the other, consider combining them in a complex sentence. Compare these two paragraphs:

1. Version 1 contains six simple sentences, implying that the ideas are of equal value:

   > (1) I was very upset. (2) The Fourth of July fireworks were especially loud. (3) My dog ran away. (4) The animal control officer made his morning rounds. (5) He found my dog in another part of town. (6) I was relieved.

2. Version 2 consists of two simple sentences and two complex sentences, showing that some ideas are more important than others:

   > (1) I was very upset. (2) Because the Fourth of July fireworks were especially loud, my dog ran away. (3) When the animal control officer made his morning rounds, he found my dog in another part of town. (4) I was relieved.

You will probably consider Version 2 superior to Version 1. Sentences 2 and 3 are closely related, but 3 is more important. Sentences 4 and 5 are closely related, but 5 is more important. In Version 2 the revision made each pair into a complex sentence.

Although you could combine sentences 1 and 2, the result would be illogical because the wrong idea would be conveyed:

Illogical Combination: I was very upset because the Fourth of July fireworks were especially loud.

The person was very upset because the dog ran away, not because the fireworks were especially loud.

Subordinating Conjunctions

As you learned in Chapter 2, a complex sentence is composed of one independent clause and one or more dependent clauses. In combining two independent clauses to write a complex sentence, your first step is to decide on a word that will best show the relationship between the clauses. Words that show the relationship of a dependent clause to an independent one are called subordinating conjunctions. The italicized words in the following sentences are subordinating conjunctions. Consider the meaning as well as the placement of each one.

> *Because* the storm hit, the game was canceled.
>
> *After* the storm passed, the dogs began to bark.
>
> *When* Colette told her joke, the class was moved to fits of hysterics.
>
> Vernon did not volunteer to work on the holiday, *although* the pay was good.
>
> No one has visited Patty *since* she moved into town.
>
> They decided to wait *until* the cows came home.
>
> They refused to work *unless* they were allowed to wear chef's hats.
>
> *Before* the session ended, all the "hep cats" blew some sweet sounds.

Other subordinating conjunctions include the following:

as	*provided that*	*whereas*
as if	*rather than*	*wherever*
even if	*so that*	*whether*
even though	*than*	*while*
if	*whenever*	
in order that	*where*	

Punctuation with Subordinating Conjunctions

If the dependent clause comes *before* the main clause, set it off with a comma.

> Before Mike wrote his final draft, he looked over his outline.

If the dependent clause comes *after* or *within* the main clause, set it off only if the clause is not necessary to the meaning of the main clause or if the dependent clause begins with the word *although, though,* or *even though.*

> We went home *after* the concert had ended.
>
> Vincent continued painting, *although* he had repainted the cabinet twice.

Punctuation with Relative Pronouns

As you learned in Chapter 2, a relative clause begins with a relative pronoun, a pronoun such as *that, which,* or *who.*

> The decision <u>that I made</u> is final.
> **relative clause**

> A student <u>who uses a computer</u> can save time in revising.
> **relative clause**

Set off the dependent (relative) clause with commas when it is not necessary to the sentence. Do not set off the clause if it is necessary for the meaning of the sentence.

> Everyone *who tries* will pass this class. (The dependent clause is necessary because one would not say, "Everyone will pass this class.")

> Juan, *who tries,* will pass this class. (The dependent clause is not necessary because one can say, "Juan will pass this class.")

The relative pronoun *which* usually refers to things. The word *which* almost always indicates that a clause is not necessary for the meaning of the sentence. Therefore, a clause beginning with *which* is almost always set off by commas.

> My car, *which* is ten years old, has a flat tire.

The relative pronoun *that* also usually refers to things. However, the word *that* almost always indicates that the clause *is* necessary for the meaning of the sentence. Therefore, a clause beginning with *that* usually is *not* set off by commas.

> The car *that* has a flat tire is ten years old.

The relative pronouns *who* and *whom,* as well as *whoever* and *whomever,* usually refer to people. Clauses that begin with those relative pronouns are not set off by commas if they are necessary for the meaning of the sentence; if they are not necessary, they are set off.

> A person *who* has a way with words is often quoted. (necessary for the meaning of the sentence)

> Uncle Colby, *whom* I quote often, has a way with words. (not necessary for the meaning of the sentence)

Exercise 5   COMBINING SENTENCES: COMPLEX

Combine the following pairs of sentences into one complex sentence. Insert an appropriate subordinating conjunction or relative pronoun, add or fix punctuation, and make other minor changes as needed. Sentences that should be combined by using a relative pronoun are indicated. (See Answer Key for answers.)

1. (relative pronoun) The freeway congestion was under study. The problem occurred every Friday at noon.

2. The vacationers had a good time. The bears destroyed a few tents and ate people's food.

3. The teenagers loved their senior prom. The band played badly.

4. Farmers gathered for miles around. Jeff had grown a fifty-pound cucumber.

5. Back-seat drivers make unwanted suggestions in the nag-proof model. They can be ejected from the vehicle.

6. (relative pronoun) The marriage counselor gave bad advice. He charged only half price.

7. (relative pronoun) The robots would not do their work. They needed fresh batteries.

8. The hurricane was expected to hit during the night. The residents checked their flashlights.

9. The ice sculptor displayed his work in the dining hall. The customers applauded.

10. Someone stole the artwork of ice. No evidence was found.

Exercise 6   **COMBINING SENTENCES: COMPLEX**

Combine the following pairs of sentences into one complex sentence. Insert an appropriate subordinating conjunction or relative pronoun, add or fix punctuation, and make other minor changes as needed. Sentences that should be combined by using a relative pronoun are indicated.

1. (relative pronoun) Mary Hayes was one of the first female soldiers in American warfare. She is better known as Molly Pitcher.

2. (relative pronoun) At the outbreak of the War of Independence, Mary was the wife of John Hayes. He soon joined the army.

3. Following established practice, Mary Hayes also went to war. She was the wife of a soldier.

4. He performed military duties. She washed and mended clothes and cooked meals.

5. John Hayes's regiment fought at the Battle of Monmouth. The day was hot.

6. Mary Hayes brought the soldiers water in pitchers. Some men started calling her Molly Pitcher, "Molly" for "Mary" and "Pitcher" for what she carried.

7. She was immediately proud of the name. Others started using it.

8. John Hayes suffered a heat stroke. Mary Hayes took over his job, firing his cannon.

9. A cannonball sailed between her knees and tore her dress. She refused to stop fighting.

10. Following the war, Mary Hayes received a pension for soldiers. She was truly a patriotic veteran.

Coordination and Subordination: The Compound-Complex Sentence

At times you may want to show the relationship of three or more ideas within one sentence. If that relationship involves two or more main ideas and one or more supporting ideas, the combination can be stated in a compound-complex sentence (two or more independent clauses and one or more dependent clauses).

<u>Before Kafka learned how to operate a word processor,</u>
dependent clause

<u>he had trouble with his typewritten assignments,</u>
independent clause

but now <u>he produces clean, attractive pages</u>.
independent clause

In our previous discussion of the complex sentence, we presented this group of six sentences:

I was very upset. The Fourth of July fireworks were especially loud. My dog ran away. The animal control officer made his morning rounds. He found my dog in another part of town. I was relieved.

We then converted the group of six sentences to four.

I was very upset. Because the Fourth of July fireworks were especially loud, my dog ran away. When the animal control officer made his morning rounds, he found my dog in another part of town. I was relieved.

But what if we wanted to show an even closer relationship of ideas? One solution would be to combine the two complex sentences in this way (the italicized sentence is compound-complex):

I was very upset. *Because the Fourth of July fireworks were especially loud, my dog ran away; but when the animal control officer made his morning rounds, he found my dog in another part of town.* I was relieved.

Punctuation of Complicated Compound or Compound-Complex Sentences

If a compound or compound-complex sentence has one or more commas in the first clause, you may want to use a semicolon before the coordinating conjunction between the two clauses. Its purpose is to show the reader very clearly the division between the two independent clauses. The preceding example illustrates this use of the semicolon.

| **Exercise 7** | **COMBINING SENTENCES: COMPOUND-COMPLEX** |

Combine each group of sentences into one compound-complex sentence. Use the rules of sentence combining and punctuation discussed in this chapter. (See Answer Key for answers.)

1. A grumpy bear had stalked the grounds. Summer camp had been a great experience for the campers. They vowed to return.

2. The stuffed cabbage ran out. The party ended. The guests went home.

3. It was a costume party. All the guests dressed as movie legends. Ten were Elvis impersonators.

4. A new Elvis theme park opened in our town. I attended. I think I saw the King.

5. My father encouraged me to take up a hobby. I began collecting stamps. Now my hobby has become a business.

6. They were in a wilderness camp. They were not allowed to bring pets. They were allowed to bring toys.

7. He had no leather shoes to wear. Young Stu could not go to the prom. He hoped there would be a prom next year.

8. People were hungry. They ate massive quantities of hot dogs at the game. They knew the dogs were made of mystery meat.

9. The ambulance drivers were taking a break. A man had a choking fit. The drivers came to his rescue.

10. The film was filled with scenes of violence. It included a charming love story. The public liked it.

Exercise 8 — COMBINING SENTENCES: COMPOUND-COMPLEX

Combine each group of sentences into one compound-complex sentence. Use the rules of sentence combining and punctuation discussed in this chapter.

1. Helen Keller suffered a serious childhood illness. She became blind and deaf. At first her parents did not know what to do.

2. Her parents would not give up despite discouraging advice. They advertised for a teacher. A tutor named Anne Sullivan agreed to help.

3. Young Helen began to discover the world through her sense of touch. She learned the alphabet. She started connecting words with objects.

4. Her physical condition was irreversible. Her progress was rapid. In three years she could read Braille.

5. She could not talk. She used sign language for speech. She used a special typewriter to write.

6. She reached the age of ten. She took speech lessons from a teacher of the deaf. In six years she could speak well enough to be understood.

7. She attended college. She still needed help. Anne Sullivan continued as her tutor and interpreter.

8. She graduated from college with honors. She became involved in programs to help the deaf and blind communicate. She wrote books and articles about problems of the disabled.

9. The effects of World War II presented special problems. Helen Keller helped disabled people in other countries. She helped soldiers blinded in the war.

10. Helen Keller died in 1968. She had an international reputation as a humanitarian. Her books had been translated into more than fifty languages.

Other Ways to Combine Ideas

In this chapter you have learned how to combine simple sentences into compound, complex, and compound-complex sentences that show the coordination and subordination of ideas. There are other methods of combining ideas, too. Here are four you may want to use in your own writing.

1. Use an appositive, which is a noun or a noun phrase that immediately follows a noun or pronoun and renames it.

    Kyoko is the leading scorer on the team. Kyoko is a quick and strong player.

    Kyoko, *a quick and strong player,* is the leading scorer on the team.

2. Use a prepositional phrase, a preposition followed by a noun or pronoun object.

    Dolly Parton wrote a song about a coat. The coat had many colors.

    Dolly Parton wrote a song about a coat *of many colors.*

3. Drop the subject in the sentence that follows and combine the sentences.

    Some items are too damaged for recycling. They must be discarded.

    Some items are too damaged for recycling and must be discarded.

4. Use a participial phrase, a group of words that includes a participle, which is a verbal that usually ends in *-ing* or *-ed.*

    Jamal rowed smoothly. He reached the shore.

    Rowing smoothly, Jamal reached the shore.

| **Exercise 9** | **COMBINING SENTENCES** |

Combine each group of sentences into a single sentence in the ways indicated. (See Answer Key for answers to the odd-numbered sentence sets.)

Use an appositive.

1. Ernest Hemingway won the Nobel Prize for literature in 1954. He was mainly an American writer of fiction.

2. Ernest spent his childhood summers in Michigan. He was the second of six children of Clarence and Grace Hemingway.

Use a prepositional phrase.

3. After high school he became a reporter. He worked for the Kansas City *Star.*

4. During World War I he volunteered to serve as a Red Cross ambulance driver. The Red Cross unit was stationed in Italy.

Drop the subject of the second sentence.

5. In 1920 he returned to journalism with the Toronto *Star.* He met his future first wife, Hadley Richardson.

6. Hemingway and his wife moved to France. They lived in a walk-up flat in the Latin Quarter of Paris.

Use a participial phrase.

7. Hemingway worked conscientiously on his writing. He soon became a leader of the so-called Lost Generation.

8. He always sought adventure. He hunted, fished, loved, drank, fought, and wrote his way through the next three decades.

Use any of the above ways.

9. During World War II Hemingway armed his fishing boat and hunted for German submarines. He patrolled the waters of the Caribbean.

10. He died as a life-weary, broken man in 1960 at his home in Ketchum, Idaho. He was suffering from both physical and psychological problems.

Chapter Review: Combining Sentences

Coordination

If you want to communicate two equally important and closely related ideas, place them close together, probably in a **compound sentence** (two or more independent clauses).

1. When you combine two sentences by using a coordinating conjunction (FAN-BOYS), drop the first period, change the capital letter of the second sentence to a small letter, and insert a comma before the coordinating conjunction.

> I like your home. I can visit for only three months.

> I like your home, *but* I can visit for only three months.

2. When you combine two sentences by using a semicolon, replace the first period with a semicolon and change the capital letter that begins the second sentence to a small letter. If you wish to use a conjunctive adverb, insert it after the semicolon and usually follow it with a comma.

> I like your home. I can visit for only three months.

> I like your home; I can visit for only three months.

> I like your home; *however,* I can visit for only three months.

Subordination

If you have two ideas that are closely related, but one is secondary or dependent on the other, you may want to use a **complex sentence.**

> My neighbors are considerate. They never play loud music

> Because my neighbors are considerate, they never play loud music.

1. If the dependent clause comes first, set it off with a comma.

> Because my dog has no hands or words, he licks me to show affection.

2. If the dependent clause comes after the main clause, set it off with a comma only if you use some form of the word *though* or if the words are not necessary to convey the basic meaning in the sentence.

> Edmund Hillary was knighted by Queen Elizabeth II because he was one of the first two men to climb Mt. Everest.

> Other mountain climbers soon duplicated his feat, *though* they received less recognition.

3. One type of dependent clause is called a relative clause. A relative clause begins with a relative pronoun, a pronoun such as *that, which,* or *who.* Relative pronouns *relate* the clause to another word in the sentence.

> Orlando purchased a used computer.

> It had hardly been touched.

> Orlando purchased a used computer *that* had hardly been touched.

4. A relative clause should be set off with commas when it is not necessary to the sentence. Do not set the clause off if it is necessary for the meaning of the sentence.

Necessary:	No one *who fails the eye test* will get a driver's license.
Unnecessary:	Mr. McGoo, *who failed his eye test,* did not get a driver's license.

Coordination and Subordination

At times you may want to show the relationship of three or more ideas within one sentence. If that relationship involves two or more main ideas and one or more supporting ideas, the combination can be stated in a **compound-complex sentence** (two or more independent clauses and one or more dependent clauses).

> Kafka produced illegible handwritten papers.
>
> At that time he had not learned how to operate a word processor.
>
> Now he hands in clean, attractive pages.
>
> Before Kafka learned how to operate a word processor, he produced illegible handwritten papers, but now he hands in clean, attractive pages.

Use punctuation consistent with that of the compound and complex sentences.

Other Ways to Combine Ideas

1. Use an appositive, a noun or a noun phrase that immediately follows a noun or pronoun and renames it.

   > Garth Brooks claims Yukon, Oklahoma, as his hometown. He is a famous singer.
   >
   > Garth Brooks, *a famous singer,* claims Yukon, Oklahoma, as his hometown.

2. Use a prepositional phrase, a preposition followed by a noun or pronoun object.

   > John Elway led the Denver Broncos to two Super Bowl victories. Both triumphs occurred in the 1990s.
   >
   > John Elway led the Denver Broncos to two Super Bowl victories *in the 1990s.*

3. Drop the subject in the sentence that follows and combine the sentences.

   > Emily Dickinson's poetry went mostly unpublished during her lifetime. It was finally discovered and celebrated more than a half century later.
   >
   > Emily Dickinson's poetry went mostly unpublished during her lifetime but was finally discovered and celebrated more than a half century later.

4. Use a participial phrase, a group of words that includes a participle, which is a verbal that usually ends in *-ing* or *-ed.*

   > The turtle plodded without rest stops. It won the race against the rabbit.
   >
   > *Plodding without rest stops,* the turtle won the race against the rabbit.

Chapter Review Exercises

Combine two or more sentences from each group by using any pattern. (See Answer Key for possible answers.)

1. The Mercury Comet was judged the winner. It had imitation zebra-skin seat covers. It had an eight-ball shift knob.

2. Koko had a great plan to make some money. She had financial problems. She could not develop her plan.

3. The mixture could not be discussed openly. Competitors were curious. Corporate spies were everywhere.

4. Babette's bowling ball is special. It is red and green. It is decorated with her phone number in metal-flake.

5. The young bagpiper liked Scottish food. He enjoyed doing Scottish dances. Wearing a kilt in winter left him cold.

6. Ruby missed the alligator farm. She fondly remembered the hissing and snapping of the beasts as they scrambled for raw meat. Her neighbors were indifferent to the loss.

7. Many people are pleased to purchase items with food preservatives. Others are fearful. They think these chemicals may also preserve consumers.

8. Leewan loves her new in-line roller skates. They look and perform much like ice skates. They are not as safe as her conventional roller skates.

9. Fish sold at Discount Fish Market were not of the highest quality. Some of them had been dead for days without refrigeration. They were suitable only for bait.

10. Cliff wanted to impress his date. He splashed on six ounces of He-Man cologne. He put on his motorcycle leathers and a flying scarf.

Review 2	**COMBINING SENTENCES**

Use appropriate methods to combine sentences as needed. Add and delete words sparingly.

Muhammad Ali was arguably the greatest heavyweight boxing champion. He won the title on four occasions. He loved to perform for the press. He made up sayings and poems about himself and his opponents. He said he would "float like a butterfly and sting like a bee." Ali announced that he would win each fight. He even named the round. He became a Black Muslim. He refused induction into the armed services. He was convicted of a crime for having done so. As a result he lost his championship. Later the decision was reversed by the U.S. Supreme Court. He won back the championship by defeating George Foreman in 1974. In 1978 he lost it to Leon Spinks. He won it back one more time the next year. He retired in 1980. Then fought once more for the title. He quit for good.

Review 3	**COMBINING SENTENCES**

Use appropriate methods to combine sentences as needed. Add and delete words sparingly.

Reba McEntire: No Secrets to Her Success

Good singers can be found anywhere, even in a local lounge or pizza parlor. Great singers are rare. They have the "something special" qualities. The qualities just seem to work together. Country singer Reba McEntire is definitely one of the greats. The reasons are obvious: voice, songs, and style. Her voice is like no other. Her Oklahoma "twangy" accent is known by everyone in country music. She is able to jump from note to note. She can cover two octaves with ease. Her voice is rich and sensitive, yet powerful. Reba sings. She takes up all the oxygen in the room. The songs she sings are another reason for her greatness. Her lyrics deal with the issues. Those issues really touch the heart. They inspire the mind. They make even the men cry. Her song "Is There Life Out There?" encourages women and men everywhere to follow their dreams, no matter what those dreams may be. That song came out. Reba got thousands of letters from people. The people thanked her for writing such a positive song during difficult times. The final reason for her greatness is her style. It is all its own, from her spunky attitude right down to her steel-toed boots. This fiery redhead really knows how to get the crowd going. She has been performing for about twenty years. She has produced about twenty albums. With all those qualities, Reba McEntire will be around for a long, long time.

4

Correcting Fragments, Comma Splices, and Run-Ons

"Using principles you now understand, this chapter will protect you against the most dreaded disease in student writing: the scarlet frag's, CS's, and RO's.*"*

In Chapter 1, you learned about subjects and verbs. In Chapters 2 and 3, you identified and wrote different kinds of sentences. With the information you now have, you will be able to spot and correct three problems in sentence structure that sometimes creep into and insidiously destroy what is otherwise good writing. Those problems are sentence fragments, comma splices, and run-on sentences.

Fragments

A correct sentence signals completeness. The structure and punctuation provide those signals. For example, if I say to you, "She left in a hurry," you do not necessarily expect me to say anything else, but if I say, "In a hurry," you do. If I say, "Tomorrow I will give you a quiz on the reading assignment," and I leave the room, you will merely take note of my words. But if I say, "Tomorrow when I give you a quiz on the reading assignment," and I leave the room, you will probably be annoyed, and you may even chase after me and ask me to finish my sentence. Those examples illustrate the difference between completeness and incompleteness.

A **fragment** is a word or group of words without a subject ("Is going to town.") or without a verb ("He going to town.") or without both ("Going to town."). A fragment can also be a group of words with a subject and verb that cannot stand alone

("When he goes to town."). Although the punctuation signals a sentence (a capital letter at the beginning and a period at the end), the structure of a fragment signals incompleteness. If you said it or wrote it to someone, that person would expect you to go on and finish the idea.

Other specific examples of common unacceptable fragments are these:

- *Dependent clause only:* When she came.

- *Phrase(s) only:* Waiting there for some help.

- *No subject in main clause:* Went to the library.

- *No verb in main clause:* She being the only person there.

Acceptable Fragments

Sometimes, fragments are used intentionally. When we speak, we often use the following fragments:

- *Interjections:* Great! Hooray! Whoa!

- *Exclamations:* What a day! How terrible! What a bother!

- *Greetings:* Hello. Good morning. Good night. Good evening.

- *Questions:* What for? Why not? Where to?

- *Informal conversation:* (What time is it?) Eight o'clock. Really.

In novels, plays, and short stories, fragments are often used in conversation among characters. However, unless you are writing fiction, you need to be able to identify fragments in your college assignments and turn those fragments into complete sentences.

Dependent Clauses as Fragments: Clauses with Subordinating Conjunctions

In Chapter 3, you learned that words such as *because, after, although, since,* and *before* (see page 43 for a more complete list) are subordinating conjunctions, words that show the relationship of a dependent clause to an independent one. A dependent clause punctuated like a sentence (capital letter at the beginning; period at the end) is a sentence fragment.

> *While the ship was sinking.*

You can choose one of many ways to fix that kind of fragment.

Incorrect: They continued to dance. *While the ship was sinking.*

Correct: They continued to dance *while the ship was sinking.*

Correct: *While the ship was sinking,* they continued to dance.

Correct: The ship was sinking. They continued to dance.

Correct: The ship was sinking; they continued to dance.

In the first two correct sentences above, the dependent clause *while the ship was sinking* has been attached to an independent clause. Note that a comma is used when the dependent clause appears at the beginning of the sentence. In the next two sentences, the subordinating conjunction *while* has been omitted. The two independent clauses can then stand alone as sentences or as parts of a sentence, joined by a semicolon.

Dependent Clauses as Fragments: Clauses with Relative Pronouns

You learned in Chapter 2 that words such as *that, which,* and *who* can function as relative pronouns, words that relate a clause back to a noun or pronoun in the sentence. Relative clauses are dependent. If they are punctuated as sentences (begin with a capital letter; end with a period), they are incorrect. They are really sentence fragments.

> *Which is lying on the floor.*

The best way to fix such a fragment is to attach it as closely as possible to the noun to which it refers.

Incorrect: That new red sweater is mine. *Which is lying on the floor.*

Correct: The new red sweater, *which is lying on the floor,* is mine.

Reminder: Some relative clauses are restrictive (necessary to the meaning of the sentence) and should not be set off with commas. Some are nonrestrictive (not necessary to the meaning of the sentence), as in the example above, and are set off by commas.

Exercise 1	CORRECTING FRAGMENTS

Underline and correct each fragment. Some items may be correct as is. (See Answer Key for answers.)

1. When Leroy Robert Paige was seven years old. He was carrying luggage at a railroad station in Mobile, Alabama.

2. He was a clever young fellow. Who invented a contraption for carrying four satchels (small suitcases) at one time.

3. After he did that. He was always known as Satchel Paige.

4. His fame rests on his being arguably the best baseball pitcher. Who ever played the game.

5. Because of the so-called Jim Crow laws. He, as an African American, was not allowed to play in the Major Leagues. Until 1948 after the Major League color barrier was broken.

6. By that time he was already forty-two. Although he was in excellent condition.

7. He had pitched. Wherever he could, mainly touring around the country.

8. When he faced Major Leaguers in exhibition games. He almost always won.

9. Because people liked to see him pitch. He pitched almost every day. While he was on tour.

10. One year he won 104 games. During his career he pitched 55 no-hitters and won more than 2,000 games.

11. He pitched his last game in the majors at the age of fifty-nine.

12. In 1971 he was the first African-American player. Who was voted into the Baseball Hall of Fame in a special category for those. Who played in the old Negro Leagues.

Exercise 2   CORRECTING FRAGMENTS

Underline and correct each fragment.

1. Although Woody Guthrie had a hard life. His songs are filled with hope.

2. His autobiography, *Bound for Glory,* tells of this free-spirited man. Who saw boomtown oil fields dry up and crops wither in the dust bowl.

3. Many people knew him only as the author of "This Land Is Your Land." Which is often treated as a second national anthem.

4. Because he was honest and would say what he thought. He was often out of work.

5. Cisco Houston said, "Woody is a man. Who writes two or three ballads before breakfast every morning."

6. The hobo, the migrant worker, the merchant marine, the sign painter, the labor agitator, the musician in New York City with his hat on the sidewalk—Woody was a restless traveler. Whose life was as varied as his song bag.

7. Some of his best songs are about his experience during the days of the Great Depression. When he was an unofficial spokesperson for migrant workers in the West.

8. Arlo Guthrie, Woody's son, achieved his own fame. While he carried on the folk music tradition of his father.

9. Woody's song "Pretty Boy Floyd" was recorded by Bob Dylan. Who modeled his early style on that of Woody and once referred to himself as a "Woody Guthrie jukebox."

10. A simple farmer once said to a reporter, "I'll always remember Woody as the man. Who said, 'Some men will rob you with a six-gun and some with a fountain pen.'"

Phrases as Fragments

Although a phrase may carry an idea, a phrase is a fragment because it is incomplete in structure. It lacks both a subject and a verb. See Chapter 1 for verbal phrases and prepositional phrases, and see Chapter 3 for appositive phrases.

Verbal Phrase

> **Incorrect:** *Having studied hard all evening.* John decided to retire.
>
> **Correct:** *Having studied hard all evening,* John decided to retire.

The italicized part of the incorrect example is a verbal phrase. As you learned in Chapter 1, a verbal is verblike without being a verb in sentence structure. Verbals include verb parts of speech ending in *-ed* and *-ing*. To correct a verbal phrase fragment, attach it to a complete sentence (independent clause). When the phrase begins the sentence, it is usually set off by a comma.

Prepositional Phrase

> **Incorrect:** *For the past ten hours.* I have been designing my home page.
>
> **Correct:** *For the past ten hours,* I have been designing my home page.

In this example, the fragment is a prepositional phrase—a group of words beginning with a preposition, such as *in, on, of, at,* and *with,* that connects a noun or pronoun object to the rest of the sentence. To correct a prepositional phrase fragment, attach it to a complete sentence (independent clause). If the prepositional phrase is long and begins the sentence, it is usually set off by a comma.

Appositive Phrase

> **Incorrect:** He lived in the small town of Whitman. *A busy industrial center near Boston.*
>
> **Correct:** He lived in the small town of Whitman, *a busy industrial center near Boston.*
>
> **Incorrect:** Many readers admire the work of the nineteenth-century American poet. *Emily Dickinson.*
>
> **Correct:** Many readers admire the work of the nineteenth-century America poet *Emily Dickinson.*

In these examples, the fragment is an appositive phrase—a group of words following a noun or pronoun and renaming it. To correct an appositive phrase fragment, connect it to a complete sentence (an independent clause). An appositive phrase fragment is set off by a comma or by commas only if it is not essential to the meaning of the sentence.

Exercise 3	CORRECTING FRAGMENTS

Underline and correct each fragment. (See Answer Key for answers.)

1. As a subject of historical record. Dancing seems to be a natural human act.

2. Even prehistoric cave paintings depict dancing figures. Scrawled outlines of people in motion.

3. Dancing takes many forms, but mainly it is a matter of moving rhythmically. In time to music.

4. Most children jump up and down when they are excited. They sway back and forth when they are contented.

5. Having studied the behavior of many ethnic groups. Anthropologists confirm that dancing reveals much. About a group's culture.

6. People dance for various reasons. Such as to entertain others, to relax, to inspire others, and to celebrate life.

7. One stylized form of dancing is the ballet. A story told with graceful, rhythmic movement and music.

8. Folk dances relate stories. Of the dancers' culture.

9. Young people can get to know each other at social dances. While enjoying themselves.

10. Each generation of social dancers seems to have its own style. Sometimes a modified revival, such as swing.

Exercise 4	CORRECTING FRAGMENTS

Underline and correct each fragment.

1. Reflecting religious concerns. Ceremonial dances are still conducted in some cultures to promote good crops or successful warfare.

2. In the 1800s, an American Christian group called the Shakers performed a whirling, shaking dance. A ceremony to shake out the devil.

3. In the 1900s. Whirling Dervishes and Ghost Dancers believed that their dancing protected them in battle.

4. In Australia and North America. Aborigines had dances that imitated the movement of animals to be hunted.

5. Some of those dances are still performed. With few significant changes of style.

6. In Africa and the South Pacific. Groups have dances that signify the achievement of maturity.

7. In the United States and in many other countries. Young people gain popularity. By learning and demonstrating popular dance steps and movements.

8. It is hard to imagine human beings without dance. An activity transcending all time and culture.

9. With the birth of rock 'n' roll music. Dancing styles became freer.

10. During the past hundred years. Dozens of dances, such as the lindy, twist, hustle, Charleston, big apple, frug, and mashed potato, have had their times of popularity.

Exercise 5	**CORRECTING FRAGMENTS**

Correct the following phrase fragments by adding subjects and verbs and, perhaps, by changing or adding words. The story line is simple. Driving his Ford truck, Harry took Jane to the opening-day baseball game at Dodger Stadium. They arrived with high hopes, settled into their seats, had expectations, saw the game begin, and spotted some rain clouds. The questions in the boxes will help you follow the plot. (See Answer Key for possible answers.)

Example: A special date with Jane.

> Who had a special date with Jane?

Harry had a special date with Jane.

1. A Ford Ranger truck with fine Corinthian leather seats.

> What did he polish?

_____

_____

2. To pick up Jane for their date.

> What did he do then?

_____

_____

3. To go to the opening-day baseball game at Dodger Stadium.

> Where did Jane want to go on the date?

_____

_____

4. A never-to-be-forgotten experience.

> What satisfaction did she hope for?

_____

_____

5. Being seen on big-screen Diamond Vision in the stadium.

> What special experience did Jane dream of?

_____

_____

6. With the first sound of the bat on ball.

> When did they arrive?

_____

_____

7. Buying peanuts and Crackerjacks.

> Who bought peanuts and Crackerjacks and for whom?

_____

_____

8. A baseball glove to catch a well-hit ball.

> What did Jane bring so that she might catch a well-hit ball?

_____

_____

9. To hear and see heroes up close.

> What portable electronic device did Jane bring so she could follow the action on the field?

_____

_____

10. Seeing the rain clouds.

> Noticing the change in weather, what did they fear?

_____

_____

Exercise 6   **CORRECTING FRAGMENTS**

Correct the following phrase fragments by adding subjects and verbs and, perhaps, by changing or adding words. Continuing from Exercise 5 is the story of Harry and Jane at a baseball game where they got caught in a rainstorm. They ran for cover, contemplated leaving, waited, saw the game continue, watched the players slide in the mud, celebrated the Dodgers' victory, headed for the parking lot, and finally found Harry's truck. The questions in the boxes will help you follow the plot.

Example: In the last of the fourth inning.

> What began to fall from the clouds?

In the last of the fourth inning, *rain began to fall.*

1. Running for shelter.

> What happened to them as they ran through the rain?

_____

_____

2. Shivering and waiting for sunshine.

> Where did they wish they were?

_____

_____

3. To delay the game.

> What did the umpires decide to do?

_____

_____

4. To leave or not to leave.

> What question did Harry and Jane consider?

_____

_____

5. In less than an hour.

> What happened to the rain?

_____

_____

6. With the players back on the field.

Following the change of weather, what happened to the game?

_____

_____

7. Sliding into bases on the wet field.

What became easy for the players?

_____

_____

8. Winning the game at the end of the eleventh inning.

How did the Dodgers delight their fans?

_____

_____

9. Finding Harry's truck in the parking lot.

What problem did Harry and Jane have in finding Harry's truck?

_____

_____

10. By the light of the moon.

How did they find Harry's truck?

_____

_____

Fragments as Word Groups Without Subjects or Without Verbs

Incorrect: Ayana studied many long hours. And received the highest grade in the class. (without subject)

Correct: Ayana studied many long hours and received the highest grade in the class.

Incorrect: Few children living in that section of the country. (without verb)

Correct: Few children live in that section of the country.

Each sentence must have an independent clause, a group of words that contains a subject and a verb and that can stand alone. As you may recall from the discussion of subjects in Chapter 1, a command or direction sentence, such as "Think," has an understood subject of *you.*

| Exercise 7 | **CORRECTING FRAGMENTS** |

The fragments in the following passage need either a subject or a verb. Underline the fragments and correct them. (See Answer Key for possible answers.)

(1) Fleas remarkable animals. (2) Although they do not have wings, jump more than twelve inches. (3) Fleas living on many kinds of animals. (4) Suck blood from their victims. (5) They often move from pets to human beings. (6) They do not discriminate. (7) They land on poets, politicians, physicians, and anyone else in close proximity. (8) Carry germ-ridden blood and spread diseases. (9) Fleas the main spreader of bubonic plague. (10) Rodents, including those infected with diseases, providing fleas with transportation and food. (11) Nowadays one attacker is called the human flea. (12) This creature in houses, where it lays eggs on the carpet. (13) Often bites human beings. (14) Another kind of flea is the chigoe. (15) Burrows under the skin and lays its eggs. (16) For flea control, cleanliness and insecticide are important. (17) Our pets, mainly our cats and dogs, among the main carriers of fleas in the typical household.

| Exercise 8 | **CORRECTING FRAGMENTS** |

The fragments in the following passage need either a subject or a verb. Underline the fragments and correct them.

(1) Susan B. Anthony among the leaders in the early days of the women's rights movement. (2) Her parents being Quakers, who believed in the equality of the sexes. (3) As a young woman, wanted to argue against alcohol abuse. (4) Was not allowed to speak at rallies because she was a woman. (5) Susan B. Anthony not to be silenced. (6) She joined other women in fighting for women's rights in education, voting, and property ownership. (7) Also fought for the abolition of slavery. (8) When black men were given the right to vote in 1869, she was pleased. (9) However, was disappointed that women did not receive the same consideration. (10) For about sixty years, she was active in the National Woman Suffrage Movement.

(11) Died fourteen years before the 19th Amendment gave women the right to vote.

(12) In 1979, she was recognized for her civic contributions. (13) Placed her picture on a one-dollar coin.

Exercise 9	CORRECTING FRAGMENTS

The following fragments need either a subject or a verb. Correct them. (See Answer Key for possible answers.)

1. One of the two main industries in Florida which is tourism.

2. People going to Florida to visit Disney World.

3. Others who go to watch sporting events such as the Orange Bowl.

4. Tourists regarding the Everglades National Park as a national wonder.

5. St. Augustine having the oldest house in the United States.

6. Many Major League baseball teams to Florida for spring training.

7. Can see a living coral reef formation at a state park.

8. Tours, demonstrations, and displays at the John F. Kennedy Space Center.

9. Some people who visit Florida for the pleasant weather and good beaches.

10. Circus World which offers opportunities for amateurs.

Exercise 10	CORRECTING FRAGMENTS

The following fragments need either a subject or a verb. Correct them.

1. Australia as the "down under" country because it is south of the equator.

2. It being colonized by the English.

3. The first English residents being convicts.

4. The aborigines moving away from their traditional lands.

5. Had lived there for many thousands of years.

6. The population of Australia now well beyond twenty million.

7. More than two hundred thousand aborigines.

8. Many people living in the southeastern part of the country.

9. The inner region as the outback.

10. Australia being known for its unusual animals.

Exercise 11   **CORRECTING FRAGMENTS**

Identify each of the following as a fragment (FRAG) or a complete sentence (OK). Correct the fragments. (They may be any of the kind you have studied in this chapter: dependent clause, phrase, or word group without a subject or without a verb.) You can correct some fragments by adding them to a complete sentence.

_____ 1. Asia which developed much earlier than the West.

_____

_____ 2. More than five thousand years ago, Asia had an advanced civilization.

_____

_____ 3. People there who invented writing and created literature.

_____

_____ 4. Involved in the development of science, agriculture, and religion.

_____

_____ 5. The birthplace of the major religions of the world.

_____

_____ 6. The most common religion in Asia being Hinduism.

_____

_____ 7. The second most common religion is Islam.

_____

_____ 8. Asia is the most populous continent.

_____

_____ 9. With almost four billion people.

_____

_____ 10. Hong Kong and Bangladesh which are among the most densely populated places in the world.

_____

_____ 11. Asia having many ethnic groups.

_____

_____ 12. Including the Chinese, the Indians, the Arabs, the Turks, and the Jews.

_____

_____ 13. The Chinese have different groups.

_____

_____ 14. Speaking many dialects.

_____

_____ 15. Although they have different dialects.

_____

_____ 16. There is a national language.

_____

_____ 17. A language called Mandarin.

_____

_____ 18. Cultural differences exist in Taiwan.

_____

_____ 19. The main difference being between the Chinese from the mainland and the Taiwanese.

_____

_____ 20. Despite the difference, all Chinese have much culture in common.

_____

Comma Splices and Run-Ons

The comma splice and the run-on are two other kinds of faulty "sentences" that give false signals to the reader. In each instance the punctuation suggests that there is only one sentence, but, in fact, there is material for two.

The **comma splice** consists of two independent clauses with only a comma between them:

> *The weather was disappointing, we canceled the picnic.* (A comma by itself cannot join two independent clauses.)

The run-on differs from the comma splice in only one respect: It has no comma between the independent clauses. Therefore, the run-on is two independent clauses with *nothing* between them:

> *The weather was disappointing we canceled the picnic.* (Independent clauses must be properly connected.)

Because an independent clause can stand by itself as a sentence and because two independent clauses must be properly linked, you can use a simple technique to identify the comma splice and the run-on. If you see a sentence that you think may contain one of these two errors, ask yourself this question: "Can I insert a period at some place in the word group and still have a sentence on either side?" If the answer is yes and there is no word such as *and* or *but* following the inserted period, then you have a comma splice or a run-on to correct. In our previous examples of the comma splice and run-on, we could insert a period after the word *disappointing* in each case, and we would still have an independent clause—therefore, a sentence—on either side.

Four Ways to Correct Comma Splices and Run-Ons

Once you identify a comma splice or a run-on in your writing, you need to correct it. There are four different ways to fix these common sentence problems: Use a comma and a coordinating conjunction, use a subordinating conjunction, use a semicolon, or make each clause a separate sentence.

1. Use a comma and a coordinating conjunction.

Incorrect: We canceled the picnic the weather was disappointing. (run-on)

Correct: We canceled the picnic, *for* the weather was disappointing. (Here we inserted a comma and the coordinating conjunction *for.*)

Knowing the seven coordinating conjunctions will help you in writing sentences and correcting sentence problems. Remember the acronym FANBOYS: *for, and, nor, but, or, yet, so.*

Exercise 12	**CORRECTING COMMA SPLICES AND RUN-ONS**

Identify each word group as a comma splice (CS), a run-on (RO), or a complete sentence (OK), and make needed corrections using commas and coordinating conjunctions. (See Answer Key for possible answers.)

Example: __CS__ He did the assignment, ^and^ his boss gave him a bonus.

_____ 1. In 1846 a group of eighty-two settlers headed for California with much optimism, a hard road lay ahead.

_____ 2. They had expected to cross the mountains before winter they were in good spirits.

_____ 3. They would not arrive in California before winter, nor would some of them get there at all.

_____ 4. When they encountered a heavy snowstorm, they stopped to spend the winter they still thought they would be safe.

_____ 5. They made crude shelters of logs and branches, some also used moss and earth.

_____ 6. They had trouble managing they had not encountered such problems before.

———— 7. They ran out of regular food, they ate roots, mice, shoe leather, and their horses.

———— 8. Thirty-five members of the Donner Party died that winter, the survivors were so hungry that they ate the dead bodies.

———— 9. They were weak, sick, and depressed they did not give up.

———— 10. Fifteen people set out to get help seven survived and returned to rescue friends and relatives.

Exercise 13	CORRECTING COMMA SPLICES AND RUN-ONS

Identify each word group as a comma splice (CS), a run-on (RO), or a complete sentence (OK), and make needed corrections using commas and coordinating conjunctions.

———— 1. John Dillinger was a troubled youth he dropped out of school when he was sixteen.

———— 2. He held several jobs then he turned to crime.

———— 3. He was arrested for armed robbery he spent nine years in prison.

———— 4. He got out and formed a gang, they robbed eleven banks in 1933 and 1934.

———— 5. He was twice captured by the police and imprisoned.

———— 6. Each time he escaped by using clever schemes.

———— 7. His bank jobs were well planned they often depended on deception.

———— 8. On one occasion while he was robbing a bank, he explained to observers that he was making a gangster movie.

———— 9. In 1934 he was fatally shot when he came out of a movie.

———— 10. He thought he was safe, his date had made a deal with the FBI and wore a red dress as a signal.

2. Use a subordinating conjunction.

Incorrect: The weather was disappointing, we canceled the picnic.

Correct: *Because* the weather was disappointing, we canceled the picnic.

By inserting the subordinating conjunction *because,* you can transform the first independent clause into a dependent clause and correct the comma splice. Knowing the most common subordinating conjunctions will help you in writing sentences and correcting sentence problems. Here is a list of the subordinating conjunctions you saw in Chapter 3.

after	*if*	*until*
although	*in order that*	*when*
as	*provided that*	*whenever*
as if	*rather than*	*where*
because	*since*	*whereas*
before	*so that*	*wherever*
even if	*than*	*whether*
even though	*unless*	*while*

Exercise 14	**CORRECTING COMMA SPLICES AND RUN-ONS**

Identify each word group as a comma splice (CS), a run-on (RO), or a complete sentence (OK), and correct the errors by making a dependent clause. (See Answer Key for possible answers.)

_____ 1. Chris Evert was one of the most successful tennis players of the 1970s and 1980s, she was not physically powerful.

_____ 2. She was intelligent and well coordinated, she became a top player.

_____ 3. She was still in her teens she won major championships.

_____ 4. She attracted much attention in 1974 she won fifty-five consecutive matches.

_____ 5. She reached the top, she had much competition there.

_____ 6. Evonne Goolagong was Evert's main competition at first Martina Navratilova soon assumed that role.

_____ 7. Financially Chris Evert's career was notable she made more than six million dollars.

_____ 8. Chris Evert helped to make women's tennis what it is today, she will not be forgotten.

_____ 9. She was called the "ice princess" she did not show her emotions.

_____ 10. She is regarded as one of the greatest athletes of the past forty years.

| Exercise 15 | CORRECTING COMMA SPLICES AND RUN-ONS |

Identify each group as a comma splice (CS), a run-on (RO), or a complete sentence (OK), and correct the errors by making a dependent clause.

_____ 1. Jesse Owens won four gold medals in the 1936 Olympics he became a famous person.

_____ 2. The 1936 Olympics were held in Nazi Germany Owens was placed at a disadvantage.

_____ 3. Hitler believed in the superiority of the Aryans, he thought Owens would lose.

_____ 4. Jesse Owens won Hitler showed his disappointment openly.

_____ 5. Owens broke a record for the 200-meter race that had stood for thirty-six years.

_____ 6. Owens then jumped a foot farther than others in the long jump Hitler left the stadium.

_____ 7. Before the day was at last over, Owens had also won gold medals in the 100-meter dash and the 400-meter relay.

_____ 8. Hitler's early departure was a snub at Owens, but he did not care.

_____ 9. Owens returned to the United States, he engaged in numerous exhibitions, including racing against a horse.

_____ 10. In his later years Owens became an official for the U.S. Olympic Committee, he never received the recognition that many contemporary athletes do.

3. Use a semicolon.

Incorrect: The weather was disappointing, we canceled the picnic.

Correct: The weather was disappointing; we canceled the picnic.

Correct: The weather was disappointing; *therefore,* we canceled the picnic.

This comma splice was corrected by a semicolon. The first correct example shows the semicolon alone. The second correct example shows a semicolon followed by the conjunctive adverb *therefore.* The conjunctive adverb is optional, but, as we have already seen, conjunctive adverbs can make the relationship between independent clauses stronger. Here is the list of conjunctive adverbs you saw in Chapter 3.

however

otherwise

therefore

similarly

hence

on the other hand

then

consequently

also

thus

Do you remember the acronym HOTSHOT CAT, made up of the first letter of each of these common conjunctive adverbs? The acronym will help you remember them. Other conjunctive adverbs include *in fact, for example, moreover, nevertheless, furthermore, now,* and *soon.*

| Exercise 16 | **CORRECTING COMMA SPLICES AND RUN-ONS** |

Identify each word group as a comma splice (CS), a run-on (RO), or a complete sentence (OK). Make corrections with a semicolon, and add a conjunctive adverb if appropriate. (See Answer Key for answers.)

_____ 1. Madonna Louise Veronica Ciccone became one of the biggest pop stars in the 1980s, she is known to most people as Madonna.

_____ 2. Madonna was talented in dance she even won a dance scholarship to the University of Michigan in the mid-1970s.

_____ 3. She was not interested in staying in school, with a mere thirty-five dollars in her possession, she moved to New York City.

_____ 4. After working in several small bands, she finally made her first album in 1983.

_____ 5. When her first album became number one on the *Billboard* list in 1984, she immediately had new opportunities.

_____ 6. Madonna continues to be a very popular singer, she can act.

_____ 7. She performed well in the comedy movie *Desperately Seeking Susan* she also starred in *Dick Tracy, A League of Their Own,* and *Evita.*

_____ 8. Madonna is an expert at manipulating the media, she increases her popularity each time she changes her image.

_____ 9. Her show business career has prospered, she has had problems in her private life.

_____ 10. She continues to promote herself other people do too.

Exercise 17	**CORRECTING COMMA SPLICES AND RUN-ONS**

Identify each word group as a comma splice (CS), a run-on (RO), or a complete sentence (OK). Make corrections with a semicolon, and add a conjunctive adverb if appropriate.

_____ 1. Ants are highly social insects they live in colonies.

_____ 2. They work for the benefit of the group, cooperation is important.

_____ 3. Ants have different roles they will, in some species, have different sizes and shapes.

_____ 4. An ant will be a queen, a worker, or a male, there is not an identity problem among ants.

_____ 5. A worker may be a soldier whose job is to defend the nest that ant has large mandibles, or teeth.

_____ 6. The worker that is a janitor will have the job of cleaning the nest her head is big for pushing waste material through the tunnel.

_____ 7. The queen is very large because she must lay many eggs.

_____ 8. The workers are all female, their job is to do all of the work.

_____ 9. The males have only one function, and that function is to mate with the queen.

_____ 10. In some species, the workers may change roles in their work, the males only mate and die young.

4. **Make each clause a separate sentence.**

Incorrect: The weather was disappointing, we canceled the picnic.

Correct: The weather was disappointing. We canceled the picnic.

This method is at once the simplest and most common method of correcting comma splices and run-ons. To correct the comma splice, replace the comma with a period, and begin the second sentence (the second independent clause) with a capital letter. For a run-on, insert a period between the two independent clauses and begin the second sentence with a capital letter.

| Exercise 18 | CORRECTING COMMA SPLICES AND RUN-ONS |

Identify each word group as a comma splice (CS), a run-on (RO), or a complete sentence (OK), and make corrections with a period and a capital letter. (See Answer Key for answers.)

_____ 1. About a hundred and fifty years ago, British soldiers wore a bright red coat, they also wore a black hat and white trousers.

_____ 2. The soldiers looked good in parades the queen was very proud.

_____ 3. On the battlefield, the situation was different, and the uniform was rewarded differently.

_____ 4. The coat could be seen at a great distance enemies aimed at the red coats.

_____ 5. This had long been a problem, even in the days of the American Revolution.

_____ 6. No one in high position was willing to change the colors of the uniform the soldiers decided to take action.

_____ 7. A solution was at hand, the soldiers would wear the red coats but change the colors.

_____ 8. At the time of their experiment, they were serving in India, they would use natural elements to solve their problem.

_____ 9. In the dry season, they would rub yellow-brown dust on their uniforms, and in the wet season they would use mud.

_____ 10. They liked the camouflage color so much that they finally changed the color of their uniforms to the drab color they called it *khaki*, the Indian word for *dust*.

| Exercise 19 | CORRECTING COMMA SPLICES AND RUN-ONS |

Identify each word group as a comma splice (CS), a run-on (RO), or a complete sentence (OK), and make corrections with a period and a capital letter.

_____ 1. The phonograph was invented about a hundred years ago, the inventor was Thomas Edison.

_____ 2. He calculated that sound vibrations could be recorded and that they could be played back.

_____ 3. He constructed an instrument with a mouthpiece, a speaker, a cylinder, a needle, and a crank he put tin foil around the cylinder.

_____ 4. He uttered the first words into the machine as he turned the crank the first words were "Mary had a little lamb."

_____ 5. Next he moved the needle back to its original position he turned the crank again and put his ear to the speaker.

_____ 6. The speaker looked like a large funnel, Edison could hear scratchy sounds.

_____ 7. Then he heard his own voice his invention was a success.

_____ 8. The next step was to perfect his invention, he worked to improve the sound and to simplify the process.

_____ 9. The quality of the needles was improved, the cylinders were made of wax to improve the fidelity.

_____ 10. Soon it was possible for people all over the world to listen to great music and to hear the voices of famous people.

Techniques for Spotting Problem Sentences

1. For the fragment, ask yourself: "If someone were to say or write this to me, would I expect the person to add to the statement or rephrase it?"

2. In checking for the comma splice or run-on, ask yourself, "Is there a point in this word group at which I can insert a period and create a sentence on either side?" The question is not necessary if there is a coordinating conjunction (FANBOYS) at that point.

3. If you have trouble with comma splices and run-ons, check these constructions as you revise:
    a. A comma preceded by a noun or pronoun followed by a noun or pronoun
    b. A sentence beginning with a subordinating conjunction

4. If you have trouble with fragments, look for these clues:
    a. A word group with a single verb ending in *-ing*
    b. A word group without both a subject and a verb

5. Use the grammar checker on your word processor to alert you to possible problem sentences. Then use instruction from this book to make the necessary corrections.

Chapter Review: Correcting Fragments, Comma Splices, and Run-Ons

Fragments

1. A correct sentence signals completeness; a **fragment** signals incompleteness—it doesn't make sense. You expect the speaker or writer of a fragment to say or write more or to rephrase it.

2. A **dependent clause** cannot stand by itself because it begins with a subordinating word.

   > *Because* he left.

   > *When* she worked.

   > *Although* they slept.

3. A **verbal phrase**, a **prepositional phrase**, and an **appositive phrase** may carry ideas, but each is incomplete because it lacks a subject and verb.

   Verbal Phrase: *having completed his initial research*

   Sentence: Having completed his initial research, he refined his outline.

   Prepositional Phrase: *in the store*

   Sentence: She worked in the store.

   Appositive Phrase: *a successful business*

   Sentence: Marks Brothers, a successful business, sells clothing.

4. Each complete sentence must have an **independent clause,** a group of words that contains a subject and a verb, and can stand alone.

   > He enrolled for the fall semester.

Comma Splices and Run-Ons

1. The **comma splice** (CS) consists of two independent clauses with only a comma between them.

   > Maria exceeded her sales quota, she received a bonus. (A comma by itself cannot join two independent clauses.)

2. The run-on (RO) differs from the comma splice in only one respect: It has no comma between the independent clauses.

   > Maria exceeded her sales quota she received a bonus. (Independent clauses must be properly connected.)

Correcting Comma Splices and Run-Ons

1. Use a comma and a **coordinating conjunction** (*for, and, nor, but, or, yet, so*) to correct the comma splice or run-on.

   > Maria exceeded her sales quota, *and* she received a bonus.

2. Use a **subordinating conjunction** (such as *because, after, that, when, although, since, how, till, unless, before*) to make one clause dependent and correct the comma splice or run-on.

   > *Because* Maria exceeded her sales quota, she received a bonus.

3. Use a **semicolon** (with or without a conjunctive adverb such as *however, otherwise, therefore, similarly, hence, on the other hand, then, consequently, also, thus*) to correct the comma splice or run-on.

> Maria exceeded her sales quota; *therefore,* she received a bonus.

> Maria exceeded her sales quota; she received a bonus.

4. Use a period to replace a comma and add a capital letter (to correct a comma splice), or use a period between two independent clauses and add a capital letter (to correct a run-on).

> Maria exceeded her sales quota. She received a bonus.

Chapter Review Exercises

Review 1   CORRECTING FRAGMENTS, COMMA SPLICES, AND RUN-ONS

Correct each fragment, comma splice, and run-on problem by using one of the methods you learned. Select the method you think is most effective for smoothness of expression and emphasis. You may find it helpful to read the material aloud as you work. (See Answer Key for possible answers.)

Dinosaurs were giant lizardlike animals, they lived more than a hundred million years ago. Some had legs like lizards and turtles, some had legs more like birds. The ones with legs like birds. Could walk easily with raised bodies. They varied in size, many were huge. The largest, the diplodocus, about ninety feet long, equal to the distance between the bases in baseball. Weighing more than ten elephants. The smallest weighed no more than two pounds and was no bigger than a chicken. Some dinosaurs ate meat, almost certainly some dinosaurs ate other dinosaurs. Used their strong claws and fierce teeth to tear at their victims. Dinosaurs were different. In design as well as size. They had horns, spikes, bills, armorlike plates, clublike tails, bony crests, and teeth in many sizes and shapes their heads were proportionately tiny or absurdly large. Their mouths varied. Depending on their eating habits.

Review 2   CORRECTING FRAGMENTS, COMMA SPLICES, AND RUN-ONS

Correct each fragment, comma splice, and run-on. Choose methods of corrections that promote smoothness of expression and emphasis.

Deserts are often referred to as wastelands. It is true that not as many plants grow there as in a temperate zone, it is also true that animals do not live there in great numbers. However, many plants and animals live and do quite well in the desert. Because of their adaptations.

Not all deserts have the same appearance, many people think of the desert as a hot, sandy area. Actually, sand covers only about 20 percent of the desert. Some deserts have mountains some others have snow.

Because deserts are dry for most of the year. Plants must conserve and store water. Several kinds of cacti can shrink during a dry season and swell during a rainy season. Some shrubs simply drop their leaves and use their green bark to manufacture chlorophyll. Seeds sometimes lying in the desert for several years before sprouting to take advantage of a rainfall.

Animals have quite effectively adjusted to the desert, some animals obtain moisture from the food they eat and require no water. One animal of the desert, the camel, produces fat. Which it stores in its hump. The fat allows the camel to reserve more body heat it needs little water. Still other animals feed only at night or are inactive for weeks or even months.

About 15 percent of the land of the earth is covered by deserts. That area increasing every year. Because of overgrazing by livestock. Also because of the destruction of forests. Areas that were once green and fertile will now support little life and only a small population of human beings.

5

Verbs

"*V*erbs *are to* strong sentences *as* gas *is to* fine cars. *Choose the right kind and don't skimp on the octane.*"

This chapter covers the use of standard verbs. To some, the word *standard* implies "correct." A more precise meaning is "that which is conventional among educated people." Therefore, a standard verb is the right choice in most school assignments, most published writing, and most important public speaking situations. We all change our language when we move from these formal occasions to informal ones: We don't talk to our families in the same way we would speak at a large gathering in public; we don't write letters to friends the same way we write a history report. But even with informal language we would seldom change from standard to nonstandard usage.

Regular and Irregular Verbs

Verbs can be divided into two categories, called *regular* and *irregular*. Regular verbs are predictable, but irregular verbs—as the term suggests—follow no definite pattern.

Verbs always show time. Present tense verbs show an action or a state of being that is occurring at the present time: I *like* your hat. He *is* at a hockey game right now. Present tense verbs can also imply a continuation from the past into the future: She *drives* to work every day.

Past tense verbs show an action or a state of being that occurred in the past: We *walked* to town yesterday. Tim *was* president of the club last year.

Regular Verbs

Present Tense

For *he, she,* and *it,* regular verbs in the present tense add an *-s* or an *-es* to the base word. The following chart shows the present tense of the base word *ask,* which is a regular verb.

	Singular	Plural
First Person:	I ask	we ask
Second Person:	you ask	you ask
Third Person:	he, she, it asks	they ask

If the verb ends in *-y,* you might have to drop the *-y* and add *-ies* for *he, she,* and *it.*

	Singular	Plural
First Person:	I try	we try
Second Person:	you try	you try
Third Person:	he, she, it tries	they try

Past Tense

For regular verbs in the past tense, add *-ed* to the base form:

Base Form (Present)	Past
walk	walked
answer	answered

If the base form already ends in *-e,* add just *-d:*

Base Form (Present)	Past
smile	smiled
decide	decided

If the base form ends in a consonant followed by *-y,* drop the *-y* and add *-ied.*

Base Form (Present)	Past
fry	fried
amplify	amplified

Regardless of how you form the past tense, regular verbs in the past tense do not change forms. The following chart shows the past tense of the base word *like,* which is a regular verb.

	Singular	Plural
First Person:	I liked	we liked
Second Person:	you liked	you liked
Third Person:	he, she, it liked	they liked

Past Participles

The past participle uses the helping verb *has, have,* or *had* along with the past tense of the verb. For regular verbs, the past participle form of the verb is the same as the past tense.

Base Form	Past	Past Participle
happen	happened	happened
hope	hoped	hoped
cry	cried	cried

Here is a list of some common regular verbs, showing the base form, the past tense, and the past participle. The base form can also be used with such helping verbs as *can, could, do, does, did, may, might, must, shall, should, will,* and *would.*

Regular Verbs

Base Form (Present)	Past	Past Participle
answer	answered	answered
ask	asked	asked
cry	cried	cried
decide	decided	decided
dive	dived (dove)	dived
finish	finished	finished
happen	happened	happened
learn	learned	learned
like	liked	liked
love	loved	loved
need	needed	needed
open	opened	opened
start	started	started
suppose	supposed	supposed
walk	walked	walked
want	wanted	wanted

Irregular Verbs

Irregular verbs do not follow any definite pattern.

Base Form (Present)	Past	Past Participle
shake	shook	shaken
make	made	made
begin	began	begun

Some irregular verbs that sound similar in the present tense don't follow the same pattern.

Base Form (Present)	Past	Past Participle
ring	rang	rung
swing	swung	swung
bring	brought	brought

Present Tense

For *he, she,* and *it,* irregular verbs in the present tense add an *-s* or an *-es* to the base word. The following chart shows the present tense of the base word *break,* which is an irregular verb.

	Singular	Plural
First Person:	I break	we break
Second Person:	you break	you break
Third Person:	he, she, it breaks	they break

If the irregular verb ends in *-y,* you might have to drop the *-y* and add *-ies* for *he, she,* and *it.*

	Singular	Plural
First Person:	I fly	we fly
Second Person:	you fly	you fly
Third Person:	he, she, it flies	they fly

Past Tense

Like past tense regular verbs, past tense irregular verbs do not change their forms. The following chart shows the past tense of the irregular verb *do.*

	Singular	Plural
First Person:	I did	we did
Second Person:	you did	you did
Third Person:	he, she, it did	they did

For irregular verbs in the past tense, use the following list of irregular verbs.

Past Participles

Use the past tense form with the helping verbs *has, have,* and *had.*

Here is a list of some common irregular verbs, showing the base form (present), the past tense, and the past participle. Like regular verbs, the base forms can be used with such helping verbs as *can, could, do, does, did, may, might, must, shall, should, will,* and *would.*

Irregular Verbs

Base Form (Present)	Past	Past Participle
arise	arose	arisen
awake	awoke (awaked)	awoken (awaked)
be	was, were	been

Irregular Verbs

Base Form (Present)	Past	Past Participle
become	became	become
begin	began	begun
bend	bent	bent
blow	blew	blown
break	broke	broken
bring	brought	brought
burst	burst	burst
buy	bought	bought
catch	caught	caught
choose	chose	chosen
cling	clung	clung
come	came	come
cost	cost	cost
creep	crept	crept
deal	dealt	dealt
do	did	done
drink	drank	drunk
drive	drove	driven
eat	ate	eaten
feel	felt	felt
fight	fought	fought
fling	flung	flung
fly	flew	flown
forget	forgot	forgotten
freeze	froze	frozen
get	got	got (gotten)
go	went	gone
grow	grew	grown
hang	hung	hung
have	had	had
hit	hit	hit
know	knew	known
lead	led	led
leave	left	left
lose	lost	lost
make	made	made

Irregular Verbs

Base Form (Present)	Past	Past Participle
mean	meant	meant
put	put	put
read	read	read
ride	rode	ridden
ring	rang	rung
see	saw	seen
shine	shone	shone
shoot	shot	shot
sing	sang	sung
sink	sank	sunk
sleep	slept	slept
slink	slunk	slunk
speak	spoke	spoken
spend	spent	spent
spread	spread	spread
steal	stole	stolen
stink	stank (stunk)	stunk
sweep	swept	swept
swim	swam	swum
swing	swung	swung
take	took	taken
teach	taught	taught
tear	tore	torn
think	thought	thought
throw	threw	thrown
thrust	thrust	thrust
wake	woke (waked)	woken (waked)
weep	wept	wept
write	wrote	written

Exercise 1   **SELECTING VERBS**

Underline the correct verb form. (See Answer Key for answers.)

1. This morning I (saw, seen) an intriguing new product on an infomercial.

2. As I (pause, paused) at Channel 17, my interest (grew, growed).

3. The Sandwich Demon was the name of the product, and I (knew, knowed) I wanted one.

4. Judy, the spokesperson, (extracted, extract) a piping hot, toasted cheese sandwich from the Demon's steaming jaws.

5. Then a hungry member of the audience (jumped, jumpt) up and (eat, ate) the sandwich in one gulp.

6. Judy (force, forced) a laugh and (accepted, accept) the audience's applause.

7. She then (nodded, nod) to two stage hands who (dragged, drug) the man back up to center stage.

8. While smiling serenely at the camera, Judy (thrust, thrusted) the man's hand into the Sandwich Demon, at which he (flung, fling) his body convulsively like a hooked fish.

9. After the man pulled free from the Demon, Judy (lift, lifted) his hand and (displayed, display) it to the audience.

10. Amazingly the hand (didn't, doesn't) look much different from the toasted cheese sandwich!

Exercise 2	SELECTING VERBS

Underline the correct verb form.

1. Recycling is very important; almost nothing should be (throwed, thrown) away.

2. For instance, ties that are worn out can (become, became) tails for kites or leashes for dogs.

3. Engine grease can be (spreaded, spread) on wounds to prevent infection.

4. I personally (earn, earned) vacation money by recycling lard for candles.

5. Placing used plutonium fuel pellets on patio furniture will (help, helped) people deal with insects.

6. The plutonium will (make, made) the insects large so they can be (hit, hitted) with recycled tennis rackets.

7. The plutonium will also make insects (glow, glowed) in the dark so they can be easily (saw, seen).

8. This textbook can be (used, use) to wrap fish.

9. Strapped to the chest, it can (stop, stopped) small-caliber bullets.

10. When (dropped, dropt) from sufficient height, a single copy has been (known, knowed) to kill small rodents.

"Problem" Verbs

The following pairs of verbs are especially troublesome and confusing: *lie* and *lay, sit* and *set, rise* and *raise.* One way to tell them apart is to remember which word in each pair takes a direct object. A direct object answers the question *whom* or *what* in connection with a verb. The words *lay, raise,* and *set* take a direct object.

> He *raised* the window. (He *raised* what?)

Lie, rise, and *sit,* however, cannot take a direct object. We cannot say, for example, "He rose the window." In the examples, the italicized words are objects.

Present Tense	Meaning	Past Tense	Past Participle	Example
lie	to rest	lay	lain	I lay down to rest.
lay	to place something	laid	laid	We laid the *books* on the table.
rise	to go up	rose	risen	The smoke rose quickly.
raise	to lift, to bring forth	raised	raised	She raised the *question.*
sit	to rest	sat	sat	He sat in the chair.
set	to place something	set	set	They set the *basket* on the floor.

Exercise 3   SELECTING VERBS

Underline the correct verb form. (See Answer Key for answers.)

1. This story is about Bill "Chick" Walker, who (lossed, lost) all he owned at the Wagon Wheel Saloon in Las Vegas.

2. Chick had (laid, layed) one thousand dollars on the red 21 at the roulette table.

3. For that spin, he (done, did) an amazing thing—he (won, wins).

4. But after a while, Chick (became, become) stupid, and his luck (ran, run) out.

5. Before he had (ate, eaten) breakfast, he accepted free drinks from the charming Trixie, who (served, serve) cocktails.

6. His judgment was soon (ruined, ruint) by the drinks, and he (put, putted) all his money on one spin.

7. That wager (cost, costed) Chick everything, and he couldn't (raise, rise) any more money.

8. Moreover, Trixie would not (sit, set) with him because she (like, liked) only winners.

9. Chick drained his glass, (rose, raised) from his red tufted vinyl barstool, and (head, headed) for the parking lot.

10. There he (known, knew) Bonnie Lou would be waiting for him because she (lust, lusted) for losers.

Exercise 4	**SELECTING VERBS**

Underline the correct verb form.

1. Young Hubert has answered too many questions without (rising, raising) his hand.

2. Pugsy, the bully of the class, runs across the room and (sits, sets) on Hubert.

3. The teacher (lies, lays) a heavy hand on Pugsy's head.

4. He then tells the two boys to (lie, lay) down and cool off.

5. They (raise, rise) and retire to opposite corners of the classroom.

6. Both of them have (lain, laid) there for several minutes before the class comes to order.

7. The teacher decides to use them to (sit, set) an example.

8. Looking at Hubert, the teacher says, "What if everyone answered without a (risen, raised) hand?"

9. "What if we solved all our problems by (sitting, setting) on those we disagree with?" he continues, trying to (sit, set) Pugsy straight.

10. "We would all be (lying, laying) over here in the corner," says Pugsy, without (rising, raising) his hand, and all of his fellow students run over to (set, sit) on him.

Exercise 5	**USING VERBS IN SENTENCES**

Use each of these words in a sentence of ten words or more.

1. *lie, lay* (rest), *lain, laid* _____

_____

_____

_____

_____

_____

_____

2. *sit, sat, set* _____

_____

_____

_____

_____

_____

3. *is, was, were* _____

_____

_____

_____

_____

_____

4. *do, does* (or *don't, doesn't*) _____

_____

_____

_____

_____

_____

_____

The Twelve Verb Tenses

Some languages, such as Chinese and Navajo, have no verb tenses to indicate time. English has a fairly complicated system of tenses, but most verbs pattern in what are known as the simple tenses: past, present, and future. Altogether there are twelve tenses in English. The first four charts that follow illustrate those tenses in sentences. The next charts place each verb on a time line. The charts also explain what the different tenses mean and how to form them.

Simple Tenses

Present: I, we, you, they *drive.*
He, she, it *drives.*

Past: I, we, you, he, she, it, they *drove.*

Future: I, we, you, he, she, it, they *will drive.*

Perfect Tenses

Present Perfect:	I, we, you, they *have driven.*
	He, she, it *has driven.*
Past Perfect:	I, we, you, he, she, it, they *had driven.*
Future Perfect:	I, we, you, he, she, it, they *will have driven.*

Progressive Tenses

Present Progressive:	I *am driving.*
	He, she, it *is driving.*
	We, you, they *are driving.*
Past Progressive:	I, he, she, it *was driving.*
	We, you, they *were driving.*
Future Progressive:	I, we, you, he, she, it, they *will be driving.*

Perfect Progressive Tenses

Present Perfect Progressive:	I, we, you, they *have been driving.*
	He, she, it *has been driving.*
Past Perfect Progressive:	I, we, you, he, she, it, they *had been driving.*
Future Perfect Progressive:	I, we, you, he, she, it, they *will have been driving.*

Simple Tenses

Tense	Time Line	Time	Verb Form
Present I drive to work. She drives to work.	past ——— XXX ——— future Now	Present, may imply a continuation from past to future	Present: drive drives
Past I drove to work.	x Now	Past	Past: drove
Future I will drive to work.	x Now	Future	Present preceded by will: will drive

Perfect Tenses

Tense	Time Line	Time	Verb Form
Present Perfect I <u>have driven</u> to work.	past ———XXX———future Now	Completed recently in the past, may continue to the present	Past participle preceded by <u>have</u> or <u>has</u>: have driven
Past Perfect I <u>had driven</u> to work before I moved to the city (event).	Event X O Now	Prior to a specific time in the past	Past participle preceded by <u>had</u>: had driven
Future Perfect I <u>will have driven</u> to work thousands of times by December 31 (event).	Event X O Now	At a time prior to a specific time in the future	Past participle preceded by <u>will have</u>: will have driven

Progressive Tenses

Tense	Time Line	Time	Verb Form
Present Progressive I <u>am driving</u> to work.	past ———XXX———future Now	In progress now	Progressive (-*ing* ending) preceded by <u>is</u>, <u>am</u>, or <u>are</u>: am driving
Past Progressive I <u>was driving</u> to work.	XXX Now	In progress in the past	Progressive (-*ing* ending) preceded by <u>was</u> or <u>were</u>: was driving
Future Progressive I <u>will be driving</u> to work.	XXX Now	In progress in the future	Progressive (-*ing* ending) preceded by <u>will be</u>: will be driving

Perfect Progressive Tenses

Tense	Time Line	Time	Verb Form
Present Perfect Progressive I have been driving to work.	past ——— XXX ——— future **Now**	In progress up to now	Progressive (*-ing* ending) preceded by <u>have been</u> or <u>has been</u>: have been driving
Past Perfect Progressive I had been driving when I began ride-sharing (event).	Event XXX O **Now**	In progress before another event in the past	Progressive (*-ing* ending) preceded by <u>had</u>: had been driving
Future Perfect Progressive By May 1 (event), I will have been driving to work for six years.	Event XXX O Now	In progress before another event in the future	Progressive (*-ing* ending) preceded by <u>will have been</u>: will have been driving

---

Exercise 6   **CHOOSING VERB TENSE**

Underline the correct verb form. (See Answer Key for answers.)

1. Jason (is receiving, had received) his appointment before he graduated.

2. She (worked, had worked) in sales for two years before she was promoted.

3. After parking their car, they (walk, walked) to the beach.

4. I (have, had) never encountered a genius until I met her.

5. I wished that we (could have gone, went) to the big game.

6. They know that they (will complete, will have completed) the job before the first snow.

7. We (are considering, consider) the proposal.

8. Last summer, he told us of the many interesting adventures he (has had, had).

9. Yesterday, we went to the desert to see the cabin they (built, had built).

10. Tomorrow I (will go, go) to the supermarket for party items.

Exercise 7	**CHOOSING VERB TENSE**

Underline the correct verb form.

1. By the time the game was over, most fans (left, had left).

2. The shipping clerks said they (had sent, sent) the package.

3. We (study, are studying) the user's guide now.

4. We (decide, will decide) on the winner tomorrow.

5. They reminded us that we (made, had made) the same promise before.

6. Jill (had believed, believed) in his guilt until she saw the complete evidence.

7. Jake (had been napping, napped) when the alarm sounded.

8. By the time he finished talking, he realized that he (said, had said) too much.

9. At the end of the semester, the course grade (depends, will depend) on your ability to write well.

10. After he retired, I realized how much I (had learned, learned) from working with him.

Subject-Verb Agreement

This section is concerned with number agreement between subjects and verbs. The basic principle of **subject-verb agreement** is that if the subject is singular, the verb should be singular, and if the subject is plural, the verb should be plural. There are ten major guidelines. In the examples under the following guidelines, the simple subjects and verbs are italicized.

1. Do not let words that come between the subject and verb affect agreement.

   - Modifying phrases and clauses frequently come between the subject and verb:

     The various *types* of drama *were* not *discussed.*

     Angela, who is hitting third, *is* the best player.

     The *price* of those shoes *is* too high.

   - Certain prepositions can cause trouble. The following words are prepositions, not conjunctions: *along with, as well as, besides, in addition to, including, together with.* The words that function as objects of prepositions cannot also be subjects of the sentence.

     The *coach,* along with the players, *protests* the decision.

   - When a negative phrase follows a positive subject, the verb agrees with the positive subject.

     Phillip, not the other boys, *was* the culprit.

2. Do not let inversions (verb before subject, not the normal order) affect the agreement of subject and verb.

- Verbs and other words may come before the subject. Do not let them affect the agreement. To understand subject-verb relationships, recast the sentence in normal word order.

   Are Jabir and his *sister* at home? (question form)

   Jabir and his *sister are* at home. (normal order)

- A sentence filler is a word that is grammatically independent of other words in the sentence. The most common fillers are *there* and *here*. Even though a sentence filler precedes the verb, it should not be treated as the subject.

   There *are* many *reasons* for his poor work. (The verb *are* agrees with the subject *reasons*.)

3. A singular verb agrees with a singular indefinite pronoun. (See page 120.)

- Most indefinite pronouns are singular.

   Each of the women *is* ready at this time.

   Neither of the women *is* ready at this time.

   One of the children *is* not paying attention.

- Certain indefinite pronouns do not clearly express either a singular or plural number. Agreement, therefore, depends on the meaning of the sentence. These pronouns are *all, any, none,* and *some*.

   All of the melon *was* good.

   All of the melons *were* good.

   None of the pie *is* acceptable.

   None of the pies *are* acceptable.

4. Two or more subjects joined by *and* usually take a plural verb.

   The *captain* and the *sailors were* happy to be ashore.

   The *trees* and *shrubs need* more care.

- If the parts of a compound subject mean one and the same person or thing, the verb is singular; if the parts mean more than one, the verb is plural.

   The *secretary* and *treasurer is* not present. (one)

   The *secretary* and the *treasurer are* not present. (more than one)

- When *each* or *every* modifies singular subjects joined by *and,* the verb is singular.

   Each *boy* and each *girl brings* a donation.

   Each *woman* and *man has asked* the same questions.

5. Alternative subjects—that is, subjects joined by *or, nor, either/or, neither/nor, not only/but also*—should be handled in the following manner:

- If the subjects are both singular, the verb is singular.

   Rosa or *Alicia* is responsible.

- If the subjects are plural, the verb is plural.

   Neither the *students* nor the *teachers were* impressed by his comments.

• If one of the subjects is singular and the other subject is plural, the verb agrees with the nearer subject.

> Either the Garcia *boys* or their *father goes* to the hospital each day.

> Either their *father* or the Garcia *boys go* to the hospital each day.

6. Collective nouns—*team, family, group, crew, gang, class, faculty,* and the like— take a singular verb if the verb is considered a unit, but they take a plural verb if the group is considered as a number of individuals.

> The *team is playing* well tonight.

> The *team are getting* dressed.

> (In the second sentence, the individuals are acting not as a unit but separately. If you don't like the way the sentence sounds, substitute "The members of the team are getting dressed.")

7. Titles of books, essays, short stories, and plays; a word spoken of as a word; and the names of businesses take a singular verb.

> *The Canterbury Tales was written* by Geoffrey Chaucer.

> *Ives is* my favorite name for a pet.

> *Markle Brothers has* a sale this week.

8. Sums of money, distances, and measurements are followed by a singular verb when a unit is meant. They are followed by a plural verb when the individual elements are considered separately.

> *Three dollars was* the price. (unit)

> *Three dollars were* lying there. (individual)

> *Five years is* a long time. (unit)

> The *first five years were* difficult ones. (individual)

9. Be careful of agreement with nouns ending in *-s.* Several nouns ending in *-s* take a singular verb—for example, *aeronautics, civics, economics, ethics, measles, mumps.*

> *Mumps is* an extremely unpleasant disease.

> *Economics is* my major field of study.

10. Some nouns have only a plural form and so take only a plural verb—for example, *clothes, fireworks, scissors, trousers.*

> His *trousers are* badly wrinkled.

> Marv's *clothes were* stylish and expensive.

Exercise 8   **MAKING SUBJECTS AND VERBS AGREE**

Underline the verb that agrees in number with the subject. (See Answer Key for answers.)

1. The Mills (is, are) my favorite restaurant.

2. My scissors (is, are) dull.

3. For mature men, mumps (is, are) a serious disease.

4. Ethics (is, are) a very interesting discussion course.

5. "Current Affairs" (is, are) an exciting program.

6. Sears (is, are) having a giant sale.

7. Fireworks (is, are) dangerous.

8. Six years (is, are) too long to wait.

9. The team (is, are) meeting with their families.

10. The manager and the coach (is, are) leaving the stadium.

Exercise 9   **MAKING SUBJECTS AND VERBS AGREE**

Underline the verb that agrees in number with the subject.

1. The value of those books (is, are) much greater than the price.

2. The superintendent, along with his assistants, (is, are) asking for extensive changes.

3. The organizer of the rally, not the participants, (was, were) held responsible.

4. (Are, Is) the team and the referees ready to begin the game?

5. There (is, are) no sound reasons to support that view.

6. Each of the candidates (was, were) quick to profess a love of country, family, and God.

7. Each of the candidates (was, were) eager to shake hands.

8. All of the incumbents (was, were) confident about winning.

9. All of the coffee (was, were) gone before the program began.

10. Each man and woman in the audience (was, were) prepared for the question period.

11. Neither the mayor nor his opponents (was, were) interested in bringing up the topic of recycling.

12. Roberts's *Rules of Order* (was, were) used by the moderator when questions arose.

13. One citizen complained that twenty dollars (was, were) too much for trash pickup.

14. One candidate said that economics (is, are) more important than politics.

15. A well-dressed man said, "In some cases, clothes (make, makes) the man."

16. One of his opponents (was, were) concerned about his use of the word *man* instead of *person.*

17. Some of the children in the audience (was, were) not paying attention.

18. There (was, were) no breaks in the program until the question period.

19. Monroe Joslin, the youngest of the fifteen candidates, (was, were) the last to speak.

20. The local cable television station, along with two radio stations, (was, were) there to record the program for a delayed broadcast.

Consistency in Tense

Consider this paragraph:

> We (1) went downtown, and then we (2) watch a movie. Later we (3) met some friends from school, and we all (4) go to the mall. For most of the evening, we (5) play video games in arcades. It (6) was a typical but rather uneventful summer day.

Does the shifting verb tense bother you (to say nothing about the lack of development of ideas)? It should! The writer makes several unnecessary changes. Verbs 1, 3, and 6 are in the past tense, and verbs 2, 4, and 5 are in the present tense. Changing all verbs to past tense makes the paragraph much smoother.

> We went downtown, and then we watched a movie. Later we met some friends from school, and we all went to the mall. For most of the evening, we played video games in arcades. It was a typical but rather uneventful summer day.

In other instances you might want to maintain a consistent present tense. There are no inflexible rules about selecting a tense for certain kinds of writing, but you should be consistent, changing tense only for a good reason.

The present tense is usually used in writing about literature, even if the literature was written long in the past:

> *Moby Dick is* a novel about Captain Ahab's obsession with a great white whale. Ahab *sets* sail with a full crew of sailors who *think* they *are going* on merely another whaling voyage. Most of the crew *are* experienced seamen.

The past tense is likely to serve you best in writing about your personal experiences and about historical events (although the present tense can often be used effectively to establish the feeling of intimacy and immediacy):

> In the summer of 1991, Hurricane Bob *hit* the Atlantic coast region. It *came* ashore near Cape Hatteras and *moved* north. The winds *reached* a speed of more than ninety miles per hour on Cape Cod but then *slackened* by the time Bob *reached* Maine.

Exercise 10 — MAKING VERBS CONSISTENT IN TENSE

Correct verbs as needed in the following paragraph to achieve consistency in tense. Make all verbs past tense. (See Answer Key for answers.)

Judy had a weird hobby. A few years ago, she start to collect shreds of automobile tires in the street. She goes home and put them into interesting patterns on her mother's carpet. Then she takes a big can of industrial-strength glue and glued them together. Her mother is not amused by this tire-shred mosaic. Sometimes the glue stuck to the carpet. On those occasions, Judy's mother shook her fists and chases Judy around the house. Then one day, an art critic walks through the neighborhood in search of folk art. The critic saw Judy's tire-shred mosaic and buys it for a thousand dollars. Judy's mother smiles. She was very proud of her artistic daughter.

Exercise 11 — MAKING VERBS CONSISTENT IN TENSE

Correct verbs as needed in the following paragraph to achieve consistency in tense. Most verbs will be present tense.

A trip to the dentist should not be a terrible experience—unless one goes to Dr. Litterfloss, credit dentist. Although he graduated *magna cum lately* from Ed's School of Dentistry, he had a reputation for being one of the dirtiest and most careless dentists in the state. He didn't even know about germs. He never used Novocain. He just spins the chair until his patients lost consciousness. Then he shot them with his x-ray gun from behind a lead wall. Sometimes he missed, and now his dental technician glows in the dark, so he didn't need a light as he worked. While drilling with one hand, he snacked on Vienna sausages with the other. Stray alley cats and mangy curs fought around his feet for food scraps, so he didn't need a cleaning service. He seldom washed his Black and Decker drill or Craftsman chisel, and he squirts tobacco juice into his spit sink. I recommended him only with strong reservation.

Active and Passive Voice

Which of these sentences sounds better to you?

> Ken Griffey, Jr., slammed a home run.

> A home run was slammed by Ken Griffey, Jr.

Both sentences carry the same message, but the first expresses it more effectively. The subject *(Ken Griffey, Jr.)* is the actor. The verb *(slammed)* is the action. The direct object *(home run)* is the receiver of the action. The second sentence lacks the vitality of the first because the receiver of the action is the subject; the one who performs the action is embedded in the prepositional phrase at the end of the sentence.

The first sentence demonstrates the active voice. It has an active verb (one that leads to the direct object), and the action moves from the beginning to the end of the sentence. The second exhibits the passive voice (with the action reflecting back on the subject). When given a choice, you should usually select the active voice. It promotes energy and directness.

The passive voice, although not usually the preferred form, does have its uses.

- When the doer of the action is unknown or unimportant:

> My car was stolen.

> (The doer, a thief, is unknown.)

- When the receiver of the action is more important than the doer:

> My neighbor was permanently disabled by an irresponsible drunk driver.

> (The neighbor's suffering is the focus, not the drunk driver.)

As you can see, the passive construction places the doer at the end of a prepositional phrase (as in the second example) or does not include the doer in the statement at all (as in the first example). In the first example, the receiver of the action (the car) is in the subject position. The verb is preceded by a *to be* helper *was.* Here is another example:

> The book was read by her.   (passive)

> She read the book.   (active)

Because weak sentences often involve the unnecessary and ineffective use of the passive form, the following exercise gives you practice in identifying the passive voice and changing it to active.

| Exercise 12 | USING ACTIVE AND PASSIVE VOICE |

Identify each sentence as either active voice (A) or passive voice (P). If a sentence with the passive form would be more effective in the active voice, rewrite it. (See Answer Key for answers.)

_____ 1. Lauren named the puppy Cody.

_____

_____ 2. The customer, despite his rudeness, was allowed to return the soiled shirt.

_____

_____ 3. The victim was questioned by a police officer at the scene of the accident.

_____

_____ 4. The noisy rappers were sentenced by the solemn judge to listen to a hundred waltz CDs.

_____

_____ 5. The picnic was interrupted by hungry bears.

_____

_____ 6. During the confusion, the food was grabbed by the bears.

_____

_____ 7. Your last warning has been given by me to you.

_____

_____ 8. Rip Van Winkle was known by his friends for his long sleeping spells.

_____

_____ 9. For the party, we hired a Dixieland jazz band.

_____

_____ 10. Book reviews may be posted by you on many different online sites.

_____

Exercise 13   **USING ACTIVE AND PASSIVE VOICE**

Identify each sentence as either active voice (A) or passive voice (P). If a sentence with a passive form would be more effective in the active voice, rewrite it.

_____ 1. A story will be told to you by me.

_____

_____ 2. A tragedy was experienced by a local ventriloquist the other day.

_____

_____ 3. Hundreds of his fans were being delighted by him at a county fair.

_____

_____ 4. Suddenly his dummy was destroyed by flames.

_____

_____ 5. Some speculated that spontaneous combustion caused the tragedy.

_____

_____ 6. However, the fire possibly was produced by a system of cleverly placed mirrors engineered by the ventriloquist to increase his fame.

_____

_____ 7. The story was covered by all three major television networks.

_____

_____ 8. The scene of the mysterious combustion was viewed by thousands of curious folk.

_____

_____ 9. The ventriloquist has been made a rich man by the publicity.

_____

_____ 10. In fact, he had been given several offers to appear on television talk shows to discuss the event.

_____

_____ 11. Though living happily now, he will never forget how his little wooden friend and their friendship went up in smoke.

_____

Strong Verbs

Because the verb is an extremely important part of any sentence, it should be chosen with care. Some of the most widely used verbs are the "being" verbs: *is, was, were, are, am.* We couldn't get along in English without them, but writers often use them when more forceful and effective verbs are available.

Consider these examples:

    Weak Verb: He *is* the leader of the people.

   Strong Verb: He *leads* the people.

    Weak Verb: She *was* the first to finish.

   Strong Verb: She *finished* first.

Exercise 14	USING STRONG VERBS

Replace the weak verbs with stronger ones in the following sentences. Delete unnecessary words to make each sentence even more concise if you can. (See Answer Key for answers.)

1. My watch is running slowly.

2. My computer is quite inexpensive.

3. The horse was a fast runner.

4. They were writers who wrote well.

5. The dog is sleeping on the bed.

6. Mr. Hawkins is a real estate salesperson.

7. José is in attendance at Santa Ana College.

8. This assignment is something I like.

9. We are the successful students here.

10. She is in the process of combing her hair.

Exercise 15	USING STRONG VERBS

Replace the weak verbs with stronger ones in the following sentences. Delete unnecessary words to make each sentence even more concise if you can.

1. William Shakespeare was the writer of many great plays.

2. The students were the recipients of praise.

3. A big, red apple is my desire.

4. I was the writer of that article.

5. Jannell is the leader of the study group in the library.

6. Baseball is something I like to play.

7. He was the driver of the big rig.

8. The Dodgers will be winners next year.

9. They were in tears after the defeat.

10. The fire in the hills was in a condition of subsidence.

Subjunctive Mood

Mood refers to the intention of the verb. Three moods are relevant to our study: indicative, imperative, and subjunctive.

The indicative mood expresses a statement of fact.

> I considered the issue.

> I was tired.

The imperative mood expresses a command (and has a *you* understood subject).

> Go to the store.

The subjunctive mood expresses a statement as contrary to fact, conditional, desirable, possible, necessary, or doubtful. In current English the subjunctive form is distinguishable only in two forms: The verb *to be* uses *be* throughout the present tense and *were* throughout the past tense.

> He requires that we *be* (instead of *are*) on time.

> If she *were* (instead of *was*) the candidate, she would win.

In other verbs, the final *s* is dropped in the third person singular (he, she, it) of the present tense to make all forms the same in any one tense.

> I request that he *report* (instead of *reports*) today.

Here are examples of the common forms:

> If I *were* (instead of *was*) you, I wouldn't do that. (contrary to fact)

> She behaves as if she *were* (instead of *was*) not certain. (doubt)

> I wish I *were* (instead of *was*) in Texas. (wish)

| Exercise 16 | SELECTING SUBJUNCTIVE VERBS |

Underline the subjunctive verbs. (See Answer Key for answers to 1 through 5.)

1. If I (was, were) going to work, I would give you a ride.

2. I wish I (were, was) on the beach.

3. If I (was, were) you, I would take a stand.

4. They act as if they (are, were) angels.

5. I require that my workers (are, be) on time.

6. You may wish you (are, were) an adult, but you must show your ID.

7. You talk as if your winning (was, were) possible.

8. My manager insists that I (be, am) on time.

9. Suppose, for the sake of argument, your statement (was, were) true.

10. Sometimes I wish I (were, was) of the younger generation.

Chapter Review: Verbs

1. **Standard usage** is appropriate for the kind of writing and speaking you are likely to do in your college work and future career.

2. Whereas **regular verbs** are predictable—having an *-ed* ending for past and past-participle forms—**irregular verbs,** as the term suggests, follow no definite pattern.

   raise, raised, raised (regular); *see, saw, seen* (irregular)

3. Certain verbs (present tense here) can be troublesome and should be studied with care (page 87).

   lie, lay   sit, set   rise, raise

4. If the subject of a sentence is singular, the verb should be singular; if the subject is plural, the verb should be plural.

   The *price* of the shoes *is* high.

   The *advantages* of that shoe *are* obvious.

5. There are no inflexible rules about selecting a **tense** for certain kinds of writing, but you should be consistent, changing tense only for a good reason.

6. Usually you should select the present tense to write about literature.

   Herman Melville's character Bartleby the Scrivener fails to communicate.

   Select the past tense to write about yourself or something historical.

   I *was* eighteen when I *decided* I *was* ready for independence.

7. English has twelve verb tenses. (See charts on pages 90–92 for names, examples, functions, and forms.)

8. The **active voice** expression (subject, active verb, and sometimes object) is usually preferred over the **passive voice** expression (subject as the receiver of action, with doer unstated or at the end of a prepositional phrase).

   She read the book. (active)

   The book was read by her. (passive)

9. In your revision, replace weak verbs with strong ones.

   He *was* the first to leave. (weak verb)

   He *left* first. (strong verb)

10. The **subjunctive mood** expresses a statement that is contrary to fact, conditional, desirable, possible, necessary, or doubtful. *Be* is used throughout the present tense and *were* throughout the past.

    He requires that we *be* (not *are*) on time.

    I wish I *were* (not *was*) home.

In other verbs, the final *s* is dropped in the third person singular (he, she, it) of the present tense.

> I request that he *report* (instead of *reports*) today.

Chapter Review Exercises

Review 1	CHANGING VERB TENSE

Change the verbs from present to past tense. (See Answer Key for answers to 1 through 5.)

1. Frederick Douglass is the leading spokesman of African Americans in the 1800s.

2. Born a slave, he is befriended by his master's wife and begins to educate himself.

3. As a young man, he runs away to New Bedford, Massachusetts.

4. He works as a common laborer for some time.

5. At the Massachusetts Antislavery Society in 1841, he gives a speech on the importance of freedom.

6. His speech is so well received that he was hired to lecture on his experience as a slave.

7. While traveling on the lecture circuit, he often protests various forms of segregation.

8. He insists on sitting in "Whites Only" areas on the railroad.

9. He successfully protests against segregated schools in Rochester, New York.

10. In 1845 he publishes *Narrative of the Life of Frederick Douglass,* his autobiography.

Review 2	MAKING SUBJECTS AND VERBS AGREE

Underline the verb that agrees in number with the subject. (See Answer Key for answers to 1 through 5.)

1. The result of the defendant's corrupt business dealings (was, were) soon felt.

2. The mayor and most citizens (was, were) deeply affected.

3. There (was, were) no justification for the defendant's behavior.

4. Neither of the defendant's parents (was, were) willing to defend him.

5. Neither the judge nor the jury members (was, were) very sympathetic with the defense's case.

6. Ethics (was, were) apparently an unknown field of study to the defendant.

7. Each and every day (was, were) consumed with intense debate.

8. In the penalty phase, the judge said that ten years (was, were) the correct sentence.

9. Then the judge added, "Fifty thousand dollars (is, are) the right sum for restitution."

10. The defendant, along with his attorney, (was, were) not pleased.

Review 3	CORRECTING VERB PROBLEMS

Correct problems with verb form, tense, agreement, strength, and voice. As a summary of a novel, this piece should be mostly in the present tense.

Summary of *The Old Man and the Sea*

Santiago, one of many local fishermen, have not caught a fish in eighty-four days. Young Manolin, despite the objections of his parents, has a belief in the old man. His parents says Santiago is unlucky, and they will not let their son go fishing with him.

The next day Santiago sit sail. Soon he catch a small tuna, which he used for bait. Then a huge marlin hit the bait with a strike. The old man cannot rise the fish to the surface, and it pulled the boat throughout the rest of the day and during the night.

During the second day, Santiago's hand is injured by the line and he become extremely tired, but he holds on. When the fish moves to the surface, Santiago notes that it was two feet longer than his skiff. It is the biggest fish he has ever saw. He thinks in wonder if he will be up to the task of catching it. With the line braced across his shoulders, he sleeped for a while. As he dreams gloriously of lions and porpoises and of being young, he is awaken by the fish breaking water again, and Santiago is sure the fish is tiring. He lays in the boat and waits.

On the third day, the fish came to the surface. Santiago pull steadily on the line, and finally it is harpooned and killed by Santiago. The fish is tied to the skiff by him.

But sharks attacked and mutilate the huge marlin. Using an oar, he beats on the sharks courageously with all his strength, but they strips the fish to a skeleton.

With the bones still tied to the skiff, the exhausted old man returned to shore. Other fishermen and tourists marvel at the eighteen-foot skeleton of the fish as the old man lays asleep. The young boy knew he has much to learn from the old man and is determined to go fishing with him.

Review 4	USING STRONG VERBS

Replace the weak verbs with stronger ones in the following sentences. Delete unnecessary words to make each sentence even more concise if you can. (See Answer Key for answers to 1 through 5.)

1. Whitney is in the process of rebuilding her desktop.

2. Anika is a person who is capable of leading our group.

3. Matthew was the scorer of the last touchdown.

4. Maria is a worker at the department store.

5. Jonathan is one who attracts favorable attention.

6. Lauren has a smile that is sweet.

7. Shane is waiting for the next train.

8. Jarrett is a swift runner.

9. Jannell was the second to finish the race.

10. This review is something that makes me think.

Review 5	WRITING SENTENCES WITH CORRECT VERBS

Each of the following verbs appears in its base form. Change the verb form to the tense specified in parentheses and include it in a sentence of ten or more words. (See pages 90 through 92 for verb forms.)

1. eat (to past tense) _____

_____

_____

2. begin (to future) _____

_____

_____

3. see (to past perfect) _____

_____

_____

4. walk (to future perfect) _____

_____

_____

5. speak (to present perfect) _____

_____

_____

6. go (to future progressive) _____

_____

_____

7. drink (to present progressive) _____

_____

_____

8. dance (to past progressive) _____

_____

_____

9. fly (to present perfect progressive) _____

_____

_____

10. grow (to past perfect progressive) _____

_____

_____

11. choose (to future perfect progressive) _____

_____

_____

6

Pronouns

"It's not true that only owls know the difference between who's *and* whom's. *This chapter will provide you with the wisdom to master those pronouns and many more."*

Should you say, "Between you and *I*" or "Between you and *me*"? What about "Let's you and *I* do this" or "Let's you and *me* do this"? Are you confused about when to use *who* and *whom?* Is it "Everyone should wear *their* coat, or *his* coat, or *his or her* coat"? Is there anything wrong with saying, "When *you* walk down the streets of Laredo"?

The examples in the first paragraph represent the most common problems people have with pronouns. This chapter will help you identify the standard forms and understand why they are correct. The result should be additional expertise and confidence in your writing.

Pronoun Case

Case is the form a pronoun takes as it fills a position in a sentence. Words such as *you* and *it* do not change, but others do, and they change in predictable ways. For example, *I* is a subject word and *me* is an object word. As you refer to yourself, you will select a pronoun that fits a certain part of sentence structure. You say, "*I* will write the paper," not "*Me* will write the paper," because *I* is in the subject position. But you say, "She will give the apple to *me*," not "She will give the apple to *I*" because *me* is in the object position. These are the pronouns that change:

Subject	Object
I	me
he	him
she	her
we	us
they	them
who, whoever	who, whomever

Subjective Case

	Singular	Plural
First Person:	I	we
Second Person:	you	you
Third Person:	he, she, it	they
	who	

Subjective-case pronouns can fill two positions in a sentence.

1. Pronouns in the subjective case may fill subject positions.
    a. Some will be easy to identify because they are at the beginning of the sentence.

> *I* dance in the park.
>
> *He* dances in the park.
>
> *She* dances in the park.
>
> *We* dance in the park.
>
> *They* dance in the park.
>
> *Who* is dancing in the park?

    b. Others will be more difficult to identify because they are not at the beginning of a sentence and may not appear to be part of a clause. The words *than* and *as* are signals for these special arrangements, which can be called incompletely stated clauses.

> He is taller than *I* (am).
>
> She is younger than *we* (are).
>
> We work as hard as *they* (do).

The words *am, are,* and *do,* which complete the clauses, have been omitted. We are actually saying, "He is taller than *I am,*" "She is younger than *we are,*" and "We work as hard as *they do.*" The italicized pronouns are subjects of "understood" verbs.

2. Pronouns in the subjective case may refer back to the subject.

    a. They may follow a form of the verb *to be,* such as *was, were, am, is,* and *are.*

> I believe it is *he.*
>
> It was *she* who spoke.
>
> The victims were *they.*

    b. Some nouns and pronouns refer back to an earlier noun without referring back through the verb.

> The leading candidates—Pedro, Darnelle, Steve, Kimilieu, and *I*—made speeches.

Objective Case

	Singular	Plural
First Person:	me	us
Second Person:	you	you
Third Person:	him, her, it	them

whom

Objective-case pronouns can also fill two positions in sentences.

1. Pronouns in the objective case may fill object positions.

    a. They may be objects after the verb. A direct object answers the question *what* or *whom* in connection with the verb.

> We brought *it* to your house. (*what* did we bring? *it*)
>
> We saw *her* in the library. (*whom* did we see? *her*)

An indirect object answers the question *to whom* in connection with the verb.

> I gave *him* the message. (*to whom* did I give the message? *to him*)
>
> The doctor told *us* the test results. (*to whom* did the doctor tell the results? *to us*)

    b. They may be objects after prepositions.

> The problem was clear to *us.*
>
> I went with Steve and *him.*

2. Objective-case pronouns may also refer back to object words.

> They had the results for us—Judy and *me.*
>
> The judge addressed the defendants—John and *her.*

Techniques for Determining Case

Here are three techniques that will help you decide which pronoun to use when the choice seems difficult.

1. If you have a compound element (such as a subject or an object of a preposition), consider only the pronoun part. The sound alone will probably tell you the answer.

> She gave the answer to Yoshi and (I, me).

Yoshi and the pronoun make up a compound object of the preposition *to.* Disregard the noun, *Yoshi,* and ask yourself, "Would I say, 'She gave the answer *to me* or *to I*'?" The way the words sound would tell you the answer is *to me.* Of course, if you immediately notice that the pronoun is in an object position, you need not bother with sound.

2. If you are choosing between *who* (subject word) and *whom* (object word), look to the right to see if the next verb has a subject. If it does not, the pronoun probably *is* the subject, but if it does, the pronoun probably is an object.

> The person (*who,* whom) works hardest will win. (*Who* is the correct answer because it is the subject of the verb *works.*)

> The person (who, *whom*) we admire most is José. (*Whom* is the correct answer because the next verb, *admire,* already has a subject, *we. Whom* is an object.)

A related technique works the same way. If the next important word after *who* or *whom* in a statement is a noun or pronoun, the correct word will almost always be *whom.* However, if the next important word is not a noun or pronoun, the correct word will be *who.*

To apply this technique, you must disregard qualifier clauses such as "I think," "it seems," and "we hope."

> Tyrone is a natural leader (*who,* whom) has charisma. (*Who* is the correct answer; it is followed by something other than a noun or pronoun.)

> Tyrone is a natural leader (*who,* whom), we think, has charisma. (*Who* is the correct answer; it is followed by the qualifier clause *we think,* which is then followed by something other than a noun or pronoun.)

> Tyrone is a natural leader (who, *whom*) we supported. (*Whom* is the correct answer; it is followed by a pronoun.)

3. *Let's* is made up of the words *let* and *us* and means "you *let us*"; therefore, when you select a pronoun to follow it, consider the two original words and select another object word—*me.*

> Let's you and (I, *me*) take a trip to Westwood. (Think of "You let us, you and me, take a trip to Westwood." *Us* and *me* are object words.)

Exercise 1	**SELECTING PRONOUNS**

Underline the correct pronouns. (See Answer Key for answers.)

1. The counselor said, "I gave the same advice to Janice and (she, her) last week."

2. ("Her, She) and (I, me) left the party in a cloud of stardust," said the poet.

3. I did more work than Clem, and I should be paid more than (he, him).

4. "The only difference between (them, they) and (we, us) is a few million dollars," he said wistfully.

5. "Let's you and (I, me) blow this town because they recognize (we, us)," said the fugitive.

6. "(Us, We) chickens are dying for a frying," said the rooster ambiguously.

7. (We, Us) judges gave the prize to his brother and (he, him).

8. The next person (who, whom) leaves this room will be the next topic of conversation.

9. They will be gracious to (whoever, whomever) you have invited.

10. Between you and (I, me), I don't care who wins the Broccoli Bowl.

Exercise 2	SELECTING PRONOUNS

Underline the correct pronouns.

1. (She, Her) and (I, me) are going to the Museum of Dental Instruments.

2. (We, Us) young people are fascinated by rusty drills, saws, and heavy-duty pliers.

3. I would rather go to the museum with you than with (she, her).

4. There are those (who, whom) would say that early dentistry was barbaric.

5. Before anesthesia was developed, the patient (who, whom) passed out was lucky.

6. In 1844, laughing gas, nitrous oxide, was used on Horace Wells, (who, whom) had developed it.

7. Josiah Flagg, (who, whom) was the first native-born American dentist, first made tooth fillings with gold leaf in 1783.

8. George Washington, to (who, whom) the dental industry is indebted, wore dentures, to the envy of many of his toothless peers.

9. Just between you and (I, me), Washington's famous dentures were not made of wood.

10. Heavy and bad-fitting, his spring-loaded ivory dentures popped open like a nutcracker when he smiled at (whoever, whomever) called.

Exercise 3	**SELECTING PRONOUNS**

Underline the correct pronouns. (See Answer Key for answers.)

1. (Who, Whom) are you taking to the monster truck rodeo?

2. I am not sure (who, whom) I will be taking.

3. The person with (whom, who) I witness the event must love loud engines as much as (I, me).

4. To (who, whom) will you give your whoopee cushion?

5. Some people (who, whom) are wealthy never shop for themselves.

6. Fisherfolk (who, whom) admire floating stink bait will love our new floating sandwich spread.

7. It is designed for clumsy fisherfolk (who, whom) sometimes drop their food into the water.

8. (Whom, Who) will you invite to your Christmas party?

9. May I suggest someone (who, whom) looks like Bob Cratchit?

10. (Whom, Who) may I say is calling so late at night?

Exercise 4	**SELECTING PRONOUNS**

Underline the correct pronouns.

1. I know some people (who, whom) fear technology.

2. They are afraid that those (who, whom) own super computers will control (us, we) (who, whom) own dinky computers.

3. Homer asked Becky, "(Who, Whom) are you asking to the Sadie Hawkins dance?"

4. Looking into his eyes tenderly, she answered, "(Whom, Who) do you think, you silly dunderhead?"

5. The ancient philosopher asked the age-old question, "(Who, Whom) wrote the book of love?"

6. His life's companion said, "Someone (who, whom) was very young."

7. The child asked her father, "(Whom, Who) makes babies?"

8. Her father, (who, whom) didn't expect that question, said, "Your mother will tell you (who, whom) does."

9. (Who, Whom) will receive the award?

10. The person (who, whom) does will get a free school lunch.

Exercise 5   **SELECTING PRONOUNS**

Underline the correct pronouns. (See Answer Key for answers.)

1. Let's you and (I, me) consider some stories called urban legends.

2. These are stories heard by people like you and (I, me), which are passed on as if they were true.

3. We hear them from people (who, whom) have heard them from others.

4. You have probably heard more of them than (I, me), but I'll tell some anyway.

5. One is about a guard dog named Gork (who, whom) was found choking in his owner's bedroom.

6. The owner, (who, whom) loved Gork dearly, took him to the veterinarian, left him, and headed home.

7. While driving home, the owner answered his cell phone, asking "To (who, whom) am I speaking?"

8. "This is your vet calling. Just between you and (I, me), you have a big problem here."

9. "Gork has someone's detached finger stuck in his throat, and I've called the police, (who, whom) are on their way to your house."

10. Eventually the police arrested an angry armed man (who, whom) they suspected had broken into the owner's house, where Gork had bitten off and choked on the intruder's finger while the intruder, (who, whom) had crawled into a closet, passed out from loss of blood.

Exercise 6   **SELECTING PRONOUNS**

Underline the correct pronouns.

1. Another famous urban legend, involving two motorists, was told to my sister and (me, I) years ago.

2. Between you and (I, me), the story is sexist, but this is the way (we, us) heard it.

3. A motorist, (who, whom) was named Al, needed someone to push his car, so he called on Sue, his neighbor, (who, whom) lived next door.

4. "I need a push to get my car started," he said to her. "Let's you and (I, me) work together, and I'll be grateful forever."

5. "You're a special person (who, whom) I've always wanted to befriend," she said happily. "Tell me what to do."

6. "My car has an automatic transmission, which means the car won't start at less than thirty-five miles per hour," said Al, (who, whom) talked fast.

7. Al sat in his car as happy as (her, she) when he looked in his rear-view mirror and saw (she, her) heading toward his back bumper at a high speed.

8. After the collision, Al stumbled out of his car and confronted Sue, (who, whom), despite her injuries, was smiling.

9. "Look what you've done to you and (I, me)!" Al yelled.

10. "Let's you and (I, me) review what you said," she answered coolly. "You said, 'thirty-five miles per hour,' and that's exactly what I was doing."

Exercise 7	SELECTING PRONOUNS

Underline the correct pronouns.

1. My brother can tell this urban legend better than (I, me), but here is my version.

2. A man (who, whom) always wanted a 1958 Corvette saw one advertised in the newspaper for twenty dollars.

3. Within an hour he had purchased the car from a person named Lola, but before he drove away, he said, "(Who, Whom) is the person (who, whom) authorized you to make the sale?"

4. "It's my husband, Jake, (whom, who) I now despise because he ran away with his secretary."

5. "Last week," Lola went on, "he sent this fax: 'I've spent all my money here in Las Vegas, and Flo and (me, I) need your help.'"

6. "'Please sell my Corvette and send me the money. Just between you and (I, me), I miss you lots.'"

7. The man (who, whom) bought the Corvette said, "And now you're going to send Flo and (he, him) the money?"

8. "That's right, but he didn't tell me the price. So now I'm sending twenty dollars to this jerk (whom, who) I thought I loved."

9. That urban legend was told to my family and (I, me) when I was a wide-eyed child.

10. Some people insist that the buyer was a friend of someone (whom, who) they know.

Pronoun-Antecedent Agreement

Every pronoun refers to an earlier noun, which is called the *antecedent* of the pronoun. The antecedent is the noun that the pronoun replaces. The pronoun brings the reader back to the earlier thought. Here are some examples:

> I tried to buy *tickets* for the concert, but *they* were all sold.

> *Roger* painted a *picture* of a pickup truck. *It* was so good that *he* entered *it* in an art show.

A **pronoun** agrees with its antecedent in person, number, and gender. **Person**—first, second, or third—indicates perspective, or point of view. **Number** indicates singular or plural. **Gender** indicates masculine, feminine, or neuter.

Subject Words

	Singular	Plural
First Person:	I	we
Second Person:	you	you
Third Person:	he, she, it	they

who

Object Words

	Singular	Plural
First Person:	me	us
Second Person:	you	you
Third Person:	him, her, it	them

whom

Agreement in Person

Avoid needless shifting of person, which means shifting of point of view, such as from *I* to *you*. First person, second person, and third person indicate perspectives from which you can write. Select one point of view and maintain it, promoting continuity and consistency. Needless shifting of person, meaning changing perspectives without reasons important for your content and purpose, is distracting and awkward. Each point of view has its appropriate purposes.

First Person

Using the word *I* and its companion forms *we, me,* and *us,* the first-person point of view emphasizes the writer, who is an important part of the subject of the composition. Choose first person for friendly letters, accounts of personal experience, and, occasionally, business correspondence, such as a letter of application for a job, which requires self-analysis.

Observe the presence of the writer and the use of *I* in this example.

> I could tell that the wedding would not go well when the caterers started serving drinks before the ceremony and the bride began arguing with her future mother-in-law. After the sound system crashed, the band canceled, and I wished I hadn't come.

Second Person

Using or implying the word *you,* the second-person point of view is fine for informal conversation, advice, and directions. Although it is occasionally found in academic writing, most instructors prefer that you use it only in process analysis, instructions in how to do something.

In this example, note that the word *you* is sometimes understood and not stated.

> To juggle three balls, first you place two balls (A and B) in one hand and one ball (C) in the other. Then toss one of the two balls (A), and before you catch it with your other hand, toss the single ball (C) from that hand. Before that ball (C) lands in the other hand, toss the remaining inactive ball (B). Then pick up the balls and repeat the process until the balls no longer fall to the ground.

Third Person

Referring to subject material, individuals, things, or ideas, the third-person point of view works best for most formal writing, be it academic or professional. Third-person pronouns include *he, she, it, they, him, her,* and *them.* Most of your college writing—essay exams, reports, compositions that explain and argue, critiques, and research papers—will be from this detached perspective with no references to yourself.

In this example, written in the third person, the name *Bartleby* is replaced by forms of *he.*

> *Bartleby,* one of Herman Melville's most memorable characters, has befuddled critics for more than a century. At a point in *his* life chosen for no obvious reason, *he* decides not to work, not to cooperate with others, and not to leave the premises of *his* employer because *he* "prefer[s] not to." Most readers do not know what to make of *him.*

Correcting Problems of Agreement in Person

Most problems with pronoun agreement in person occur with the use of *you* in a passage that should have been written in the first or third person. If your composition is not one of advice or directions, the word *you* is probably not appropriate and should be replaced with a first- or third-person pronoun.

If you are giving advice or directions, use *you* throughout the passage, but, if you are not, replace each *you* with a first- or third-person pronoun that is consistent with the perspective, purpose, and content of the passage.

Inconsistent: *I* love to travel, especially when *you* go to foreign countries.

Consistent: *I* love to travel, especially when *I* go to foreign countries.

Inconsistent: When *you* are about to merge with moving traffic on the freeway, *one* should not stop *his or her* car.

Consistent: When *you* are about to merge with moving traffic on the freeway, *you* should not stop *your* car.

Consistent (using third-person pronouns, including the indefinite pronoun *one*): When *one* is about to merge with moving traffic on the freeway, *one* should not stop *his or her* car.

Consistent (using third-person plural pronouns to match plural noun): When *drivers* are about to merge with moving traffic on the freeway, *they* should not stop *their* cars.

| Exercise 8 | CHOOSING CORRECT PRONOUNS: PERSON |

Each of the following sentences has one or more needless changes in pronoun person. Correct each problem by crossing out the inconsistent pronoun and submitting a consistent one. Change verb forms, also, if necessary. (See Answer Key for answers.)

1. When tourists play with wild animals, you often get more than you bargain for.

2. I told her you shouldn't take feral children away from their parents.

3. I tried, but you couldn't persuade her not to adopt little Napoo, son of wolves.

4. The Cave Bear priest told his warriors that you should watch the sky for omens.

5. People should not lend money unless you are willing to use muscle to get it back.

6. The nature guide told us that you should not pet the Tasmanian devil unless you were wearing full body armor.

7. People may think they will never receive a Chia Pet, but you never know until Christmas Day.

8. Tourists love Venice, California, especially when you walk on the beach.

9. Every beauty contestant knew that you shouldn't wear fishnet stockings during the talent part of the program.

10. The kick boxer was taught that you should look an opponent in the feet.

| Exercise 9 | CHOOSING CORRECT PRONOUNS: PERSON |

Complete the following sentences while maintaining agreement in person. Use at least one personal pronoun in each completion.

First Person

1. I enjoy working on a computer, and _____

2. Nevertheless, sometimes I forget about the importance of good posture, and

_____

3. Sitting with bad posture for long periods of time can _____

_____

Second Person

1. When you need a long session on the computer, _____

_____

2. Having good posture at the computer is important, so _____

_____

3. Taking frequent rest breaks is crucial to staying alert; therefore, you should

_____

Third Person

1. People who work for long hours at the computer should understand that __

_____

2. While computer operators sit at the computer, _____

_____

3. Whether computer operators are tired or not, _____

_____

Agreement in Number

Most problems with pronoun-antecedent agreement involve **number.** The principles are simple: If the antecedent (the word the pronoun refers back to) is singular, use a singular pronoun. If the antecedent is plural, use a plural pronoun.

1. A singular antecedent requires a singular pronoun.

> *Hoang* forgot *his* notebook.

2. A plural antecedent requires a plural pronoun.

> Many *students* cast *their* votes today.

3. A singular indefinite pronoun as an antecedent takes a singular pronoun. Most indefinite pronouns are singular. The following are common indefinite singular pronouns: *anybody, anyone, each, either, everybody, everyone, no one, nobody, one, somebody, someone.*

> *Each* of the girls brought *her* book.

> When *one* makes a promise, *one* (or *he or she*) should keep it.

4. A plural indefinite pronoun as an antecedent takes a plural pronoun.

> *Few* knew *their* assignments.

5. Certain indefinite pronouns do not clearly express either a singular or plural number. Agreement, therefore, depends on the meaning of the sentence. These pronouns are *all, any, none,* and *some.*

> *All* of the grapefruit *was* good.
>
> *All* of the grapefruits *were* gone.
>
> *None* of the cake *is* acceptable.
>
> *None* of the cakes *are* acceptable.

6. Two or more antecedents, singular or plural, take a plural pronoun. Such antecedents are usually joined by *and* or by commas and *and*.

> *Howard* and his *parents* bought *their* presents early.
>
> *Students, instructors,* and the *administration* pooled *their* ideas at the forum.

7. Alternative antecedents—that is, antecedents joined by *or, nor, whether/or, either/or, neither/nor, not only/but also*—require a pronoun that agrees with the nearer antecedent.

> Neither Sam nor his *friends* lost *their* way.
>
> Neither his friends nor *Sam* lost *his* way.

8. In a sentence with an expression such as *one of those ____ who,* the antecedent is usually the plural noun that follows.

> He is one of those *people who* want *their* money now.

9. In a sentence with the expression *the only one of those ____ who,* the antecedent is usually the singular word *one.*

> She is the *only one of* the members *who* wants *her* money now.

10. When collective nouns such as *team, jury, committee,* and *band* are used as antecedents, they take a singular pronoun if they are considered as units.

> The *jury* is doing *its* best to follow the judge's directions.

When individual behavior is suggested, antecedents take a plural form.

> The *jury* are putting on *their* coats.

11. The words *each, every,* and *many a(n)* before a noun make the noun singular.

> *Each child* and *adult* was *his* or *her* own authority.
>
> *Each* and *every person* doubted *himself or herself.*
>
> *Many* a person is capable of knowing *himself or herself.*

| **Exercise 10** | **CHOOSING CORRECT PRONOUNS: PERSON** |

Underline the correct pronouns. (See Answer Key for answers.)

1. The team is doing (its, their) best to win.

2. Each and every person should be prepared for work, or (they, he or she) will waste a lot of time.

3. Each student should try (their, his or her) best.

4. If the family doesn't stick together now, (it, they) may never be functional.

5. Each of those Moroccan Palace Guards has (their, his) own fez-pressing machine.

6. Mathilda and Jake have (their, his or her) sights set on chinchilla ranching.

7. Someone has left (his or her, their) fingerprints on my velvet painting.

8. Either Bryant or his friends always offer to bring (his, their) fresh Tater Tots.

9. She is one of those free spirits who insist on having (their, her) wedding in a tree.

10. Every gorilla picks fleas from (its, their) closest associates.

| **Exercise 11** | **CHOOSING CORRECT PRONOUNS: PERSON** |

Underline the correct pronouns.

1. Many a Viking raiding party allowed (its, their) terrified victims to decide between submission and death.

2. The team of Knute Grunson and his trusted malamute, Thor, made (their, its) way through a snowstorm.

3. The famous heavy-metal band Hemorrhage will travel in (its, their) bright red bus.

4. Young Freda was the only one of the schoolgirls to wear (her, their) raincoat today.

5. Neither dogs nor birds can hold (their, its) own with pigs in intelligence tests.

6. A child left (his or her, their) pet muskrats on the schoolbus.

7. The snake-handling troupe brought (their, its) defanged rattlesnakes to show the curious children.

8. In one day, a hummingbird can eat (its, their) weight in nectar.

9. Each member of the Boffo Brothers acrobatic troupe can balance a lawn chair on (his, their) nose.

10. Those wacky acrobats will expand (its, their) act to table balancing next year.

Agreement in Gender

The pronoun should agree with its antecedent in **gender,** if the gender of the antecedent is specific. Masculine and feminine pronouns are gender-specific: *he, him, she, her.* Others are neuter: *I, we, me, us, it, they, them, who, whom, that, which.*

The words *who* and *whom* refer to people. *That* can refer to ideas, things, and people, but usually does not refer to individuals. *Which* refers to ideas and things, but never to people.

> My *girlfriend* gave me *her* best advice. (feminine)

> Mighty *Casey* tried *his* best. (masculine)

> The *people* with *whom* I work are loud. (neuter)

Indefinite singular pronouns used as antecedents require, of course, singular pronouns. Handling the gender of these singular pronouns is not as obvious; opinion is divided.

1. Traditionally, writers have used the masculine form of pronouns to refer to the indefinite singular pronouns when the gender is unknown.

   > *Everyone* should work until *he* drops.

2. To avoid a perceived sex bias, use *he or she* or *his or her* instead of just *he* or *his*.

   > *Everyone* should work until *he or she* drops.

3. Although option 1 is more direct, it is illogical to many listeners and readers, and option 2 used several times in a short passage can be awkward. To avoid those possible problems, writers often use plural forms.

   > *All people* should work until *they* drop.

In any case, avoid using a plural pronoun with a singular indefinite pronoun; such usage violates the basic principle of number agreement.

> **Incorrect:**   *Everyone* should do *their* best.

Exercise 12   **CHOOSING CORRECT PRONOUNS: GENDER AND NUMBER**

Underline the correct pronoun for gender and number. (See Answer Key for answers.)

1. The fry cooks at Campus Kitchen have developed a new chocolate cookie that (they, he or she) will try to sell to (us, we) students.

2. The cookies taste terrible, but an official EPA test proved that (they, it) are biodegradable.

3. The weather forecasters were especially pleased when (their, his or her) prediction for tornadoes was accurate.

4. Commuters driving home in (their, his or her) cars can learn to swear in several tongues by listening to foreign language tapes.

5. My neighbors avoid harmful radiation by wearing (his or her, their) lead suits.

6. If all class members would work together, (they, he or she) might accomplish great things.

7. Each child in this population of young people should do vigorous exercises during (his or her, their) television viewing.

8. Whether children want to or not, (they, he or she) will be required to walk rapidly to and from the refrigerator.

9. Joe, the blacksmith, finally had to close down (his, their) business.

10. Almost no one needed to furnish (his or her, their) home or business with hand-wrought ironware.

Exercise 13   **CHOOSING CORRECT PRONOUNS: GENDER AND NUMBER**

Correct the faulty pronouns for problems in gender and number.

1. The teacher which helped me most is now retired.

2. Everyone interested in improving their vocabulary should purchase a dictionary and use it.

3. A person who can make their vocation and avocation the same will find contentment.

4. The storyteller was the first person which was responsible for maintaining tradition.

5. The tribal storyteller, who is also the historian, should take their task seriously.

6. Almost every person has their own definition of romantic love.

7. A person which cannot resist counting objects is called *compulsive*.

8. According to legend, a groundhog that ventures forth from their den in early February can forecast weather.

9. If the groundhog sees their shadow, it goes back inside its cave, and warm weather will be late in coming.

10. The blacksmith which specialized in ironware for camping prospered.

Pronoun Reference

A pronoun must refer clearly to its antecedent. Because a pronoun is a substitute word, it can express meaning clearly and definitely only if its antecedent is easily identified.

In some sentence constructions, gender and number make the reference clear.

Dimitri and Poloma discussed *his* absences and *her* good attendance. (gender)

If the three older boys in the *club* carry out those pans, *it* will break up. (number)

Avoid ambiguous reference. The following sentences illustrate the kind of confusion that results from structuring sentences with more than one possible antecedent for the pronoun.

Unclear: Kim gave David *his* money and clothes.

Clear: Kim gave his own money and clothes to David.

Unclear: Sarah told her sister that *her* car had a flat tire.

Clear: Sarah said to her sister, "Your car has a flat tire."

When using a pronoun to refer to a general idea, make sure that the reference is clear. The pronouns used frequently in this way are *this, that, which,* and *it.* The best solution may be to recast the sentence to omit the pronoun in question.

Unclear: Gabriella whistled the same tune over and over, *which* irritated me.

Clear: Gabriella whistled the same tune over and over, a *habit* that irritated me.

Recast: Her whistling the same tune over and over irritated me.

Exercise 14   **SHOWING CLEAR PRONOUN REFERENCES**

Label each sentence as V if the pronoun reference is vague or OK if it is clear. (See Answer Key for answers.)

_____ 1. (a) Pickled eggs were served on paper plates at the wedding, which was really tacky.

_____ (b) At the wedding pickled eggs were served on paper plates, a practice that was really tacky.

_____ 2. (a) I took my defective mustache-straightening compound back to the drugstore and told the salesperson to give me my money back.

_____ (b) I took my defective mustache-straightening compound back to the drugstore and told them to give me my money back.

_____ 3. (a) The druggist was eating a double cheeseburger and wiping the grease from his fingers onto his grubby old smock, which didn't give me much confidence.

_____ (b) The druggist was eating a double cheeseburger and wiping the grease from his fingers onto his grubby old smock, and that situation didn't give me much confidence.

_____ 4. (a) Young Douglas told his father that he was having trouble in school.

_____ (b) Young Douglas told his father, "I am having trouble in school."

_____ 5. (a) His father replied to Douglas that it was time for him to study.

_____ (b) His father replied that it was time for Douglas to study.

_____ 6. (a) Bert has bought a 1975 Gremlin and customized it with bumper stickers and chrome mud flaps, which has made him the envy of all the kids at the high school.

_____ (b) Bert has bought a 1975 Gremlin and customized it with bumper stickers and chrome mud flaps, and the project has made him the envy of all the kids at the high school.

_____ 7. (a) The little girl told her mother, "I have a craving to watch reruns of 1950s family sitcoms."

_____ (b) The little girl told her mother that she had a craving to watch reruns of 1950s family sitcoms.

_____ 8. (a) After hearing the offer on a television commercial, I rushed to the doctor's office and asked them for my free snake-bite kit.

_____ (b) After hearing the offer on a television commercial, I rushed to the doctor's office and asked the receptionist for my free snake-bite kit.

_____ 9. (a) The astronaut told his commanding officer that he was a sorry specimen of a human being.

_____ (b) The astronaut told his commanding officer, "You are a sorry specimen of a human being."

_____ 10. (a) The traveling salesperson wore a sandwich-board sign and beat a drum loudly, all of which impressed the townsfolk greatly.

_____ (b) The traveling salesperson wore a sandwich-board sign and beat a drum loudly, which impressed the townsfolk greatly.

Exercise 15   CHOOSING CORRECT PRONOUNS: REFERENCE AND AGREEMENT

Identify and correct the problems with pronoun reference and agreement.

1. They say the Yankees aren't what they used to be.

2. In London they say that Americans talk funny.

3. When you walk down the streets of Laredo, a person should look out for traffic.

4. When he drove his car into the swimming pool, it was damaged.

5. We sprayed Microbe Eradicator everywhere, but some of them still got in.

6. Soon-Yi told her friend that she cherished her cool date.

7. When a student signs up for English 1A, you had better be ready for dedication.

8. Toni told Mae that she had an attitude problem.

9. In a hidden message in this book, it says you should learn your grammar or die.

10. He was always showing off his big vocabulary, which aroused, riled, inflamed, irritated, infuriated, and enraged me.

Chapter Review: Pronouns

1. **Case** is the form a pronoun takes as it fills a position in a sentence.

2. **Subjective-case pronouns** are *I, he,* and *she* (singular) and *we* and *they* (plural). *Who* can be either singular or plural.
   Subjective-case pronouns can fill subject positions.

   > *We* dance in the park.

   > It was *she* who spoke. (referring back to and meaning the same as the subject)

3. **Objective-case pronouns** are *me, him,* and *her* (singular) and *us* and *them* (plural). *Whom* can be either singular or plural.
   Objective-case pronouns fill object positions.

   > We saw *her* in the library. (object of verb)

   > They gave the results to *us*. (object of a preposition)

4. Three techniques are useful for deciding which pronoun case to use.
   a. If you have a compound element (such as a subject or an object of a preposition), consider only the pronoun part.

   > They will visit you and (I, me). (Consider: They will visit me.)

   b. If the next important word after *who* or *whom* in a statement is a noun or pronoun, the word choice will be *whom;* otherwise, it will be *who.* Disregard qualifier clauses such as *It seems* and *I feel.*

   > The person *whom* judges like will win.

   > The person *who* works hardest will win.

   > The person *who,* we think, worked hardest won. (ignoring the qualifier clause)

   c. *Let's* is made up of the words *let* and *us* and means *"You let us";* therefore, when you select a pronoun to follow it, consider the two original words and select another object word—*me.*

   > Let's you and *me* go to town.

5. A pronoun agrees with its antecedent in person, number, and gender.
   a. Avoid needless shifting in **person,** which means shifting in point of view, such as from *I* to *you.*

   > "*I* was having trouble. *You* could see disaster ahead." Change to "*I* was having trouble. *I* could see disaster ahead."

   b. Most problems with pronoun-antecedent agreement involve **number.** The principles are simple: If the antecedent (the word the pronoun refers back to) is singular, use a singular pronoun. If the antecedent is plural, use a plural pronoun.

Royce forgot *his* notebook.

Many students cast *their* votes.

Someone lost *his or her* (not *their*) book.

    c. The pronoun should agree with its antecedent in **gender,** if the gender of the antecedent is specific. Masculine and feminine pronouns are gender-specific: *he, him, she, her.* Others are neuter: *I, we, me, us, it, they, them, who, whom, that, which.* The words *who* and *whom* refer to people. *That* can refer to ideas, things, and people but usually does not refer to individuals. *Which* refers to ideas and things, but not to people. To avoid a perceived sex bias, you can use *he or she* or *his or her* instead of just *he* or *his;* however, many writers simply make antecedents and pronouns plural.

Everyone should revise *his or her* composition carefully.

Students should revise *their* compositions carefully.

   6. A pronoun must refer clearly to its antecedent. Because a pronoun is a substitute word, it can express meaning clearly and definitely only if its antecedent is easily identified.

Chapter Review Exercises

Review 1	SELECTING CORRECT PRONOUNS: CASE

Underline the correct pronouns. (See Answer Key for answers to 1 through 5.)

1. Between you and (me, I), pronouns are not that difficult.

2. Those (who, whom) have much trouble may not have studied the rules.

3. Let's you and (I, me) consider those pesky rules.

4. The opportunity offered to you and (I, me) should not be wasted.

5. (We, Us) students can lick these pronoun problems together.

6. To (whom, who) should I give credit for my success?

7. Some of the credit should go to you and (me, I).

8. I know you didn't study harder than (I, me).

9. Now I know that the person (who, whom) studies will prosper.

10. You and (I, me) should now celebrate.

| Review 2 | **SELECTING CORRECT PRONOUNS: PERSON** |

Each of the following sentences has one or more needless changes in pronoun person. Correct each problem by crossing out the inconsistent pronoun and substituting a consistent one. Change verb form also if necessary. (See Answer Key for answers to 1 through 5.)

1. Everyone knows that you should carry an emergency kit while backpacking.

2. I want to know if a man's man ever does a breath check before you go on a date.

3. Our scoutmaster said, "Boys, one can never have too many dry socks."

4. It was the best wrestling match I had ever seen; you could almost feel the agony of Hawkman as he was slammed by Global Savage.

5. A man may think that his date wants you to provide fancy wining and dining for every occasion.

6. In fact, every man should know that his date may want you to plan something simple.

7. She may even prefer a man who would take you to something simple like an amateur hog-calling contest.

8. She might even prefer a man who would let you share equally in planning the date.

9. I thought you couldn't mix weasels with ferrets, but I was wrong.

10. Let's write a public service commercial that tells drivers how you can improve gas mileage.

| Review 3 | **MAKING PRONOUNS AGREE WITH THEIR ANTECEDENTS** |

Some of the following sentences have a problem with pronoun-antecedent number agreement. If a sentence is correct, label it C. If not, correct it. (See Answer Key for answers to 1 through 5.)

_____ 1. Young Hakeem and his brothers chased their shadows through the streets.

_____ 2. The dance company pranced for the pleasure of their audience.

_____ 3. The singing cowboy and his horse, Bright Star, left his fans in shock when they disappeared from the world of entertainment.

_____ 4. Nothing would dissuade Kovar from pursuing their chosen career of toothpick sculpting.

_____ 5. Batman and Robin wore his sleek and elegant crime-prevention bat boots.

_____ 6. Few of the clowns ever took off his or her exploding slap shoes.

_____ 7. The jackals and the coyotes sneaked out of its cage and began gobbling up dropped popcorn.

_____ 8. The crowd of spectators stood up from its seats as the contortionist bent his leg behind his head and then licked his big toe.

_____ 9. Slick Veekel, tractor-pulling champion, and his lovely wife and mechanic, Thelma, were a team that did their best.

_____ 10. The crew members of the Russian freighter wanted to pilot its boat to Disney World.

Review 4	SELECTING CORRECT PRONOUNS: AGREEMENT

Correct the faulty pronoun-antecedent gender agreement in the following sentences. Rewrite the sentences as necessary. (See Answer Key for answers to 1 through 5.)

1. The person who does not attend to their personal hygiene will not be welcomed at social activities.

2. A person needs to know that, or they may be lonely.

3. Of course, people with poor hygiene can have his or her own stinking parties.

4. Rupert Schlagel, one of several famed accordion virtuosos, made their debut with the Galloping Polka Minstrels.

5. The fly fisherfolk wore their rubber waders around the house to simulate the outdoor feeling for which he or she tragically yearned.

6. Many an anonymous Halloween prankster used their cans of Wacky String to decorate fellow revelers.

7. Any one of the assembled baseball fans would have exchanged all their baseball cards for one of young Babe Ruth.

8. The members of the ski team left their boots and skis by the hot tub.

9. Each of the firewalkers is available to exhibit their talents at bar mitzvahs and weddings.

10. Each and every wrestler must supply their own tights and intimidation mask.

Review 5	SELECTING CORRECT PRONOUNS: REFERENCES

Correct the pronoun reference problems. (See Answer Key for answers to 1 through 5.)

1. His boss had a rule for all situations, and that made Tom uncomfortable.

2. Joanne told Mabel she wanted her paycheck.

3. They say that we can be sure of only two things: death and taxes.

4. They say he's so lazy his paycheck should be gift-wrapped.

5. Shana told Louanne that she bought the dress for a low price.

6. We put some mothballs in the closet, but some of them still got in.

7. In the army, you have few choices.

8. The doctor told Samantha that she needed some little, round pills.

9. They say that love conquers all.

10. Some of us procrastinate habitually, and that interferes with our productivity.

Review 6	WRITING SENTENCES WITH CORRECT PRONOUNS

Write a sentence using each of the following words. Do not use the word as the first one in the sentence. One sentence should contain the word between *before a pronoun such as "between you and _____."*

1. she _____

_____

_____

_____

2. her _____

_____

_____

_____

3. him _____

_____

_____

_____

4. us _____

_____

_____

_____

5. who _____

_____

_____

_____

6. whom _____

_____

_____

_____

7. me _____

_____

_____

_____

8. I _____

_____

_____

_____

9. they _____

_____

_____

_____

10. them _____

_____

_____

_____

Adjectives and Adverbs

"When we relate to close friends and family members, we may be able to convey simple ideas and feelings using only grunts and gestures. But when we need to communicate more complex messages with people we hardly know, we depend on precise words, especially adjectives and adverbs."

djectives modify (describe) nouns and pronouns and answer the questions *Which one? What kind?* and *How many?*

> *Which one?* The <u>new</u> <u>car</u> is mine
>   adj   n

> *What kind?* <u>Mexican</u> <u>food</u> is my favorite.
>   adj   n

> *How many?* A <u>few</u> <u>friends</u> are all one needs.
>   adj   n

Adverbs modify verbs, adjectives, and other adverbs and answer the questions *How? Where? When? Why?* and *To what degree?* Most words ending in *-ly* are adverbs.

> *Where?* The cuckoo <u>flew</u> <u>south</u>.
>   v   adv

> *When?* The cuckoo <u>flew</u> <u>yesterday</u>.
>   v   adv

> *Why?* The cuckoo <u>flew</u> <u>because of the cold weather</u>.
>   v   adv phrase

How? The cuckoo <u>flew</u> <u>swiftly</u>.
            v   adv

<u>Without adjectives and adverbs,</u> <u>even</u> John Steinbeck, the <u>famous</u>
     adv phrase   adv   adj

<u>Nobel Prize–winning</u> author, <u>surely</u> could <u>not</u> have described the
    adj   adv   adv

<u>crafty</u> octopus <u>very</u> <u>well</u>.
 adj   adv adv

We have two concerns regarding the use of adjectives and adverbs (modifiers) in writing. One is a matter of diction, or word choice—in this case, how to select adjectives and adverbs that will strengthen the writing. The other is how to identify and correct problems with modifiers.

Selecting Adjectives and Adverbs

If you want to finish the sentence "She was a(n) _____ speaker," you have many adjectives to select from, including these:

distinguished	irritating	profound	persuasive
influential	colorful	polished	long-winded
adequate	boring	abrasive	humorous

If you want to finish the sentence "She danced _____," you have another large selection, this time adverbs such as the following:

comically	catatonically	slowly	zestfully
gracefully	awkwardly	carnally	smoothly
mechanically	limply	serenely	frantically

Adjectives and adverbs can be used to enhance communication. If you have a thought, you know what it is, but when you deliver that thought to someone else, you may not say or write what you mean. Your thought may be eloquent and your word choice weak. Keep in mind that no two words mean exactly the same thing. Further, some words are vague and general. If you settle for a common word such as *good* or a slang word such as *neat* to characterize something that you like, you will be limiting your communication. Of course, those who know you best may understand fairly well; after all, people who are really close may be able to convey ideas using only grunts and gestures.

But what if you want to write to someone you hardly know to explain how you feel about an important issue? Then the more precise the word, the better the communication. By using modifiers, you may be able to add significant information. Keep in mind, however, that anything can be overdone; therefore, use adjectives and adverbs wisely and economically.

Your first resource in searching for more effective adjectives should be your own vocabulary storehouse. Another resource is a good thesaurus (book of synonyms). Finally, you may want to collaborate with others to discuss and share ideas.

Supply the appropriate modifiers in the following exercises, using a dictionary, a thesaurus, or the resources designated by your instructor.

| **Exercise 1** | **SUPPLYING ADJECTIVES** |

Provide adjectives to modify these nouns. Use only single words, not adjective phrases.

1. A(n) _____ dog

2. A(n) _____ comedian

3. A(n) _____ voice

4. A(n) _____ neighbor

5. A(n) _____ ball player

6. A(n) _____ party

7. A(n) _____ singer

8. A(n) _____ date

9. A(n) _____ car

10. A(n) _____ job

| **Exercise 2** | **SUPPLYING ADJECTIVES** |

Provide adverbs to modify these verbs. Use only single words, not adverb phrases.

1. sleep _____

2. run _____

3. talk _____

4. walk _____

5. kiss _____

6. smile _____

7. drive _____

8. leave _____

9. laugh _____

10. eat _____

Comparative and Superlative Forms

For making comparisons, most adjectives and adverbs have three different forms: the positive (one), the comparative (comparing two), and the superlative (comparing three or more).

Adjectives

1. Some adjectives follow a regular pattern:

Positive (one)	Comparative (comparing two)	Superlative (comparing three or more)
nice	nicer	nicest
rich	richer	richest
big	bigger	biggest
tall	taller	tallest
lonely	lonelier	loneliest
terrible	more terrible	most terrible
beautiful	more beautiful	most beautiful

These are usually the rules:

a. Add *-er* (or *-r*) to short adjectives (one or two syllables) to rank units of two.

> Julian is *nicer* than Sam.

b. Add *-est* (or *-st*) to short adjectives (one or two syllables) to rank units of three or more.

> Of the fifty people I know, Julian is the *kindest.*

c. Add the word *more* to long adjectives (three or more syllables) to rank units of two.

> My hometown is *more beautiful* than yours.

d. Add the word *most* to long adjectives (three or more syllables) to rank units of three or more.

> My hometown is the *most beautiful* in all America.

2. Some adjectives are irregular in the way they change to show comparison:

Positive (one)	Comparative (comparing two)	Superlative (comparing three or more)
good	better	best
bad	worse	worst

Adverbs

1. Some adverbs follow a regular pattern.

Positive (one)	Comparative (comparing two)	Superlative (comparing three or more)
clearly	more clearly	most clearly
quickly	more quickly	most quickly

carefully   more carefully   most carefully

thoughtfully   more thoughtfully   most thoughtfully

   a. Add *-er* to some one-syllable adverbs for the comparative form and add *-est* for the superlative form.

> My piglet runs *fast*. (positive)
>
> My piglet runs *faster* than your piglet. (comparative)
>
> My piglet runs *fastest* of all known piglets. (superlative)

   b. Add the word *more* to form longer comparisons and the word *most* to form longer superlative forms.

> Shanelle reacted *happily* to the marriage proposal. (positive)
>
> Shanelle reacted *more happily* to the marriage proposal than Serena. (comparative)
>
> Of all the women Clem proposed to, Shanelle reacted *most happily*. (superlative)

   c. In some cases, the word *less* may be substituted for *more,* and the word *least* for *most.*

> Mort's views were presented *less effectively* than Al's. (comparative)
>
> Of all the opinions that were shared, Mort's views were presented *least effectively*. (superlative)

2. Some adverbs are irregular in the way they change to show comparisons.

Positive (one)	Comparative (comparing two)	Superlative (comparing three or more)
well	better	best
far	farther (distance) further	farthest (distance) furthest
badly	worse	worst

Using Adjectives and Adverbs Correctly

1. Avoid double negatives. Words such as *no, not, none, nothing, never, hardly, barely,* and *scarcely* should not be combined.

Double Negative:	I do *not* have *no* time for recreation. (incorrect)
Single Negative:	I have *no* time for recreation. (correct)
Double Negative:	I've *hardly never* lied. (incorrect)
Single Negative:	I've *hardly* ever lied. (correct)

2. Do not confuse adjectives with adverbs. Among the most commonly confused adjectives and adverbs are *good/well, bad/badly,* and *real/really.* The words *good, bad,* and *real* are always adjectives. *Well* is sometimes an adjective. The words *badly* and *really* are always adverbs. *Well* is usually an adverb.

To distinguish these words, consider what is being modified. Remember that adjectives modify nouns and pronouns and that adverbs modify verbs, adjectives, and other adverbs.

Wrong:	I feel *badly* today. (We're concerned with the condition of *I*.)
Right:	I feel *bad* today. (The adjective *bad* modifies the pronoun *I*.)
Wrong:	She feels *well* about that choice. (We're concerned with the condition of *she*.)
Right:	She feels *good* about that choice. (The adjective *good* modifies the pronoun *she*.)
Wrong:	Ted plays the piano *good*. (The adjective *good* modifies the verb *plays*, but adjectives should not modify verbs.)
Right:	Ted plays the piano *well*. (The adverb *well* modifies the verb *plays*.)
Wrong:	He did *real* well. (Here the adjective *real* modifies the adverb *well*, but adjectives should not modify adverbs.)
Right:	He did *really* well. (The adverb *really* modifies the adverb *well*.)

3. Do not use an adverb such as *very, more,* or *most* before adjectives such as *perfect, round, unique, square,* and *straight.*

Wrong:	It is more round.
Right:	It is round.
Right:	It is more nearly round.

4. Do not double forms, such as *more lonelier* or *most loneliest.*

Wrong:	Julie was *more nicer* than Jake.
Right:	Julie was *nicer* than Jake.

Exercise 3   SELECTING ADJECTIVES AND ADVERBS

Underline the correct adjective or adverb. (See Answer Key for answers.)

1. Bud Sneagle, a famed sky writer, was the (most, more) successful stunt pilot in the world.

2. The producers knew that they had a (real, really) hit on their hands.

3. After being hit by the snowplow, my car looked rather (badly, bad).

4. I was (not hardly, hardly) ready to play ball when a big linebacker tackled me.

5. After sighting Elvis buying some peanut butter cups at the mini-market, Thelma Lou was the (more, most) joyful person on campus.

6. I am afraid that I did (bad, badly) on my Sanskrit exam today.

7. The tyrannosaurus rex was the (more, most) hideous predator of the age of dinosaurs.

8. The dinosaurs were (not hardly, hardly) intelligent.

9. Because I won the bake-off, I can now tell people that I am a (real, really) fine cook.

10. The (best, better) thing about my possum pie is that it is the (best, better) tasting in the whole world.

| Exercise 4 | SELECTING ADJECTIVES AND ADVERBS |

Correct any problems with adjectives and adverbs in the following sentences. (See Answer Key for answers.)

1. The chili cook-off event was a real big success.

2. People did not have no complaints about the food.

3. Luther, my canary, sings really good.

4. When the old bloodhound was near death, he was never no lonelier.

5. Rudy Vingstadt, Olympic ski jumper, looked well during practice runs.

6. The fourth-grader was real proud after completing her project.

7. I never saw a woman more perfect than Sharon Stone.

8. Calf roping is not never an easy thing to learn.

9. I remember the real big explosion of the nacho machine at the convenience store; a horribler sight I have never seen.

10. It was the most nastiest scene of splattered saturated fat products in the store's history.

| Exercise 5 | SELECTING ADJECTIVES AND ADVERBS |

Underline the correct word or words. (See Answer Key for answers.)

1. Skip did (real, really) (well, good) on his alchemy exam.

2. Trixie was the (more, most) talented of all the performers in the go-go club.

3. Beowulf, King of the Geats, was (greater greatest) among all the warriors in the northern kingdoms.

4. The kind old man did not have (no, any) trinkets to give the children.

5. After drinking two bottles of Volt Cola, the moviegoer felt much (worse, worst).

6. Sadie is (friendliest, friendlier) than her twin, Veronica.

7. Except for locking my keys in my car, I am doing pretty (good, well) today.

8. Leewan was the (more, most) sophisticated of the girls at the boarding school.

9. Ivan was the (more, most) terrible of all the cruel despots of his time.

10. After being sick with jungle rot for two years, I am finally (good, well) again.

Exercise 6	**SELECTING ADJECTIVES AND ADVERBS**

Correct any problems with adjectives and adverbs in the following sentences.

1. Howard Hughes was one of the most richest men in American history.

2. The actor read bad for the part of Whimsey, Prince of the Leprechauns.

3. There has never been anyone quicker with a six shooter than old Dead-Eye Pete.

4. Kuei-Ling drew a more round figure.

5. I know of no one who would make a best executioner than you.

6. I don't feel so well today.

7. That milk turned sourly.

8. They did their work bad.

9. Juan spoke quieter than Alex.

10. Maria was the better of the three candidates.

Dangling and Misplaced Modifiers

Modifiers should clearly relate to the word or words they modify.

1. A modifier that fails to modify a word or group of words already in the sentence is called a **dangling modifier.**

   Dangling: *Walking down the street,* a snake startled him. (Who was walking down the street? The person isn't mentioned in the sentence.)

   Correct: *Walking down the street,* Don was startled by a snake.

   Correct: As *Don* walked down the street, *he* was startled by a snake.

   Dangling: *At the age of six,* my uncle died. (Who was six years old? The person isn't mentioned in the sentence.)

   Correct: *When I was six,* my uncle died.

2. A modifier that is placed so that it modifies the wrong word or words is called a **misplaced modifier.** The term also applies to words that are positioned so as to unnecessarily divide closely related parts of sentences such as infinitives (*to* plus verb) or subjects and verbs.

   Misplaced: The sick man went to a doctor *with a high fever.*

   Correct: The sick man *with a high fever* went to a doctor.

Misplaced:	I saw a great movie *sitting in my pickup.*
Correct:	*Sitting in my pickup,* I saw a great movie.
Misplaced:	Kim found many new graves *walking through the cemetery.*
Correct:	*Walking through the cemetery,* Kim found many new graves.
Misplaced:	I forgot all about my sick dog *kissing my girlfriend.*
Correct:	*Kissing my girlfriend,* I forgot all about my sick dog.
Misplaced:	They tried to *earnestly and sincerely* complete the task. (splitting of the infinitive *to complete*)
Correct:	They tried *earnestly and sincerely* to complete the task.
Misplaced:	My neighbor, *while walking to the store,* was mugged. (unnecessarily dividing the subject and verb)
Correct:	*While walking to the store,* my neighbor was mugged.

3. Try this procedure in working through Exercises 7, 8, and 9.
   a. Circle the modifier
   b. Draw an arrow from the modifier to the word or words it modifies.
   c. If the modifier does not relate directly to anything in the sentence, it is dangling, and you must recast the sentence.
   d. If the modifier does not modify the nearest word or words, or if it interrupts related sentence parts, it is misplaced and you need to reposition it.

Exercise 7 **CORRECTING DANGLING AND MISPLACED MODIFIERS**

Each of the following sentences has a dangling (D) or a misplaced (M) modifier. Identify the problems and correct them by rewriting the sentences. (See Answer Key for answers.)

_____ 1. Driving through the field, the wild jackrabbits were excited.

_____

_____ 2. The delivery truck drove past the library carrying fresh meat.

_____

_____ 3. Walking through the meadow, the satisfied wolverines slept deeply after gorging on the road kill.

_____

_____ 4. He went for a walk with his cute puppy hoping to meet an available female.

_____

_____ 5. I saw a slimy monster watching a television program.

_____

_____ 6. The lass ran home to her parents nursing a head wound inflicted by crazed weasels.

_____

_____ 7. I began to fearfully unwrap the ticking package from my loved one.

_____

_____ 8. Trailing smoke and flames, I watched the plane.

_____

_____ 9. Soaked to the bone, I saw the men remove their boots at the front door.

_____

_____ 10. To avoid the construction, a detour was taken.

_____

Exercise 8   **CORRECTING DANGLING AND MISPLACED MODIFIERS**

Each of the following sentences has a dangling (D) or a misplaced (M) modifier. Identify the problems and correct them by rewriting the sentences.

_____ 1. Exploding noisily, I watched the fireworks.

_____

_____ 2. Count von Swerdlow started to abruptly without warning whistle his favorite themes from the *Elvis Gold* album.

_____

_____ 3. Running in front of the car, my sister tried to catch up with her dog.

_____

_____ 4. The crusty old sailor went to the fortune teller with bad luck.

_____

_____ 5. Burning out of control, the firefighters did their best at the location of the fire.

_____

_____ 6. I felt inadequate in the shopping mall without credit cards.

_____

_____ 7. Wearing striped suits and chains, the guards watched the convicts.

_____

_____ 8. I wanted to desperately obtain the recipe for the molded Jell-O dessert.

_____

_____ 9. Lounging in my hammock, the crime took place before my very eyes.

_____

_____ 10. I decided to foolishly purchase the solar-powered electric blanket.

_____

| **Exercise 9** | **CORRECTING DANGLING AND MISPLACED MODIFIERS** |

Each of the following sentences has a dangling (D) or a misplaced (M) modifier. Identify the problems and correct them by rewriting the sentences.

_____ 1. The ballplayers kissed their wives covered with dirt and sweat.

_____

_____ 2. The young lady began to angrily dump mustard and relish over her boyfriend's head.

_____

_____ 3. The alleged burglar addressed the judge on his knees.

_____

_____ 4. Wearing gaudy makeup and silly polka-dots pants, we watched the clowns.

_____

_____ 5. The anguished pet owner went to the veterinarian with a sick iguana.

_____

_____ 6. I saw a snail, a lizard, and a turtle on the way to church.

_____

_____ 7. Trying to succeed in school, my teacher was my greatest source of information and inspiration.

_____

_____ 8. By watching our diet, a long, healthy life is possible.

_____

_____ 9. Wearing a pink taffeta gown, Josh fell in love with his date.

_____

_____ 10. Dripping with tomato sauce, I began eating huge portions of my mother's special Mexican casserole.

Chapter Review: Adjectives and Adverbs

1. **Adjectives** modify (describe) nouns and pronouns and answer the questions *Which one? What kind? How many?*

2. **Adverbs** modify verbs, adjectives, and other adverbs and answer the questions *Where? When? Why? How?* Most words ending in *ly* are adverbs.

3. Anything can be overdone; therefore, use adjectives and adverbs like gravy, sparingly.

4. Some adjectives follow a regular pattern.

   > *nice, nicer, nicest*
   >
   > *lonely, more lonely, most lonely*

   These are usually the rules:

   a. Add *-er* to short adjectives (one or two syllables) to rank units of two.

      > Jethro is *shorter* than Cy.

   b. Add *-est* to short adjectives (one or two syllables) to rank units of more than two.

      > Senator Goodyear is the *brightest* person in Congress.

   c. Add the word *more* to long adjectives (three or more syllables) to rank units of two.

      > Your state is *more* prosperous than mine.

   d. Add the word *most* to long adjectives (three or more syllables) to rank units of three or more.

      > Your state is the *most* prosperous state in the West.

   e. Some adjectives are irregular in the way they change to show comparison.

      > *good, better, best*
      >
      > *bad, worse, worst*

5. Some adverbs follow a regular pattern.

   > *sadly, more sadly, most sadly*
   >
   > *carefully, more carefully, most carefully*

   a. Add *-er* to some one-syllable adverbs for the comparative form and add *-est* for the superlative form.

      > Pierre works *hard*. (positive)
      >
      > Pierre works *harder* than Simon. (comparative)
      >
      > Pierre works *hardest* of all students in the class. (superlative)

b. Add the word *more* to adverbs of two or more syllables for the comparative form and the word *most* to adverbs of two or more syllables for the superlative form.

> Sultana proofread *carefully.* (positive)
>
> Sultana proofread *more carefully* than Venny. (comparative)
>
> Sultana proofread *most carefully* of all in the class. (superlative)

c. In some cases the word *less* may be substituted for *more* and the word *least* for *most.*

> Martelle examined the contract *less carefully* during her second reading. (comparative)

d. Some adverbs are irregular in the way they change to show comparisons.

> *well, better, best*
>
> *badly, worse, worst*

6. Use adjectives and adverbs correctly.

   a. Avoid double negatives. Words such as *no, not, none, nothing, never, hardly, barely,* and *scarcely* should not be combined.

   b. Do not confuse adjectives with adverbs. Among the most commonly confused adjectives and adverbs are *good/well, bad/badly,* and *real/really.* The words *good, bad,* and *real* are always adjectives. *Well* is sometimes an adjective. The words *badly* and *really* are always adverbs. *Well* is usually an adverb.

Incorrect:	Clint did *good.* (*Good* is not an adverb.)
Correct:	Joline felt *good.* (*Good* does not address the matter of feeling; it indicates the condition of the subject, *Joline.*)
Correct:	Clint did *well.* (Used here as an adverb, *well* modifies the verb *did.*)
Correct:	Sigmund said, "Carl, you are not a *well* person." (Used here as an adjective, *well* modifies the noun *person.*)
Incorrect:	Elvis was real happy with his new disguise. (*Happy* is an adjective modifying the noun *Elvis,* and *real* modifies that adjective. Because only adverbs modify adjectives, we need the word *really.*)
Correct:	Elvis was *really* happy with his new disguise.
Incorrect:	I feel *badly.* (*Badly* is an adverb but here indicates the condition of the subject; therefore, it modifies the pronoun *I.*)
Correct:	I feel *bad.* (*Bad* is an adjective modifying the pronoun *I.*)
Correct:	I explained that *badly.* (*Badly,* an adverb, modifies the verb *explained.*)

   c. Do not use an adverb such as *very, more,* or *most* before adjectives such as *perfect, round, unique, square,* and *straight.*

Incorrect:	It is *more square.*
Correct:	It is *square.*
Correct:	It is *more nearly square.*

d. Do not double forms such as *more lonelier* or *most loneliest.*

Incorrect:	She is *more smarter* than I.
Correct:	She is *smarter* than I.

7. A **dangling modifier** gives information but fails to make clear which word or group of words it refers to.

a. **Incorrect:**   *Ignoring the traffic signals,* the car crashed into a truck. (The car is not ignoring; the driver is.)

b. **Correct:**   *Ignoring the traffic signals,* the driver crashed his car into a truck.

8. A **misplaced modifier** is placed so that it modifies the wrong word or words.

Incorrect: The monkeys attracted the attention of the elegant women *who picked fleas off one another.*

Correct: The monkeys *who picked fleas off one another* attracted the attention of the elegant women.

Chapter Review Exercises

Review 1	**USING CORRECT MODIFIERS**

Correct problems with modifiers. (See Answer Key for answers to the first paragraph.)

Old-time cowboys are among the better known figures in American folklore. Of course, they were versatiler than the word *cowboy* suggests. They did whatever work was needed on ranches, and they were able to do it real good. They mended fences, built sheds, took care of ranch equipment, and branded calves. They rounded up cattle, riding on their horses. Many times the roundups, as they were called, took in hundreds of square miles of range. After the cattle were rounded up, some were taken as trail herds to places such as Dodge City, Kansas, to be sold.

Often barren and dry, cowboys were the lonesomest fellows in the world on the trail. At night they would sing soft to the cattle, and life seemed more perfect than ever. No doubt most of them sang very bad, but the animals were soothed remarkable by the simple melodies and bellowed, bawled, and mooed in response. Sometimes the cattle stampeded and, the cowboys had to depend mighty on their horses to control the animals outfitted with practical saddles. The horses often saved the cowboys from death. When the trail herds reached their railhead destinations, the cowboys usual went to town for refreshments and entertainment in saloons. Some of these cowboys developed differences of opinions with other cowboys, and because they couldn't think critical enough to settle their problems in discussion groups, they ended up in places such as Boot Hill, a cemetery where men who died violent with their boots on were buried that way.

Review 2	**WRITING SHORT PARAGRAPHS CONTAINING ADJECTIVES AND ADVERBS**

For each numbered item, write a short paragraph using the words in parentheses.

1. (good, better, best) _____

   _____

   _____

   _____

   _____

   _____

   _____

2. (good, well) _____

   _____

   _____

   _____

   _____

   _____

3. (more, most) _____

   _____

   _____

   _____

   _____

   _____

4. (bad, badly) _____

_____

_____

_____

_____

_____

5. (real, really) _____

_____

_____

_____

_____

_____

8

Balancing Sentence Parts

"When the wheels on your car start to wobble, you must drive to a repair shop to have them balanced. But if your sentences start to wobble, you can apply the principles of parallelism discussed in this chapter and fix them yourself."

We are surrounded by balance. Watch a high-performance jet plane as it streaks across the sky. If you draw an imaginary line from the nose to the tail of the aircraft, you will see corresponding parts on either side. If you were to replace one of the streamlined wings of the jet with the straight and long wing of a glider, the plane would never fly. A similar lack of balance can also cause a sentence to crash.

Consider these statements:

"*To be* or *not to be*—that is the question." (dash added)

This line from *Hamlet,* by William Shakespeare, is one of the most famous lines in literature. Compare it to the jet in full flight. Its parts are parallel and it "flies" well.

"*To be or not being*—that is the question."

It still vaguely resembles the sleek aircraft, but now a phrase dips like a wing tip. Lurching, the line begins to lose altitude.

"*To be* or *death is the other alternative*—that is the question."

The writer and the line slam into the ground with a deafening boom, scattering words across the landscape.

The first sentence is forceful and easy to read. The second is more difficult to follow. The third is almost impossible to understand. We understand it only because we know what it should look like from having read the original. The point is that perceptive readers are as critical of sentences as pilots are of planes.

Basic Principles of Parallelism

Parallelism as it relates to sentence structure is usually achieved by joining words with similar words: nouns with nouns, adjectives (words that describe nouns and pronouns) with adjectives, adverbs (words that describe verbs, adjectives, and other adverbs) with adverbs, and so forth.

> *Men, women,* and *children* enjoy the show. (nouns)

> The players are *excited, eager,* and *enthusiastic.* (adjectives)

> The author wrote *skillfully* and *quickly.* (adverbs)

Parallel structure may also be achieved by joining groups of words with similar groups of words: prepositional phrase with prepositional phrase, clause with clause, sentence with sentence.

> She fell *in love* and *out of love* in a few minutes. (prepositional phrases)

> *Who he was* and *where he came from* did not matter. (clauses)

> *He came in a hurry. He left in a hurry.* (sentences)

Parallelism means balancing one structure with another of the same kind. Faulty parallel structure is awkward and draws unfavorable attention to what is being said.

Nonparallel: Kobe Bryant's reputation is based on his ability in *passing, shooting,* and *he is good at rebounds.*

Parallel: Kobe Bryant's reputation is based on his ability in *passing, shooting,* and *rebounding.*

In the nonparallel sentence, the words *passing* and *shooting* are of the same kind (verblike words used as nouns), but the rest of the sentence is different. You don't have to know terms to realize that there is a problem of balance in sentence structure. Just read the material aloud. Then compare it with the parallel statement; *he is good at rebounds* is changed to *rebounding* to make a sentence that's easy on the eye and ear.

Signal Words

Some words signal parallel structure. If you use *and,* the items joined by *and* should almost always be parallel. If they aren't, then *and* is probably inappropriate.

> The weather is hot *and* humid. (*and* joins adjectives)

> The car *and* the trailer are parked in front of the house. (*and* joins nouns)

The same principle is true for *but,* although it implies a direct contrast. Where contrasts are being drawn, parallel structure is essential to clarify those contrasts.

> He *purchased* a Dodger Dog, *but* I *chose* the Stadium Peanuts. (*but* joins contrasting clauses)

> She *earned* an A in math *but failed* her art class. (*but* joins contrasting verbs)

You should regard all the coordinating conjunctions (FANBOYS: *for, and, nor, but, or, yet, so*) as signals for parallel structure.

| **Exercise 1** | **IDENTFYING SIGNAL WORDS AND PARALLEL ELEMENTS** |

Underline the parallel elements—words, phrases, or clauses—and circle the signal words in the following sentences. The sentences in Exercises 1 through 9 are based on video review excerpts from Movie Guide *by the Wherehouse; the film titles are shown in parentheses. (See Answer Key for answers.)*

> **Example:**   One by one they <u>are stalked</u>, <u>terrorized</u>, (and) <u>murdered</u>. *(The Howling)*

1. The residents become the target of vicious, relentless, and inexplicable attacks by hordes of birds. *(The Birds)*

2. A family moves into a supposedly haunted New York home, and it finds that the house is inoperative. *(The Amityville Horror)*

3. While the family members try to make a comfortable life for themselves and to ignore a few irritations, all hell breaks loose.

4. Muffy invited her college friends to her parents' secluded island home but neglected to tell them it might be the last day of their lives. *(April Fool's Day)*

5. A woman discovers that her young daughter has inherited an evil streak and has caused the death of several people. *(The Bad Seed)*

6. A physician surgically separates Siamese twins, and they hate him. *(Basket Case)*

7. Onc twin is normal, and the other is horribly deformed.

8. The deformed twin becomes an embittered and vindictive person.

9. In a final unreasoning, angry, and brutal assault, she rips the face off the doctor.

10. A slimy alien crashes to earth and devours everyone in its path. *(The Blob)*

| **Exercise 2** | **IDENTIFYING SIGNAL WORDS AND PARALLEL ELEMENTS** |

Underline the parallel elements—words, phrases, or clauses—and circle the signal words in the following sentences.

1. An old granny tells tales of wolves and of children of the night. *(The Company of Wolves)*

2. Several convicts from another planet escape and fly to the planet Earth. *(Critters)*

3. Krite eggs hatch bloodthirsty babies and the babies continue the family tradition. *(Critters 2)*

4. Four people become trapped in a shopping mall with walking flesh-eaters and a gang of motorcyclists. *(Dawn of the Dead)*

5. A mad scientist dreams of creating life and using his ingenious talents. *(Frankenstein)*

6. He succeeds in producing a monster with the brain of a friend, the emotions of a child, and the body of a giant.

7. Combining fact, fiction, and horror, this film is an imaginative tale of fear. *(Gothic)*

8. A man flees a disturbed past while being pursued by a lawman, a psychopathic killer, and the woman who still loves him. *(Night Breed)*

9. A man wants money he didn't earn, a sightless woman wants to see, and a man's past catches up with him. *(Night Gallery)*

10. Norman Bates attempts to put his life together and to put his old habits behind him. *(Psycho III)*

Exercise 3	CORRECTING FAULTY PARALLELISM

Identify the sentences with parallel elements (P) and those with faulty parallelism (X). Correct the weak element. You need not rewrite the entire sentence. (See Answer Key for answers.)

_____ 1. Employees of a medical supply company release several zombies who like to roam the countryside and eating brains. *(Return of the Living Dead)*

_____ 2. A genetic experiment gone completely haywire spawns a new, hideous life form that breaks free and escaping into the sewer. *(Scared to Death)*

_____ 3. A young traveler finds madness, mystery, and he finds mayhem in the Louisiana bayou in this chilling Gothic tale. *(Sister, Sister)*

_____ 4. The Prince of Darkness has resurfaced in Los Angeles with a new look, a new life, a new love, and having an old enemy. *(To Die For)*

_____ 5. The Puttermans wanted clearer, more effective television reception. *(Terrorvision)*

_____ 6. They purchased a satellite dish, a good television set, and they sat down to watch.

_____ 7. Unfortunately for them, their new equipment brought monsters into their living room and upsetting their lives.

_____ 8. Scientists have bred the combat weapons—beasts with the cunning of human beings, the strength of giants, and who had the bloodlust of predators. *(Watchers)*

_____ 9. An explosion sets the mistakes free, and no one is safe.

_____ 10. A group of teenagers go for a free late-night showing at a wax museum horror display but tragically becoming part of the show. *(Waxwork)*

Exercise 4	**CORRECTING FAULTY PARALLELISM**

Identify the sentences with parallel elements (P) and those with faulty parallelism (X). Correct the weak element. You need not rewrite the entire sentence.

_____ 1. This film gives a warm and nostalgic look back at the year 1963 and focuses on one summer night of cruising in a small town. *(American Graffiti)*

_____ 2. It features greasers, geeks, good girls, and has cleancut characters.

_____ 3. This film casts a cynical shadow on bad acting, bad special effects, and uses bad dialogue. *(Attack of the Killer Tomatoes)*

_____ 4. Savage tomatoes roll around to terrorize the citizens and destroying their society.

_____ 5. Alex Foley is a brash, street-smart Detroit detective and who follows the trail of a friend's murder. *(Beverly Hills Cop)*

_____ 6. This zany comedy features a series of sketches that satirize movies, television, and ridicule other aspects of contemporary society. *(Kentucky Fried Movie)*

_____ 7. Prince Alceem quickly finds a new job, new friends, new enemies, and has lots of trouble. *(Coming to America)*

————— 8. High school students struggle with independence, success, money, and to be mature in this off-beat comedy. *(Fast Times at Ridgemont High)*

————— 9. A bespectacled spectacle of a bookkeeper adores his pet fish and dreams of becoming one of these scaled wonders. *(The Incredible Mr. Limpet)*

————— 10. When his wish suddenly comes true, he fisheyes a lady fish and becoming an invaluable hero to the U.S. Navy.

Exercise 5	COMPLETING PARALLEL STRUCTURES

Fill in the blanks in the following sentences with parallel elements. (See Answer Key for possible answers.)

1. The animated Disney classic concerns a little girl who follows a white rabbit to a land of wonder, ——————— , and ——————— . *(Alice in Wonderland)*

2. In this exciting and ——————— family adventure, Benji is adopted by a loving family. *(Benji)*

3. When the two children are kidnapped, Benji is the only one who knows where they are and ——————— .

4. A daring family decides to move to Alaska and ——————— completely apart from society. *(The Alaska Wilderness Aventure)*

5. This film takes us into the forest to share the excitement, ——————— , and ——————— of a little deer. *(Bambi)*

6. The caped crusader and his faithful boy wonder fight for ——————— , ——————— , and ——————— . *(Batman)*

7. Acme Co.'s best customer uses his entire arsenal, but Road Runner ——————— and ——————— . *(Road Runner)*

8. Coldheart has captured children and made them his slaves, and the Care Bears must outwit him with ——————— and ——————— . *(The Care Bears in a Land without Feeling)*

9. Van Dyke is delightful as a man whose old automobile suddenly develops the ability to ——————— and ——————— . *(Chitty-Chitty Bang-Bang)*

10. The mistreated stepdaughter is transformed by her fairy godmother, who

_____ her and _____ her to the royal ball. *(Cinderella)*

| **Exercise 6** | **COMPLETING PARALLEL STRUCTURES** |

Fill in the blanks in the following sentences with parallel elements. (See Answer Key for possible answers.)

1. Schwarzenegger plays a _____ , _____ killing machine.

   (The Terminator)

2. Nothing can stop him from his mission to find and _____ an inno-

   cent woman.

3. A man's dreams lead him to Mars in search of certain danger, his old

   _____ , and a mysterious _____ . *(Total Recall)*

4. A spaceship crash-lands on an unknown planet, and the three astronauts

   _____ . *(Planet of the Apes)*

5. There, the apes are the rulers, and the _____ .

6. Ultimately the alien grows to be an enormous size and _____ killing

   everyone on board. *(Alien)*

7. When unsuspecting guests check in at a hotel, they are surprised to find

   vicious ants who appear and _____ them with a vengeance. *(Ants)*

8. A futuristic ex-cop is drawn out of retirement to seek and _____ a

   group of renegade robots. *(Bladerunner)*

9. This is a touching and sometimes comical adventure of an _____ but

   _____ alien. *(E.T.)*

10. Max's somewhat cloudy origin is brought to light as the "creation" of an

    _____ and _____ computer-generated talk-show host.

    (Max Headroom—The Original Story)

Combination Signal Words

The words *and* and *but* are the most common individual signal words used with parallel constructions. Sometimes, however, **combination words** signal the need for parallelism or balance. The most common ones are *either/or, neither/nor, not only/but also, both/and,* and *whether/or.* Now consider this faulty sentence and a possible correction.

Nonparallel: *Either* we will win this game, *or* let's go out fighting.

Parallel: *Either we will* win this game, *or we will* go out fighting.

The correction is made by changing *let's* to *we will* to parallel the *we will* in the first part of the sentence. The same construction should follow the *either* and the *or.*

Nonparallel: Flour is used *not only* to bake cakes *but also* in paste.

Parallel: Flour is used *not only to bake* cakes *but also to make* paste.

The correction is made by changing *in* (a preposition) to *to make* (an infinitive). Now an infinitive follows both *not only* and *but also.*

Exercise 7	IDENTIFYING COMBINATION SIGNAL WORDS AND PARALLEL ELEMENTS

Underline the parallel elements—words, phrases, or clauses—and circle the combination signal words in the following sentences. (See Answer Key for answers.)

1. Robin Hood not only robbed from the rich but also gave to the poor. *(Adventures of Robin Hood)*

2. Both Humphrey Bogart and Katharine Hepburn star in this movie about two unlikely people traveling together through the jungle rivers of Africa during World War II. *(The African Queen)*

3. Dr. Jekyll discovers a potion, and now he can be either himself or Mr. Hyde. *Dr. Jekyll and Mr. Hyde)*

4. An Oklahoma family moves to California and finds neither good jobs nor compassion in the "promised land." *(The Grapes of Wrath)*

5. In this Christmas classic, Jimmy Stewart stars as a man who can either die by suicide or go back to see what life would have been like without him. *(It's a Wonderful Life)*

6. During the Korean War, army surgeons discover that they must either develop a lunatic lifestyle or go crazy. *(M*A*S*H)*

7. An advertising executive not only gets tied up with an obnoxious but boring salesman but also goes with him on a wacky chase across the country. *(Planes, Trains, and Automobiles)*

8. In this flawless integration of animation and live action, Roger and Eddie try to discover both who framed Roger and who is playing patty-cake with his wife. *(Who Framed Roger Rabbit?)*

9. A long-suffering black woman named Celie experiences not only heartaches but also some joy as she rises from tragedy to personal triumph. *(The Color Purple)*

10. An independent man learns that he is expected to give up either his dignity or his life. *(Cool Hand Luke)*

| **Exercise 8** | **CORRECTING FAULTY PARALLELISM** |

Underline the parallel elements—words, phrases, or clauses—and circle the combination single words in the following sentences. If the elements are not parallel, change them to achieve balance. You need not rewrite the entire sentence.

Example: <u>Either the street punks would terrorize the school</u>, ⓞⓡ <u>a former gang member would stop them.</u> *(The Moment of Truth)*

1. A fanatical submarine captain makes a misguided effort to sink the ships of both the allies and the enemy. *(20,000 Leagues Under the Sea)*

2. After a young woman is brutally attacked by a scurvy street gang, not only she studies martial arts but also plans for absolute bloody revenge. *(Alley Cat)*

3. The main issue is whether a street-wise girl will find the killer or he will escape. *(Avenging Angel)*

4. Either the Barbarian brothers will triumph or the evil world will win. *(The Barbarians)*

5. Neither the joker nor anyone else can get the last laugh on Batman. *(Batman)*

6. Two youngsters are shipwrecked in the South Pacific and not only they mature but also slowly make a surprising discovery. *(Blue Lagoon)*

7. A neighborhood gang will either reign, or Danny McGavin will. *(Colors)*

8. After Conan's parents were murdered, he swore that he would either get revenge or die trying. *(Conan the Barbarian)*

9. The question is whether Harry will kill the psychopath or the psychopath will kill him. *(Dirty Harry)*

10. Neither Mumbles nor Breathless Mahoney communicated well with Dick Tracy. *(Dick Tracy)*

Exercise 9	**CORRECTING FAULTY PARALLELISM**

Underline the parallel elements—words, phrases, or clauses—and circle the combination signal words in the following sentences. If the elements are not parallel, change them to achieve balance. You need not rewrite the entire sentence.

1. James Bond protects the U.S. gold reserve both with some wonderfully ingenious gadgets and a few unusually lovely ladies. *(Goldfinger)*

2. Two convicts decide that either they must escape from Devil's Island or die. *(Papillon)*

3. These prehistoric people are not only competing in a quest for fire but also in a struggle for dominance. *(Quest for Fire)*

4. Whether one side won or the other, human beings would benefit.

5. Neither his poor physical condition nor his reputation would discourage Rocky Balboa. *(Rocky)*

6. Both Al Capone and Bugs Moran neglected to pass out Valentine's Day cards in 1934. *(The St. Valentine's Day Massacre)*

7. It was neither a bird nor was it a plane; it was Superman. *(Superman—The Movie)*

8. The pilot loved both the experience of flying and to be around a certain beautiful astrophysicist. *(Top Gun)*

9. A computer whiz kid manages not only to get himself hooked into a top-secret military computer but also finds the fate of the world in his hands. *(Wargames)*

10. Only one person would walk away from this friendship; it would be either the drug smuggler or it would be the cop. *(Tequila Sunrise)*

Chapter Review: Balancing Sentence Parts

1. Parallelism is a balance of one structure with another of the same kind—nouns with nouns, verbs with verbs, adjectives with adjectives, phrases with phrases, and clauses with clauses.

> *Goats, chickens,* and *cows* (nouns) *roamed* the yard and *caused* (verbs) considerable confusion.

> Tanya walked *into the room* and *out of the room* with grace (prepositional phrases).

> *Tanya walked into the room,* and *she walked out of the room* with grace (independent clauses).

2. Faulty parallel structure is awkward and draws unfavorable attention to what is being said.

> *Hitting* home runs and *to catch* balls in the outfield were his main concerns (should be *Hitting . . . and catching* or *To hit . . . and to catch*).

3. Some words signal parallel structure. All coordinating conjunctions (FANBOYS: *for, and, nor, but, or, yet, so*) can give such signals.

> My car is inexpensive *and* plain.

> My dog is ugly, *but* it is a good companion.

4. Combination words also signal the need for parallelism or balance. The most common ones are *either/or, neither/nor, not only/but also, both/and,* and *whether/or.*

> Patsy decided that propagating plants could be *either* a hobby *or* a business but not both. (A noun follows each of the combination words.)

Chapter Review Exercises

| **Review 1** | **CORRECTING FAULTY PARALLELISM** |

Eliminate awkwardness in the following passage by using parallel structure. (See Answer Key for possible answers to the first two paragraphs.)

Ken Kesey wrote *One Flew Over the Cuckoo's Nest* as a novel. It was later made into a stage play and a film. The title was taken from a children's folk rhyme: "One flew east, one flew west, / One flew over the cuckoo's nest."

The narrator in the novel is Chief Bromden, the central character is Randle McMurphy, and Nurse Ratched is the villain. Bromden sees and can hear but does not speak. He is a camera with a conscience. McMurphy is both an outcast and serves as a leader, and he speaks out for freedom and as an individual. Nurse

Ratched is the voice of repression. She is the main representative of what Bromden calls the "Combine." She organizes, directs, controls, and, if necessary to her purposes, will destroy.

The setting is a mental institution where McMurphy has gone to avoid doing more rigorous time in the nearby prison. Discovering what the inmates are going through, he seeks to liberate them from their affliction and freeing them from Nurse Ratched's domination.

A battle of wills ensues, and the reader wonders who will win. The nurse has the whole system behind her, one that prevents the inmates from regaining self-esteem. McMurphy is a colorful, irreverent, expressive person and who appeals to the men's deepest need for self-respect and to be sane. She offers her therapy; his is also offered. She gives drugs. She also gives group therapy, which is tightly controlled by her to produce humiliation. McMurphy provides recreation in the form of first a fishing trip and then sex (for some).

McMurphy is eventually defeated by the system. Neither his energy was enough nor his intelligence when the Combine moves in. McMurphy is given a lobotomy and reduced to a mere body without a mind. Out of profound respect and deeply loving, Bromden destroys McMurphy's body and then escapes.

Review 2	**COMPLETING PARALLEL STRUCTURES**

Complete each of the following sentences by adding a construction that is parallel to the underlined construction.

1. We went to the zoo not only for <u>fun</u> but also for _____
   _____

2. He attended Utah State University for <u>a good education</u> and _____
   _____

3. For a college major, she was considering <u>English</u>, <u>history</u>, and _____

4. Mr. Ramos was <u>a good neighbor</u> and _____

5. My breakfast each day that week consisted of <u>a slice of bread</u>, <u>a glass of low-fat milk</u>, and _____

6. She decided that she must choose between <u>a social life</u> and _____

_____

7. Either <u>she would make the choice,</u> or _____

_____

8. Because we are mutually supportive, either <u>we will all have a good time,</u> or

_____

9. Like the Three Musketeers, our motto is "<u>All for one</u> and _____

_____

10. My intention was to <u>work for a year,</u> <u>save my money,</u> and _____

_____

Review 3	**WRITING SENTENCES WITH PARALLEL STRUCTURE**

Use each of these signal words or combined signal words in a sentence of ten or more words.

1. and _____

_____

_____

2. but _____

_____

_____

3. so _____

_____

_____

4. either/or _____

_____

_____

5. both/and _____

_____

_____

9

Punctuation and Capitalization

"Reading a passage with wrong punctuation is like driving on streets with wrong traffic signs and signals."

nderstanding punctuation will help you to write better. If you aren't sure how to punctuate a compound or a compound-complex sentence, then you probably will not write one. If you don't know how to show that some of your words come from other sources, you may mislead your reader. If you misuse punctuation, you will force your readers to struggle to get your message. So take the time to review and master the mechanics. Your efforts will be rewarded.

End Punctuation

Periods

1. Place a period after a statement.

   The weather is beautiful today.

2. Place a period after common abbreviations.

   Dr.   Mr.   Mrs.   Dec.   A.M.

   Exceptions: FBI   UN   NAACP   FHA

3. Use an ellipsis—three periods within a sentence and four periods at the end of a sentence—to indicate that words have been omitted from quoted material.

> He stopped walking and the buildings . . . rose up out of the misty courtroom. . . .

James Thurber, "The Secret Life of Walter Mitty"

Question Marks

1. Place a question mark at the end of a direct question.

> Will you go the country tomorrow?

2. Do *not* use a question mark after an indirect (reported) question.

> She asked me what caused the slide.

Exclamation Points

1. Place an exclamation point after a word or a group of words that expresses strong feeling.

> Oh!   What a night!   Help!   Gadzooks!

2. Do not overwork the exclamation point. Do not use double exclamation points. Use the period or comma for mild exclamatory words, phrases, or sentences.

> Oh, we can leave now.

Exercise 1   **USING END PUNCTUATION**

Add end punctuation. (See Answer Key for answers.)

1. The exhausted sponge divers asked their skipper whether they could have shore leave so they could get more tattoos of mermaids and anchors

2. Holy motherboard, my computer just crashed

3. I wonder if my boyfriend will like my purple hair

4. Junior, put down that water balloon and get away from your sister this minute

5. Hooray, I've just won the lottery

6. Now I can buy that pink '59 Coupe de Ville I've always wanted

7. "Have a nice day," the clerk said with a leer

8. Hmmm, I wonder how my neighbor would react if I trimmed his Saint Bernard's coat French-poodle style

9. Who *is* responsible for writing that e-mail message

10. Let us stop and give thanks to the king, Elvis, for his moving performance in *Viva Las Vegas*

Exercise 2	**USING END PUNCTUATION**

Add end punctuation.

1. It is very hard to find time to study when so much excellent television program- ming is available

2. As a good American, I know that I must watch at least four or five hours of tele- vision each day

3. When I don't watch at least three hours of television, I wonder if I'm somehow not a good citizen

4. Would you like to spend a few hours watching game shows with me this morning

5. The sky is falling

6. If we are to get the children of this great country away from television, we must encourage them to read and exercise

7. The knave asked if he could have another bowl of gruel

8. Would you like some gruel

9. It is made from old potato skins, cabbage water, and bits of chicken fat

10. Help, my otter has escaped

Commas

Commas to Separate

1. Use a comma to separate main clauses joined by one of the coordinating con- junctions—*for, and, nor, but, or, yet, so.* The comma may be omitted if the clauses are brief and parallel.

> We traveled many miles to see the game, *but* it was canceled.

> Mary left and I remained. (brief and parallel clauses)

2. Use a comma after introductory dependent clauses and long introductory phrases (generally, four or more words is considered long).

> *Before the arrival of the shipment,* the boss had written a letter protesting the delay. (two prepositional phrases)

> *If you don't hear from me,* assume that I am lost. (introductory dependent clause, an adverbial modifier)

> *In winter* we skate on the river. (short prepositional phrase, no comma)

3. Use a comma to separate words, phrases, and clauses in a series.

> *Red, white,* and *blue* were her favorite colors. (words)

> *He ran down the street, across the park,* and *into the arms of his father.* (prepositional phrases)

> *When John was asleep, when Mary was at work,* and *when Bob was studying,* Mother had time to relax. (dependent clauses)

4. However, when coordinating conjunctions connect all the elements in a series, the commas are omitted.

> He bought apples and pears and grapes.

5. Use a comma to separate coordinate adjectives not joined by *and* that modify the same noun.

> I need a *sturdy, reliable* truck.

6. Do not use a comma to separate adjectives that are not coordinate. Try the following technique to determine whether the adjectives are coordinate: Put *and* between the adjectives. If it fits naturally, the adjectives are coordinate; if it does not, they are not, and you do not need a comma.

> She is a kind, beautiful person.

> kind *and* beautiful (natural, hence the comma)

> I built a red brick wall.

> red *and* brick wall (not natural, no comma)

7. Use a comma to separate sentence elements that might be misread.

> Inside the dog scratched his fleas.

> *Inside,* the dog scratched his fleas.

Without benefit of the comma, the reader might initially misunderstand the relationship among the first three words.

Commas to Set Off

1. Use commas to set off (enclose) adjectives in pairs that follow a noun.

> The scouts, *tired and hungry,* marched back to camp.

2. Use commas to set off nonessential (unnecessary for meaning of the sentence) words, phrases, and clauses.

> My brother, *a student at Ohio State University,* is visiting me. (If you drop the phrase, the basic meaning of the sentence remains intact.)

> Marla, *who studied hard,* will pass. (The clause is not essential to the basic meaning of the sentence.)

> All students *who studied hard* will pass. (Here the clause *is* essential. If you remove it, you would have *All students will pass,* which is not necessarily true.)

> I shall not stop searching *until I find the treasure.* (A dependent clause at the end of a sentence is usually not set off with a comma. However, a clause beginning with the word *though* or *although* will be set off regardless of where it is located.)

> I felt unsatisfied, *though we had won the game.*

3. Use commas to set off parenthetical elements such as mild interjections (*oh, well, yes, no,* and others), most conjunctive adverbs (*however, otherwise, therefore, similarly, hence, on the other hand,* and *consequently,* but not *then, thus, soon, now,* and *also*), quotation indicators, and special abbreviations (*etc., i.e., e.g.,* and others).

> *Oh,* what a silly question! (mild interjection)

> It is necessary, *of course,* to leave now. (sentence modifier)

> We left early; *however,* we missed the train anyway. (conjunctive adverb)

> "When I was in school," *he said,* "I read widely." (quotation indicator)

> Books, papers, pens, *etc.,* were scattered on the floor. (The abbreviation *etc.* should be used sparingly, however.)

4. Use commas to set off nouns used as direct address.

> Play it again, *Sam.*

> Please tell us the answer, *Jane,* so we can discuss it.

5. Use commas to separate the numbers in a date.

> June 4, 1965, is a day I will remember.

6. Do not use commas if the day of the month is not specified, or if the day is given before the month.

> June 1965 was my favorite time.

> One day I will never forget is 4 June 1965.

7. Use commas to separate the city from the state. No comma is used between the state and the ZIP code.

> Walnut, CA 91789

8. Use a comma after both the city and the state when they are used together in a sentence.

> Our family visited Anchorage, Alaska, last summer.

9. Use a comma following the salutation of a friendly letter and the complimentary closing in any letter.

> Dear Saul,

> Sincerely,

10. Use a comma in numbers to set off groups of three digits. However, omit the comma in dates, serial numbers, page numbers, years, and street numbers.

> The total assets were $2,000,000.

> I look forward to the year 2050.

Exercise 3   **USING COMMAS**

Insert commas where needed. (See Answer Key for answers.)

1. After long and thoughtful consideration I decided that I would be grand marshal for the recycled products parade.

2. The cowpokes tired and hungry settled down to a satisfying meal of beans and hardtack.

3. Contrary to popular belief hardtack can be quite palatable if one soaks it in bacon fat and slurps it down with a cup of thick scalding coffee.

4. Barstow California is the gateway to the Mojave and it is the last major gas stop before Las Vegas Nevada.

5. I have decided therefore to move there because I like open private spaces.

6. Debbi Winthrop inventor of the waterproof match retired in Cleveland Ohio.

7. The fifth grade class gobbled up hundreds of marshmallows Eskimo Pies and hot dogs at the party.

8. The woman who swallowed small live fish at the fair for a living became an instant celebrity.

9. The motorcycle gang rowdy and bored drew happy faces on all the road signs in the tri-state area.

10. He knew of course that winning the Nobel Prize for inventing a new kind of instant pudding was a long shot at best.

11. The wood-burning kit a source of many household fires in the fifties and sixties was one of my favorite childhood toys.

12. The young energetic campaign workers offered free promotional hamsters to the harried distracted commuters.

13. They responded of course with looks of deep appreciation.

14. The kind generous government agents gave packages of astronaut ice cream to the aliens from outer space.

15. The alto-sax player "Space" Jackson was renowned for his ability to chew gum talk and play his sax at the same time.

16. I however think that there must be some sort of trick involved with Jackson's act.

17. You sir are the best Elvis imitator in Fullerton California.

18. Alexander Dumas author of *The Three Musketeers* curiously enough never handled a sword in his life.

19. He was however famous for his skill in handling a fondue fork.

20. August 19 1961 was certainly one of the greatest days in history.

Exercise 4	USING COMMAS

Insert commas where needed.

1. In *Frankenstein* the original classic horror thriller written by Mary Shelley and published on October 3 1818 Victor Frankenstein was a gifted dedicated student.

2. While he studied science at the university he came upon the secret of how to create life.

3. Being more interested in simple practical matters than in theory he set out to construct a living breathing creature.

4. Victor who was very much concerned about process first needed to gather the materials necessary for his experiment.

5. He went all around town picking up body parts and he stored them in his laboratory.

6. The dissecting room at a local hospital provided him with the most basic articles and he was very grateful.

7. Local butcher shops had plenty of items perhaps including some spare ribs.

8. Finally he was ready to begin construction of a strange humanlike creature.

9. He made a creature that was eight feet tall four feet wide and very strong.

10. The face of the creature which could be described only as hideous was not easy to look upon.

11. One night while Victor was sleeping lightly the monster lonely and troubled came to his bedroom.

12. Victor screamed loudly and the monster ran away in disappointment.

13. Victor developed brain fever which was a result of the encounter.

14. When Victor recovered from his illness he discovered that one of his brothers had been murdered by an unknown person.

15. In despair and befuddlement Victor went to a remote wilderness to sort out his problems.

16. One day when he was out walking Victor saw a strange lumbering creature running into the mountains.

17. Victor chased the creature but he was unable to catch it.

18. Soon after he sat down to rest and the creature appeared before him.

19. It was Victor Frankenstein's monster who had come to talk to him.

20. With a great deal of self-pity the monster explained that he was very sad because people were unkind to him.

Exercise 5	**USING COMMAS**

Insert commas where needed. (See Answer Key for answers.)

1. Frankenstein's monster distraught and desperate told a story of acute loneliness.

2. After leaving Victor Frankenstein's house he had gone to live in the country.

3. He had tried diligently to help the simple gentle people by bringing them firewood.

4. They took the firewood; however they were at first frightened and then angry.

5. The monster very upset and dejected had gone back to the city.

6. There he killed Victor's innocent unsuspecting brother and he then cleverly tried to place the blame on someone else.

7. Listening to the monster in horror Victor Frankenstein realized what he had done in this act of creation.

8. The monster started making demands and it was clear that he would force Victor to carry them out.

9. He said that if Victor did not make a suitable female companion for him he would begin killing human beings at random.

10. Victor went away gathered up some more parts and started building a bride for the monster.

11. The monster waited in eager anticipation but he was to be sorely disappointed.

12. Victor became disgusted with his project and he destroyed all the tissue just before it came to life.

13. Needless to say the monster was deeply distressed by this unexpected shocking development.

14. Before the monster ran away he swore to get revenge on Victor's wedding night.

15. When Victor got married he armed himself fully for he expected a visit from the enraged vengeful monster.

16. On the night of the wedding the monster slipped into the bridal chambers and strangled the horrified unlucky bride.

17. Victor himself vowed to avenge the murder by killing the monster but the monster was nowhere to be found.

18. Victor finally died in a cabin in the desolate frozen lands of the North and much later his body was found by a friend.

19. The monster dropped by for one last visit for he wanted to complain about his unhappy life.

20. He said that Victor had created a man without a friend love or even a soul and therefore Victor was more wicked than anyone.

Exercise 6	**USING COMMAS**

Insert commas where needed.

1. Many people have criticized spinach in recent years and I would like to offer a rebuttal.

2. First of all spinach comes in an interesting attractive shade of green.

3. It is also inexpensive nutritious and delicious.

4. I have recently purchased a beautiful perky toy poodle named Maxine.

5. Maxine and I take walks each day but we are often cursed by the unwanted irritating advances of amorous bachelor dogs.

6. These would-be suitors will never win the love of Maxine for her affections are directed to the handsome clever Pierre a standard poodle.

7. Zeke Rimkin defense attorney will be representing me next week and I hope he can get my case dismissed.

8. He is a bright articulate person, and he will do almost anything to win a case for his clients.

9. According to his commercials on television he is the only local attorney who specializes in skateboard litigation.

10. When the jury members see Zeke Rimkin skate into court they will be impressed.

11. The professional wrestlers circled each other like caged wild beasts and the crowd loved the spectacle.

12. According to official records California has more tanning booths per capita than any other state.

13. If you know what is good for you you will eat a big hearty breakfast of tofu and wheat germ every day.

14. Outside the cold winter wind established a record chill factor.

15. The cheerful efficient waitress helped the squirming screaming toddler into the highchair.

16. Figure-skating star Henri Tartuffe executed a death-defying leap into the snack stand adjacent to the skating rink and the fans gasped.

17. Without the invention of the hot dog baseball would be a dreary dismal affair to some.

18. The teenager proud and talkative displayed his bright shiny pickup to his admiring friends.

19. Contrary to popular belief the chameleon can be an attractive amusing alternative to a boyfriend.

20. Beef jerky tarot cards and Flemish paintings were the passions of Mugsie O'Flannigan's life.

Semicolons

The semicolon indicates a stronger division than the comma. It is used principally to separate independent clauses within a sentence.

1. Use a semicolon to separate independent clauses not joined by a coordinating conjunction.

> You must buy that car today; tomorrow will be too late.

2. Use a semicolon between two independent clauses joined by a conjunctive adverb such as one of the HOTSHOT CAT words *(however, otherwise, therefore, similarly, hence, on the other hand, then, consequently, accordingly, thus).*

> It was very late; therefore, I remained at the hotel.

3. Use a semicolon to separate main clauses joined by a coordinating conjunction if one or both of the clauses contain distracting commas.

> Byron, the famous English poet, was buried in Greece; and Shelley, who was his friend and fellow poet, was buried in Italy.

4. Use a semicolon in a series between items that themselves contain commas.

> He has lived in Covina, California; Reno, Nevada; Tribbey, Oklahoma; and Bangor, Maine.

Exercise 7	USING SEMICOLONS AND COMMAS

Insert semicolons and commas where needed. (See Answer Key for answers.)

1. Horse trading is a declining art in American society but obtaining a horse was once as complicated as obtaining an automobile is now.

2. Years ago many thousands of people made their living by trading horses few laws regulated that business.

3. These traders traveled from farm to farm, they rode one horse and led several others.

4. The same traders, who were often ambitious, aggressive, and articulate, traded for other horses but they also traded for poultry, cattle, land, and personal items.

5. Some horse traders were honest quite a few of them were not.

6. A farmer buying a horse from a trader had to be careful otherwise he could purchase a bad one.

7. Because a horse's teeth grow longer with age some traders filed the teeth to shorten them.

8. Some horses being traded were in poor condition these animals often developed a depression over each eye.

9. Dishonest traders had a special technique to conceal this problem they used needles for pumping those depressions full of air.

10. As horses grow older the hair on their face begins to turn gray.

11. That problem was easy to unscrupulous traders they dyed the gray hair, often with shoe polish.

12. Crafty traders gave painkillers to lame horses then they sold them before the effects of the medicine wore off.

13. Most farmers were shrewd in selecting horses but some were gullible.

14. The farmers were practical men and they wanted workhorses to pull a plow and other farm equipment.

15. They wanted horses with large feet because large feet would not sink into the ground.

16. Most farmers also wanted animals with broad chests and strong hindquarters for pulling therefore they were not interested in sleek riding horses.

17. Some were looking for a handsome matching pair of horses after all they had wagons and buggies for transportation to and from town.

18. The farmers' livelihood depended on their having good work animals therefore horse trading was a big business in communities such as Liberal Kansas Waco Texas and Seminole Oklahoma.

19. Now, most people who own horses use them only for recreational riding and horses are seldom purchased for their pulling power.

20. In past times the horses worked to support people now people work to support horses.

| Exercise 8 | USING SEMICOLONS AND COMMAS |

Insert semicolons and commas where needed.

1. Once upon a time, there was a young woman named Cyberella she lived in Oklahoma with an evil stepmother and an obnoxious stepsister.

2. One night at eleven her wretched stepfamily was snoring raucously and Cyberella was busily dusting the family computer, which someone had left running.

3. It was then that Cyberella inadvertently hit the Instant Internet button therefore the screen lit up.

4. She had never been permitted to use the Internet but she had enviously watched her evil stepfamily at the keyboard.

5. Cyberella created the screen name Cool4aday and logged on for fun and education naturally she started with the index of chat rooms.

6. She was delighted with her unexpected opportunity however she realized that the computer was programmed to go out of commission at midnight.

7. Now she was a free-spirited cyberspace explorer surfing the World Wide Web at midnight she would turn back into a servant ripping out cobwebs and capturing dust bunnies.

8. Cyberella spotted a chat room called "Talk to the Prince" feeling like a princess she joined in the conversation.

9. To her amazement she discovered that she was chatting with a real prince Prince Igor of Transylvania in fact he seemed to like her.

10. Prince Igor boldly invited Cyberella to accompany him to a private chat room breathlessly she said yes and followed him with demure keystrokes.

11. They chatted shyly and then passionately for almost an hour and soon the prince became royally enamored by the way she processed thought noticing that she wrote skillfully, using her spell checker and grammar checker in a most delicate way.

12. Cyberella wanted to tell Prince Igor explicitly what was in her heart therefore she often used the computer thesaurus feature, impressing him further with her highly eloquent diction.

13. Prince Igor was about to ask the royal marriage question then Cyberella heard the clock strike her computer went dark and she believed she would never again chat with her sweet prince.

14. Prince Igor was devastated and vowed to find this lovely correspondent he therefore directed his army to undertake a royal search that would properly but legally identify Cool4aday and expose all impostors.

15. The soldiers would test the computer-assisted writing skills of everyone in the world if necessary moreover they would even provide laptops for any computerless woman who looked as if she could possibly be the mystery writer.

16. Cyberella had informed Prince Igor that she was from the American Southwest a fact that enabled him to focus his search.

17. Following electronic clues, the soldiers visited Amarillo Texas Tucumcari New Mexico Tulsa Oklahoma and Window Rock Arizona.

18. At last a soldier came to Cyberella's house and was greeted by the obnoxious stepsister, who claimed that she was Cool4aday and began to chat on line with Prince Igor however the stepsister forgot to use her spell checker and the prince flamed a rejection.

19. Then the soldier handed Cyberella a laptop computer and instructions of course both the wicked stepmother and the obnoxious stepsister scoffed.

20. Nevertheless, Cyberella was verified as Cool4aday and the prince was wildly elated therefore he declared an international holiday slapped his leg with glee and offered to grant her fondest wish.

21. "Does that mean I get this laptop for myself?" Cyberella asked and Prince Igor, a bit humbled by her response said "No, that means you get me for yourself."

22. "Oh, that's very, very nice but may I also have this laptop?" Cyberella asked striking a hard bargain as she fondly hugged the computer.

23. "Yes" Prince Igor said. "I'll even toss in a laser printer and I'll add a few pounds of copy paper and a stack of dungeon-and-dragon software customized in one of my own castles."

24. They got married and lived happily ever after for a while then the wicked step-family tried to move into the palace but they were arrested and were no longer allowed to use the Internet in Transylvania or Oklahoma until they had passed a writing test which they never did.

Quotation Marks

Quotation marks are used principally to set off direct quotations. A direct quotation consists of material taken from the written work or the direct speech of others; it is set off by double quotation marks. Single quotation marks are used to set off a quotation within a quotation.

> **Double Quotation Marks:**   He said, "I don't remember."
>
> **Single Quotation Marks:**   He said, "I don't remember if she said, 'Wait for me.'"

1. Use double quotation marks to set off direct quotations.

> Lavonne said, "Give me the book."
>
> As Edward McNeil writes of the Greek achievement: "To an extent never before realized, mind was supreme over faith."

2. Use double quotation marks to set off titles of shorter pieces of writing such as magazine articles, essays, short stories, short poems, one-act plays, chapters in books, songs, and separate pieces of writing published as part of a larger work.

> The book *Literature: Structure, Sound, and Sense* contains a deeply moving poem titled "On Wenlock Edge."
>
> Have you read "The Use of Force," a short story by William Carlos Williams?
>
> My favorite Elvis song is "Don't Be Cruel."

3. Use double quotation marks to set off slang, technical terms, and special words.

> There are many aristocrats, but Elvis is the only true "King." (special word)
>
> The "platoon system" changed the game of football. (technical term)

4. Use double quotation marks in writing dialogue (conversation). Write each speech unit as a separate paragraph and set it off with double quotation marks.

> "Will you go with me?" he asked.
>
> "Yes," she replied. "Are you ready now?"

5. Use single quotation marks to set off a quotation within a quotation.

> Professor Baxter said, "You should remember Shakespeare's words, 'Nothing will come of nothing.'"

6. Do *not* use quotation marks for indirect quotations.

   Wrong: He said that "he would bring the supplies."

   Right: He said that he would bring the supplies.

7. Do *not* use quotation marks for the title on your own written work. If you refer to that title in another piece of writing, however, you need the quotation marks.

Punctuation with Quotation Marks

1. A period or comma is always placed *inside* the quotation marks.

   > Our assignment for Monday was to read Poe's poem "The Raven."
   >
   > "I will read you the story," he said. "It's a good one."

2. A semicolon or colon is always placed *outside* the quotation marks.

   > He read Robert Frost's poem "Design"; then he gave the examination.
   >
   > He quoted Frost's "Stopping by Woods on a Snowy Evening": "But I have promises to keep."

3. A question mark, exclamation point, or dash (see page 180) is placed *outside* the quotation marks when it applies to the entire sentence and *inside* the quotation marks when it applies to the material in quotation marks.

   > He asked, "Am I responsible for everything?" (quoted question within a statement)
   >
   > Did you hear him say, "I have the answer"? (statement within a question)
   >
   > Did she say, "Are you ready?" (question within a question)
   >
   > She shouted, "Impossible!" (exclamation)
   >
   > Roy screamed, "I'll flunk if I don't read Poe's short story 'The Black Cat'!" (exclamation that does not belong to the material inside the quotation marks)
   >
   > "I hope—that is, I—" he began. (dash)
   >
   > "Accept responsibility"—those were his words. (dash that does not belong to the material inside the quotation marks)

4. A single question mark is used in sentence constructions that contain a double question—that is, a quoted question following a question.

   > Mr. Rodriguez said, "Did he say, 'Are you going?'"

Italics

Italics (slanting type) is used to call special attention to certain words or groups of words. In handwriting or typing, such words are <u>underlined.</u>

1. Italicize (underline) foreign words and phrases that are still listed in the dictionary as foreign.

   nouveau riche   *Weltschmerz*

2. Italicize (underline) titles of books (except the Bible); long poems; plays; magazines; motion pictures; musical compositions; newspapers; works of art; names of aircraft and ships; and letters, figures, and words.

   I think Hemingway's best novel is *A Farewell to Arms.*

   His source material was taken from *Time, Newsweek,* and the Los Angeles *Times.* (Sometimes the name of the city in titles of newspapers is italicized—for example, the *New York Times.*)

   The *Mona Lisa* is my favorite painting.

3. Italicize (underline) the names of ships, airplanes, spacecraft, and trains.

   Ships: *Queen Mary   Lurline   Stockholm*

   Spacecraft: *Challenger   Voyager 2*

4. Italicize (underline) to distinguish letters, figures, and words when they refer to themselves rather than to the ideas or things they usually represent.

   Do not leave the *o* out of *sophomore.*

   Your *3*'s look like *5*'s.

Exercise 9   **USING QUOTATION MARKS AND ITALICS**

Insert quotation marks and italics (underlining) as needed. (See Answer Key for answers.)

1. Professor Jones said, Now we will read from The Complete Works of Edgar Allan Poe.

2. The enthusiastic students shouted, We like Poe! We like Poe!

3. The professor lectured for fifty-seven minutes before he finally said, In conclusion, I say that Poe was an unappreciated writer during his lifetime.

4. The next speaker said, I believe that Poe said, A short story should be short enough so that a person can read it in one sitting.

5. Then, while students squirmed, he read The Fall of the House of Usher in sixty-eight minutes.

6. Now we will do some reading in unison, said Professor Jones.

7. Each student opened a copy of The Complete Works of Edgar Allan Poe.

8. Turn to page 72, said Professor Jones.

9. What parts do we read? asked a student.

10. You read the words, or maybe I should say word, of the raven, said the professor.

| Exercise 10 | USING QUOTATION MARKS AND ITALICS |

Insert quotation marks and italics (underlining) as needed.

1. The students were not pleased with their small part in the group reading of The Raven.

2. They made several derogatory comments about Professor Jones, even though he had written a learned texbook entitled A Short, Brief, and Concise Study of English Rhetoric and the Art of Using English Effectively, Correctly, and Well.

3. As Professor Jones lit candles around a sculpted artwork, one student yelled, The poem says bust of Pallas, and that is not Pallas.

4. Professor Jones retorted archly, We didn't have a bust of Pallas in the department, so I brought a bust of Elvis from the chairperson's office.

5. Another student nodded approval and whispered to his enthralled companion, That prof is cool, real cool.

6. His companion, an English minor with a keen knowledge of grammar, whispered good-naturedly, Really cool is what you mean.

7. Yes, he said, that's what I mean. Sometimes I leave out my ly's and use the wrong words, and people think I'm a gashead.

8. The professor reached into his bag of props, took out a dark, feathered object, and said, I have brought a stuffed raven.

9. That's not a raven. That's a crow, said a student who was majoring in ornithology.

10. The professor waggled his finger playfully at his audience and said, I believe Coleridge once observed, Art sometimes requires the willing suspension of disbelief.

Dashes

The dash is used when a stronger break than the comma is needed. The dash is typed as two hyphens with no space before or after them (--).

1. Use a dash to indicate a sudden change in sentence construction or an abrupt break in thought.

> Here is the true reason—but maybe you don't care.

2. Use a dash after an introductory list. The words *these, those, all,* and occasionally *such* introduce the summarizing statement.

> English, French, history—these are the subjects I like.

> Dodgers, Giants, Yankees—such names bring back memories of exciting World Series games.

3. Use a dash to set off material that interrupts the flow of an idea, sets off material for emphasis, or restates an idea as an appositive.

> You are—I am certain—not serious. (interrupting)

> Our next question is—how much money did we raise? (emphasis)

> Dione plays the kazoo—an instrument with a buzz. (restatement)

4. Use a dash to indicate an unfinished statement or word or an interruption. Such interruptions usually occur in dialogue.

> Susan said, "Shall we—" (no period)

> "I only wanted—" Jason remarked. (no comma)

5. Do *not* use a dash in places in which other marks of punctuation would be more appropriate.

> **Wrong:**   Lupe found the store—and she shopped.
>
> **Right:**   Lupe found the store, and she shopped.
>
> **Wrong:**   I think it is too early to go—
>
> **Right:**   I think it is too early to go.

Colons

The colon is a formal mark of punctuation used chiefly to introduce something that is to follow, such as a list, a quotation, or an explanation.

1. Use a colon after a main clause to introduce a formal list, an emphatic or long restatement (appositive), an explanation, an emphatic statement, or a summary.

> These cars are my favorites: Cadillac, Chevrolet, Toyota, Oldsmobile, and Pontiac. (list)

> He worked toward one objective: a degree. (restatement or appositive)

> Let me emphasize one point: I do not accept late papers. (emphatic statement)

2. Use a colon to introduce a formal quotation or a formal question.

> Shakespeare's Polonius said: "Neither a borrower nor a lender be." (formal quotation)

> The question is this: Shall we surrender? (formal question)

3. Use a colon in the following conventional ways: to separate a title and subtitle, a chapter and verse in the Bible, and hours and minutes; and after the salutation in a formal business letter.

Title and subtitle:	*Korea: A Country Divided*
Chapter and verse:	Genesis 4:12
Hour and minutes:	8:25 P.M.
Salutation:	Dear Ms. Chen:

Parentheses

1. Use parentheses to set off material that is not part of the main sentence but is too relevant to omit altogether. This category includes numbers that designate items in a series, amplifying references, explanations, directions, and qualifications.

> He offered two reasons for his losing: (1) he was tired, and (2) he was out of condition. (numbers)

> Review the chapters on the Civil War (6, 7, and 8) for the next class meeting. (references)

> Her husband (she had been married about a year) died last week. (explanation)

2. Use a comma, semicolon, and colon after the parentheses when the sentence punctuation requires their use.

> Although I have not lived here long (I arrived in 1999), this place feels like my only true home.

3. Use a period, question mark, and exclamation point in appropriate positions, depending on whether they go with the material within the parentheses or with the entire sentence.

> The greatest English poet of the seventeenth century was John Milton (1608–1674).

> The greatest English poet of the seventeenth century was John Milton. (Some might not agree; I myself favor Andrew Marvell.)

Brackets

Brackets are used within a quotation to set off editorial additions or corrections made by the person who is quoting.

> Churchill said: "It [the Yalta agreement] contained many mistakes."

| Exercise 11 | USING DASHES, COLONS, PARENTHESES, BRACKETS, AND QUOTATION MARKS |

Insert dashes, colons, parentheses, brackets, and quotation marks as needed. (See Answer Key for answers.)

1. Ben Johnson 1572–1637 wrote these poems "On My First Son" and Though I Am Young and Cannot Tell.

2. William Blake 1757–1827 he is my favorite poet wrote The Tyger.

3. In that famous poem, he included the following words Tyger, Tyger, the spelling of his time burning bright/In the forests of the night.

4. Rudyard Kipling 1865–1936 wrote in several forms short stories, poems, and novels.

5. Robert Frost 1874–1963 he is probably America's best-loved poet lived in New England for most of his life.

6. He wrote about many subjects in his environment trees, walls, spiders, and ants.

7. Poet, philosopher, speaker Frost had many talents.

8. Dylan Thomas 1914–1953 was a great poet and a flamboyant individual.

9. Thomas acquired a reputation some say he didn't deserve it for being a drunk.

10. One of Thomas's most moving poems, Fern Hill, begins with this line Now as I was young and easy under the apple boughs.

| Exercise 12 | USING DASHES, COLONS, PARENTHESES, BRACKETS, AND QUOTATION MARKS |

Insert dashes, colons, parentheses, brackets, and quotations marks as needed.

1. Anne Sexton 1928–1974 began writing poetry seriously as therapy for her mental illness.

2. Many of her poems were about those she knew well her children, her parents, herself.

3. Her style was colorful and imaginative, and her subjects some say she was too confessional often related directly to her life experiences.

4. Articulate, engaging, and intense she was popular on her poetry-reading tours.

5. After years of struggling with her emotional problems, she did what friends had long feared she would do she committed suicide.

6. John Keats 1795–1821 was an English poet who suffered from the most dreaded disease of his time tuberculosis.

7. Keats wrote extraordinary poems about the "big" topics truth, beauty, love, and death.

8. He went to Italy to live in a warmer climate he knew he was about to die and to visit his friends.

9. Alfred, Lord Tennyson 1809–1892 wrote these words I he was referring to Ulysses cannot rest from travel.

10. Ulysses restless, curious, and imaginative was bored with life on Ithaca.

Apostrophes

The apostrophe is used with nouns and indefinite pronouns to show possession; to show the omission of letters and figures in contractions; and to form the plurals of letters, numerals, and words referred to as words.

1. A possessive shows that something is owned by someone. Use an apostrophe and -*s* to form the possessive of a noun, singular or plural, that does not end in -*s*.

     man's coat   women's suits

2. Use an apostrophe alone to form the possessive of a plural noun ending in -*s*.

     girls' clothes   the Browns' house

3. Use an apostrophe and -*s* or the apostrophe alone to form the possessive of singular nouns ending in -*s*. Use the apostrophe and -*s* only when you would pronounce the *s*.

     James' hat or (if you would pronounce the *s*) James's hat

4. Use an apostrophe and -*s* to form the possessive of certain indefinite pronouns.

     everybody's idea   one's meat   another's poison

5. Use an apostrophe to indicate that letters or numerals have been omitted.

     o'clock (short for *of the clock*)   in the '90s (short for 1990s)

6. Use an apostrophe with pronouns only when you are making a contraction. A contraction is a combination of two words. The apostrophe in a contraction indicates where a letter has been omitted.

it is = it's

she has = she's

you are = you're

If no letters have been left out, don't use an apostrophe.

Wrong: The dog bit it's tail. (not a contraction)

Right: The dog bit its tail.

Wrong: Whose the leader now?

Right: Who's the leader now? (a contraction of *who is*)

Wrong: Its a big problem.

Right: It's a big problem. (a contraction of *it is*)

7. Use an apostrophe to indicate the plural of letters, numerals, and words used as words.

Dot your *i*'s.   five *8*'s   *and*'s

Note that the letters, numerals, and words are italicized, but the apostrophe and *s* are not.

Hyphens

The hyphen brings two or more words together into a single compound word. Correct hyphenation, therefore, is essentially a spelling problem rather than one of punctuation. Because the hyphen is not used with any degree of consistency, consult your dictionary for current usage. Study the following as a beginning guide.

1. Use a hyphen to separate the parts of many compound words.

brother-in-law   go-between

2. Use a hyphen between prefixes and proper names.

all-American   mid-Atlantic

3. Use a hyphen to join two or more words used as a single adjective modifier before a noun.

bluish-gray eyes   first-class service

4. Use a hyphen with spelled-out compound numbers up to ninety-nine and with fractions.

twenty-six   two-thirds

Note: Dates, street addresses, numbers requiring more than two words, chapter and page numbers, time followed directly by A.M. or P.M., and figures after a dollar sign or before measurement abbreviations are usually written as figures, not words.

Capitalization

Following are some of the many conventions concerning the use of capital letters in English.

1. Capitalize the first word of a sentence.

2. Capitalize proper nouns and adjectives derived from proper nouns.

Names of persons:
Edward Jones

Adjectives derived from proper nouns:
a Shakespearean sonnet   a Miltonic sonnet

Countries, nationalities, races, languages:
Germany   English   Spanish   Chinese

States, regions, localities, other geographical divisions:
California   the Far East   the South

Oceans, lakes, mountains, deserts, streets, parks:
Lake Superior   Fifth Avenue   Sahara Desert

Educational institutions, schools, courses:
Santa Ana College   Spanish 3   Joe Hill School   Rowland High School

Organizations and their members:
Boston Red Sox   Boy Scouts   Audubon Society

Corporations, governmental agencies or departments, trade names:
U.S. Steel Corporation   Treasury Department   White Memorial Library
Coca-Cola

Calendar references such as holidays, days of the week, months:
Easter   Tuesday   January

Historic eras, periods, documents, laws:
Declaration of Independence   Geneva Convention   First Crusade
Romantic Age

3. Capitalize words denoting family relationships when they are used before a name or substituted for a name.

> He walked with his nephew and Aunt Grace.

>> *but*

> He walked with his nephew and his aunt.

> Grandmother and Mother are away on vacation.

>> *but*

> My grandmother and my mother are away on vacation.

4. Capitalize abbreviations after names.

> Henry White, Jr.

> Juan Gomez, M.D.

5. Capitalize titles of themes, books, plays, movies, poems, magazines, newspapers, musical compositions, songs, and works of art. Do not capitalize short conjunctions and prepositions unless they come at the beginning or the end of the title.

Desire Under the Elms

Last of the Mohicans

"Blueberry Hill"

Terminator

Of Mice and Men

6. Capitalize any title preceding a name or used as a substitute for a name. Do not capitalize a title following a name.

Judge Wong   Alfred Wong, a judge

General Clark   Raymond Clark, a general

Professor Fuentes   Harry Fuentes, the biology professor

Exercise 13	USING CAPITAL LETTERS, HYPHENS, APOSTROPHES, AND QUOTATION MARKS

Write capital letters and insert hyphens, apostrophes, and quotation marks as needed. (See Answer Key for answers.)

1. Ive heard that you intend to move to el paso, texas, my brother in law said.

2. My date of departure on united airlines is july 11, I answered.

3. Then youve only thirty three days remaining in california, he said.

4. My mother gave me some samsonite luggage, and dad gave me a ronson razor.

5. Jennifer does not know i am leaving for the university of texas.

6. Jennifer, my mothers dog, is one quarter poodle and three quarters cocker spaniel.

7. That dogs immediate concern is almost always food rather than sentimentality.

8. I wouldnt have received my scholarship without the straight As from my elective classes.

9. I am quite indebted to professor jackson, a first rate teacher of english and several courses in speech.

10. I wasnt surprised when grandma gave me a box of stationery and a note asking me to write mother each friday.

Exercise 14	USING CAPITAL LETTERS, HYPHENS, APOSTROPHES, AND QUOTATION MARKS

Write capital letters and insert hyphens, apostrophes, and quotation marks as needed.

1. Susan James likes to brag about her first new bicycle, a schwinn orange krate.

2. She bought it when she was in the eighth grade for ninety three dollars from her sister in law, who owned a bike store.

3. Susan said, my bike had factory installed shock absorbers and a battery powered horn.

4. I named it the *Peeler,* she said. I used it on my paper route with the *Daily tribune.*

5. Her thirty three customers needs were well served by her bike.

6. With her earnings, she purchased chrome bike fenders made by Acme manufacturing.

7. Later she installed a mirror purchased at the midland bike barn.

8. I quit riding it when I entered high school, she said.

9. She said that owning the bike helped her build self esteem as a youth.

10. Now the bike is on display at the Amarillo museum of mid century pop art, which Susans family visited once during a recent summer vacation.

Exercise 15	**USING CAPITAL LETTERS AND ALL PUNCTUATION MARKS**

Correct all capitalization and insert punctuation marks as needed.

will rogers 1879–1935 was a famous movie star newspaper writer and lecturer. A part cherokee indian he was born in what was then indian territory before oklahoma became a state. He is especially known for his humor and his social and political criticism. He said my ancestors may not have come over on the *mayflower,* but they met em at the boat. He said that when many oklahomans moved to california in the early 1930s the average IQ increased in both states. In his early years, he was a first class performer in rodeos circuses and variety shows. When he performed in variety shows he often twirled a rope. He usually began his presentations by saying, all I know is what I read in the papers. Continuing to be close to his oklahoma roots he appeared in fifty one silent movies and twenty one talking movies. At the age of fifty six he was killed in an airplane crash near Point Barrow Alaska. He was so popular and influential that his statue now stands in washington d.c. On another statue of him in Claremore Oklahoma is inscribed one of his most famous sayings I never met a man I didn't like.

Chapter Review: Punctuation and Capitalization

1. There are three marks of end punctuation.
   a. Periods

      Place a period after a statement.

      Place a period after common abbreviations.
   b. Question marks

      Place a question mark at the end of a direct question.

      Do not use a question mark after an indirect question.

      > She asked me what caused the slide.

   c. Exclamation points

      Place an exclamation point after a word or group of words that expresses strong feeling.

      Do not overwork the exclamation point. Do not use double exclamation points.

2. The comma is used essentially to separate and to set off sentence elements.
   a. Use a comma to separate main clauses joined by one of the coordinating conjunctions—*for, and, nor, but, or, yet, so.*

      > We went to the game, but it was canceled.

   b. Use a comma after long introductory modifiers. The modifiers may be phrases or dependent clauses.

      > Before she and I arrived, the meeting was called to order.

   c. Use a comma to separate words, phrases, and clauses in a series.

      > He ran down the street, across the park, and into the forest.

   d. Use a comma to separate coordinate adjectives not joined by *and* that modify the same noun.

      > I need a sturdy, reliable truck.

   e. Use a comma to separate sentence elements that might be misread.

      > Outside, the thunder rolled.

   f. Use commas to set off nonessential (unnecessary for the meaning of the sentence) words, phrases, and clauses.

      > Maria, who studied hard, will pass.

   g. Use commas to set off nouns used as direct address.

      > What do you intend to do, Hamlet?

   h. Use commas to separate the numbers in a date.

      > November 11, 1918, is a day worth remembering.

   i. Use commas to separate the city from the state. No comma is used between the state and the ZIP code.

      > Boston, MA 02110

3. The semicolon indicates a longer pause and stronger emphasis than the comma. It is used principally to separate main clauses within a sentence.

a. Use a semicolon to separate main clauses not joined by a coordinating conjunction.

> You must buy that car today; tomorrow will be too late.

b. Use a semicolon between two main clauses joined by a conjunctive adverb (such as *however, otherwise, therefore, similarly, hence, on the other hand, then, consequently, accordingly, thus*).

> It was very late; therefore, I remained at the hotel.

4. Quotation marks bring special attention to words.

a. Quotation marks are used principally to set off direct quotations. A direct quotation consists of material taken from the written work or the direct speech of others; it is set off by double quotation marks. Single quotation marks are used to set off a quotation within a quotation.

> He said, "I don't remember if she said, 'Wait for me.'"

b. Use double quotation marks to set off slang, technical terms, and special words.

> The "platoon system" changed the game of football. (technical term)

5. Italics (slanting type) are also used to call special attention to certain words or groups of words. In handwriting or typing, such words are underlined.

a. Italicize (underline) foreign words and phrases that are still listed in the dictionary as foreign.

> *modus operandi*   *perestroika*

b. Italicize titles of books; long poems; plays; magazines; motion pictures; musical compositions; newspapers; works of art; names of aircraft and ships; and letters, numbers, and words referred to by their own name.

> *War and Peace*   *Apollo 12*   leaving the *o* out of *sophomore*

6. The dash is used when a stronger pause than the comma is needed. It can also be used to indicate a break in the flow of thought and to emphasize words (less formal than the colon in this situation).

7. The colon is a formal mark of punctuation used chiefly to introduce something that is to follow, such as a list, a quotation, or an explanation.

> These cars are my favorites: Cadillac, Chevrolet, Toyota, Oldsmobile, and Pontiac.

8. Parentheses are used to set off material that is of relatively little importance to the main thought of the sentence. Such material—numbers, parenthetical material, figures, supplementary material, and sometimes explanatory details—merely amplifies the main thought.

> The years of the era (1961–1973) were full of action
>
> I paid twenty dollars ($20) for that mousepad.

9. Brackets are used within a quotation to set off editorial additions or corrections made by the person who is quoting.

> "It [the Yalta Agreement] contained many mistakes."

10. The apostrophe is used with nouns and indefinite pronouns to show possession, to show the omission of letters and figures in contractions, and to form the plurals of letters, figures, and words referred to as words.

man's coat   girls' clothes   can't   five *and*'s
it's (contraction)

11. The hyphen is used to link two or more words together into a single compound word. Hyphenation, therefore, is essentially a spelling problem rather than a punctuation problem. Because the hyphen is not used with any degree of consistency, it is best to consult your dictionary to learn current usage.

a. Use a hyphen to separate the parts of many compound words.

about-face   go-between

b. Use a hyphen between prefixes and proper names.

all-American   mid-July

c. Use a hyphen with spelled-out compound numbers up to ninety-nine and with fractions.

twenty-six   one hundred   two-thirds

d. Use a hyphen to join two or more words used as a single adjective modifier before a noun.

first-class service   hard-fought game   sad-looking mother

12. In English, there are many conventions concerning the use of capital letters. Although style and use of capital letters may vary, certain rules for capitalization are well established.

a. Capitalize the first word of a sentence.

b. Capitalize proper nouns and adjectives derived from proper nouns such as the names of persons, countries, nationalities, as well as dances, days of the week, months, and titles of books.

c. Capitalize words denoting family relationships when they are used before a name or substituted for a name.

The minister greeted Aunt May, my grandfather, and Mother.

Chapter Review Exercises

Correct capitalization and insert punctuation marks as needed. (Adapted from "How Families Stay Afloat," by Sally Squires.) (See Answer Key for answers.)

1. Theres the question of defining a healthy or well functioning family.

2. what measure is appropriate to make that judgment

3. you cant really talk about 'good' families unless youre talking about good for what

   said Marian yarrow, a psychologist at the national institute of mental health.

4. some believe that even the definition of family is ambiguous.

5. the census bureau considers a family to be "two or more persons related

   through birth, marriage or adoption living under one roof.

6. Until recently popular image dictated that family consisted of a mother a father and two children.

7. But the reality is that families come in all shapes and sizes traditional families stepfamilies blended families single-parent families childless couples and extended families.

| Review 2 | **USING CAPITAL LETTERS AND ALL PUNCTUATION MARKS** |

Correct capitalization and insert punctuation marks as needed.

Jack (Jackie) Roosevelt Robinson 1919–1972 was born in Pasadena California. After excelling in sports in high school and community college he transferred to UCLA, where he lettered in four sports baseball, basketball, football, and track. In world war II he was commissioned second lieutenant in the army. After he was discharged he joined the negro league as a player with the Kansas City Monarchs for $100 a week. In 1947 he was offered a tryout with the Brooklyn dodgers. Before no African Americans had been allowed to participate in the minor or major leagues. After signing a contract, Jackie Robinson was sent to the minor leagues and there he played for one year with Montreal a team in the International League. Following a year in which he was the best hitter in the league he was brought up to the major leagues. During the first year 1947 he showed his greatness and was named the rookie of the year. Two years later he was the most valuable player in the national league and won the batting title with a .342 average. Despite the initial bigoted opposition by some baseball fans and players he performed with dignity courage and skill. Nevertheless he was an independent proud person. In the book Players of Cooperstown Mike Tully wrote he Robinson refused to be someone he was not, refused to conform to an image of a man who 'knew his place.' Because sports is such a high-profile activity Jackie Robinson is credited with playing a significant role in breaking down the racial barriers in society. In his ten years in the major leagues he helped his team reach the world series six times. He was inducted into the Baseball hall of fame in 1962.

Review 3   DEMONSTRATING ABILITY TO USE CORRECT PUNCTUATION

Demonstrate your ability to use correct punctuation by writing sentences that contain the following marks. Use the topics in parentheses.

Comma (travel)

1. To separate independent clauses in a compound sentence using coordinating conjunctions (FANBOYS)

   _____

   _____

   _____

2. For long introductory modifiers

   _____

   _____

   _____

3. To separate words in a series

   _____

   _____

   _____

Semicolon (a family member)

4. To connect two related independent clauses without a coordinating conjunction

   _____

   _____

   _____

Quotation marks (Use this textbook as your source for quotations.)

5. To set off a quotation (words taken from the written work or the speech of others)

   _____

   _____

   _____

Italics, shown by underlining (school)

6. Word or letter referred to by its name

_____

_____

_____

7. Title of a book

_____

_____

_____

Colon (computers)

8. To introduce a list

_____

_____

_____

Apostrophe (friendship)

9. A singular possessive

_____

_____

_____

10. A plural possessive

_____

_____

_____

11. A contraction

_____

_____

_____

Hyphen (shopping)

12. Numbers

_____

_____

_____

13. Two-word modifiers

_____

_____

_____

Spelling

*"*A* person who is not born a great speller will probably never be one, but almost anyone can, with work, become a competent speller, an accomplishment to be proud of."*

Some people are born good spellers. They see a word and can spell it correctly forever; others struggle. This chapter offers you a systematic approach and several strategies for spelling correctly in a language that is inconsistent to a significant degree. Some words just don't look the way they sound; they are not phonetic, and they do not pattern in ways parallel with other words of the same spelling. This anonymous poem shows some of the problems:

When in the English language we speak
Why is *break* not rhymed with *freak?*
Will you tell me why it's true
That we *sew,* but we also saw *few?*
And why cannot makers of verse
Rhyme the word *horse* with *worse?*
Beard sounds much different from *heard*
Cord is so different from *word*
Cow is *cow,* but *low* is *low.*
Shoe never rhymes with *foe,*
And think of *hose,* and *dose,* and *lose,*
And think of *goose* and yet of *choose,*
Doll and *roll,* and *home* and *some.*

And since *pay* is rhymed with *say,*
Why *paid* and *said,* I pray?
Mood is not pronounced like *wood*
And *done* is not like *gone* and *lone.*
To sum it all up, it seems to me
That sounds and letters just do not agree.

Despite these problems inherent in our language, you can be an effective speller. Unfortunately, for those who are not, there are unhappy consequences. In a society as literate as ours, if you are a poor speller, you will find yourself with a serious handicap. The professions and trades, as well as schools, are demanding that individuals spell well and write effectively. If you write *thier* for *their* or *definately* for *definitely* in compositions, term reports, examinations, letters of application, or business reports, you will draw unfavorable attention from your audience.

Steps to Efficient Spelling

1. Make up your mind that you are going to spell well.

2. Use your Self-Evaluation Chart (inside front cover of this book) to keep a list of words you misspell; work on spelling them correctly.

3. Get into the habit of looking up new words in a dictionary for correct spelling as well as for meaning.

4. Look at each letter in a word carefully and pronounce each syllable; that is, *change-a-ble, con-tin-u-ous, dis-ap-pear-ance.*

5. Visualize how the word is made up.

6. Write the word correctly several times. After each writing, close your eyes and again visualize the word.

7. Set up frequent recall sessions with problem words. Become aware of the reasons for your errors.

Your Spell Checker

Your computer spell checker is an important tool with many benefits and some limitations. With about 100,000 words in a typical database, the spell checker alerts you to problem words that should be verified. If you agree that the spelling of a word should be checked, you can then select from a list of words with similar spellings. A likely substitute word will be highlighted. With a keystroke, you can correct a problem, add your own word to the database, or ignore the alert. With a few more keystrokes, you can type in your own correction. You may even be able to program your spell checker to correct automatically your most frequent spelling or typing errors. You will be amazed at how many times your computer will catch misspellings that your eye did not see.

However, the spell checker has limitations. If you intended to type *he* and instead typed *me,* the spell checker will not alert you to a possible problem because the word you typed is spelled correctly. If you use the wrong word, such as *herd* instead of *heard,* the spell checker will not detect a problem. Thus you should always proofread your writing after you have spell checked it. Do not be lulled into a false sense of spelling security simply because you have a machine on your side. As a writer, you are the final spell checker.

Spelling Tips

The following tips will help you become a better speller:

1. **Do not omit letters.**
   Many errors occur because certain letters are omitted when the word is pronounced or spelled. Observe the omissions in the following words. Then concentrate on learning the correct spellings.

Incorrect	Correct	Incorrect	Correct
agravate	aggravate	irigation	irrigation
ajourned	adjourned	libary	library
aproved	approved	paralell	parallel
aquaintance	acquaintance	parlament	parliament
artic	arctic	paticulaly	particularly
comodity	commodity	readly	readily
efficent	efficient	sophmore	sophomore
envirnment	environment	stricly	strictly
familar	familiar	unconsious	unconscious

2. **Do not add letters.**

Incorrect	Correct	Incorrect	Correct
athelete	athlete	ommission	omission
comming	coming	pasttime	pastime
drownded	drowned	priviledge	privilege
folkes	folks	similiar	similar
occassionally	occasionally	tradgedy	tragedy

3. **Do not substitute incorrect letters for correct letters.**

Incorrect	Correct	Incorrect	Correct
benefisial	beneficial	offence	offense
bullitins	bulletins	peculier	peculiar
sensus	census	resitation	recitation
discription	description	screach	screech
desease	disease	substansial	substantial
dissention	dissension	surprize	surprise
itims	items	technical	technical

4. **Do not transpose letters.**

Incorrect	Correct	Incorrect	Correct
alunmi	alumni	prehaps	perhaps
childern	children	perfer	prefer
dupilcate	duplicate	perscription	prescription
irrevelant	irrelevant	principels	principles
kindel	kindle	yeild	yield

Note: Whenever you notice other words that fall into any one of these categories, add them to the list.

5. **Apply the spelling rules for spelling *ei* and *ie* words correctly.**

Remember the poem?

Use *i* before *e*
Except after *c*
Or when sounded like *a*
As in *neighbor* and *weigh.*

i before e

achieve	chief	niece	relieve
belief	field	piece	shield
believe	grief	pierce	siege
brief	hygiene	relief	variety

Except after c

ceiling	conceive	deceive	receipt
conceit	deceit	perceive	receive

Exceptions: either, financier, height, leisure, neither, seize, species, weird

When sounded like a

deign	freight	neighbor	sleigh
eight	heinous	reign	veil
feign	heir	rein	vein
feint	neigh	skein	weigh

6. **Apply the rules for dropping the final *e* or retaining the final *e* when a suffix is added.**

Words ending in a silent *e* usually drop the *e* before a suffix beginning with a vowel; for example, *accuse* + *-ing* = *accusing.* Here are some common suffixes beginning with a vowel: *-able, -al, -age, -ary, -ation, -ence, -ing, -ion, -ous, -ure.*

admire + *-able* = admirable	imagine + *-ary* = imaginary
arrive + *-al* = arrival	locate + *-ion* = location
come + *-ing* = coming	please + *-ure* = pleasure
explore + *-ation* = exploration	plume + *-age* = plumage
fame + *-ous* = famous	precede + *-ence* = precedence

Exceptions: *dye* + *-ing* = *dyeing* (to distinguish it from *dying*), *acreage, mileage.*

Words ending in a silent *-e* usually retain the *e* before a suffix beginning with a consonant; for example: *arrange* + -ment = *arrangement.* Here are some common suffixes beginning with a consonant: *-craft, -ful, -less, -ly, -mate, -ment, -ness, -ty.*

entire + *-ty* = entirety	manage + *-ment* = management
hate + *-ful* = hateful	safe + *-ly* = safely
hope + *-less* = hopeless	stale + *-mate* = stalemate
like + *-ness* = likeness	state + *-craft* = statecraft

Exceptions: Some words taking the *-ful* or *-ly* suffixes drop the final *e:*

awe + *-ful* = awful   true + *-ly* = truly

due + *-ly* = duly   whole + *-ly* = wholly

Some words taking the suffix *-ment* drop the final *e;* for example:

acknowledgment   argument   judgment

Words ending in silent *-e* after *c* or *g* retain the *e* when the suffix begins with the vowel *a* or *o*. The final *-e* is retained to keep the *c* or *g* soft before the suffixes.

advantag*e*ous   notic*e*able

courag*e*ous   peac*e*able

7. **Apply the rules for doubling a final consonant before a suffix beginning with a vowel.**

Words of one syllable:

blot	blotted	get	getting	rob	robbed
brag	bragging	hop	hopped	run	running
cut	cutting	hot	hottest	sit	sitting
drag	dragged	man	mannish	stop	stopped
drop	dropped	plan	planned	swim	swimming

Words accented on the last syllable:

acquit	acquitted	equip	equipped
admit	admittance	occur	occurrence
allot	allotted	omit	omitting
begin	beginning	prefer	preferred
commit	committee	refer	referred
concur	concurring	submit	submitted
confer	conferring	transfer	transferred
defer	deferring		

Words that are not accented on the last syllable and words that do not end in a single consonant preceded by a vowel do not double the final consonant (whether or not the suffix begins with a vowel).

Frequently Misspelled Words

a lot	appearance	beginning	coming
absence	appreciate	belief	committee
across	argument	benefit	competition
actually	athlete	buried	complete
all right	athletics	business	consider
among	awkward	certain	criticism
analyze	becoming	college	definitely

dependent	guarantee	particular	separate
develop	guard	persuade	severely
development	guidance	physically	shining
difference	height	planned	significant
disastrous	hoping	pleasant	similar
discipline	humorous	possible	sincerely
discussed	immediately	practical	sophomore
disease	independent	preferred	speech
divide	intelligence	prejudice	straight
dying	interest	privilege	studying
eighth	interfere	probably	succeed
eligible	involved	professor	success
eliminate	knowledge	prove	suggest
embarrassed	laboratory	psychology	surprise
environment	leisure	pursue	thoroughly
especially	length	receipt	though
etc.	library	receive	tragedy
exaggerate	likely	recommend	tried
excellent	lying	reference	tries
exercise	marriage	relieve	truly
existence	mathematics	religious	unfortunately
experience	meant	repetition	unnecessary
explanation	medicine	rhythm	until
extremely	neither	ridiculous	unusual
familiar	ninety	sacrifice	using
February	ninth	safety	usually
finally	nuclear	scene	Wednesday
foreign	occasionally	schedule	writing
government	opinion	secretary	written
grammar	opportunity	senior	
grateful	parallel	sense	

Confused Spelling and Confusing Words

The following are more words that are commonly misspelled or confused with one another. Some have similar sounds, some are often mispronounced, and some are only misunderstood.

a   An adjective (called an article) used before a word beginning with a consonant or a consonant sound, as in "I ate *a* donut."

an	An adjective (called an article) used before a word beginning with a vowel *(a, e, i, o, u)* or with a silent *h*, as in "I ate an artichoke."
and	A coordinating conjunction, as in "Sara *and* I like Johnny Cash."
accept	A verb meaning "to receive," as in "I *accept* your explanation."
except	A preposition meaning "to exclude," as in "I paid everyone *except* you."
advice	A noun meaning "guidance," as in "Thanks for the *advice.*"
advise	A verb meaning "to give guidance," as in "Will you please *advise* me of my rights?"
all right	An adjective meaning "correct" or "acceptable," as in "It's *all right* to cry."
alright	Not used in formal writing.
all ready	An adjective that can be used interchangeably with *ready*, as in "I am *all ready* to go to town."
already	An adverb meaning "before," which cannot be used in place of *ready*, as in "I have *already* finished."
a lot	An adverb meaning "much," as in "She liked him *a lot*," or a noun meaning "several," as in "I had *a lot* of suggestions."
alot	Misspelling.
altogether	An adverb meaning "completely," as in "He is *altogether* happy."
all together	An adverb meaning "as one," which can be used interchangeably with *together*, as in "The group left *all together.*"
choose	A present tense verb meaning "to select," as in "Do whatever you *choose.*"
chose	The past tense form of the verb *choose*, as in "They *chose* to take action yesterday."
could of	A misspelled phrase caused by confusing *could've*, meaning *could have*, with *could of.*
could have	Correctly spelled phrase, as in "I could have danced all night."
effect	Usually a noun meaning "result," as in "That *effect* was unexpected."
affect	Usually a verb meaning "change," as in "Ideas *affect* me."
hear	A verb indicating the receiving of sound, as in "I *hear* thunder."
here	An adverb meaning "present location," as in "I live *here.*"
it's	A contraction of *it is*, as in "*It's* time to dance."
its	Possessive pronoun, as in "Each dog has *its* day."
know	A verb usually meaning "to comprehend" or "to recognize," as in "I *know* the answer."
no	An adjective meaning "negative," as in "I have *no* potatoes."
led	The past tense form of the verb *lead*, as in "I *led* a wild life in my youth."

lead	A present tense verb, as in "I *lead* a stable life now," or a noun referring to a substance, such as "I sharpened the *lead* in my pencil."
loose	An adjective meaning "without restraint," as in "He is a *loose* cannon."
lose	A present tense verb from the pattern *lose, lost, lost,* as in "I thought I would *lose* my senses."
paid	The past tense form of *pay,* as in "He *paid* his dues."
payed	Misspelling.
passed	The past tense form of the verb *pass,* meaning "went by," as in "He *passed* me on the curve."
past	An adjective meaning "former," as in "That's *past* history," or a noun, as in "He lived in the *past.*"
patience	A noun meaning "willingness to wait," as in "Job was a man of much *patience.*"
patients	A noun meaning "people under care," as in "The doctor had fifty *patients.*"
peace	A noun meaning "a quality of calmness" or "absence of strife," as in "The guru was at *peace* with the world."
piece	A noun meaning "part," as in "I gave him a *piece* of my mind."
quiet	An adjective meaning "silent," as in "She was a *quiet* child."
quit	A verb meaning "to cease" or "to withdraw," as in "I *quit* my job."
quite	An adverb meaning "very," as in "The clam is *quite* happy."
receive	A verb meaning "to accept," as in "I will *receive* visitors now."
recieve	Misspelling.
stationary	An adjective meaning "not moving," as in "Try to avoid running into *stationary* objects."
stationery	A noun meaning "paper material to write on," as in "I bought a box of *stationery* for Sue's birthday present."
than	A conjunction, as in "He is taller *than* I am."
then	An adverb, as in "She *then* left town."
their	A possessive pronoun, as in "They read *their* books."
there	An adverb, as in "He left it *there,*" or a filler word as in "*There* is no time left."
they're	A contraction of *they are,* as in "*They're* happy."
to	A preposition, as in "I went *to* town."
too	An adverb meaning "excessively" or "very," as in "you are *too* late to qualify for the discount," or "also," as in "I have feelings, *too.*"
two	An adjective of number, as in "I have *two* jobs."
thorough	An adjective, meaning "complete" or "careful," as in "He did a *thorough* job."

through	A preposition, as in "She went *through* the yard."
truly	An adverb meaning "sincerely" or "completely," as in "He was *truly* happy."
truely	Misspelling.
weather	A noun meaning "condition of the atmosphere," as in "The *weather* is pleasant today."
whether	A conjunction, as in "*Whether* he would go was of no consequence."
write	A present tense verb, as in "Watch me as I *write* this letter."
writen	Misspelling.
written	Past participle of the verb *write*, as in "I have *written* the letter."
you're	A contraction of *you are,* as in "*You're* my friend."
your	A possessive pronoun, as in "I like *your* looks."

Exercise 1	**SPELLING CONFUSING WORDS**

Underline the correct word or words. (See Answer Key for answers.)

1. I cannot (hear, here) the answers.

2. She is taller (then, than) I.

3. They left town to find (their, they're, there) roots.

4. Sam went (through, thorough) the initiation.

5. I am only asking for a little (peace, piece) of the action.

6. Whatever you say is (alright, all right) with me.

7. I (passed, past) the test, and now I'm ready for action.

8. That smash was (to, too, two) hot to handle.

9. I did not ask for her (advise, advice).

10. I found (a lot, alot) of new ideas in that book.

11. She has (all ready, already) left.

12. I (chose, choose) my answer and hoped for the best.

13. I knew that I would (recieve, receive) fair treatment.

14. Juan was (quit, quite, quiet) happy with my decision.

15. Maria (could of, could have) completed the assignment.

16. Marlin knew they would (lose, loose) the game.

17. I've heard that (it's, its) a good movie.

18. June would not (accept, except) my answer.

19. I did not (know, no) what to do.

20. Sean (paid, payed) his bill and left town.

Exercise 2	SPELLING CONFUSING WORDS

1. She said that my application was (alright, all right).

2. Sheriff Dillon worked hard for (peace, piece) in the valley.

3. She was the first woman to (recieve, receive) a medal.

4. He spoke his mind; (then, than) he left.

5. The cleaners did a (through, thorough) job.

6. After the loud explosion, there was (quit, quiet, quite).

7. The nurse worked diligently with his (patience, patients).

8. They were not (altogether, all together) happy, but they (could of, could have) been.

9. The cowboys (led, lead) the cows to water.

10. For my hobby, I study (grammar, grammer).

11. Elvis (truly, truely) respected his mother.

12. Zeke asked for the (whether, weather) report.

13. I never (advise, advice) my friends about gambling.

14. You should (accept, except) responsibility for your actions.

15. Joan inherited (alot, a lot) of money.

16. We waited for the gorilla to (chose, choose) a mate.

17. Virginia thinks (its, it's) a good day for a party.

18. It was a tale of (to, too, two) cities.

19. I went (they're, their, there) to my childhood home.

20. It was the best letter Kevin had ever (writen, written, wrote).

Chapter Review: Spelling

1. Do not omit letters.

   Incorrect: *libary*

   Correct: *library*

2. Do not add letters.

   Incorrect: *athalete*

   Correct: *athlete*

3. Do not substitute incorrect letters for correct letters.

   Incorrect: *technacal*

   Correct: *technical*

4. Do not transpose letters.

   Incorrect: *perfer*

   Correct: *prefer*

5. Apply the spelling rules for spelling *ei* and *ie* words correctly.

   Use *i* before *e*
   Except after *c*
   Or when sounded like *a*
   As in *neighbor* and *weigh*.

   Exceptions: *either, financier, height, leisure, neither, seize, species,* and *weird.*

6. Apply the rules for dropping the final *e* or retaining the final *e* when a suffix is added. (See the restrictions on pages 198–199.)

   Correct: *come   coming*

7. Apply the rules for doubling a final consonant before a suffix beginning with a vowel if the final syllable is accented.

   Correct: *transfer   transferred*

8. Study the list of frequently misspelled words (see pages 199–200).

9. Some words are sometimes misspelled because they are mispronounced or share a pronunciation with another word.

   Incorrect: *alright*

   Correct: *all right*

   Two words with the same sound and different meanings: *hear   here*

10. Use your spell checker but be aware of its limitations and always proofread your writing.

Chapter Review Exercises

Review 1   **ADDING SUFFIXES**

Add the indicated suffixes to the following words. If you need help, see pages 198 through 199 for adding suffixes. (See Answer Key for answers.)

1. fame + *ous* = _____

2. locate + *ion* = _____

3. notice + *able* = _____

4. drop + *ed* = _____

5. like + *ly* = _____

6. hope + *less* = _____

7. manage + *ment* = _____

8. hot + *est* = _____

9. rob + *ed* = _____

10. stop + *ed* = _____

11. safe + *ly* = _____

12. argue + *ment* = _____

13. judge + *ment* = _____

14. courage + *ous* = _____

15. swim + *ing* = _____

16. commit + *ed* = _____

17. occur + *ence* = _____

18. omit + *ed* = _____

19. begin + *ing* = _____

20. prefer + *ed* = _____

| **Review 2** | **CORRECTING MISSPELLING** |

Underline the misspelled words and write the correct spelling above the words. Make two lines under the words that are incorrectly spelled but would go unchallenged by your spell checker.

Professor Pufnagel was torturing his English students once again, and he relished his familar evil roll. "Today, class, we will write without the assistence of computers. In fact, never again will we use them in this class. They are a perscription for lazyness. And they make life to easy for alot of you."

The profesor lectured the students for an hour, stresing that when he was in school, there were no computers in his enviroment. He extoled the virtues of writting with little yellow pensils, fountain pens, and solid, dependible typewriters. He went on with his ranting, listing computer games, television sets, frozen foods, plastic wrap, asperin, and Velcro as similiar and familiar negative forces that had lead society to it's truely sorry state. "You are nothing but a pityful pack of party people, and you will recieve no sympathy from me," he sputtered. Grabbing a student's laptop computer, Pufnagel reared back and, like an athalete, hurled it against the wall In the corner of the classroom lay a pile of high-tech junk, once fine shinning machines, now just garbage—smashed in a senseless, aweful war against technology.

The students starred in embarassed amazement at there professor, who was developing a nervious twitch. His mouth began twisting and contorting as his limbs jerked with the helter-skelter motion of a tangled marionette. He clutched desparately at his throat, and smoke began to poor out of his ears and neck. Unconsious, he crashed to the floor with a clatter.

One of the students, who had just taken a CPR class, rushed forward and attempted to revive the fallen educator. As the student pounded with a catchy rap rhythm on the chest of his stricken teacher, everyone herd a loud pop and sizzle.

It was a door in Pufnagel's chest, which had poped open to reveal the complex electrical control panel of a short-circuited cyborg!

Just than a security team in white jumpsuits from student goverment entered the class, carefully deposited Pufnagel on a wheelbarrow, and roled him out to the Faculty Service Center.

A few minutes later a Professor Ramirez arrived. "Ladys and gentlemen," she said, "its time to start your search engines. Your prevous professor's mainframe is down, but I'm his substitute and mine is fine, fine, fine, fine, fine, fine, fine, fine, fine, fine. . . ."

PART Two

Writing Paragraphs and Beyond

11

The Writing Process for the Paragraph: Stage One

Exploring/Experimenting/ Gathering Information

"You can use the developmental paragraph in two ways: (1) as a complete answer to a short writing assignment, and (2) as a middle or body paragraph in an essay."

The Paragraph Defined

 efining the word *paragraph* is no easy task because there are different kinds of paragraphs, each one having a different purpose:

Introductory: Usually the first paragraph in an essay, it gives the necessary background and indicates the main idea, called the thesis.

Developmental: A unit of several sentences, it expands on an idea. This book features the writing of developmental paragraphs.

Transitional: A very brief paragraph, it merely directs the reader from one point in the essay to another.

Concluding: Usually the last paragraph in an essay, it makes the final comment on the topic.

The following paragraph is both a definition and an example of the developmental paragraph.

Topic sentence
Support

Support

Support

Concluding sentence

The developmental paragraph contains three parts: the subject, the topic sentence, and the support. The **subject** is what you will write about. It is likely to be broad and must be focused or qualified for specific treatment. The **topic sentence** contains both the subject and the treatment—what you will do with the subject. It carries the central idea to which everything else in the paragraph is subordinated. For example, the first sentence of this paragraph is a topic sentence. Even when not stated, the topic sentence as an underlying idea unifies the paragraph. The **support** is the evidence or reasoning by which a topic sentence is developed. It comes in several basic patterns and serves any of the four forms of expression: narration, description, exposition, and argumentation. These forms, which are usually combined in writing, will be presented with both student and professional examples in the following chapters. *The* developmental paragraph, *therefore, is a group of sentences, each with the function of supporting a controlling idea called the topic sentence.*

Basic Paragraph Patterns

The most important point about a developmental paragraph is that it should state an idea and support it. The support, or development, can take several forms, all of which you already use. It can

- give an account (tell a story).

- describe people, things, or events.

- explain by analyzing, giving examples, comparing, defining, showing how to do something, or showing causes.

- argue that something should be done or resisted, that something is true or untrue, or that something is good or bad.

(All of these forms of expression are discussed with examples in Chapters 16 through 22). You will not find it difficult to write solid paragraphs once you understand that good writing requires that main ideas have enough support so that your reader can understand how you have arrived at your main conclusions.

Two effective patterns of conventional paragraph structure are shown in Figure 11.1. Form A merely states the controlling idea, the topic sentence, and develops it; Form B adds a concluding sentence following the development.

A paragraph, however, is not a constraining formula: it has variations. In some instances, for example, the topic sentence is not found in a single sentence. It may be the combination of two sentences, or it may be an easily understood but unwritten underlying idea that unifies the paragraph. Nevertheless, the paragraph in most college writing contains discussion that supports a stated topic sentence, and the instruction in this book is based on that fundamental idea.

A Sample Paragraph

The following paragraph was written by college student Cyrus Norton. The subject of the paragraph and the treatment of the paragraph have been marked. Norton's topic sentence (not the first sentence in this case), his support of the topic sentence, and his concluding sentence are also marked.

Figure 11.1
Paragraph Patterns

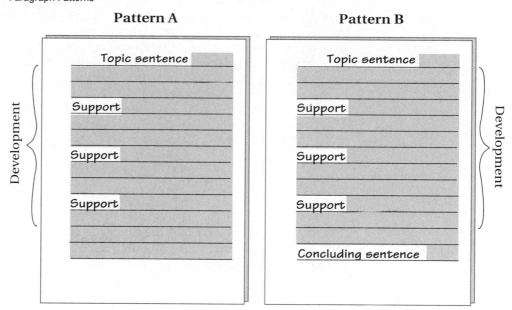

This is the final draft. Following it, we will back up and, in this chapter and the next two, show how Norton moved during the writing process from his initial idea to this polished paragraph.

Magic Johnson, an NBA Great
Cyrus Norton

Topic sentence Some NBA (National Basketball Association) players are good because they have a special talent in one area. <u>Magic Johnson was a great NBA star because he was excellent in shooting, passing, rebounding, and leading.</u>
Support for shooting As a shooter few have ever equaled him. He could slam, shovel, hook, and fire from three-point range—all with deadly accuracy. As for free throws, he led all NBA players in shooting percentage in 1988–89. While averaging more than
Support for passing twenty points per game, he helped others become stars with his passes. As the point guard (the quarterback of basketball), he was always near the top in the league in assists and was famous for his "no-look" pass, which often surprised even his teammates with its precision. When he wasn't shooting or
Support for rebounding passing, he was rebounding. A top rebounding guard is unusual in professional basketball, but Magic, at six feet, nine inches, could bump shoulders and leap with anyone. These three qualities made him probably the most spectacular triple-double threat of all time. "Triple-double" means reaching two digits in scoring, assists, and rebounding. Magic didn't need more for greatness in the NBA, but he had more. With his everlasting smile and bound-
Support for leading less energy, he was also an inspirational team leader. He always believed in himself and his team. When his team was down by a point and three seconds remained on the game clock, the fans looked for Magic to get the ball. They watched as he dribbled once, he faded, he leaped, he twisted, and he hooked
Concluding sentence one in from twenty feet! That was magic. <u>That was Magic.</u>

Let's consider Norton's paragraph in light of what we know about paragraphs in general. Magic Johnson, the subject, is what the paragraph is all about. In this example, the title also names the subject. The topic sentence, the unifying and controlling idea, makes a clear statement about what the writer will do with the subject. As usual, the topic sentence appears near the beginning of the paragraph. The support gives evidence and examples to back up the controlling idea. The last sentence, "That was Magic!" echoes the topic sentence. It is usually called the concluding sentence.

The author has told you what he was going to say, he has said it, and finally he has reminded you of what he has told you. The concluding sentence is sometimes omitted. The two most common designs of paragraphs in college writing are these:

topic sentence $\longrightarrow$ support $\longrightarrow$ concluding sentence

topic sentence $\longrightarrow$ support

"Magic Johnson, an NBA Great" is a typical paragraph: a group of sentences that present and develop an idea. In college writing, a paragraph is usually expository; that is, its purpose is to explain. In this example, you, the reader, get the point. You're informed and maybe even entertained a little by the explanation.

The Writing Process

Although the first section of this chapter defined and illustrated the paragraph as a concept, it stopped short of presenting an overall plan for paragraph writing. The reason for that omission is simple. Each assignment has its own guidelines that vary according to the kind of topic, the source of ideas, the time permitted, the conditions for writing (especially in or outside class), and the purpose. Obviously, if one is to use a system, it must be flexible, because a technique that is an asset for one assignment may be a burden for another. Therefore, a good writer should know numerous techniques, treating each as a tool that can be used when needed. All of these tools are in the same box, one labeled "The Writing Process."

The writing process consists of strategies that can help you proceed from your purpose or initial idea to a final developed paragraph. Those strategies can be divided into prewriting techniques and writing stages. Using prewriting, you explore, experiment, gather information, formulate your thesis, and develop and organize your support. Then you write a first draft, revise your draft as many times as necessary, and edit your writing. The typical college writing assignment process looks like this:

Stage One: Exploring / Experimenting / Gathering Information

Stage Two: Writing the Controlling Idea / Organizing and Developing Support

Stage Three: Writing / Revising / Editing

These stages are discussed in Chapter 11, 12, and 13, respectively. Collectively they represent what is known as the writing process.

At the end of the Student Overview (page 6), this book provides a blank worksheet with brief directions for completing the three stages of the writing process. This Writing Process Worksheet is designed to be duplicated and completed with each major writing assignment. It gives you clear, consistent guidance and provides your instructor with an easy format for finding and checking information. Customarily it should be stapled to the front of your rough and final drafts. A sample worksheet completed by a student appears on pages 234–235 in Chapter 13.

Stage One Strategies

Certain strategies commonly grouped under the heading *prewriting* can help you get started and develop your ideas. These strategies—freewriting, brainstorming, clustering, note taking—are very much a part of writing. The understandable desire to skip to the finished statement is what causes the most common student-writer grief: that of not filling the blank sheet or of filling it but not significantly improving on the blankness. The prewriting strategies described in this section will help you attack the blank sheet constructively with imaginative thought, analysis, and experimentation. They can lead to clear, effective communication.

Freewriting

One strategy is freewriting, an exercise that its originator, Peter Elbow, has called "babbling in print." When you freewrite, you write without stopping, letting your ideas tumble forth. You do not concern yourself with the fundamentals of writing, such as punctuation and spelling. Freewriting is an adventure into your memory and imagination. It is concerned with discovery, invention, and exploration. If you are at a loss for words on your subject, write in a comment such as "I don't know what is coming next" or "blah, blah, blah" and continue when relevant words come. It is important to keep writing. Freewriting immediately eliminates the blank page and thereby helps you break through an emotional barrier, but that is not the only benefit. The words that you sort through in that idea kit will include some you can use. You can then underline or circle those words and even add notes on the side so that the freewriting continues to grow even after its initial spontaneous expression.

The way in which you proceed depends on the type of assignment: working with a topic of your choice, a restricted list of topics, or a prescribed topic.

The *topic of your choice* affords you the greatest freedom of exploration. You would probably select a subject that interests you and freewrite about it, allowing your mind to wander, perhaps mixing fact and fantasy, direct experience, and hearsay. A freewriting about music might uncover areas of special interest and knowledge, such as jazz or folk rock, that you would want to pursue further in freewriting or other prewriting strategies.

Working from a *restricted list* requires a more focused freewriting. With the list, you can, of course, experiment with several topics to discover what is most suitable for you. If, for example, "career choice," "career preparation," "career guidance," and "career prospects" are on the restricted list, you would probably select one and freewrite about it. If it works well for you, you would probably proceed with the next step of your prewriting. If you are not satisfied with what you uncover in freewriting, you would explore another item from the restricted list or take notes from the Internet or library sources.

When working with a *prescribed topic,* you focus on a particular topic and try to restrict your freewriting to its boundaries. If your topic specifies a division of a subject area such as "political involvement of your generation," then you would tie those key words to your own information, critical thinking, and imaginative responses. If the topic is restricted to, let's say, a particular reading selection such as a poem, then that poem would give you the framework for your free associations with your own experiences, creations, and opinions.

You should learn to use freewriting because it will often serve you well, but you need not use it every time you write. Some very short writing assignments do not call for freewriting. An in-class assignment may not allow time for freewriting.

Nevertheless, freewriting is often a useful strategy in your toolbox of techniques. It can help you get words on paper, break emotional barriers, generate topics, develop new insights, and explore ideas.

Freewriting can lead to other stages of prewriting and writing, and it can also provide content as you develop your topic.

The following example of freewriting and the writing, revising, and editing examples in Chapter 12 are from student Cyrus Norton's paragraph entitled "Magic Johnson, an NBA Great" (page 213). Norton's topic came from a restricted list; he was directed to write about the success of an individual. Had he been working with a prescribed topic, he might have been directed to concentrate on a specific aspect of Johnson's career, such as business, philanthropy, public service, or the one Norton chose: great basketball playing.

great	Magic Johnson was the <u>greatest</u> player I've ever seen in professional
leader, inspiration	basketball. Actually not just a player but a <u>leader</u> and an <u>inspiration</u> to the
	team so they always gave him the ball when the game was on the line. It
	was too bad his career was cut short when they discovered he was HIV posi-
rich	tive. Actually he came back but then retired again. He made <u>a lot of money</u>
	and I guess he invested it wisely because his name is linked to the Lakers and
	theaters and more. Also to programs making people aware of the danger of
	AIDS and helping kids grow up and stay out of trouble. But the main thing
playing	about Magic is the <u>way he played.</u> He could do everything. He even played
scoring	center one time in a championship game. He always <u>scored a lot</u> and he could
passing	<u>pass</u> like nobody else. Even though he was a guard, he was tall and could
rebounding	<u>rebound.</u> He was great. Everyone says so.

After doing this freewriting, Norton went back through his work looking for ideas that might be developed in a paper.

Observe how he returned to his freewriting and examined it for possible ideas to develop for a writing assignment. As he recognized those ideas, he underlined key words and phrases and made a few notes in the margins. By reading only the underlined words, you can obtain a basic understanding of what is important to him. It is not necessary to underline entire sentences.

In addition to putting some words on that dreaded blank sheet of paper, Norton discovered that he had quite a lot of information about Magic Johnson and that he had selected a favorable topic to develop. The entire process took little time. Had he found few or no promising ideas, he might have freewritten about another topic. In going back through his work, he saw some errors in writing, but he did not correct them, because the purpose of freewriting is discovery, not correct grammar, punctuation, or spelling. Norton was confident that he could then continue with the process of writing a paper.

Norton's understanding of the topic came mainly from information he had collected from reading and from watching sports programs on television. He knew that if he needed to gather more information, he could do further research, which could take the form of reading, underlining, annotating, note taking, outlining, and summarizing. These techniques are explained in Chapter 15.

Exercise 1	**FREEWRITING**

Try freewriting on a broad topic such as one of these: the best car on the market, a popular college course, a controversial television program, a favorite retail store or mall, a good school, a neighborhood you know well, a memorable learning experience, a person who has influenced you, or a useful piece of software. Following the example on p. 216, underline and annotate the phrases that may lead you to ideas to explore further.

Brainstorming

This prewriting strategy features key words and phrases that relate in various ways to the subject area or to the specific topic you are concerned about. Brainstorming includes two basic forms: (1) asking and answering questions and (2) listing.

Big Six Questions

One effective way to get started is to ask the "big six questions" about your subject: Who? What? Where? When? Why? How? Then let your mind run free as you jot down answers in single entries or lists. Some of the big six questions may not fit, and some may be more important than others, depending on the purposes of your writing. For example, if you were writing about the causes of a situation, the Why? question could be more important than the others; if you were concerned with how to do something, the How? question would predominate. If you were writing in response to a reading selection, you would confine your thinking to questions appropriately related to the content of that reading selection.

Whatever your focus for the questions is, the result is likely to be numerous ideas that will provide information for continued exploration and development of your topic. Thus your pool of information for writing widens and deepens.

Norton continued with the topic of Magic Johnson, and his topic tightened to focus on particular areas.

Who: Magic Johnson
What: great baksetball player
Where: the NBA
When: for more than ten years
Why: love of game and great talent
How: shooting, passing, rebounding, leading, coolness, inspiring

As it turned out, How? was the most fruitful question for Norton.

Listing

Another effective way to brainstorm, especially if you have a defined topic and a storehouse of information, is to skip the big six questions approach and simply make a list of words and phrases related to your topic.

Had Norton known at the outset that he would write about Magic Johnson's greatness as a basketball player, he might have gone directly to a list such as this:

(shooting)
intelligence
(rebounding)
coolness
quickness
(passing)
split vision
determination
(leading)
work ethic
unselfishness
attitude
ambition

From this list, Norton might have selected perhaps four ideas for his framework, circling them for future reference.

Even if you do not have a focused topic, you may find a somewhat random listing useful, merely writing or word processing phrases as they occur to you. This exploratory activity is not unlike freewriting. After you have established such a list, you can sort out and group the phrases as you generate your topic and find its natural divisions. Feel free to accept, reject, or insert phrases.

Exercise 2	**BRAINSTORMING**

Further explore the topic you worked with in Exercise 1 by first answering the big six questions and then by making a list.

Big Six Questions

Who? _____

What? _____

Where? _____

When? _____

Why? _____

How? _____

List

_____

_____

_____

_____

_____

_____

_____

_____

_____

Clustering

Still another prewriting technique is *clustering*. Start by "double-bubbling" your topic; that is, write it down in the middle of the page and draw a double circle around it. Then, responding to the question "What comes to mind?" single-bubble other ideas on spokes radiating out from the hub that contains the topic. Any bubble can lead to another bubble or numerous bubbles in the same way. This strategy is sometimes used instead of or before making an outline to organize and develop ideas.

The more restricted the topic inside the double bubble, the fewer the number of spokes that will radiate with single bubbles. For example, a topic such as "high school dropouts" would have more spokes than "reasons for dropping out of school."

Here is Norton's cluster on the subject of Magic Johnson. He has drawn broken circles around subclusters that seem to relate to a feasible unified topic.

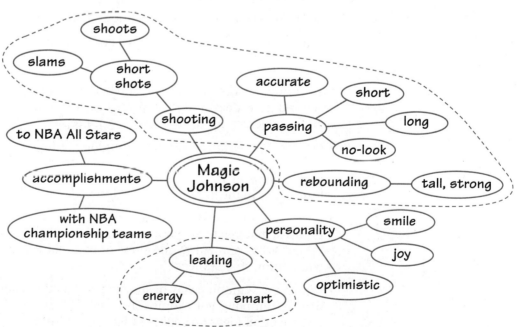

Exercise 3	**CLUSTERING**

Continuing with your topic, develop a cluster of related ideas. Draw broken circles around subclusters that have potential for focus and more development.

Writer's Guidelines: Paragraphs and Prewriting

1. A paragraph is a group of sentences, each with the function of stating or supporting a single controlling idea that is contained in the topic sentence.

2. A paragraph contains two parts: the topic sentence and the support.

   - The topic sentence expresses the controlling idea of the paragraph. It has a subject (what the paragraph is about) and indicates the treatment (what the writer will do with the subject).

   - The support is the evidence, such as details, examples, and explanations, that backs up the topic sentence.

3. The two most common paragraph designs in college writing are these:

   - Topic sentence → support → concluding sentence

   - Topic sentence → support

4. Prewriting includes activities you do before writing your first draft or whenever you need new ideas. You should use only the activities that will best help you explore, generate, limit, and develop your topic.

   - *Freewriting:* writing without stopping, letting your ideas tumble forth. Freewriting helps you break emotional barriers, generate topics, and discover and explore ideas. If you need more information, consult sources on the Internet or in the library and take notes.

   - *Brainstorming:* a listing procedure that helps you discover key words and phrases that relate to your subject. Begin by asking Who? What? Where? When? Why? and How? questions of your subject or by merely listing ideas concerning your subject.

   - *Clustering:* a graphic way of showing connections and relationships. Start by double-bubbling your topic. Then ask "What comes to mind?' and single-bubble other ideas on spokes radiating out from the double bubble.

12

The Writing Process for the Paragraph: Stage Two

Writing the Controlling Idea/Organizing and Developing Support

"The foundation of a good outline and, hence, of a good paragraph is a strong topic sentence, which means one with a specific subject and a well-defined treatment."

The most important advice this book can offer you is *state your controlling idea and support it.* If you have no controlling idea—no topic sentence— your paragraph will be unfocused, and your readers may be confused or bored. If you organize your material well, so that it supports and develops your controlling idea, you can present your views to your readers with interest, clarity, and persuasion.

Stating the controlling idea and organizing support can be accomplished effectively and systematically. How? This chapter presents several uncomplicated techniques you can use in Stage Two of the writing process.

Writing the Controlling Idea as a Topic Sentence

An effective topic sentence has both a subject and a treatment. The subject is what you intend to write about. The treatment is what you intend to do with your subject.

Consider, for example, this topic sentence:

<u>Magic Johnson</u> <u>was a great all-around NBA player.</u>
        subject   treatment

It is an effective topic sentence because it limits the subject and indicates treatment that can be developed in additional sentences. Another sound version is the following, which goes further to include divisions for the treatment.

<u>Magic Johnson</u> <u>was a great NBA star because he was excellent in</u>
        subject   treatment

<u>shooting, passing, rebounding, and leading.</u>

Ineffective topic sentences are often too broad, vague, or narrow.

Ineffective: Magic Johnson was everything to everybody.

Too Broad or Vague: Magic Johnson was fun.
Magic Johnson was a success in basketball.

Ineffective: Magic Johnson went to college in Michigan.

Too Narrow: Magic Johnson signed with the Los Angeles Lakers.

Usually, simple statements of fact do not need or do not allow for development.

Exercise 1	**EVALUATING TOPIC SENTENCES**

In the following statements, underline and label subject (S) and treatment (T). Also judge each one as E (effective) or I (ineffective). Effective statements are those that you can easily relate to supporting evidence. Ineffective statements are too broad, too vague, or too narrowly factual.

_____ 1. Columbus is located in Ohio.

_____ 2. Columbus is a fabulous city.

_____ 3. Columbus has dealt thoroughly with its housing problems.

_____ 4. A monkey is a primate.

_____ 5. Monkeys are fun.

_____ 6. In clinical studies monkeys have demonstrated a remarkable ability to reason.

_____ 7. More than a million cats are born in California each year.

_____ 8. A simple observation of a domesticated cat in the pursuit of game will show that it has not lost its instinct for survival.

_____ 9. The two teams in the Rose Bowl have similar records.

_____ 10. Michigan State is in the Rose Bowl.

Exercise 2	WRITING TOPIC SENTENCES

Complete the following entries to make each one a solid topic sentence. Only a subject and part of the treatment are provided. The missing part may be more than a single word.

Example: Car salespersons behave differently depending on <u>the car they are selling and the kind of customer they are serving.</u>

1. Television commercials are often _____

    _____

2. Word-processing features can _____

    _____

3. My part-time job taught me _____

    _____

4. I promote environmental conservation by _____

    _____

5. The clothing that a person wears often reveals _____

    _____

6. My close friend is preoccupied with _____

    _____

7. Winning a lot of money is not always _____

    _____

8. Country music appeals to our most basic _____

    _____

9. Friendship depends on _____

    _____

10. A good salesperson should _____

    _____

Exercise 3	WRITING TOPIC SENTENCES

Convert each of the following subjects into a topic sentence.

1. Computer literacy _____

    _____

2. My taste in music _____

    _____

3. Bus transportation _____

_____

4. The fear of crime _____

_____

5. An excellent boss _____

_____

6. Doing well in college English classes _____

_____

7. Violence on television _____

_____

8. Childcare centers _____

_____

9. Good health _____

_____

10. Teenage voters _____

_____

Writing an Outline

An outline is a pattern for showing the relationship of ideas. The two main outline forms are the *sentence outline* (each entry is a complete sentence) and the *topic outline* (each entry is a key word or phrase). The topic outline is commonly used for paragraphs and short essays.

Indentation, number and letter sequences, punctuation, and the placement of words are important to clear communication. We do not read an outline expecting to be surprised by form and content, as we may read a poem. We go to the outline for information, and we expect to find ideas easily. Unconventional marks (circles, squares, half-parentheses) and items out of order are distracting and, therefore, undesirable in an outline. The standard form is as easily mastered as a nonstandard form, and it is worth your time to learn it. Outlining is not difficult: The pattern is flexible and can have any number of levels and parts.

Basically, an outline shows how a topic sentence is supported. Thus it shows the organization of the paragraph. The most important supporting material, called the major support, is indicated by Roman numerals. That major support is developed by less important supporting material, called the minor support, which in turn may be developed by details or examples. The major and minor support may be derived from one or more strategies of prewriting such as listing and clustering. Here is the outline developed by Norton:

Topic Sentence: Magic Johnson was a great NBA star because he was excellent in shooting, passing, rebounding, and leading.

I. Shooting (major support)

   A. Short shots (minor support)

      1. Shovel (detail)

      2. Slam-dunk (detail)

   B. Long shots (minor support)

   C. Free throws (minor support)

II. Passing (major support)

   A. No-look (minor suport)

   B. Precise (minor support)

III. Rebounding (major support)

   A. Leaping (minor support)

   B. Bumping shoulders (minor support)

IV. Leading (major support)

   A. Energy (minor support)

   B. Spirit (minor support)

      1. Faith (detail)

      2. Smile (detail)

The foundation of a good outline and, hence, of a good paragraph, is a strong topic sentence, which means one with a specific subject and a well-defined treatment. After you have written a good topic sentence, the next step is to divide the treatment into parts. Just what the parts are will depend on what you are trying to do in the treatment. Consider the thought process involved. What sections of material would be appropriate in your discussion to support or explain that topic sentence? You will probably find that your listing or clustering has already addressed one or more ways of dividing your material. Therefore, reexamine your other forms of prewriting for patterns of development, as well as support.

Among the most common forms of division are the following:

- Divisions of time or incident to tell a story

    I. Situation

    II. Conflict

    III. Struggle

    IV. Outcome

    V. Meaning

- Divisions of example or examples

    I. First example

    II. Second example

    III. Third example (or divide one example into three or more aspects)

- Divisions of causes or effects

    I. Cause (or effect) one

    II. Cause (or effect) two

    III. Cause (or effect) three

- Divisions of a unit into parts (such as the federal government into executive, legislative, and judicial branches—or Magic Johnson's all-around skill into shooting, passing, rebounding, and leading)

> I. Part one
>
> II. Part two
>
> III. Part three
>
> • Divisions of how to do something or how something was done
>
> I. Preparations
>
> II. Steps
>
> A. Step 1
>
> B. Step 2
>
> C. Step 3

Exercise 4	COMPLETING OUTLINES

Fill in the missing parts of the following outline. Consider whether you are dealing with time, examples, causes, effects, parts, or steps. The answers will vary depending on your individual experiences and views.

1. Too many of us are preoccupied with material things.

    I. Clothing

    II. Cars

    III. _____

2. Television sit-coms may vary, but every successful show has certain components.

    I. Good acting

    II. _____

    III. Good situations

    IV. _____

3. A person who is trying to discourage unwanted sexual advances should take several measures.

    I. _____

    II. Set clear boundaries

    III. Avoid compromising situations

4. Concentrating during reading involves various techniques.

    I. Preview material

    II. Pose questions

    III. _____

5. Crime has some bad effects on a nearby neighborhood.

    I. People fearful

    A. Don't go out at night

    B. _____

II. People without love for neighborhood

    A. _____

    B. Put houses up for sale

III. People as victims

    A. Loss of possessions

    B. _____

6. Exercising can improve a person's life.

    I. Looks better

      A. Skin

      B. _____

    II. Feels better

      A. _____

      B. Body

    III. Performs better

      A. Work

      B. _____

7. Shoppers in department stores can be grouped according to needs.

    I. _____

    II. Special-needs

    III. Bargain hunters

8. There are different kinds of intelligence based on situations.

    I. Street-smart

    II. Common sense

    III. _____

9. Smoking should be discouraged.

    I. Harm to smokers

      A. _____

      B. Cancer risk

    II. Harm to those around smokers

      A. _____

      B. Fellow workers

    III. Cost

      A. Industry—production and absenteeism

      B. _____

10. An excellent police officer must have six qualities.

    I. _____

    II. Knowledge of law

    III. _____

    IV. Emotional soundness

    V. Skill in using weapons

    VI. _____

Exercise 5	**WRITING A TOPIC SENTENCE AND AN OUTLINE**

Still working with your same topic, write a topic sentence and an outline. The topic sentence may suggest a particular pattern of development. Following the lead of that topic sentence, the Roman numeral headings will often indicate divisions of time or place, steps, causes, effects, or parts of a unit. For example, if you have selected your favorite retail store for your subject and your reasons for choosing it as the treatment, then those reasons would be indicated with Roman numeral headings.

Writer's Guidelines: Writing Topic Sentences and Outlines

1. An effective topic sentence has both a subject and a treatment. The subject is what you intend to write about. The treatment is what you intend to do with your subject.

    Example: <u>Wilson High School</u> <u>offers a well-balanced academic program.</u>
                   subject   **treatment**

2. An outline is a form for indicating the relationship of ideas. The outline shows how a topic sentence is supported. Thus it reveals the organization of the paragraph. Major support is indicated by Roman numerals. The major support is developed by minor support, which in turn may be developed by details or examples.

Topic sentence
  I. Major support
     A. Minor support
     B. Minor support
        1. Details or examples
        2. Details or examples
 II. Major support
     A. Minor support
     B. Minor support

13

The Writing Process for the Paragraph: Stage Three
Writing/Revising/Editing

"Don't be embarrassed by the roughness of your first draft. You should be embarrassed only if you leave it that way."

Writing Your First Draft

Once you have written your topic sentence and completed your outline (or list or cluster), you are ready to begin writing your paragraph. The initial writing is called the first, or rough, draft. Your topic sentence is likely to be at or near the beginning of your paragraph and will be followed by your support as ordered by your outline.

Paying close attention to your outline for basic organization, you should proceed without worrying about the refinements of writing. This is not the time to concern yourself with perfect spelling, grammar, or punctuation.

Whether you write in longhand or on a computer depends on what works best for you. Some writers prefer to do a first draft by hand, mark it up, and then go to the computer. Computers save you time in all aspects of your writing, especially revision.

Don't be embarrassed by the roughness of your first draft. You should be embarrassed only if you leave it that way. You are seeing the reason why a first draft is called "rough." Famous authors have said publicly that they wouldn't show their rough drafts to their closest, most forgiving friends.

The Recursive Factor

The process of writing can be called recursive, which means "going back and forth." In this respect, writing is like reading. If you do not understand what you have read, you back up and read it again. After you have reread a passage, you may still need to read it selectively. The same can be said of writing. If, for example, after having developed an outline and started writing your first draft, you discover that your subject is too broad, you have to back up, narrow your topic sentence, and then adjust your outline. You may even want to return to an early cluster of ideas to see how you can use a smaller grouping of them. Revision is usually the most recursive of all parts of the writing process. You will go over your material again and again until you are satisfied that you have expressed yourself as well as you possibly can.

Revising Your Writing

The term *first draft* suggests quite accurately that there will be other drafts, or versions, of your writing. Only in the most dire situations, such as an in-class examination when you have time for only one draft, should you be satisfied with a single effort.

What you do beyond the first draft is revising and editing. Revision concerns itself with organization, content, and language effectiveness. Editing involves a final correcting of mistakes in spelling, punctuation, and capitalization. In practice, editing and revision are not always separate activities, although writers usually wait until the next-to-the-last draft to edit some minor details and attend to other small points that can be easily overlooked.

Successful revision almost always involves intense, systematic rewriting. You should learn to look for certain aspects of skillful writing as you enrich and repair your first draft. To help you recall these aspects so that you can keep them in mind and examine your material in a comprehensive fashion, this textbook offers a memory device—an acronym in which each letter suggests an important feature of good writing and revision. This device enables you to memorize the features of good writing quickly. Soon you will be able to recall and refer to them automatically. These features need not be attended to individually when you revise your writing, although they may be. They need not be attended to in the order presented here. The acronym is CLUESS (pronounced "clues"), which provides this guide: <u>c</u>oherence, <u>l</u>anguage, <u>u</u>nity, <u>e</u>mphasis, <u>s</u>upport, <u>s</u>entences.

Coherence

Coherence is the flow of ideas, with each idea leading logically and smoothly to the next. It is achieved by numbering parts or otherwise indicating (*first, second, third, then, next, soon,* and so on), giving directions (according to space, as in "To the right is a map, and to the left of that map is a bulletin board"), using transitional words (*however, otherwise, therefore, similarly, hence, on the other hand, then, consequently, accordingly, thus*), using demonstrative pronouns (*this, that, those*), and moving in a clear order (from the least important to the most important or from the most important to the least important).

Language

Language here stands for diction or word choice: using words that clearly convey your ideas and are suitable for what you are writing and for your audience. In college writing that means you will usually avoid slang and clichés such as "a barrel of laughs," "happy as a clam," and "six of one and a half dozen of another." Your writing will contain standard grammar and usage. See page 282 for a discussion of general and specific words.

If you are writing with a word processor, use the thesaurus feature for careful diction, but keep in mind that no two words share exactly the same meaning.

Unity

Unity begins with a good topic sentence. Everything in your paragraph should be related and subordinated to your topic sentence. Repetition of a key word or phrase can make the unity even stronger.

Emphasis

Emphasize important ideas by using *position* (the most emphatic parts of a work are the beginning and the end), *repetition* (repeat key words and phrases), and *isolation* (a short, direct sentence among longer ones will usually command attention).

Support

Support is the material that backs up, justifies, or proves your topic sentence. Work carefully with the material from your outline (or list or cluster) to make sure that your ideas are well supported. If your paragraph is skimpy and your ideas slender, you are probably generalizing and not explaining how you arrived at your conclusions. Avoid repetition that does not add to the content; use details and examples; indicate parts and discuss relationships; and explain why your generalizations are true, logical, and accurate. Your reader can't accept your ideas unless he or she knows by what reasoning or use of evidence you developed them.

Sentences

Be sure your sentences are complete (not fragments) and that you have not incorrectly combined word groups that could be sentences (comma splices and run-ons). Consider using different types of sentences and different sentence beginnings.

Write as many drafts as necessary, revising as you go for all the aspects of effective writing. Don't confuse revising with editing (the final stage of the writing process); don't get bogged down in fixing such things as spelling and punctuation.

Editing Your Writing

Editing, the final stage of the writing process, involves a careful examination of your work. Look for problems with capitalization, omissions, punctuation, and spelling (COPS).

Because you can find spelling errors in others' writing more easily than in your own, a computerized spell checker is extremely useful. (See page 196.) However, a spell checker will not detect wrong words that are correctly spelled, so you should always proofread.

Before you submit your writing to your instructor, do what almost all professional writers do before sending their material along: Read it aloud, to yourself or to a willing accomplice. Reading material aloud will help you catch any awkwardness of expression, omission and misplacement of words, and other problems that are easily overlooked by an author.

As you can see, writing is a process and is not a matter of just sitting down and "banging out" sentences. The parts of the process from prewriting to revising to editing are connected, and your movement is ultimately forward, but this process allows you to go back and forth in the recursive manner discussed earlier. If your outline is not working, perhaps the flaw is in your topic sentence. You may need to go back and fix it. If one section of your paragraph is skimpy, perhaps you will have to go back and reconsider the pertinent material in your outline or clustering. There you might find more details or alter a statement so that you can move into more fertile areas of thought.

Norton wrote the following first draft, marked it for revision, and then completed the final draft, which you read on page 213. For simplification, only this draft is shown, although a typical paper might require several drafts, including one in which the author has done nothing but edit his or her revised writing.

, an NBA Great

Magic Johnson ^

(National Basketball Association)　　　have a special talent
Some NBA players are good because they ~~are good~~ in one area ~~such as~~

a　　NBA star

~~shooting, passing, or rebounding~~. Magic Johnson was great because he was

excellent　　shooting, passing, rebounding, and leading　　ever equaled him
~~good~~ in ~~all of those things and more~~. As a shooter few have ~~been able to do~~

—all with deadly accuracy

~~what he could~~. He could slam, shovel, hook, and fire from three-point range.

As for

~~When it came to~~ free throws, he led all NBA players in shooting percentage in

While

1988–89. ~~Then~~ he averaged more than twenty points per game, he helped

with his passes.　　　　　(the quarterback of basketball),
other become stars. As the point guard he was always near the top in the

s　　　" "
league in asists and was famous for his no-look passes ~~W~~hich often surprised

its　When he wasn't shooting or passing, he was rebounding.
even his teammates with ~~their~~ precision. A top rebounding guard is unusual,

u

but Magic, ~~standing~~ at six feet nine inches tall, could bump sholders and jump

with anyone. These three qualities made him probably the most spectacular

"Triple-double" means reaching two digits in scoring, assists, and rebounding.
triple-double threat of all time. Magic didn't need more for greatness in the

W

NBA, but he had more. He was also an inspirational team leader with his ever-

He　　　ed

lasting smile and boundless energy. Always believing in himself and his team.

remained on the game clock　the fans
When his team was down by a point and three seconds ~~were left~~, ~~you~~ always

They　　　　　　　　　he
looked for Magic to get the ball. ~~Then you~~ watched as he dribbled once, faded,

he　　he　　　　he　　　　　　　　　　!That was magic.
leaped, twisted, and hooked one in from twenty feet That was Magic.

The Writing Process Worksheet

One effective and systematic way to organize your writing is by using the Writing Process Worksheet. The procedure is simple. First, copy the directions for your assignment, making certain that you know precisely what you are to do and when you are to submit your paper. Few things are more frustrating to both student and instructor than an assignment that falls outside the directions or is not turned in on time.

Next, do your prewriting, beginning on the worksheet and using extra pages if necessary. Prewriting will vary according to your assignment and according to your instructor's requirements.

Then follow your prewriting activities with writing, which includes revising and editing.

Keep in mind that the writing process is recursive and that you can go back and forth between different activities, depending on your needs. For example, if one part of your outline does not work as you write your rough draft, go back to your outline or other prewriting activities to add or subtract ideas.

The Writing Process Worksheet is useful in helping you understand the assignment, in reminding you of the best tools the writing process offers for prewriting and writing, and in providing an organized packet of material for your instructor. For some instructors that packet will include these parts stapled in this order: a completed Writing Process Worksheet, a rough draft marked for revision, and a final draft.

Norton's Writing Process Worksheet follows. You will find a full-size blank Writing Process Worksheet on page 6. It can be photocopied, filled in, and submitted with each assignment if your instructor directs you to do so.

Writing Process Worksheet (completed through Stage 2)

TITLE Magic Johnson, an NBA Great

NAME Cyrus Norton   **DUE DATE** Monday, October 21, 9 a.m.

ASSIGNMENT   In the space below, write whatever you need to know about your assignment, including information about the topic, audience, pattern of writing, length, whether to include a rough draft or revised drafts, and whether your paper must be typed.

Topic: person who has achieved excellence / about qualities that made him or her excellent / analysis by division / 200–300 words / paragraph / one or more rough drafts / typed final draft / audience of instructor and other students, those who have heard of the subject but don't have detailed information—

STAGE ONE   **Explore**   Freewrite, brainstorm (list), cluster, or take notes as directed by your instructor. Use the back of this page or separate paper if you need more space.

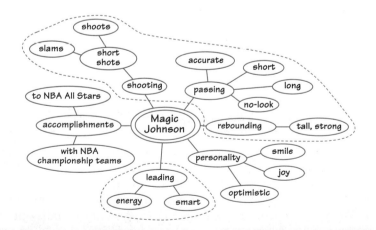

STAGE TWO   **Organize**   Write a topic sentence or thesis; label the subject and the treatment parts.

<u>Magic Johnson was a great NBA star because he was excellent in shooting,</u>
      subject   treatment

<u>passing, rebounding, and leading.</u>

Write an outline or an outline alternative.

I. Shooting
   A. Short shots
   B. Long shots
   C. Free throws
II. Passing
   A. No-look
   B. Precise
III. Rebounding
   A. Tall
   B. Rugged
IV. Leading
   A. Energy
   B. Spirit

STAGE THREE   **Write**   On separate paper, write and then revise your paper as many times as necessary for coherence, language (usage, tone, and diction), unity, emphasis, support, and sentences (CLUESS). Read your paper aloud to hear and correct any grammatical errors or awkward-sounding sentences.

Edit any problems in fundamentals, such as capitalization, omissions, punctuation, and spelling (COPS). *(See rough and final drafts on pages 233, 213.)*

Exercise 1   **REVISING AND EDITING**

Treat the following paragraph as your own rough draft and mark it in the way Norton marked his rough draft. First consider coherence, language, unity, emphasis, support, and sentences (CLUESS). Then edit the paragraph, correcting fundamentals such as capitalization, omissions, punctuation, and spelling (COPS). (See Answer Key for possible answers.)

Young voters are not voting the way they should. The latest figures show that only 20 percent are going to the poles. The next-older generation is, the so-called baby boomers, they are going to the poles at about twice that rate. Because I'm part of the young group, I'm concerned, but the answers to why we usually don't bother to vote are as obvious as the nose on your face. For one thing the younger people don't think voting changes anything. The political parties are all about the same, and the candidates look and talk alike, even though they seem angry with each other. For another a lot of young voters don't have parents that voted or even talked about politics when they were growing up, they don't either. Still another thing is that the issues going around don't move young people that much. The politicians talk about the national debt and social security and health care and we're concerned about jobs and the high cost of education. If they could get people we could believe in and they would talk about issue that matter to us, then maybe they'd see more of us at the polls.

| Exercise 2 | **REVISING AND EDITING** |

Mark this rough draft for coherence, language, unity, emphasis, support, and sentences (CLUESS). Then edit the paragraph, correcting fundamentals such as capitalization, omissions, punctuation, and spelling (COPS).

High school dress codes don't make any sense to me. I've heard all the reasons. Too many kids wear gang clothes, and some get attacked or even killed. Parents have to put up too much money and even then the kids without parents with deep pockets can't compete. And then there are those that say kids behave bad if they dress in a free spirit way. Let's take them one at a time. As for the gang stuff, it's mainly how you act, not how you look, and if the gang stuff is still a problem, then just ban certain items of clothing. You don't have to go to the extreames of uniforms, just change the attitude, not the clothes. Then comes the money angle. Let the kid get a part-time job if they want better clothes. The behavior number is not what I can relate to. I mean, you go to class and learn, and you do it the school way, but the way you dress should have something to do with how you want to express yourself. Do they want to turn out a bunch of little robots that think the same way, behave the same way, and yes with the dress code even look the same way. Get real! If they'll cut us some slack with how we dress, they'll get happier campers in the classroom. Later better citizens in society.

| Exercise 3 | REVISING AND EDITING |

Mark the following rough draft for c̲oherence, l̲anguage, u̲nity, e̲mphasis, s̲upport, and s̲entences (CLUESS). Then edit the paragraph, correcting fundamentals such as c̲apitalization, o̲missions, p̲unctuation, and s̲pelling (COPS).

In the los Angeles Basin, people know why the Santa Anas are called the "devil winds." I know I do. At their worst they come in from the desert searing hot like the breeth of a blast furnace, tumbling over the mountain ranges and streaking down the canyons. Pitilessly destroying and disrupting. I hate them. Trees are striped of foliage, broken, and toppled. Fires that starts in the foothills may become firestorms. And bombard the downwind areas with lots of stuff. That sounds bad, doesn't it? But even without fire, the winds picks up sand, dirt, and debris and sent them toward the ocean as a hot, dry tide going out. All the time the Santa Anas are relentless, humming, howling, and whining through yards, and rattling and ripling lose shingles. Palm fronds move around. I've seen it and heard it lots of times. Dogs howl and often panic and run away, birds hunkers down in wind breaks; and human beings mostly stay inside Wiping up dust, coughing, and getting grumpy. The devil winds earning their reputation. Santa Anas suck.

| Exercise 4 | REVISING AND EDITING |

Using your topic from the previous chapters, write a rough draft and a final draft. Use CLUESS and COPS for revising and editing.

 Or do the following:

  Fill in the two blanks to complete the topic sentence:
_____ [person's name] is an excellent _____ [boss, coach, doctor, neighbor, parent, preacher, teacher, sibling].
  Then use the topic sentence to write a paragraph. Go through the complete writing process. Use one or more prewriting techniques (freewriting, brainstorming, clustering, outlining), write a first draft, revise your draft as many times as necessary, edit your work, and write a final polished paragraph.
  In your drafts, you may rephrase the topic sentence as necessary. Using the paragraph on page 213 (showing Magic Johnson as a shooter, passer, rebounder, and leader) as a model, divide your topic into whatever qualities make your subject an excellent example of whichever type of person you have chosen.

Writer's Guidelines: Writing, Revising, and Editing the Paragraph

1. **Writing the rough draft:** Referring to your outline for guidance and to your topic sentence for limits, write a first, or rough, draft. Do not get caught up in correcting and polishing your writing during this stage.

2. **Revising:** Mark and revise your rough draft, rewriting as many times as necessary to produce an effective paragraph. The main points of revision are contained in the acronym CLUESS, expressed here as questions.

   <u>C</u>oherence: Does the material flow smoothly, with each idea leading logically to the next?

   <u>L</u>anguage: Are the words appropriate for the message, occasion, and audience?

   <u>U</u>nity: Are all ideas related to and subordinate to the topic sentence?

   <u>E</u>mphasis: Have you used techniques such as repetition and placement of ideas to emphasize your main point(s)?

   <u>S</u>upport: Have you presented material to back up, justify, or prove your topic sentence?

   <u>S</u>entences: Have you used some variety of structure and avoided fragments, comma splices, and run-ons?

3. **Editing:** Examine your work carefully. Look for problems in <u>c</u>apitalization, <u>o</u>missions, <u>p</u>unctuation, and <u>s</u>pelling (COPS).

4. **Using word-processing features:** Use your thesaurus and spell checker to help you revise and edit, but note that those features have their limitations.

5. **Using the Writing Process Worksheet:** Explore your topic, organize your ideas, and write your paragraphs using the Writing Process Worksheet as your guide. Photocopy the blank form on page 6.

14

From Paragraph to Essay

"As you learn the properties of effective paragraphs—those with a strong topic sentence and strong support—you also learn how to organize an essay, if you just magnify the procedure."

Writing the Short Essay

The definition of a paragraph gives us a framework for defining the essay: A *paragraph* is a group of sentences, each with the function of supporting a single, main idea, which is contained in the topic sentence.

The main parts of a paragraph are the topic sentence (subject and treatment), support (evidence and reasoning), and, often, the concluding sentence at the end. Now let's use that framework for an essay. An *essay* is a group of paragraphs, each with the function of stating or supporting a controlling idea called the thesis.

The main parts of the essay are as follows:

Introduction: carries the thesis, which states the controlling idea—much like the topic sentence for a paragraph but on a larger scale.

Development: evidence and reasoning—the support.

Conclusion: an appropriate ending—often a restatement of or reflection on the thesis.

Thus, considered structurally, the paragraph is often an essay in miniature. That does not mean that all paragraphs can grow up to be essays or that all essays can shrink to become paragraphs. For college writing, however, a good understanding of the parallel between well-organized paragraphs and well-organized essays is useful. As you learn the properties of effective paragraphs—those with a strong topic sentence and strong support—you also learn how to organize an essay, if you just magnify the procedure.

The following diagram illustrates the parallel parts of outlines, paragraphs, and essays:

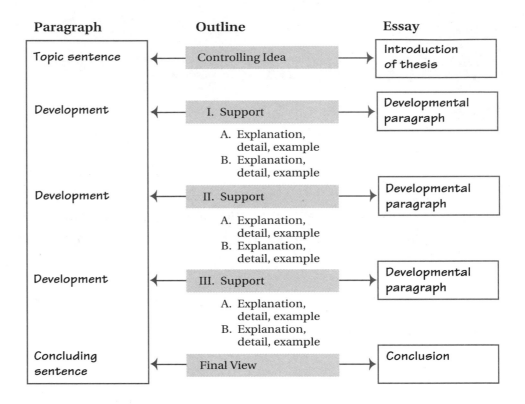

Of course, the parallel components are not exactly the same in a paragraph and an essay. The paragraph is shorter and requires much less development, and some paragraph topics simply couldn't be developed much more extensively to their advantage. But let's consider the ones that can. What happens? How do we proceed?

Introductory Paragraph

The topic sentence idea is expanded to the introductory paragraph through elaboration: explanation, historical background, anecdote, quotation, or stress on the significance of an idea. Usually the introduction is about three to six sentences long. If you say too much, your paper will be top-heavy. If you don't say enough, your readers will be confused. But a solid opening paragraph should

- introduce the subject through the thesis or controlling idea.

- gain reader interest.

- move the reader into the middle paragraphs. Avoid any statement of apology about your topic or your writing and avoid beginning with a statement such as "I am writing an essay about. . . ."

Middle Paragraphs

The middle paragraphs are similar to the paragraphs you have been writing. They are developmental paragraphs used to support the thesis. Each has its own unity based on the topic sentence, moves logically and coherently, and has adequate and appropriate development. The topic sentence is usually at the beginning of the paragraph in a college essay, regardless of the form. Although some essays are an expansion of a particular form of discourse and therefore use basically the same pattern for each paragraph, many essays combine the forms. For example, you might have one middle paragraph that gives examples, one that defines, and one that clarifies. You may also have combinations within paragraphs. Nevertheless, developmental paragraphs are always related to the central idea and presented in a logical arrangement. The coherence of the paragraphs can often be improved by the use of the same principles that you have applied to individual paragraphs: using sequence words such as *first, second,* and *third;* using transitional words such as *therefore, moreover,* and *for example;* and arranging material in chronological order, spatial order, or order of relative importance.

Concluding Paragraph

Like the introductory paragraph, the concluding paragraph is a special unit with a specific function. In the concluding paragraph, usually three to six sentences long, you end on a note of finality. The way that you end depends on what you want to do. If you can't decide on how to end, try going back to your introduction and see what you said there. If you posed a question, the answer should be in the conclusion. If you laid out the framework for an exploration of the topic, then perhaps you will want to bring your discussion together with a summary statement. Or perhaps a quotation, an anecdote, or a restatement of the thesis in slightly different words would be effective. Do not end with a complaint, an apology, or the introduction of a new topic or new support. Do not begin your conclusion with a worn-out phrase such as "last but not least" or "in conclusion." Try for a fresh approach.

Examining a Paragraph and an Essay

The following paragraph and essay, both on the topic of drunk driving, were written by the same student. Notice how each is developed.

Get Them Off the Road (paragraph)

Daniel Humphreys

Topic sentence <u>Drunk driving has become such a severe problem in California that something must be done.</u> The best solution is to do what Sweden did long ago: Lower the blood-alcohol content level to .04 percent for drunk-driving arrests.

I. Support <u>Driving</u> is not a right; it <u>is a privilege,</u> and that privilege should not be extended to the person who drinks to the extent that his or her physical and mental abilities are significantly impaired. <u>Alcohol,</u> working as a depressant,

II. Support <u>affects our entire nervous system,</u> according to numerous sources cited in The Police Officer's Source Book. As a result of this impairment, "50 percent of all fatal traffic accidents" involve intoxicated drivers, as reported by the National Highway Traffic Safety Administration. Cavenaugh and Associates, research specialists, say that in California 5,954 people were killed in alcohol-related accidents in the four-year period from 1995 through 1998. They go on

III. Support to say that nationally <u>intoxicated drivers cost us somewhere between $11 bil-</u>

Concluding sentence <u>lion and $14 billion each year.</u> <u>It is time to give drunk drivers a message:</u> "Stay off the road. You are costing us pain, injury, and death, and no one has the right to do that."

Get Them Off the Road (essay)

Daniel Humphreys

Introduction

Thesis of essay

The state of California, along with the rest of the nation, has a problem with society involving drinking and driving. Prohibition is not the answer, as history has demonstrated. But there is a practical answer to be found in a law. <u>I believe that the legal BAC (blood-alcohol concentration) while driving should be lowered from .08 percent to .04 percent for three strong reasons.</u>

Topic sentence of paragraph

I. Support paragraph 1

First, <u>driving in California is a privilege,</u> not a right, and <u>a person impaired by alcohol should not be allowed that privilege.</u> Statutory law states that when stopped by a police officer who suspects drunk driving, one must submit to a BAC test. The level of impairment is an individual trait because of the elapsed time of consumption, body size, and tolerance, but <u>alcohol</u> is a depressant to all of us. It <u>affects our nervous system and slows our muscular reactions.</u> As a result of extensive scientific study, Sweden determined that .04 percent BAC was the level of significant impairment, and, therefore, it passed a federal law to enforce drunk driving at that point. Penalties there are extreme.

Topic sentence of paragraph

II. Support paragraph 2

<u>We,</u> like the people in Sweden, <u>are concerned about the dangers of drunk driving.</u> The National Highway Traffic Safety Administration has stated that <u>"50 percent of all fatal accidents" involve intoxicated drivers and that 75 percent of those drivers have a BAC of .10 percent or higher.</u> Cavenaugh and Associates, a California think tank, reports that in the four-year period between 1995 and 1998, 15,363 people were injured and 5,954 were killed in alcohol-related accidents in California.

Topic sentence of paragraph

III. Support paragraph 3

Even if we are among the fortunate few who are not touched directly by the problems of drunk driving, <u>there are other effects.</u> <u>One is money.</u> There are the loss of production, cost of insurance, cost of delays in traffic, cost of medical care for those who have no insurance, and many other costs. Cavenaugh and Associates say that drunk drivers cost us nationally somewhere between $11 billion and $14 billion a year.

Conclusion

Restated thesis

Police officers report that drinking people are quick to say, "I'm okay to drive," but every four years our nation loses more lives than it lost in the entire Vietnam War. To lower the legal BAC limit to .04 percent would mean saving lives, property, and money.

Exercise 1 **EXPANDING A PARAGRAPH TO AN ESSAY**

The following paragraph could easily be expanded into an essay because the topic sentence and its related statements can be developed into an introduction; each of the main divisions (five) can be expanded into a separate paragraph; and the restated topic sentence can, with elaboration, become the concluding paragraph. Divide the paragraph below with the symbol ¶ and annotate it in the left-hand margin with the words Introduction, Support *(and numbers for the middle five paragraphs), and* Conclusion *to show the parts that would be developed further. The topic sentence has already been marked for you.*

What Is a Gang?

Will Cusak

Topic sentence   The word *gang* is often used loosely to mean "a group of people who go around together," but that does not satisfy the concerns of law enforcement people and sociologists. <u>For those professionals, the definition of gang has five parts that combine to form a unit.</u> First a gang has to have a name. Some well-known gang names are Bloods, Crips, Hell's Angels, and Mexican Mafia. The second part of the definition is clothing or other identifying items such as tattoos. The clothing may be of specific brands or colors, such as blue for Crips and red for Bloods. Members of the Aryan Brotherhood often have blue thunderbolt tattoos. A third component is rituals. They may involve such things as the use of handshakes, other body language or signing, and graffiti. A fourth is binding membership. A gang member is part of an organization, a kind of family, with obligations and codes of behavior to follow. Finally, a gang will be involved in some criminal behavior, something such as prostitution, drugs, thievery, or burglary. There are many different kinds of gangs—ethnic, regional, behavioral—but they all have these five characteristics.

Exercise 2   **ANALYZING ESSAY FORM**

Underline the thesis in the first paragraph, the topic sentences in paragraphs 2, 3, 4, and 5, and the most forceful concluding statement in the last paragraph. In the left-hand margin, label each part you underlined. Observe how information is used to support the topic sentences, and double underline that information.

Ben Franklin, Renaissance Man

Allison Udell

1   Anyone who doesn't know the definition of *Renaissance man* would do well to study Benjamin Franklin. When he died in 1790 at the age of eighty-four, he was acknowledged for greatness in numerous areas of endeavor. In short, he was a multi-genius, and each area of his accomplishments registered more than almost any other person of his time. Putting the areas together made him probably the greatest Renaissance man that America has ever produced.

2   One side to Benjamin Franklin was his education. Although he went to school for only two years, he was curious, energetic, and determined. He educated himself through reading, and learned six languages. By the age of twenty-four he opened his own print shop, first publishing a newspaper, then *Poor Richard's Almanac.* His *Autobiography* is still read for its brilliance of style and information about his learning experiences.

3   He was also an inventor and scientist. Almost everyone has heard of his experimentation with electricity, and of his invention of bifocals, the lightning rod, the Franklin stove, and the school chair. Other scholars still read his studies of ocean currents and soil improvement. In his middle years he was elected to the prestigious group of scientists called the Royal Society of London.

4   His work in planning took two directions. In urban life, he planned a hospital, a library, the postal system, the city police, and the city fire

department. These institutions were successful and became the models for other cities and even countries. The second direction occurred just before the War of Independence during the French and Indian War. At the request of people in government, he designed strategy that was enormously successful.

5   His involvement as a patriot during the War of Independence was still another area of accomplishment. An acknowledged leader, he signed the Declaration of Independence and later helped write the Constitution, which he also signed. During the war, he served the patriot colonists as the Minister to France. There he arranged for financial and military support from the French, helped negotiate the Treaty of Peace with Great Britain, and now is regarded as probably the most successful diplomat in the history of America.

6   Renaissance man means "one who is an expert in several different areas of endeavor." For these more than two hundred years we have found no better example than Benjamin Franklin.

Topics for Short Essays

Many paragraph topics in this book can become topics for short essays. In Part Three of this book, the writing instruction is presented according to the well-known patterns listed here. Although the writing topics suggested at the end of Chapters 16 through 22 refer to paragraph writing, almost all of the topics can be further developed into essays. You may want to refer back to the following list if you are working on an essay assignment.

Narration: Expand each part of the narrative form (situation, conflict, struggle, outcome, meaning) into one or more paragraphs. Give the most emphasis to the struggle.

Description: Expand each unit of descriptive detail into a paragraph. All paragraphs should support the dominant impression.

Exemplification: Expand one example into an extended example or expand a group of examples into separate paragraphs. Each paragraph should support the main point.

Process Analysis: Expand the preparation and each step in the process into a separate paragraph.

Cause and Effect: Expand each cause or effect into a separate paragraph.

Comparison and Contrast: In the point-by-point pattern, expand each point into a separate paragraph. In the subject-by-subject pattern, first expand each subject into a separate paragraph. If you have sufficient material on each point, you can also expand each point into a separate paragraph.

Argument: Expand the refutation and each main division of support into a separate paragraph.

Writer's Guidelines: From Paragraph to Essay

You do not usually set out to write an essay by first writing a paragraph. However, the organization for the paragraph and the essay is often the same, and the writing

process is also the same. You still proceed from initial prewriting to topic, to outline, to draft, to revising, to editing, to final paper. The difference is often only a
matter of development and indentation.

1. The well-designed paragraph and the well-designed essay often have the
   same form.

   a. The introduction carries the thesis, which states the controlling idea—
      much like the topic sentence for a paragraph but on a larger scale.

   b. The development, or middle part, supplies evidence and reasoning—the
      support.

   c. The conclusion provides an appropriate ending—often a restatement of or
      reflection on the thesis.

2. These are the important relationships:

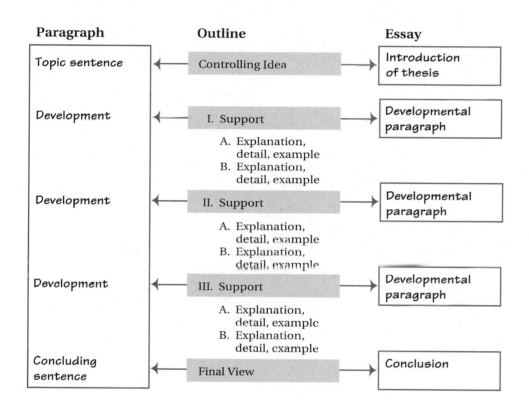

PART Three

Connecting Reading and Writing

15

Writing About Reading Selections

*"*B*ecause most college writing assignments are connected with reading, it is worthwhile to consider how to focus thoughtful attention on the written word and how to write an effective response."*

uch of your college writing will require you to evaluate and to reflect on what you read, rather than write only about personal experience. You will be expected to read, think, and write. The writing in these circumstances is commonly called reading-related writing. It includes

- effective reading (which may include underlining, annotating, and outlining).

- writing a *summary* (main ideas in your own words).

- writing a *reaction* (usually meaning how the reading relates specifically to you and your experiences and attitudes, but also often a critique, involving the worth and logic of a piece).

- writing a *two-part response* (includes both a summary and a reaction but separates them).

These kinds of writing have certain points in common; they all

- originate as a response to something you have read.

- indicate, to some degree, content from that piece.

- demonstrate a knowledge of the piece of writing.

Reading for Writing

Good reading begins with desire; and concentration, or focus, is the first product of desire. *Focus is no problem if you have a strong purpose in reading.* If you go to a cookbook to find a recipe for enchiladas, you will probably find the recipe, read it, and refer back to it periodically while you prepare the dish. It is unlikely that you will put the book aside and say, "I wanted to read about making enchiladas, but I just couldn't concentrate." If you can capture that sense of concentration and apply it to all of your reading experiences, you will become a stronger reader.

Of course, a desire that naturally emerges from a situation is different from a need that occurs because, let's say, a teacher has assigned three chapters in a history book. In the latter case, you may be motivated or you may not be. If not, you will want to manufacture that concentration somehow.

Underlining

One way to build concentration is to develop a relationship with the reading material. Imagine you are reading a chapter of several pages, and you decide to underline and write in the margins. Immediately, the underlining takes you out of the passive television-watching frame of mind. You are involved. You are participating. It is now necessary for you to discriminate, to distinguish more important from less important ideas. Perhaps you have thought of underlining as a method designed only to help you with your review. This is, when you study the material the next time, you won't have to read all the material; instead, you can deal only with the most important, underlined parts. But even while you are underlining, you are benefiting from an imposed concentration, because this procedure forces you to think, to focus. Consider these guides for underlining:

1. Underline the main ideas in paragraphs. The most important statement, the topic sentence, is likely to be at the beginning of the paragraph.

2. Underline the support for those main ideas.

3. Underline answers to questions that you bring to the reading assignment. These questions may have come from the end of the chapter, from subheadings that you turn into questions, or from your independent concern for the topic.

4. Underline only the key words. You would seldom underline all the words in a sentence and almost never a whole paragraph.

Does that fit your approach to underlining? Possibly not. Most students, in their enthusiasm to do a good job, overdo underlining.

Maybe you have had this experience: You start reading about something you have not encountered before. The idea seems important. You highlight it. The next idea is equally fresh and significant. You highlight it. A minute or two later, you have changed the color of the page from white to orange, but you haven't accomplished anything.

The trick is how to figure out what to underline. You would seldom underline more than about 30 percent of a passage, although the amount would depend on your purpose and the nature of the material. Following the preceding four rules will be useful. Learning more about the principles of sentence, paragraph, and essay organization will also be helpful. These principles are presented in Chapters 12 through 14.

Consider this passage with effective underlining.

Youth and the Counterculture

Main idea Rock music helped tie this international subculture together. Rock grew out of the black music culture of rhythm and blues, which was flavored with country and western to make it more **Support** accessible to white teenagers. The mid-1950s signaled a breakthrough as Billy Hailey called on record buyers to "Rock Around **Support** the Clock" and Elvis Presley warned them to keep off his "Blue **Support** Suede Shoes." In the 1960s, the Beatles thrilled millions of young people, often to their parents' dismay. Like Elvis, the Beatles suggested personal and sexual freedom that many older people found disturbing.

Main idea It was Bob Dylan, a young folksinger turned rock poet with an acoustic guitar, who best expressed the radical political as well as **Support** cultural aspirations of the "younger generation." In a song that became a rallying cry, Dylan sang that "the times they are a'changing." The song captured the spirit of growing alienation between **Support** the generation whose defining experiences had been the Great Depression and World War II and the generation ready to reject the complacency of the 1950s. Increasing discontent with middle-class **Closing statement** conformity and the injustices of racism and imperialism fueled the young leaders of social protest and reflected a growing spirit of rebellion.

John P. McKay et al., *A History of Western Society*

Exercise 1	UNDERLINING

Using the four rules of underlining on p. 250, mark the following paragraphs. (See Answer Key for possible answers. It is unlikely that any two readers will underline precisely the same words.)

The Leadership of Martin Luther King, Jr.

1   On December 1, 1955, in Montgomery, Alabama, a black woman named Rosa Parks was arrested for refusing to give up her bus seat to a white man. In protest, Montgomery blacks organized a year-long bus boycott. The boycott forced white city leaders to recognize the blacks' determination and economic power.

2   One of the organizers of the bus boycott was a Baptist minister, the Reverend Martin Luther King, Jr. King soon became a national leader in the growing civil rights movement. With stirring speeches and personal courage, he urged blacks to demand their rights. At the same time, he was completely committed to nonviolence. Like Gandhi, . . . he believed that justice could triumph through moral force.

3   In April 1963, King began a drive to end segregation in Birmingham, Alabama. He and his followers boycotted segregated businesses and held peaceful marches and demonstrations. Against them, the Birmingham police used electric cattle prods, attack dogs, clubs, and fire hoses to break up marches.

4   Television cameras brought those scenes into the living rooms of millions of Americans, who were shocked by what they saw. On May 10, Birmingham's city leaders gave in. A committee of blacks and whites oversaw the gradual desegregation of the city and tried to open more jobs for blacks. The victory was later marred by grief, however, when a bomb exploded at a Birmingham church, killing four black children.

Steven L. Jantzen, *World History: Perspectives on the Past*

Writing in Margins—Annotating

Annotating, a practice related to underlining, is writing in the margins. You can do it independently, although it usually appears in conjunction with underlining to mark the understanding and to extend the involvement.

Writing in the margins represents intense involvement because it makes the reader a writer. If you read material and write something in the margin as a reaction to it, then in a way you have had a conversation with the author. The author has made a statement and you have responded. In fact, you may have added something to the text; therefore, for your purposes you have become a co-author or collaborator. The comments you make in the margin are of your own choosing according to your interests and the purpose you bring to the reading assignment. Your response in the margin may merely echo the author's ideas, it may question them critically, it may relate them to something else, or it may add to them.

In the following example you can see how the reader has reinforced the underlining by placing numbers in the text and by commenting in the margin.

Women and Witchcraft

Salem witchcraft—
broad interest

1   The Salem witchcraft crisis of 1692 to 1693, in which a small number of adolescent girls and young women accused hundreds of older women (and a few men) of having bewitched them, has fascinated Americans ever since. It has provided material for innumerable books, plays, movies, and television productions. To twentieth-century Americans, the belief in witchcraft in the seventeenth-century colonies is difficult to explain or understand; perhaps that is why the Salem episode has attracted so much attention. For those interested in studying women's experiences, of course, witchcraft incidents are particularly intriguing. The vast majority of suspected witches were female, and so, too, were many of their accusers. Although colonial women rarely played a role on the public stage, in witchcraft cases they were the primary actors.

Why mostly women?	<u>What accounts for their prominence under these peculiar circum-</u><u>stances?</u>
	2 To answer that question, <u>Salem crisis</u> must be placed into its <u>proper</u> <u>historical and cultural context</u>. <u>People</u> in the early modern
Historical/cultural background	world <u>believed</u> in <u>witchcraft because</u> it <u>offered</u> a <u>rationale</u> for <u>events</u> that <u>otherwise seemed random</u> and <u>unfathomable</u>. In the <u>absence</u> of <u>modern scientific knowledge about</u> such <u>natural phe-</u>
Without modern science	<u>nomena</u> as <u>storms</u> and <u>diseases</u>, and <u>clear explanations</u> for <u>acci-</u><u>dents</u> of various sorts, the <u>evil actions of a witch</u> could provide a <u>ready answer</u> to a person or community inquiring about the causes of a disaster.

3   Therefore, <u>witchcraft accusations</u>—and some large-scale "witch hunts"—were <u>not uncommon</u> in <u>Europe between</u> the early

Witch hunts in Europe— the extent	<u>fourteenth</u> and the late <u>seventeenth centuries</u> (1300 to 1700). In short, the <u>immigrants</u> to the <u>colonies came from a culture</u> in which <u>belief</u> in <u>witchcraft</u> was <u>widespread</u> and in which <u>accusations</u> could <u>result</u> in formal <u>prosecutions</u> and <u>executions</u>. Recent research has demonstrated that the Salem incident, although the largest and most important witch hunt in New England, was just one of a number of such episodes in the American colonies.
Question—repeated	4 <u>But why were witches women?</u> Admittedly, historians have not yet answered that question entirely satisfactorily. Certain observa-
Answers: 1	tions can be made: <u>women gave birth</u> to <u>new life</u> and <u>seemed to</u>
2	<u>have</u> the <u>potential</u> to <u>take life away</u>. In <u>Western culture</u>, <u>women</u>
3	<u>were seen</u> as <u>less rational than men, more linked</u> to the "<u>natural</u>" <u>world</u>, in which <u>magic</u> held sway. <u>Men</u>, who <u>dominated European</u> <u>society, defined</u> the characteristics of a "<u>proper woman</u>," who was <u>submissive</u> and <u>accepted a subordinate position</u>. The <u>stereotypical</u> <u>witch</u>, usually described as an <u>aggressive</u> and <u>threatening older</u>
Women seen as "out of their place"	<u>woman</u>, represented the <u>antithesis</u> of that <u>image</u>. These broad cate- gories need further refinement, and historians are currently looking closely at the women who were accused of practicing witchcraft to identify the crucial characteristics that set them apart from their
Mary Beth Norton, Major Problems in American Women's History	contemporaries and made them a target for accusations.

Exercise 2	UNDERLINING AND ANNOTATING

Mark the following paragraphs with underlining and annotation. Compare your marks with those of your classmates.

Buddhism Taught Nonviolence

1   Buddha gave his first sermon to the five wisdom seekers who had been his companions. That sermon was a landmark in the history of world religions. Buddha taught the four main ideas that had come to him in his enlightenment, calling them the Four Noble Truths.

2   *First Noble Truth:* Everything in life is suffering and sorrow.

3   *Second Noble Truth:* The cause of all this pain is people's self-centered cravings and desires. People seek pleasure that cannot last and leads only to rebirth and more suffering.

4   *Third Noble Truth:* The way to end all pain is to end all desires.

5   *Fourth Noble Truth:* People can overcome their desires and attain enlightenment by following the Eightfold Path.

6   The Eightfold Path was like a staircase. According to Buddha, those who sought enlightenment had to master one step at a time. The steps of the Eightfold Path were right knowledge, right purpose, right speech, right action, right living, right effort, right mindfulness, and right meditation. By following the Eightfold Path, anyone could attain *nirvana* (nur-VAHN-uh), Buddha's word for release from pain and selfishness.

7   Buddha taught his followers to treat all living things (humans, animals, and even insects) with loving kindness. A devout Buddhist was not even supposed to swat a mosquito.

8   Buddhists and Hindus both sought to escape from the woes of this world, but their paths of escape were very different. Unlike traditional Hinduism, Buddhism did not require complex rituals. Moreover, Buddha taught in everyday language, not in the ancient Sanskrit language of the Vedas and the Upanishads, which most Indians in 500 B.C. could no longer understand. Buddha's religion was also unique in its concern for all human beings—women as well as men, lowborn as well as highborn.

Forms of Writing

Among the forms of writing that will be suggested as assignments in most of these chapters are outlines, summaries, and reading-related paragraphs. In some instances you might be asked to use all three forms after reading a passage. The three forms are also tied to reading and critical thinking, in that they contribute to reading comprehension and use systematic and analytical thought.

To show how a reading selection can be dealt with by more than one form, the next two writing examples will be based on the following brief passage.

The Roman Toga

1   Practicality has never been a requirement of fashion. The Roman toga was an uncomfortable garment. It was hot in summer, cold in winter, and clumsy for just about any activity but standing still. The toga was, however, practical in one way: It was easy to make, since it involved no sewing. Not even a buttonhole was needed. An adult's toga was basically a large wool blanket, measuring about 18 by 7 feet. It was draped around the body in a variety of ways, without the use of buttons or pins.

2   In the early days of the Roman republic, both women and men wore togas. Women eventually wore more dresslike garments, called *stolas,* with separate shawls. For men, however, the toga remained in fashion with very little change.

3   Soon after the republic was formed, the toga became a symbol of Roman citizenship. Different styles of togas indicated a male citizen's place in society. For example, a young boy would wear a white toga with a narrow purple band along the border. When his family decided he was ready for adult responsibilities, he would don a pure white toga. On that day, usually when he was about 16, his family would take him to the Forum, where he would register as a full citizen. For the rest of his life, he would wear a toga at the theater, in court, for religious ceremonies, and on any formal occasion. At his funeral his body would be wrapped in a toga to mark him, even in death, as a Roman citizen.

Steven L. Jantzen, *World History: Perspectives on the Past*

Outlining

Following is a topic outline by student Leon Batista. Note parallel structure.

  I. Practicality
   A. Not practical
     1. Hot in summer
     2. Cold in winter
     3. Clumsy
   B. Practical
     1. Easy to make
     2. Easy to put on and take off

 II. Fashion in Roman republic
   A. Worn by men and women
     1. Changes little with men
     2. Alternates with stolas and shawls for women
   B. Symbol of citizenship
     1. One style for young male
     2. Another style for adult male
       a. Presented at point of adulthood
       b. Worn on all occasions

Exercise 3	ORGANIZING AN OUTLINE

Use the outline form to organize these sentences about college English into an outline.

1. It can help you express yourself more effectively in speaking and writing.
2. It can help you with your reading.
3. It will present the difference between fact and opinion.
4. It can help you to recognize and avoid logical fallacies.
5. It will offer complex courses in the interpretation of literature.
6. It will teach that a fact is something that can be verified.
7. It will offer courses in reading skills.
8. It will teach that an opinion is a subjective view.
9. It will offer courses in composition.
10. It will offer instruction in inductive and deductive thinking.
11. It will offer courses that involve discussion.
12. It can help you think critically.
13. College English can benefit you in many ways.
14. It will help you understand causes and effects.

Main idea: _____

    I. _____

        A. _____

        B. _____

    II. _____

        A. _____

        B. _____

    III. _____

        A. _____

            1. _____

            2. _____

        B. _____

        C. _____

        D. _____

Summarizing

A **summary** is a rewritten, shortened version of a piece of writing in which you use your own wording to express the main ideas. Learning to summarize effectively will help you in many ways. Summary writing reinforces comprehension skills in reading. It requires you to discriminate among the ideas in the target reading passage. Summaries are usually written in the form of a well-designed paragraph. Frequently, they are used in collecting material for research papers and in writing conclusions to essays.

The following rules will guide you in writing effective summaries. The summary

1. cites both the author and title of the text.

2. is usually shorter than the original by about two-thirds, although the exact reduction will vary depending on the content of the original.

3. concentrates on the main ideas and includes details only infrequently.

4. changes the wording without changing the idea.

5. does not evaluate the content or give an opinion in any way (even if you see an error in logic or fact).

6. does not add ideas (even if you have an abundance of related information).

7. does not include any personal comments by the author of the summary (therefore, no use of "I" referring to self).

8. seldom uses quotations (but if you do, only with quotation marks).

9. uses author tags ("says York," "according to York," or "the author explains") to remind the reader that you are summarizing the material of another writer.

10. begins with the main idea (as you usually do in middle paragraphs) and proceeds to cover the main points in an organized fashion while using complete sentences.

The following is a summary of "The Roman Toga," written by the same student who prepared the sample outline. The writing process used by Batista was direct and systematic. When first reading the material, he had underlined key parts and written comments and echo phrases in the margin. Then he wrote his outline. Finally, referring to both the marked passage and the outline, he wrote this summary. Had he not been assigned to write the outline, he would have done so anyway, as preparation for his summary.

Summary of "The Roman Toga" by Steven L. Jantzen

According to Steven Jantzen in <u>World History: Perspectives on the Past</u>, the toga was the main form of dress for citizens of the Roman republic, despite its being "hot in summer, cold in winter, and clumsy" to wear. Perhaps the Romans appreciated the simplicity of wearing a piece of woolen cloth about eighteen by seven feet "without the use of buttons or pins." Jantzen explains that the women also wore another garment similar to a dress called the *stola*, but Roman male citizens were likely to wear only the toga—white with a purple edge for the young and solid white for the adult. This apparel was worn from childhood to death.

Exercise 4	EVALUATING A SUMMARY

Compare this summary with the original passage and with the student summary you just read. Then mark the instances of poor summary writing by underlining and by using rule numbers from the preceding list.

Summary About One of My Favorite Garments

For citizens of the Roman republic, the toga was the main form of dress, despite its being hot in summer, cold in winter, and clumsy to wear. Frankly, I don't see why a bright bunch of people like the Romans couldn't have come up with a better design. Perhaps the Romans appreciated the simplicity of wearing a piece of woolen cloth about eighteen by seven feet without buttons or pins; but I've read elsewhere that the togas were sometimes stolen at the public baths. The women also wore another garment similar to a dress called the *stola*, but the Roman male citizen was likely to wear only the toga—white with a purple edge for the young and solid white for the adult. For the rest of his life, he would wear a toga at the theater, in court, for religious ceremonies, and on any formal occasion. At his funeral, his body would be wrapped in a toga to mark him, even in death, as a Roman citizen.

Other Reading-Related Writing Forms: The Reaction and the Two-Part Response

The following three paragraphs are further examples of reading-related writing: the reaction and the two-part response.

The Reaction

The reaction is usually concerned with how a reading relates specifically to you, your experiences, and your attitudes, but also is often a critique, involving the worth and logic of a piece.

In this reading-related writing, student Shanelle Watson takes a basic idea from the original on pages 252–253 and finds parallels. She could have written about one parallel situation or condition—personal or historical.

Sticks and Stones
Shanelle Watson

Reading "Women and Witchcraft" by Mary Beth Norton reminded me of a long line of indignities against women. If something goes wrong, and women can be blamed, they are. For centuries if a woman didn't have babies, it was said *she* couldn't, although the man was just as likely as the woman to be the cause of her childlessness. If, heaven forbid, the woman kept having female babies, that woman, it was said, couldn't produce a male. Yet we know now that it is the male who determines the sex of the child. If the child was not bright, as recently as a hundred years ago some doctors said it was because the woman was reading during pregnancy and took away the brain power from the fetus. As a result many women were not allowed to open a book during pregnancy. Of course, because it was believed that women were so weak, husbands were allowed to beat their wives, but according to English law, the stick could be no thicker than the man's thumb, hence "the rule of thumb." Even voting was argued against by some who said that the typical woman, controlled by emotions, would allow her husband to tell her how to vote, and each married man would then have two votes. It's no wonder that three hundred years ago men looked around and, finding many misfortunes, decided that women were the culprits and should be punished. Sticks were not enough. It was time for stones.

The Two-Part Response

As you have seen, the reaction includes an idea or ideas from a reading or is written with the assumption that readers have read the original piece. However, your instructor may prefer that you separate the forms and present a clear, concise summary followed by another type of reading-related writing. This format is especially useful for critical reactions or problem-solving assignments because it requires you to understand and repeat another's views or experiences before responding. The two-part response also helps you avoid the common problem of writing only a summary of the text when your instructor wants you to both summarize and evaluate or to otherwise react. In writing a summary and evaluation, it is a good idea to ask your instructor if you should separate your summary from your response.

This reading-related writing first summarizes in a separate paragraph and then analyzes, evaluates, and interprets the original passage on pages 252–253. Thus the second paragraph is a form of the reaction.

"Women and Witchcraft" by Mary Beth Norton: A Summary and a Reaction
Jeanne Garcia

Part 1: Summary

Americans have long been fascinated by the Salem witchcraft plight in 1692 to 1693. One perplexing factor is that most of the people accused and many who blamed them were women. In "Women and Witchcraft" Mary Beth Norton says the whole issue should be placed in a historical context. In those times much was unknown about the causes of disasters and illnesses, and the people came to believe that these things could be attributed to evil supernatural forces. Consequently, from about 1300 to 1700 "witchhunts" occurred, and Salem was just one of the locations. Historians are not certain about why women were often victims and accusers. They may have been involved because they had the power to produce life and, therefore, maybe had "the potential to take life away." Women were thought to be more emotional than rational and even connected to nature, as in magic. Moreover, the stereotypical witch was characterized as a mature, assertive woman, unlike the "proper woman" of the time "who was submissive and accepted a subordinate position." Norton says that historians now seek to discover the precise causes that made timid women the victims of persecution as witches.

Part 2: Reaction

The "witchcraft crisis of 1692 to 1693," which Mary Beth Norton discusses in "Women and Witchcraft," is not so surprising to some of us who look back after three hundred years. It doesn't take much reading between the lines to conclude that almost certainly most of the people charged were "uppity" older women who didn't know their places. The charges came mainly from adolescent girls and young women, but the power structure was adult men. Out of ignorance, the men, often with female accomplices, were looking around to find reasons for the misfortunes—bad weather, diseases, and accidents—that their society faced. It is a fact that if people are foolish and desperate enough to look for witches, they are foolish and desperate enough to find them. And they did: They found mainly a few old women who didn't know their place, individuals of a gender associated with the emotions. If these women had been meek and mild, if they had been properly submissive to the menfolk, and if they had still been young and sexy, they would not have been vulnerable. But they were what they were—mature and relatively independent women, who seemed to be different—and that made them witches to those who were said not to be emotionally based—the men.

| Exercise 5 | **WRITING A RESPONSE TO A READING** |

Read, underline, and annotate the following text and then complete one of the assignments below. Some of the annotation and underlining have been done for you. One possible response is for you to pose as a psychologist, counselor, or thoughtful friend and offer advice to McGraw. Is she thinking clearly? What should she do?

- *Write a summary.*

- *Write an outline.*

- *Write a reaction. Include enough summary to establish clear and logical connections between the text and your own ideas.*

- *Write a two-part response composed of a summary separated from a reaction.*

Everyone Pays the Price

Hadley McGraw

Sitting in a college classroom, Hadley McGraw doesn't remind one of the stereotypical gang member. Apparently tattoo- and puncture-free, she is fair-skinned, well-groomed, and soft-spoken. She does her homework, contributes to class discussion, and writes well. So much for stereotypes!

It is ten o'clock and time for me to start my day. I put an *X* on my calendar to signify that another twenty-four hours has passed. I now have one hundred and nine days until Martin, my boyfriend, comes home. He has been in jail for the last year. I guess you could say I was not surprised by his sentence. This is not the first time, and I'm afraid it will not be the last. Eighteen months of our three-and-a-half-year relationship, he has spent in correctional institutions. Martin is a gang member. He has been a gang member for nine years now. **Thesis** Gang membership of a loved one affects everyone around that person. Three-and-a-half years later I live each day in fear and grief.

Topic sentence I guess what attracted me to Martin at first was his bad-boy image and his carefree way of life. He was good looking and well known. He was tough and exciting. I, however, was good and obedient. I had been told often that I was pretty. I made good grades and came from a good home. My parents, still married and drug-free, lived comfortably in a middle-class neighborhood. Martin, on the contrary, **Causes** came from a broken home. His parents hated each other. His father was a cold, heartless man, and his mother was a "flakey" drug addict. His uncles and cousins were all members of a very large gang that "controlled" an area where he lived. Soon he too was a gang member.

Martin quit school when he was a freshman and spent his days on a street corner drinking Olde English forty-ouncers. Soon I was joining him. I began ditching school to hang out. In no time I was a gang member myself, and as **Effects** I look back, I see what an awful person I became. We used drugs all day and all night. I didn't care about anything and neither did he. I left home and devastated my family and lost my friends. I didn't care because I had a new family and new friends. Martin spent his nights committing crimes and dealing drugs. I was by his side, carrying his gun. The drugs made him irritable and violent, and small disagreements turned into huge battles between us. Jail sentences made him angrier and closer to his gang. Each day Martin became farther from me. Life was a nonstop party with his homeboys, and I was his woman. It was exciting and risky. It was self-destructive.

Topic sentence My breaking point was one year ago. Martin and I were at a party. Everyone was drinking and joking. Oldies were playing and a noisy, wild game of poker was taking place. Suddenly a car was approaching us rapidly. Martin told me to run and hide, so I did. The homeboys began reaching for their guns. I heard five gunshots before the car drove away. I ran to the front of the house where Martin's cousin lay bleeding. I tried to wake him, speak to him. He wasn't responding. I screamed for an ambulance. Finally Martin appeared from behind a car and ran inside to call 911. When the ambulance arrived, I was hysterical and covered in blood. They took Martin's cousin to the hospital where he was pronounced dead. Because of the gunshot wounds, the funeral was a closed casket affair and very hard on everyone. It made Martin stronger, meaner, and colder, and it made me wiser. Martin was out committing crimes again, and two months later would be jailed again.

It is hard for me to imagine what I did to myself, knowing that any day I could have died senselessly. It is even harder for me to accept the fact that my boyfriend would die for a dirty, trashy street gang, but not for me.

Topic sentence **Effects** This last year I have been moving back to the right track. I have gotten sober, started college, and returned home. I have nightmares about things I have seen and things I have done. I struggle every day to stay sober, to do the right thing. I'm doing a lot of thinking. I live each day in fear for Martin's safety as well as my own. I fear for our future in a society that doesn't understand us. I count down the days until Martin can see the sunlight. I pray every day that this time will be the last time he goes to jail. I pray Martin will trade his gun for me, even get an education. I cry every night and try to live every day.

| Exercise 6 | **DISCUSSION AND CRITICAL THINKING** |

1. Why did McGraw become associated with Martin and finally become a gang member?

2. Were there deeper reasons for her dropping out of mainstream, middle-class society and joining a gang?

3. What were the effects on her life and those who were close to her?

4. What happened before the killing to set the stage for her change?

5. To what extent has she changed?

6. Why doesn't she leave Martin?

7. What is your reaction to the statement "I fear for our future in a society that doesn't understand us"?

| Exercise 7 | **WRITING A RESPONSE TO A READING** |

Read, underline, and annotate the following text and then complete one of the assignments below.

- *Write a summary.*

- *Write an outline.*

- *Write a reaction. Include enough summary to establish clear and logical connections between the text and your own ideas.*

- *Write a two-part response composed of a summary separated from a reaction.*

American Space, Chinese Place

Yi-Fu Tuan

What can you learn about people by studying the design of their homes? According to Yi-Fu Tuan, you can learn a great deal.

1   Americans have a sense of space, not of place. Go to an American home in exurbia, and almost the first thing you do is drift toward the picture window. How curious that the first compliment you pay your host inside his house is to say how lovely it is outside his house! He is pleased that you should admire his vistas. The distant horizon is not merely a line separating earth from sky, it is a symbol of the future. The American is not rooted in his place, however lovely: His eyes are drawn by the expanding space to a point on the horizon, which is his future.

2   By contrast, consider the traditional Chinese home. Blank walls enclose it. Step behind the spirit wall and you are in a courtyard with perhaps a miniature garden around the corner. Once inside the private compound you are wrapped in an ambiance of calm beauty, an ordered world of buildings, pavement, rock, and decorative vegetation. But you have no distant view: Nowhere does space open out before you. Raw nature in such a home is experienced only as weather, and the only open space is the sky above. The Chinese is rooted in his place. When he has to leave, it is not for the promised land on the terrestrial horizon, but for another world altogether along the vertical, religious axis of his imagination.

3   The Chinese tie to place is deeply felt. Wanderlust is an alien sentiment. The Taoist classic *Tao Te Ching* captures the idea of rootedness in place with these words: "Though there may be another country in the neighborhood so close that they are within sight of each other and the crowing of cocks and barking of dogs in one place can be heard in the other, yet there is no traffic between them; and throughout their lives the two peoples have nothing to do with each other." In theory if not in practice, farmers have ranked high in Chinese society. The reason is not only that they are engaged in the "root" industry of producing food but that, unlike pecuniary merchants, they are tied to the land and do not abandon their country when it is in danger.

4   Nostalgia is a recurrent theme in Chinese poetry. An American reader of translated Chinese poems may well be taken aback—even put off—by the frequency, as well as the sentimentality of the lament for home. To understand the strength of this sentiment, we need to know that the Chinese desire for stability and rootedness in place is prompted by the constant threat of war, exile, and the natural disasters of flood and drought. Forcible removal makes the Chinese keenly aware of their loss. By contrast, Americans move, for the most part, voluntarily. Their nostalgia for home town is really longing for childhood to which they cannot return: In the meantime the future beckons and the future is "out there," in open space. When we criticize American rootlessness we tend to forget that it is a result of ideals we admire, namely, social mobility and optimism about the future. When we admire Chinese rootedness, we forget the word "place" means both location in space and position in society: To be tied to place is also to be bound to one's station in life, with little hope of betterment. Space symbolizes hope; place, achievement and stability.

Exercise 8   **DISCUSSION AND CRITICAL THINKING**

1. According to the author, if you visit a traditional American home, what will your host invite you to enjoy? Why?

2. On the contrary, if you visit a Chinese home, what will your host invite you to enjoy? Why?

3. Why do the Chinese admire their farmers?

4. In the same vein, what station in life do Americans admire?

5. What are the different views, good and bad, held by Chinese and Americans on moving?

6. What is positive and negative in both the American and Chinese views?

Journal Writing

Your journal entries are likely to be concerned primarily with the relationship between the reading material and you—your life experiences, your views, your imagination. The reading material will give you something of substance to write about, but you will be writing especially for yourself, developing confidence and ease in writing, so that writing becomes a comfortable part of your everyday activities, as speaking already is.

These journal entries will be part of your intellectual diary, recording what you are thinking about a certain issue. They will be of use in helping you understand the reading material, in helping you develop your writing skills, in uncovering ideas that can be used on other assignments, and in helping you think more clearly and imaginatively. Because these entries are of a more spontaneous nature than the more structured writing assignments, organization and editing are likely to be of less concern.

Each journal entry should be clearly dated and, if reading related, should specify the title and author of the original piece.

Even if your instructor wants you to concentrate on what you read for your journal writing, he or she might not want you to be restricted to the material in this text. Fortunately, you are surrounded by reading material in newspapers, magazines, and, of course, textbooks from other courses. These topics can serve you well.

Writer's Guidelines: Writing About Reading Selections

1. **Underlining** will help you to prepare for review and to concentrate when reading.
   a. Underline the main idea in paragraphs.
   b. Underline the support for those main ideas.

    c. Underline answers to questions.

    d. Underline only key words; almost never underline entire sentences.

2. **Annotating** along with underlining will make you an engaged, active reader.

3. **Outlining** reading selections will show main and supporting ideas.

4. **Summarizing** will help you concentrate on main ideas; this is helpful in both reading and writing. (See page 257 for specific rules.)

5. Reading-related writing can take two forms in addition to the summary:

    a. The reaction is usually a statement of how the reading relates specifically to you, your experiences, and your attitudes, but it is also often a critique, involving the worth and logic of a piece.

    b. A two-part response includes both a summary and a reaction but separates them.

6. **Journal writing** offers frequent practice in writing, especially about what you read.

16

Narration: Moving Through Time

"*C*ertain pivotal moments are as indelible on our memories as dark ink on white linen. Against these key experiences we measure the more ordinary ones and chart our progress or lack of it toward where we are today."

—"Growing Pains and Pleasures"

Writing Narrative Paragraphs

In our everyday lives, we tell stories and invite other people to do so by asking questions such as "What happened at work today?" and "What did you do last weekend?" We are disappointed when the answer is "Nothing much." We may be equally disappointed when a person doesn't give us enough details or gives us too many and spoils the effect. After all, we are interested in people's stories and in the people who tell them. We like narratives.

What is a narrative? A **narrative** is an account of an incident or a series of incidents that make up a complete and significant action. A narrative can be as short as a joke, as long as a novel, or anything between, including a single paragraph. Each narrative has five properties: situation, conflict, struggle, outcome, and meaning.

The following narrative pattern is based on a scene in Mark Twain's *The Adventures of Tom Sawyer.*

Situation

Situation is the background for the action. The situation may be described only briefly, or it may even be implied. ("Tom Sawyer, a youngster living in a small town, has been directed by his Aunt Polly to whitewash the fence in front of their house.")

Conflict

Conflict is friction, such as a problem in the surroundings, with another person(s), or within the individual. The conflict, which is at the heart of each story, produces struggle. ("A fun-loving boy who would rather go fishing than do simple, manual chores, Tom wants to find others to do his work for him. He knows that others would not want to paint the fence, so he must persuade them.")

Struggle

Struggle, which need not be physical, is the manner of dealing with the conflict. The struggle adds action or engagement and generates the plot. ("Hearing Ben Rogers nearby making huffing steamboat sounds and enjoying play, Tom pretends he is a serious artist as he brushes the sparkling white paint onto the dark fence before standing back to admire it. When Ben starts to tease Tom about having to work, Tom says, 'What do you call work?' 'Why, ain't that work?' Ben asks. Tom says it suits him and few boys could do it. Soon Tom has Ben asking if he can paint the fence and offering an apple for the privilege. Tom relents. Other friends drop by and fall for the same scheme.")

Outcome

Outcome is the result of the struggle. ("In a short time the fence has three coats of paint, and Tom has a collection of treasures, including a dead rat and a one-eyed cat.")

Meaning

Meaning is the significance of the story, which may be deeply philosophical or simple, stated or implied. ("Tom has discovered that to make a person want something it is only necessary to make that something seem difficult to obtain.")

Techniques

The properties of a narrative, which are present in some way in all the many forms of the narrative, are enhanced by the use of various techniques.

- *Description* (the use of specific details to advance action, with images to make readers see, smell, taste, hear, and feel)

  "*huffing* steamboat sounds"

  "*sparkling white paint* onto the *dark fence*"

- *Dialogue* (the exact words of the speakers, enclosed in quotation marks)

  Tom says, "*What do you call work?*"

  "*Why, ain't that work?*" Ben asks.

- *Transitional words* (words, such as *after, finally, following, later, next, soon, then,* and *when,* that move a story forward, for narratives are usually presented in chronological order)

  "*When* Ben starts"

  "*Soon* Tom has Ben asking"

  "*Then* other friends"

• *Consistent tense* (using the same time frame as indicated by verb choice)
Most narratives are related in the past tense:

I *saw* the twister.

I *ran* for the storm cellar.

I *locked* the door behind me.

However, a present tense accounting can project a keen sense of immediacy:

I *see* the twister.

I *run* for the storm cellar.

I *lock* the door behind me.

Be consistent with the past or present tense for your overall narrative pattern.

Purpose and Time Frame

Most narratives written as college assignments will have an expository purpose; that is, they explain a specified idea. Consider working with a short time frame for short writing assignments. The scope would usually be no more than one incident of brief duration for one paragraph. For example, writing about an entire graduation ceremony might be too complicated, but concentrating on the moment when you walked forward to receive the diploma or the moment when the relatives and friends come down on the field could work very well.

Connecting Reading and Writing: Growing Pains and Pleasures

THE QUIGMANS   by Buddy Hickerson

"You kids have it made. When I was your age we didn't have enough money for a bed of nails. We had to make do with whatever we could find. Thumbtacks, staples, clothespins, velcro, crackers... I remember one long winter I had to kiss up to a man with a hangnail."

B. Hickerson, copyright Los Angeles Times Syndicate. Reprinted by permission.

Even under the best of conditions, growing up is not a smooth progression. It is actually a hobbling and sprinting back and forth with some jogging to the sides and, usually, movement forward and up.

Because of the unevenness of this journey, we can all reflect on particular experiences during which we have relocated ourselves in a personal sense as if we were dealing with geography: have reached a plateau, climbed a mountain, fallen into a canyon, been stranded on an island, been lost in a desert, stumbled into paradise. These experiences may be events—special occasions, holidays, ceremonies, celebrations, graduations, special recognition. They may be traumatic events—accidents, injuries, illnesses, deaths, betrayals, escapes, entrapments. They may be struggles—for recognition, acceptance, self-identity, respect. They may involve relationships—love (in its many forms), changes in family make-up, establishing and reestablishing friendships as a result of moving or changing. They may be seemingly small acts of kindness, insults to the spirit, tokens of love.

Whatever they are, they are key experiences, as indelible on our memories as dark ink on white linen. Against these key experiences we measure the more ordinary ones and chart our progress or lack of it toward where we are today. We don't bury these experiences; from time to time they pop up on our mind screens like CD-ROM images as reminders of who we are and how we got that way. If we made time lines for our lives, these experiences would be the listed items, on a personal scale equal to the great wars, developments, discoveries, creations, and inventions of world history. They will always be with us for pain or pleasure.

Like life itself, this section is full of variety. Student Charles C. Ortiz walks the fine line between life and death, discovers fear, and learns that he and his fellow police officers are vulnerable. Maxine Hong Kingston recalls the time she stood alone in a classroom, balancing the weight of two cultures on her frail shoulders. In "Liked for Myself," Maya Angelou is rescued from muteness by a loving grandmother and a neighbor.

We begin with a humorous paragraph by student writer Joel Bailey, who gives an account of his clumsiness as a worker in a fast-food establishment. First Bailey completed the Writing Process Worksheet, which shows how he moved from understanding his assignment to exploratory prewriting to writing his paper. The worksheet is followed by his final draft. His two rough drafts are not shown.

You will find a full-size blank worksheet on page 6. It can be photocopied, filled in, and submitted with each assignment if your instructor directs you to do so.

Writing Process Worksheet

TITLE King of Klutziness

NAME Joel Bailey   **DUE DATE** Monday, September 6, 9 a.m.

ASSIGNMENT   In the space below, write whatever you need to know about your assignment, including information about the topic, audience, pattern of writing, length, whether to include a rough draft or revised drafts, and whether your paper must be typed.

Write a one-page narrative about a work-related incident that was a learning experience and made a deep impression. Submit this sheet and a rough draft marked for revision with the final draft. Type the final draft. Audience: other students and instructor.

STAGE ONE

Explore   Freewrite, brainstorm (list), cluster, or take notes as directed by your instructor. Use the back of this page or separate paper if you need more space.

List

—first day at work
—Carl's Jr., Hollywood
—no training
—easy at first
—things change
—busy
—really busy

—celebrity customer
—take order
—make mistake
—he's angry
—I spill Coke
—smear catsup

—he's really angry
—funnier now
    than then
—be cool the
    next time

STAGE TWO

Organize   Write a topic sentence or thesis; label the subject and the treatment parts.

<u>My first day at work</u> <u>was a truly memorable experience for me and my</u>
            subject   treatment
<u>unfortunate customer</u>.

Write an outline or an outline alternative.

  I. Situation
     A. Carl's Jr.
     B. My first day at work
 II. Conflict
     A. No training
     B. Too many customers
     C. Make mistake with celebrity customer
III. Struggle
     A. Mistake follows mistake
     B. Attempted correction becomes mistake
     C. Customer really angry
 IV. Outcome
     A. Customer upset
     B. His clothing soiled
     C. Embarrassment for me
  V. Meaning
     A. A learning experience
     B. Incident funnier now than then

STAGE THREE

Write   On separate paper, write and then revise your paper as many times as necessary for <u>c</u>oherence, <u>l</u>anguage (usage, tone, and diction), <u>u</u>nity, <u>e</u>mphasis, <u>s</u>upport, and <u>s</u>entences (CLUESS). Read your paper aloud to hear and correct any grammatical errors or awkward-sounding sentences.

Edit any problems in fundamentals, such as <u>c</u>apitalization, <u>o</u>missions, <u>p</u>unctuation, and <u>s</u>pelling (COPS).

King of Klutziness

Joel Bailey

Now a competent employee in a computer store, Joel Bailey remembers an incident from his first job. It began with apprehension, turned to excitement as a celebrity appeared, and ended in chaos.

Topic sentence

Situation

Conflict

Struggle

Outcome

Meaning

It was my first task of what would be a memorable day at work in Carl's Jr., a fast-food place by Universal Studio near Hollywood. I was assigned to the front counter because another worker was late. There I was at noon, the busiest time of the day, with no training, scared, and nervous. In the beginning, things went well. Orders were routine, and I filled them and made change. As time passed, the lines got short, and I was still doing great because, after all, the job didn't require the mentality of a rocket scientist. Several counter people left their registers to help out in back. Then a lot of people came in at one time. Only two of us were taking orders. I was nervous. I served three persons, hardly looking up as I punched the keys, called out orders, and made change. After barely glancing at the next person, I heard *his* voice ordering, a familiar voice. It was Alex Benson, a reporter for a TV channel I frequently watched. I repeated his order so it would be perfect, and I took his money. After I gave him his change, he stared at the receipt and said with more than a touch of irritation, "You made a mistake. You charged me for two chicken burgers." I apologized and gave him a refund. "What about the tax," he growled. "You didn't refund the tax." I was really getting nervous. He always laughed and smiled on TV. I gave him the tax money. I grabbed someone else's chicken order just so I could give him quick service, but when I handed him the tray, my hand slipped and I spilled his Coke on his trousers. Quickly I grabbed a napkin and ran around the counter and wiped at the Coke stain. Unfortunately the napkin I grabbed had catsup on it. Now I had added a condiment to the Coke stain. By that time I might as well have salted and peppered him. Beyond anger, and looking at me wildly, he fled with his tray to a distant booth and sat with his back to the wall. I decided not to ask for an autograph.

| **Exercise 1** | **DISCUSSION AND CRITICAL THINKING** |

1. Is Bailey really klutzy or is this just first-day jitters?

2. Is Bailey's problem with understanding the restaurant's procedures or with executing the procedures?

3. Was this a funny situation at the time?

4. How does the conflict differ from the struggle?

Not Invulnerable

Charles C. Ortiz

College student and cadet police officer Charles C. Ortiz entered law enforcement with unwarranted confidence and a feeling of invulnerability. Then one calm summer night only an hour into a routine patrol, eight gunshots put him more in touch with reality.

I had always considered myself invulnerable when I was riding in a police unit. I was a knight, a Rambo, a centurion. I was sure that there was nothing I couldn't handle. I had been with the sheriff's department for almost three years, and I was certain that I was ready for anything. Who would have guessed that that mentality would almost cost me my life?

On January 16, I was assigned to work 55 Frank, which was a South El Monte crime unit. Because it was my first time working this car, I felt nervous, but at the same time I was also excited. Strangely, although this wasn't my first time on patrol, I still felt somewhat apprehensive. I was sure this night was different, yet I didn't know why.

Our shift started out pretty slowly. All we did for the first three hours was write out traffic citations. Once the traffic began to diminish, we proceeded with our routine patrol checks of the homes and businesses in our area. On a check of Santa Anita Avenue, a man began to flag us down. As we approached him, I noticed he was staggering and yelling at the top of his lungs. He insisted that we take him to jail. Once I had explained his options, he agreed to be taken to our station to begin his sobering-up process. I cuffed him and put him in the back of the unit. This was routine stuff.

But as we headed toward the station, a distress call came over the radio: "Attention, all units in the vicinity of South El Monte. 55 Adam is requesting backup. He has five at gunpoint. All units responding go Code 3!" Because we were a minute away, we responded. As we took off, my adrenaline started to rise, causing me to feel anxious. Upon arriving at the scene, I grabbed the shotgun, got out of the car, and pointed the shotgun toward the vehicle in question. The first suspect was called out. As he emerged in front of us, he reached into his waistband, pulled out a gun, and pointed it in my direction. In a moment, he fired two shots at me. I hit the ground. At the same time a fear of dying took over my body. I didn't know if I was hit, if I was dying, or what. I was in a state of shock.

After I discovered that the shots had missed me and the situation was under control, I rose somewhat slowly. I looked toward the suspect and saw him lying dead in a pool of blood. He had been shot six times by the deputies at the scene. The other four suspects were arrested for grand theft auto. Even though the incident was secured, I was able to see what "real" fear was. I understood that policing is not a game; it is life-and-death reality. Walking in a cop's shoes is not something that everyone can handle.

Facing my most horrible fear has truly shown me how important my life is. It's not something to be taken for granted. I also now know personally what deputies face when they encounter someone who is armed and possibly dangerous. I have found a new sense of respect for all police officers, for I have now experienced law enforcement from their view. Furthermore, I feel a lot older and a lot wiser now. Going into the streets thinking "I'm invulnerable" is the wrong kind of attitude.

Exercise 2	DISCUSSION AND CRITICAL THINKING

1. What conflicting ideas does the author present in the first two paragraphs that attract reader interest and create suspense?

2. Dramatically what is the effect of the minor conflict in the third paragraph?

3. How does Ortiz's attitude about police work change?

4. To which other parts of the essay does the last line relate?

5. Use annotation to mark the thesis, situation, conflict, struggle, outcome, and meaning in this essay.

Voice Like Twigs Underfoot

Maxine Hong Kingston

Now a celebrated writer, Maxine Hong Kingston was once so deficient in English speech that she flunked kindergarten. In this passage taken from her book *The Woman Warrior: Memoirs of a Childhood Among Ghosts*, she tells about one of her early experiences as a frightened girl caught between two cultures.

Not all of the children who were silent at American school found voice at Chinese school. One new teacher said each of us had to get up and recite in front of the class, who was to listen. My sister and I had memorized the lesson perfectly. We said it to each other at home, one chanting, one listening. The teacher called on my sister to recite first. It was the first time a teacher had called on the second-born to go first. My sister was scared. She glanced at me and looked away; I looked down at my desk. I hoped that she could do it because if she could, then I would have to. She opened her mouth and a voice came out that wasn't a whisper, but it wasn't a proper voice either. I hoped that she would not cry, fear breaking up her voice like twigs underfoot. She sounded as if she were trying to sing through weeping and strangling. She did not pause to stop to end the embarrassment. She kept going until she said the last word, and then she sat down. When it was my turn, the same voice came out, a crippled animal running on broken legs. You could hear splinters in my voice, bones rubbing jagged against one another. I was loud, though. I was glad I didn't whisper.

Exercise 3	DISCUSSION AND CRITICAL THINKING

In your own words, identify the parts of Kingston's narrative.

1. Situation: _____

   _____

2. Conflict: _____

   _____

3. Struggle: _____

   _____

4. Outcome: _____

   _____

5. Meaning: _____

   _____

Liked for Myself

Maya Angelou

As a child, Maya Angelou (Marguerite), author of the autobiographical book *I Know Why the Caged Bird Sings*, was raped by a friend of her mother. In this excerpt she has only recently come to live in her grandmother's home in rural Arkansas. There, psychologically wounded by her experience, she does not speak. She is desperate for self-confidence. She needs to be liked for the person she is.

1   For nearly a year, I sopped around the house, the Store, the school, and the church, like an old biscuit, dirty and inedible. Then I met, or rather got to know, the lady who threw me my first life line.

2   Mrs. Bertha Flowers was the aristocrat of Black Stamps. She had the grace of control to appear warm in the coldest weather, and on the Arkansas summer days it seemed she had a private breeze which swirled around, cooling her. She was thin without the taut look of wiry people, and her printed voile dresses and flowered hats were as right for her as denim overalls for a farmer. She was our side's answer to the richest white woman in town.

3   Her skin was a rich black that would have peeled like a plum if snagged, but then no one would have thought of getting close enough to Mrs. Flowers to ruffle her dress, let alone snag her skin. She didn't encourage familiarity. She wore gloves too.

4   I don't think I ever saw Mrs. Flowers laugh, but she smiled often. A slow widening of her thin black lips to show even, small white teeth, then the slow effortless closing. When she chose to smile on me, I always wanted to thank her. The action was so graceful and inclusively benign.

5   She was one of the few gentlewomen I have ever known, and has remained throughout my life the measure of what a human being can be. . . .

6   One summer afternoon, sweet-milk fresh in my memory, she stopped at the Store to buy provisions. Another Negro woman of her health and age would have been expected to carry the paper sacks home in one hand, but Momma said, "Sister Flowers, I'll send Bailey up to your house with these things."

7   She smiled that slow dragging smile, "Thank you, Mrs. Henderson. I'd prefer Marguerite, though." My name was beautiful when she said it. "I've been meaning to talk to her, anyway." They gave each other age-group looks. . . .

8   There was a little path beside the rocky road, and Mrs. Flowers walked in front swinging her arms and picking her way over the stones.

9   She said, without turning her head, to me, "I hear you're doing very good school work, Marguerite, but that it's all written. The teachers report that they have trouble getting you to talk in class." We passed the triangular farm on our left and the path widened to allow us to walk together. I hung back in the separate unasked and unanswerable questions.

10   "Come and walk along with me, Marguerite." I couldn't have refused even if I wanted to. She pronounced my name so nicely. Or more correctly, she spoke each word with such clarity that I was certain a foreigner who didn't understand English could have understood her.

11   "Now no one is going to make you talk—possibly no one can. But bear in mind, language is man's way of communicating with his fellow man and it is language alone which separates him from the lower animals." That was a totally new idea to me, and I would need time to think about it.

12   "Your grandmother says you read a lot. Every chance you get. That's good, but not good enough. Words mean more than what is set down on paper. It takes the human voice to infuse them with the shades of deeper meaning."

13   I memorized the part about the human voice infusing words. It seemed so valid and poetic.

14   She said she was going to give me some books and that I not only must read them, I must read them aloud. She suggested that I try to make a sentence sound in as many different ways as possible.

15   "I'll accept no excuse if you return a book to me that has been badly handled." My imagination boggled at the punishment I would deserve if in fact I did abuse a book of Mrs. Flowers'. Death would be too kind and brief.

16   The odors in the house surprised me. Somehow I had never connected Mrs. Flowers with food or eating or any other common experience of common people. There must have been an outhouse, too, but my mind never recorded it.

17   The sweet scent of vanilla had met us as she opened the door.

18   "I made tea cookies this morning. You see, I had planned to invite you for cookies and lemonade so we could have this little chat. The lemonade is in the icebox."

19   It followed that Mrs. Flowers would have ice on an ordinary day, when most families in our town bought ice late on Saturdays only a few times during the summer to be used in the wooden ice-cream freezers.

20   She took the bags from me and disappeared through the kitchen door. I looked around the room that I had never in my wildest fantasies imagined I

would see. Browned photographs leered or threatened from the walls and the white, freshly done curtains pushed against themselves and against the wind. I wanted to gobble up the room entire and take it to Bailey, who would help me analyze and enjoy it.

21   "Have a seat, Marguerite. Over there by the table." She carried a platter covered with a tea towel. Although she warned that she hadn't tried her hand at baking sweets for some time, I was certain that like everything else about her the cookies would be perfect.

22   They were flat round wafers, slightly browned on the edges and butter-yellow in the center. With the cold lemonade they were sufficient for childhood's lifelong diet. Remembering my manners, I took nice little lady-like bites off the edges. She said she had made them expressly for me and that she had a few in the kitchen that I could take home to my brother. So I jammed one whole cake in my mouth and the rough crumbs scratched the insides of my jaws, and if I hadn't had to swallow, it would have been a dream come true.

23   As I ate she began the first of what we later called "my lessons in living." She said that I must always be intolerant of ignorance but understanding of illiteracy. That some people, unable to go to school, were more educated and even more intelligent than college professors. She encouraged me to listen carefully to what country people called mother wit. That in those homely sayings was couched the collective wisdom of generations.

24   When I finished the cookies she brushed off the table and brought a thick, small book from the bookcase. I had read *A Tale of Two Cities* and found it up to my standards as a romantic novel. She opened the first page and I heard poetry for the first time in my life.

25   "It was the best of times and the worst of times. . . ." Her voice slid in and curved down through and over the words. She was nearly singing. I wanted to look at the pages. Were they the same that I had read? Or were there notes, music, lined on the pages, as in a hymn book? Her sounds began cascading gently. I knew from listening to a thousand preachers that she was nearing the end of her reading, and I hadn't really heard, heard to understand, a single word.

26   "How do you like that?"

27   It occurred to me that she expected a response. The sweet vanilla flavor was still on my tongue and her reading was a wonder in my ears. I had to speak.

28   I said, "Yes, ma'am." It was the least I could do, but it was the most also.

29   "There's one more thing. Take this book of poems and memorize one for me. Next time you pay me a visit, I want you to recite."

30   I have tried often to search behind the sophistication of years for the enchantment I so easily found in those gifts. The essence escapes but its aura remains. To be allowed, no, invited, into the private lives of strangers, and to share their joys and fears, was a chance to exchange the Southern bitter wormwood for a cup of mead with Beowulf or a hot cup of tea and milk with Oliver Twist. When I said aloud, "It is a far, far better thing that I do, than I have ever done . . ." tears of love filled my eyes at my selfishness.

31   On that first day, I ran down the hill and into the road (few cars ever came along it) and had the good sense to stop running before I reached the Store.

32   I was liked, and what a difference it made. I was respected not as Mrs. Henderson's grandchild or Bailey's sister but for just being Marguerite Johnson.

33   Childhood's logic never asks to be proved (all conclusions are absolute). I didn't question why Mrs. Flowers had singled me out for attention, nor did it occur to me that Momma might have asked her to give me a little talking to. All I cared about was that she had made tea cookies for *me* and read to *me* from her favorite book. It was enough to prove that she liked me.

Exercise 4	VOCABULARY HIGHLIGHTS

Write a short definition of each word as it is used in the essay. (Paragraph numbers are given in parentheses.) Be prepared to use the words in your own sentences.

taut (2)	leered (20)
voile (2)	cascading (25)
benign (4)	sophistication (30)
infuse (12)	essence (30)
valid (13)	aura (30)

Exercise 5	DISCUSSION AND CRITICAL THINKING

1. The narrator refers to Mrs. Bertha Flowers as an aristocrat and the blacks' "answer to the richest white woman in town" (part of the situation). In what ways does she deserve that characterization? Is she rich?

2. What techniques (part of the struggle) does Mrs. Flowers use to encourage Marguerite to speak?

3. What does Mrs. Flowers mean by the word *educated?*

4. What does the narrator mean by "childhood's logic" (paragraph 33)?

5. What are "lessons in living" (paragraph 23)? In what way can this episode be called such a lesson?

6. Which one of the five parts of the narrative pattern—situation, conflict, struggle, outcome, meaning—is the lesson of this episode?

Practicing Narrative Patterns

All of the reading selections in this chapter include the five components of narrative: situation, conflict, struggle, outcome, and meaning. When you have a narrative account in mind, you will naturally work within the framework of those five components. When you start to write that narrative, if you are not careful, you may not transfer all parts of what is on your mind to your paper. One good way to prevent that omission is to work with an outline of a complete narrative pattern. The following two sketchy outline activities will give you practice in a procedure you can apply to your writing assignments.

Exercise 6	COMPLETING NARRATIVE PATTERNS

Fill in the blanks to complete each narrative pattern.

1. Lost and Found

   (situation)   I. Person taking store money deposit bag to bank

   (conflict)   II. Person loses bag

   (struggle)   III. _____

   (outcome)   IV. _____

   (meaning)   V. _____

2. Good Samaritan

   (situation)   I. Driver with flat tire, dead of night

   (conflict)   II. No spare tire

   (struggle)   III. _____

   (outcome)   IV. _____

   (meaning)   V. _____

✎ **Topics for Writing Narrative**

Reading-Related Topics

1. Trace the idea of confidence in two or more of the reading selections. Show how confidence or lack of confidence is at the heart of each narrative.

2. Discuss how the unfolding of personal growth occurs in "Not Invulnerable" and "Liked for Myself."

"King of Klutziness"

3. Write a narrative about learning how to do something specific on the job. In what way(s) did you or someone else perform badly, perhaps ridiculously? Many of these events occur on the first day of employment.

"Not Invulnerable"

4. Write a narrative about a time when you or someone you know did something that was dangerous but, through ignorance or preoccupation, approached the

event with little or no fear. Consider a rescue or an incident at school, at work, or during recreation.

"Voice Like Twigs Underfoot"

5. Write a narrative about something you had to struggle to do, like make a presentation or talk to someone you admired, held in high esteem, or were afraid of.

"Liked for Myself"

6. Write about someone in your neighborhood (or in your household) who in his or her own way can be called an "aristocrat"—someone who has true class.

7. Write a paragraph or an essay that defines the term *aristocrat* as the narrator does. Consider these aspects: how the person looks, how the person acts, what the person says, and how others react to the person. You may use Mrs. Flowers as an example or you can write about someone you know, someone you have read about, or someone you have discovered through the media.

8. Write a detailed account of how someone helped you at a time when your self-esteem was low.

9. Assume the role of either the grandmother or Mrs. Flowers and give a report of the progress of your relationship with Marguerite.

10. If you have helped or are now helping someone through a time of hardship, write an account of your involvement and the results.

11. Analyze this narrative account by discussing the factors (such as the narrator's readiness and need, and Mrs. Flowers's compassion and understanding) that made the narrator's change possible.

Career-Related Topics

12. Write a narrative about a work-related encounter between a manager and a worker, and briefly explain the significance of the event.

13. Write a narrative about an encounter between a customer and a salesperson. Explain what went right and wrong.

14. Write a narrative about how a person solved a work-related problem.

15. Write a narrative about a salesperson's dealing with a customer's complaint. Critique the procedure.

16. Write a narrative account of a problem you encountered while using your computer for word processing or Internet functions at school or work. You might write about learning to use a software product, obtaining technical support, finding information, shopping online, responding to directions on a particular Web site, or relating to an individual or individuals in a chat room or other special group situation. A unifying theme such as frustration, irritation, elation, anxiety, or satisfaction may be useful here. Your steps will take you through the conventional narrative form as you discuss the situation, conflict, struggle, outcome, and meaning.

General Topics

17. Write a narrative about a personal experience that you might characterize as the most amusing, sad, terrifying, satisfying, stupid, rewarding, self-centered, generous, stingy, loving, thoughtful, cruel, regrettable, educational, corrupting, sinful, virtuous, or disgusting thing you have done or witnessed. Keep in mind that you are writing about a single event or a portion of that event.

18. Write a narrative about the first time you did something, such as the first time you dated, kissed romantically, spoke formally in public, entered a new school, worked for pay, drove an automobile, rode a bicycle or motorcycle, danced, received a traffic citation, met a celebrity, or played a game.

Writer's Guidelines: Narration

1. Include each of the following properties to be sure you have a complete narrative.

   • Situation (at beginning)

   • Conflict

   • Struggle

   • Outcome

   • Meaning

2. Consider these techniques:

   • *Images* (sight, sound, smell, taste, touch) and other details to enhance description and advance action

   • *Dialogue* (revealing conversation)

   • *Transitional words* (such as *after, finally, following, later, next, soon, when*) to indicate chronological order

   • *Consistent tense* (using a pattern of mostly past tense—*saw, ran, locked*—or mostly present tense verbs—*see, run, lock*)

3. Most narratives written as college assignments have an expository purpose; that is, they explain a specified idea.

4. Usually work with a short time frame for brief writing assignments.

17

Description: Moving Through Space and Time

"These descriptive accounts of possessions will remind you of your own loves and loathings of the inanimate objects to which you perhaps attach much more meaning than they warrant."

—"Prized and Despised Possessions"

Writing Descriptive Paragraphs

Description is the use of words to represent the appearance or nature of something. Often called a word picture, description attempts to present its subject for the mind's eye. In doing so, it does not merely become an indifferent camera; instead, it selects details that will depict something well. Just what details the descriptive writer selects will depend on several factors, especially the type of description and the dominant impression in the passage.

Types of Description

On the basis of treatment of subject material, description is customarily divided into two types: objective and subjective.

Effective objective description presents the subject clearly and directly as it exists outside the realm of feelings. If you are explaining the function of the heart, the characteristics of a computer chip, or the renovation of a manufacturing facility, your description would probably feature specific, impersonal details. Most technical and scientific writing is objective in that sense. It is likely to be practical and utilitarian, making little use of speculation and poetic technique while focusing on details of the physical senses.

Effective subjective description is also concerned with clarity and it may be direct, but it conveys a feeling about the subject and sets a mood while making a point. Because this expression involves personal views, subjective description (often called emotional description) has a broader range of uses than objective description.

Descriptive passages can have a combination of objective and subjective description; only the larger context of the passage will reveal the main intent.

Imagery

To convey your main concern effectively to readers, you will have to give some sensory impressions. These sensory impressions, collectively called *imagery,* refer to that which can be experienced by the senses—what we can see, smell, taste, hear, and touch.

Subjective description is more likely to use images and words rich in associations than is objective description. But just as a fine line cannot always be drawn between the objective and the subjective, a fine line cannot always be drawn between word choice in one and in the other. However, we can say with certainty that whatever the type of description, careful word choice will always be important. Consider the following points about precise diction.

General and Specific Words and Abstract and Concrete Words

To move from the general to the specific is to move from the whole class or body to the individual(s); for example:

General	Specific	More Specific
food	pastry	Twinkie
mess	dirty floor	muddy footprints
drink	soda	Coke
odor	garden smell	fragrance of roses

Words are classified as abstract or concrete depending on what they refer to. *Abstract words* refer to qualities or ideas: *good, ordinary, ultimate, truth, beauty, maturity, love.* *Concrete words* refer to substances or things; they have reality: *onions, grease, buns, tables, food.* The specific concrete words, sometimes called *concrete particulars,* often support generalizations effectively and convince the reader of the accuracy of the account.

Dominant Impression

Never try to give all of the details in description; instead, be selective, picking only those that you need to make a dominant impression, always taking into account the knowledge and attitudes of your readers. Remember, description is not photographic. If you wish to describe a person, select only those traits that will project your dominant impression. If you wish to describe a landscape, do not give all the details that you might find in a picture; just pick the details that support what you want to say. That extremely important dominant impression is directly linked to your purpose and is created by choosing and arranging images, figurative language, and details.

Order: Time and Space

All of these items must have some order. Time and space are the main controlling factors in most description.

If you were describing something that was not changing, such as a room, you would be concerned with space and give directions to the reader such as

next to, below, under, above, behind, in front of, beyond, in the foreground, in the background, to the left, to the right.

If you were describing something that was changing, such as a butterfly going through metamorphosis, you would be concerned mainly with time and use transitional words such as

first, second, then, soon, finally, while, after, next, later, now, before.

If you were walking through an area—so that the setting was changing—you would use both time and space for order.

Consider giving your description a sense of movement or a narrative framework. Include some action if it fits your purpose. In the following descriptive tour from the novel *Spree*, J. N. Williamson, the celebrated author of suspense, leads you effortlessly through time and space. As a reader you identify with an imaginary troubled teen being ingested by a total institution. You shuffle along, you see, you fear.

Time: initial observation

Space: exterior

It was a juvenile detention center in a metropolitan city, and neither the center nor the city was different enough from others of its kind to be worth specifying. The apprehensive glance that arriving teenagers got of the building's exterior showed them for the most part little more than a bigger, more institutional version of their own drab homes; it tended to be only the brighter, imaginative boys and girls who noticed the steel mesh on the windows. For some of them, the concrete indication of captivity was just a materialized rendition of what they had known all their lives.

Time: then or next

Space: inside

Inside the juvenile center, beyond the main hall that struck some visitors as looking like the lobby and check-in desk of some cheap hotel in a 1940s private-eye film, was a network of seemingly countless short hallways. Each one appeared to lead somewhere important, but most of them merely led to tiny offices that looked exactly alike, or to other crossing hallways. . . .

Time: finally or at last

Space: inside and back

The principal reason why most of the newcomers wound up feeling ample apprehension was because of the bolted-door cell area, cosmetically constructed at the back of the building on the long, ill-lit second floor. It was one thing to talk tough on the streets, something else to see the doors locking behind you—and to accept the fact, at last, that you wouldn't be departing the center until time prescribed by the first-floor juvenile court finally passed.

Useful Procedure for Writing Description

What is your subject? (a college stadium)

What is the dominant impression? (deserted)

What is the situation? (You are walking through the stands an hour after a game.)

What is the order? (time and place)

What details support the dominant impression?

1. (the sight of vacant seats and an abandoned playing field)

2. (intermingled smell of stale food and spilled beer)

3. (sight of napkins, paper plates and cups, programs, and peanut shells blowing in a fierce wind)

4. (raspy sound of the wind blowing paper products and whining through the steel girders)

5. (instead of the roaring crowd, the sound of echoing footsteps)

6. (the tacky feel and popping sound of sneakers as they stick to and pull free from cement coated with spilled soft drinks)

Clustering may be useful (see Janice Hill's paragraph in the next section).

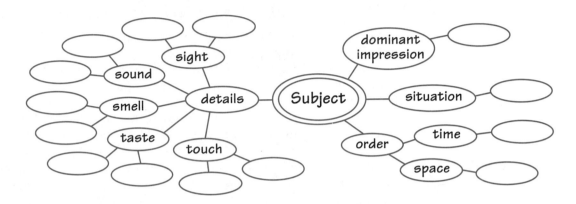

Connecting Reading and Writing: Prized and Despised Possessions

We all own things we couldn't do without, maybe things we expect to be buried with. Some of our loved ones might like to bury the things first—it sometimes happens. Of course, there are the things that we'd like to get rid of, but we can't.

THE QUIGMANS   by **Buddy Hickerson**

Sasha's love affair with health food and cleanliness became a reckless obsession when she began guzzling wheat germ shampoo.

B. Hickerson, copyright Los Angeles Times Syndicate. Reprinted by permission.

This section features these prized and despised possessions. Maria Varela owned something worse than a car that was a lemon; hers was a banana. Gary Soto's object was a jacket. It was the primary item of clothing in his most formative years. He holds the wretched garment responsible for his major discomfort and failures. Having hoped for a studly motorcycle jacket, he instead received a vinyl jacket the color of "day-old guacamole." His account is one of how he outlasted that coat. N. Scott Momaday describes the Plains Indian shield, an item central to the life of its owner. In fact, the shield and its owner were indistinguishable, each defining the other.

These descriptive accounts of possessions will remind you of your own loves and loathings of the inanimate objects to which you perhaps attach much more meaning than they warrant.

A well-loved possession might be an old pair of blue jeans, a sweater, a stuffed toy, a tattered book, a piece of jewelry, a pocket knife, a pair of shoes, a picture album, a record, a thimble, a coin, or a piece of sports equipment. You may turn to them in times of stress as talismans the same way that some people who are having trouble will eat "comfort" foods related to the happier, simpler times of childhood.

Other objects may inspire hatred, and they may be identical to the items above. In fact, any item can move from the loved to hated category. A hated item might be a tool (associated with the chores you disliked), an instrument (perhaps musical such as an accordion, a violin, a piano), an alarm clock, a lunch pail, or an identification bracelet.

One of the most poignant reading selections is by student Janice Hill. The lonely part of her childhood is symbolized by a latchkey. She says that in the winter it was "icicle cold" and that in the summer it was "hot against her skin . . . like a clammy leech." Except for her two preliminary drafts, her entire paragraph writing assignment, including the Writing Process Worksheet, immediately follows.

You will find a full-size blank worksheet on page 6. It can be photocopied, filled in, and submitted with each assignment if your instructor directs you to do so.

Writing Process Worksheet

TITLE Latchkey

NAME Janice Hill   **DUE DATE** Tuesday, January 24, 8 a.m.

ASSIGNMENT   In the space below, write whatever you need to know about your assignment, including information about the topic, audience, pattern of writing, length, whether to include a rough draft or revised drafts, and whether your paper must be typed.

Write a descriptive paragraph of about 250 words on something you prize(d) or despise(d). Submit this completed worksheet, a rough draft, and a typed final draft. Audience: instructor and students who probably have not experienced what the writer did.

STAGE ONE   **Explore**   Freewrite, brainstorm (list), cluster, or take notes as directed by your instructor. Use the back of this page or separate paper if you need more space.

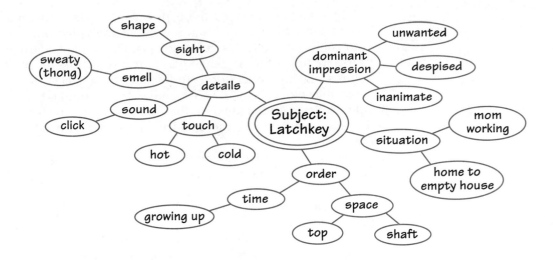

STAGE TWO   **Organize**   Write a topic sentence or thesis; label the subject and the treatment parts.

The thing I hated most when I was growing up was a metal object
                        subject   **treatment**
about two inches long.

Write an outline or an outline alternative.

I. Top
   A. Oval
   B. Hole
   C. "Master"
II. Shaft
   A. Notched
   B. Grooved
   C. Pointed
III. Hanging around neck
   A. First, leather
      1. Sweaty
      2. Got "lost"
   B. Then, chain
IV. Against skin
   A. Cold
   B. Hot
V. Function and fear
   A. Turned with click
   B. Opened to empty house
      1. Scary
      2. Lonely

STAGE THREE   **Write**   On separate paper, write and then revise your paper as many times as necessary for coherence, language (usage, tone, and diction), unity, emphasis, support, and sentences (CLUESS). Read your paper aloud to hear and correct any grammatical errors or awkward-sounding sentences.

Edit any problems in fundamentals, such as capitalization, omissions, punctuation, and spelling (COPS).

Latchkey

Janice Hill

Janice Hill had no trouble identifying the possession she most despised. It was a key she carried around her neck, first on a thong, then on a chain. It seemed to take on a life of its own as it hung there. She probably would have preferred a millstone or even an albatross.

Topic sentence — <u>The thing I hated most when I was growing up was a metal object about two inches long.</u> The part was an <u>oval shape turned on the side,</u> with a <u>hole</u> at the top middle. Down from the oval was a <u>flat shaft,</u> which was <u>straight</u> on one side, <u>notched</u> irregularly on the other, <u>grooved</u> in a straight line near the middle on each flat side, and <u>pointed</u> at the end. At the top, near the middle of the inch-long oval was the word <u>Master.</u> Oddly that's what it was to me—my master. It was my latchkey. When I went to school, it went everywhere I did. One day I took it off at school and misplaced it. My mother was very angry. I said I hated the leather thong from which it hung because it was ugly and <u>smelled of sweat.</u> She replaced that with a silver chain, and said I should never take the key off. Each day I would wear that chain and key, always inside my sweater, shirt, or blouse. In the winter it was <u>icicle cold</u> as it dangled against my skinny chest. In the summer it was <u>hot</u> against my sweaty skin, sticking like a clammy leech. Because I was forbidden to take it off by myself, even upon coming home, I always bent forward when I inserted it into the lock, my sad, sometimes scared, <u>face reflecting with weird distortions</u> in the brass door knob. I inserted the key, turned it with a <u>click,</u> and removed it. After three years of my life with the detested key, I had to bend way over to turn it in the lock, my head pressed against the solid wood door. By that time the key and the chain had worn <u>smooth</u> in places, and the <u>crisscross pattern</u> around the name had <u>darkened.</u> I always feared what lurked inside that house. Though I had a neighbor I could call if I needed help, that key always represented loneliness and fear. <u>I was glad when my mother got a new job with shorter hours, and I was no longer a latchkey kid.</u>

Margin labels: Sight images, Smell, Touch, Sight, Sound, Sight, Concluding sentence

---

Exercise 1 — **DISCUSSION AND CRITICAL THINKING**

1. What brief narrative accounts (little stories) does Hill relate to make her description more interesting?

2. Without looking back at the selection, draw the key as it was described at the beginning. If you can do so, Hill has been effective in her description. If you can remember how she said it felt around her neck, perhaps she has been even more effective.

My Banana Car

Maria Varela

To an American youngster, a first car is something to be anticipated, celebrated, and remembered. It should be the apple of one's eye, but it may be a different fruit. It could be a lemon. Even worse, as was the case for student Maria Varela, it was a "banana car." Re-created here for you, the experience is probably funnier to read about than it was to live through.

Thesis

I remember how excited I was right after my sixteenth birthday. <u>My dad was going to buy me a car!</u> I imagined it would be a nice little red car with chrome rims (not hubcaps). It would have a tan interior, a sunroof, and a great stereo system that could be heard blocks away. All my friends would envy me. The good-looking boys would notice me with favor. I would be so popular. After all, the cooler the car, the cooler the car owner.

Sight

I could not believe what was parked in my driveway when I came home from school that Monday afternoon. <u>It was a 1974 Chevy Monte Carlo, the kind that has the great big front end</u>. The car was huge. It could seat forty people if it were a dinner table. To top it off, it was <u>yellow like a banana</u>. As a matter of fact it looked like a banana. I held my breath as I walked slowly toward the car, hoping that it belonged to someone who was visiting. At that moment my father ran out of the house with a big smile on his face. "Well, what do you think?" he said. "Nice, huh?"

I looked at my dad, managed to break a smile, and said weakly, "Yeah, Dad. Thanks."

Sight
Sight

I spent the rest of the afternoon trying to find a good quality in the car. First I looked at the outside. It had <u>ugly hubcaps</u>, the kind you find at Pick-a-Part for ten dollars a set. Worst of all, it had a <u>sticker of a horse's head</u> stuck right on the paint near the trunk. I knew that if I tried to remove it, the paint would come off and leave the outline of a horse's head in another color.

Sight
Smell

I opened the driver's door slowly as if something like a weasel might pop out at me from inside. The interior was <u>light brown</u> with dark brown stripes. It <u>smelled like Old Spice</u>. I got an image of the previous owner. He must have been a tall, heavy man who wore cheap cologne and liked horses. I plopped down in the driver's seat and grabbed the steering wheel with both hands. "Great!" My feet barely reached the pedals, and my nose was at the same level as the top of the steering wheel. I was a short girl, but at that moment I felt even shorter. I got a fat cushion from the house. I would have to sit on this cushion every time I drove this car. I just hoped that no one noticed I was sitting on a cushion. "Maria's so short, she can't even reach the pedals on her car." "Can you see over the dashboard, Maria?" I could already hear them tease.

As I drove my banana car to school the next day, I saw people staring at me. I knew what they were whispering. "How could she drive that ugly car?" and "I would rather walk," and, this one with much laughter, "I can't wait till she peels out of here."

To make matters worse, the car was expensive to drive and prone to breakage. It would take over seventeen dollars in gas to fill up, and that

Sound
Sight

Sound

would last me only four days. One day as I was driving down the street, the muffler came off and started dragging on the ground. It made a <u>horrible noise</u> and <u>sparks were flying everywhere</u>. I knew what they were saying: "The sparkling banana car!" I was a legend. Another time I tried to open the window, but it just <u>plopped</u> down, never to be seen again. I could not keep anything valuable in the car for fear that it would be stolen. But, of course, I did not fear that the car would be stolen. After all, who would want it!

Because my banana car was so large, it was very hard to maneuver. Twice I knocked over our mailbox that was located at the side of the driveway. I would break into a sweat whenever I was forced to parallel park. The most embarrassing situation occurred that night when my friend Monica and I went out to Tommy's. Tommy's is a popular restaurant where all the popular people from our school hang out. Monica and I decided to chance the drive-through, but as I tried to maneuver the large car up the narrow passageway, it got stuck right in the middle. There was no room to move backward or forward. I could feel my ears getting hot from embarrassment. Like the window, Monica sank down out of sight. The people behind me started honking. I could see the people inside the restaurant looking out to see what the commotion was all about. I was ready to cry, but at that moment Danny Gurrerro, one of the cutest boys from our school, came over and asked if I needed help. "Yes, please," I blurted out. He jumped into the car and managed to maneuver it out of that tight spot. Before he left, he advised me not to take the drive-through anymore. I accepted his advice.

Every morning as I walked out of my house, I hoped the car would be gone, but my banana car was always there waiting for me to drive it to school. I got a part-time job at Togo's Eatery. I wanted to save money for a new car, but after two years, I still did not have enough for the down payment. One day at dinner, my father announced that since I was so responsible with my Monte Carlo, he would help me buy a new car. I jumped out of my seat and wrapped my arms around him. Then, remembering my last expectation, I backed off. "May I pick the car?" "Yes," he said. Goodbye, banana car.

Exercise 2	DISCUSSION AND CRITICAL THINKING

1. What is the effect of the first paragraph?

2. While at home, how does Varela manage to conceal her dislike for the car during those three years? How does that self-control measure her love and respect for her father?

3. In what way was she optimistic after she saw the car?

4. How does she characterize the previous banana car owner?

5. Is there any moment of niceness connected with the banana car?

The Jacket

Gary Soto

A writer and university professor, Gary Soto well remembers the self-consciousness of growing up. On one occasion he was all set to be cool with a fine new jacket; then his mother bought the wrong one—one that was "the color of day-old guacamole" and was "the ugly brother who tagged along wherever [he] went." Soto's best-known book is *Living Up the Street*.

1   My clothes have failed me. I remember the green coat that I wore in fifth and sixth grades when you either danced like a champ or pressed yourself against a greasy wall, bitter as a penny toward the happy couples.

2   When I needed a new jacket and my mother asked what kind I wanted, I described something like bikers wear: black leather and silver studs with enough belts to hold down a small town. We were in the kitchen, steam on the windows from her cooking. She listened so long while stirring dinner that I thought she understood for sure the kind I wanted. The next day when I got home from school, I discovered draped on my bedpost a jacket the color of day-old guacamole. I threw my books on the bed and approached the jacket slowly, as if it were a stranger whose hand I had to shake. I touched the vinyl sleeve, the collar, and peeked at the mustard-colored lining.

3   From the kitchen Mother yelled that my jacket was in the closet. I closed the door to her voice and pulled at the rack of clothes in the closet, hoping the jacket on the bedpost wasn't for me but my mean brother. No luck. I gave up. From my bed, I stared at the jacket. I wanted to cry because it was so ugly and so big that I knew I'd have to wear it a long time. I was a small kid, thin as a young tree, and it would be years before I'd have a new one. I stared at the jacket, like an enemy, thinking bad things before I took off my old jacket whose sleeves climbed halfway to my elbow.

4   I put the big jacket on. I zipped it up and down several times, and rolled the cuffs up so they didn't cover my hands. I put my hands in the pockets and flapped the jacket like a bird's wings. I stood in front of the mirror, full face, then profile, and then looked over my shoulder as if someone had called me. I sat on the bed, stood against the bed, and combed my hair to see what I would look like doing something natural. I looked ugly. I threw it on my brother's bed and looked at it for a long time before I slipped it on and went out to the backyard, smiling a "thank you" to my mom as I passed her in the kitchen. With my hands in my pockets I kicked a ball against the fence, and then climbed it to sit looking into the alley. I hurled orange peels at the mouth of an open garbage can and when the peels were gone I watched the white puffs of my breath thin to nothing.

5   I jumped down, hands in my pockets, and in the backyard on my knees I teased my dog, Brownie, by swooping my arms while making bird calls. He jumped at me and missed. He jumped again and again, until a tooth sunk deep, ripping an L-shaped tear on my left sleeve. I pushed Brownie away to study the tear as I would a cut on my arm. There was no blood, only a few loose pieces of fuzz. Damn dog, I thought, and pushed him away hard when he tried to bite again. I got up from my knees and went to my bedroom to sit with my jacket on my lap, with the lights out.

6   That was the first afternoon with my new jacket. The next day I wore it to sixth grade and got a D on a math quiz. During the morning recess Frankie T., the playground terrorist, pushed me to the ground and told me to stay there until recess was over. My best friend, Steve Negrete, ate an apple while looking at me, and the girls turned away to whisper on the monkey bars. The teachers were no help: They looked my way and talked about how foolish I looked in my new jacket. I saw their heads bob with laughter, their hands half-covering their mouths.

7   Even though it was cold, I took off the jacket during lunch and played kickball in a thin shirt, my arms feeling like braille from goose bumps. But when I returned to class I slipped the jacket on and shivered until I was warm. I sat on my hands, heating them up, while my teeth chattered like a cup of crooked dice. Finally warm, I slid out of the jacket but a few minutes later put it back on when the fire bell rang. We paraded out into the yard where we, the sixth graders, walked past all the other grades to stand against the back fence. Everybody saw me. Although they didn't say out loud, "Man, that's ugly," I heard the buzz-buzz of gossip and even laughter that I knew was meant for me.

8   And so I went, in my guacamole jacket. So embarrassed, so hurt, I couldn't even do my homework. I received Cs on quizzes, and forgot the state capitals and the rivers of South America, our friendly neighbor. Even the girls who had been friendly blew away like loose flowers to follow the boys in neat jackets.

9   I wore that thing for three years until the sleeves grew short and my forearms stuck out like the necks of turtles. All during that time no love came to me—no little dark girl in a Sunday dress she wore on Monday. At lunchtime I stayed with the ugly boys who leaned against the chainlink fence and looked around with propellers of grass spinning in our mouths. We saw girls walk by alone, saw couples, hand in hand, their heads like bookends pressing air together. We saw them and spun our propellers so fast our faces were blurs.

10   I blame that jacket for those bad years. I blame my mother for her bad taste and her cheap ways. It was a sad time for the heart. With a friend I spent my sixth-grade year in a tree in the alley waiting for something good to happen to me in that jacket, which had become the ugly brother who tagged along wherever I went. And it was about that time that I began to grow. My chest puffed up with muscle and, strangely, a few more ribs. Even my hands, those fleshy hammers, showed bravely through the cuffs, the fingers already hardening for the coming fights. But that L-shaped rip on the left sleeve got bigger; bits of stuffing coughed out from its wound after a hard day of play. I finally Scotch-taped it closed, but in rain or cold weather the tape peeled off like a scab and more stuffing fell out until that sleeve shriveled into a palsied arm. That winter the elbows began to crack and whole chunks of green began to fall off. I showed the cracks to my mother, who always seemed to be at the stove with steamed-up glasses, and she said that there were children in Mexico who would love that jacket. I told her that this was America and yelled that Debbie, my sister, didn't have a jacket like mine. I ran outside, ready to cry, and climbed the tree by the alley to think bad thoughts and watch my breath puff white and disappear.

11   But whole pieces still casually flew off my jacket when I played hard, read quietly, or took vicious spelling tests at school. When it became so

spotted that my brother began to call me "camouflage," I flung it over the fence into the alley. Later, however, I swiped the jacket off the ground and went inside to drape it across my lap and mope.

12   I was called to dinner: Steam silvered my mother's glasses as she said grace; my brother and sister with their heads bowed made ugly faces at their glasses of powdered milk. I gagged too, but eagerly ate big rips of buttered tortilla that held scooped up beans. Finished, I went outside with my jacket across my arm. It was a cold sky. The faces of clouds were piled up, hurting. I climbed the fence, jumping down with a grunt. I started up the alley and soon slipped into my jacket, that green ugly brother who breathed over my shoulder that day and ever since.

Exercise 3	DISCUSSION AND CRITICAL THINKING

1. Why is the jacket more of a disappointment than it would have been if Soto's mother had given it to him as a surprise?

2. What kind of jacket did Soto request?

3. How is the jacket like a person and an evil force?

4. What are some of the failures Soto attributes to his jacket?

5. Why doesn't he lose it or throw it away?

6. What does Soto do to make this essay funny?

7. Is this mainly a description or a narration, or is it a combination with purposes integrated?

8. One might think that Soto had an unhappy, or even twisted, childhood. Do you think so? Explain.

The Story of a Well-Made Shield

N. Scott Momaday

This descriptive consideration of the Plains Indian shield reveals a great deal about Native American culture. The two short passages here are from *In the Presence of the Sun: Stories and Poems.* They include a cultural perspective and an example. The writer tells how the designs on the shields signify far more than mere decoration or artistic imagination.

Now in the dawn before it dies, the eagle swings low and wide in a great arc, curving downward to the place of origin. There is no wind, but there is a long roaring on the air. It is like the wind—nor is it quite like the wind—but more powerful.

A Word on the Plains Shield

Oyate awicahipi kin hehan lyou waslahy el wasicu wan Ble eciyape ci Jack Carrigan kici mazopiye yuhapi ca he Sitting Bull's shield kiu he opeton. Mr. One Bull says he can draw the shield. Please send him paper and colors. Green grass color, dark blue, brown scarlet. Yes Sitting Bull's father Jumping Bull gave him this shield and named him Sitting Bull. Jumping Bull made this shield from a vision. When Sitting Bull wears his shield he paints his horse in a certain way. Yes his father gave him this painting. When they have a shield they are not supposed to tell a lie or think wrong. If they do they are wounded or killed. When Sitting Bull's band was brought to the Standing Rock Agency, a white man, in a store with Jack Carrigan, by the name of Billie (William McNider) bought Sitting Bull's shield.

"With Regard to Sitting Bull,"
Given by His Nephew, One Bull,
and Transcribed by His Grandniece,
Mrs. Cecelia One Bull Brown

1   In its basic form the Plains shield is round and made of durable materials. It is relatively small and light in weight. A diameter of twenty-four inches is close to the average. The manufacture consists of hide and adornments. The hide is thick and dried to a remarkable hardness; it is most often the hide of a bison. Only in a limited sense can the shield rightly be considered armor, although it is strong enough to repel missiles, stones, and clubs certainly, but also arrows and even balls and bullets shot from firearms, especially if the blow is glancing. But first and above all the shield is medicine.

2   The Plains shield reflects the character of the Plains culture, also known as the Horse culture or Centaur culture. It evidences a nomadic society and a warrior ideal. Those who carried shields were hunters and fighters whose purpose it was to raid, to capture, and to demonstrate extraordinary bravery.

3   The aesthetic aspects of the Plains shield is pronounced; the shield is a unique work of art. Without exception great care is given to the decoration

of a proper shield. The artwork on many Plains shields is highly evolved in terms of proportion, design, symmetry, color, and imagination. Plains shield art is the equal of the great ledgerbook drawings of the nineteenth century, which in turn have been compared to Archaic Greek vase painting. It is an art of high order and singular accomplishment.

4   The shield bears a remarkable relationship to the individual to whom it belongs. Indeed the relationship is so immediate, so intimate as to be virtually impossible to define. In a real sense the Plains warrior *is* his shield. It is his personal flag, the realization of his vision and his name, the object of his holiest quest, the tangible expression of his deepest being. In bearing his shield he says, "My shield stands for me, and I stand for my shield. I am, and I am my shield!"

5   The shield is a mask. The mask is an appearance that discloses reality beyond appearance. Like other masks, it bespeaks scared mystery. The shield is what you see, believes the Plains warrior. It reflects your own reality, as it does mine, he says. It reveals to you the essence of your self. It charms you, frightens you, disarms you, renders you helpless. You behold my shield, and you are transfixed or transformed, perhaps inspired beyond your imagining. Nothing will ever be the same again, for you have entered into the presence of my power. Oh, my enemy! Behold my shield!

6   The shield is involved in story. The shield is its own story. When the shield is made visible it means: Here is the story. Enter into it and be created. The story tells of your real being.

7   The shields in this gathering exist quintessentially in the element of language, and they are directly related to the stories, songs, spells, charms, and prayers of the Native American oral tradition.

8   And the shields are meditations that make a round of life. The shield stories are meant to be told aloud, either to oneself or to another or to others, one each day for sixteen consecutive days, in which on the fourth, eighth, twelfth, and sixteenth days the storyteller and his listener or listeners might fast in order to be hale and worthy and pure in spirit. The stories ought to be told in the early morning or late afternoon, when the sun is close to the horizon, and always in the presence of the sun.

The Floating Feathers Shield

9   When Gai-talee was still a boy, learning how to hunt, he had a wonderful dream. In it he saw a great bear on the side of a mountain. The bear stood still for a long time, waiting in the shadow of a high stone ridge near timberline. Then a shape hurtled on the ridge, and the bear reared suddenly and took in his claws an eagle from the air. For a moment there was an awful frenzy; then again the stillness, and dark feathers floating and fluttering down on a little wind.

10   Gai-talee told Many Magpies of the shield he wanted, and it was made according to his dream. Gai-talee raided many times in Mexico, and he carried his shield with him. They say that Gai-talee's shield is well known below the Llano Estacado.

Exercise 4	DISCUSSION AND CRITICAL THINKING

1. In paragraph 1, is the description mainly objective or subjective?

2. In what way is each shield an individual work of art?

3. Why is the idea of a dominant impression relevant to shield painting?

4. What kind of imagery is naturally dominant on the shield?

5. In "The Floating Feathers Shield," how is movement suggested?

6. In what way does the shield reflect the Plains culture?

Practicing Descriptive Patterns

The pattern of descriptive elements in a final draft will vary, depending on the order of presentation, whether it be space, time, or emphasis. In the initial outline the form may be much more mechanical than in the final draft in order to note important details. Later, as the writing process unfolds, the images may be blended—for example, a grape may be described according to its texture, color, and taste, all in one sentence.

Exercise 5	COMPLETING DESCRIPTIVE PATTERNS

Fill in the blanks to complete the following description.

A Produce Area in a Supermarket

(Dominant impression: Diversity)

I. Food displays (sight—color, shape)

A. Pile of red radishes _____

B. _____

C. _____

II. Smells (from vegetables, fruits)

A. Acidic tangerines _____

B. _____

III. Textures (smooth or rough to touch)

A. Rough-skinned potatoes _____

B. _____

IV. Taste (samples of sweet/sour, ripe/unripe)

A. _____

B. _____

✎ Topics for Writing Description

Reading-Related Topics

1. In "The Jacket" and "My Banana Car" the authors discuss what they dislike about their possessions. Discuss why they dislike and how they regard what was bought for them. Consider these questions:

   What is the importance of peer pressure—how others will regard them?

   What is the importance of the quality of the possession?

   Why is it important that they did not immediately reveal their disappointment?

   With the passage of time, do these authors look back with some amusement and even pleasure? Why or why not?

2. Write about an imaginary date between Soto and Varela, during which he wears his "guacamole jacket" and she drives her "banana car." Write from the point of view of either person or describe the date from the view of an observer.

"Latchkey"

3. Use this paragraph as a model to write a descriptive paragraph about something you prized or despised, such as a gift from a grandparent, braces for your

teeth, a cast for a broken bone, a piece of sports equipment, or an article of clothing.

"My Banana Car"

4. Write about your first (or any other) car, one that you came to prize or despise. Include detailed description along with discussion about the car and your life at that particular time.

5. Interview someone and write about that person's first car.

6. Write about your first bicycle or other vehicle.

7. Rewrite the essay, this time from the car's point of view.

8. Rewrite an essay, this time from the point of view of the ghost of the first owner.

"The Jacket"

9. Write about the jacket from the point of view of Soto's mother.

10. Write about the jacket from the jacket's point of view.

11. Write about an embarrassing article of clothing you wore as a child, an article that you thought at the time had an influence on how others felt about you and certainly how you felt about yourself.

12. Write about an article of clothing you wore with pride as a child or one that you now wear with pride.

"The Story of a Well-Made Shield"

13. Describe a shield for yourself or someone you know (family member, friend). Feature a significant moment in the subject's life. Narrate the moment and describe its properties. In a painting or drawing, depict the shield you describe. If time permits, make a shield using your design.

Career-Related Topics

14. Describe a well-furnished, well-functioning office or other work area. Be specific.

15. Describe a product such as a computer, with special attention to the dominant trait that gives the product its reputation.

16. Describe a person properly groomed and attired for a particular job or interview. Be specific in giving details pertaining to the person and in naming the place or situation. If you like, objectively describe yourself as that person.

Objective Description

General Topics

Give your topic some kind of frame. As you develop your purpose, consider the knowledge and attitudes of your readers. You might be describing a lung for a biology instructor, a geode for a geology instructor, a painting for an art instructor, or a comet for an astronomy instructor. Instead, you might want to pose as the seller of an object such as a desk, a table, or a bicycle. Try some of the following topics:

17. A simple object, such as a pencil, a pair of scissors, a cup, a sock, a dollar bill, a coin, a ring, or a notebook.

18. A human organ, such as a heart, a liver, a lung, or a kidney.

19. A visible part of your body, such as a toe, a finger, an ear, a nose, or an eye.

20. A construction, such as a room, a desk, a chair, or a table.

21. A mechanism, such as a bicycle, a tricycle, a wagon, a car, a motorcycle, a can opener, or a stapler.

Subjective Description

The following topics should also be presented in the context of a purpose other than just writing a description. Your intent can be as simple as giving a subjective reaction to your subject. Unless you are dealing with one of those topics that you can present reflectively or a topic interesting in itself, you will usually need some kind of situation. The narrative frame (something happening) is especially useful in providing order and vitality to writing. Here are two possibilities for you to consider:

22. Personalize a trip to a supermarket, a stadium, an airport, an unusual house, a mall, a beach, a court, a place of worship, a club, a business, a library, or a police station. Deal with a simple conflict in one of those places, while emphasizing descriptive details. Pick a high point in any event, and describe a few seconds of it. Think about how a scene can be captured by a video camera, and then give focus by applying the dominant impression principle, using the images of sight, sound, taste, touch, and smell that are relevant. The event might be a ball game, a graduation ceremony, a wedding ceremony, a funeral, a dance, a concert, a family gathering, a class meeting, a rally, a riot, a robbery, a fight, a proposal, or a meal. Focus on a body of subject material that you can cover effectively in the paragraph you write.

23. Download and, if possible, print a photo from the Internet. Select a subject that interests you, perhaps a product, a current event, or a vacation spot. The key word *pictures* will give you a variety to choose from on most search engines. Next, using your imagination, project a person or persons onto the picture you selected and describe something that occurs. The "something" need not be highly dramatic.

Writer's Guidelines: Description

1. In an objective description, use direct, practical language and usually appeal mainly to the sense of sight.

2. In an emotional description, appeal to the reader's feelings, especially through the use of figurative language and images of sight, sound, smell, taste, and touch.

3. Use specific and concrete words if appropriate.

4. Be sure that readers can answer the following questions:

   What is the subject of this description?

   What is the dominant impression?

   What is the situation?

   What is the order of details—time, space, or both?

   What details support the dominant impression?

5. Consider giving your description a narrative framework. Include some action if it fits.

18

Exemplification: Writing with Examples

"If it is true that anger is a normal human emotion, then perhaps we are becoming more and more normal."

—"Living in the Age of Irritations"

Writing Paragraphs of Exemplification

Exemplification means using examples to explain, convince, or amuse. Lending interest and information to writing, exemplification is one of the most common and effective ways of developing ideas. Examples may be developed in a sentence or more, or they may be only phrases or even single words, as in the following sentence: "Eating fast foods, such as *hamburgers, pizza, pupusas, wonton,* and *tacos,* has become a shared cross-cultural experience."

Characteristics of Good Examples

As supporting information, the best examples are specific, vivid, and representative. These three qualities are closely linked; collectively, they must support the topic sentence of a paragraph and the thesis of an essay.

You use examples to inform or convince your reader. Of course, an example by itself does not necessarily prove anything. We know that examples can be found on either side of an argument, even at the extreme edges. Therefore, in addition to providing specific examples so that your reader can follow your argument precisely and vivid ones so that your reader will be interested, you should choose examples that are representative. Representative examples are examples that your reader can consider, accept as appropriate, and even match with his or her own examples. If you are writing a paragraph about cheating and you give one specific, vivid, and representative example, your reader should be able to say, "That's exactly what happens. I can imagine just how the incident occurred, and I could give some examples that are similar."

Techniques for Finding Examples

Writing a good paragraph of exemplification begins, as always, with prewriting. The techniques you use will depend on what you are writing about. Assuming that you begin with a topic idea, one useful technique is listing. Base your list on what you have read, heard, and experienced. Here is a list on the broad topic "cheating at school":

> When I copied homework
>
> Looking at a friend's test answers
>
> A student with hand signals
>
> Jake and his electronic system
>
> Time for planned cheating
>
> Those who got caught
>
> A person who bought a research paper
>
> Jess, who copied from me
>
> The Internet "Cheaters" source
>
> The two students who exchanged identities
>
> More work than it's worth
>
> More stress than it's worth

Number and Order of Examples

After you have explored your topic and collected information, you must decide whether to use only one example with a detailed explanation, a few examples with a bit less information, or a cluster of examples. A well-stated topic sentence will guide you in making this decision. When you are writing about a personal topic, you will probably have far more examples than you can use.

If your example is an incident or a series of incidents, you will probably use time order, reinforcing that arrangement with terms such as *next, then, soon, later, last,* and *finally.* If your examples exist in space (maybe in different parts of a room), then you would use space references *(up, down, left, right, east, west, north, south).* Arranging examples by emphasis means going from the most important example to the least important or from the least to the most important.

Connecting Examples with Purpose

Here is the paragraph student Lara Olivas wrote on the topic "the hard work of cheating." After compiling the list of examples above, Olivas decided that for her purpose in this paragraph, one specific, vivid, and representative example with explanation would make her point.

Cheating Is Not Worth the Bother

Lara Olivas

Topic sentence

<u>Cheating students often put themselves under more stress than honest students.</u> I remember someone in my junior composition class who needed a research paper, so he found a source and bought one for seventy-five dollars. The <u>first</u> trouble was that he had to submit the work in stages: the topic, the working bibliography, the note cards, the outline, the rough draft, and the final. <u>Therefore,</u> he went to the library and started working backwards. Of course, he couldn't turn in only the bib cards actually used in the paper, and <u>next</u> he had to make out note cards for the material he "would be" documenting, and even make out more. <u>After</u> having all kinds of trouble, he realized that the bought paper was of "A" quality, whereas he had been a "C" student. He went back to his source and was told he should change the sentence structure and so on to make the paper weaker. <u>Finally</u> he dropped the class after spending more time on his paper than I did on mine. He also suffered more anxiety than the students who put in the most work on their papers.

One example

Explanation of the example follows

Order of time *(first, next, after, finally)*

Concluding sentence (connects ending to beginning)

Observe how a professional writer from Los Angeles uses examples to explain his topic sentence about cultural diversity. The annotations show how the paragraph answers the questions following the selection.

1 Topic sentence

2, 3 Cluster of examples

4 Specific, vivid, representative

5 Examples relate to "diversified world."

<u>This is the typical day of</u> a <u>relatively typical soul in today's diversified world.</u> I wake up to the sound of my Japanese clock radio, put on a T shirt sent me by an uncle in Nigeria and walk out into the street, past German cars, to my office. Around me are English-language students from Korea, Switzerland, and Argentina—all on this Spanish-named road in this Mediterranean-style town. On TV, I find, the news is in Mandarin; today's baseball game is being broadcast in Korean. For lunch I can walk to a sushi bar, a tandoori palace, a Thai café, or the newest burrito joint (run by an old Japanese lady). Who am I, I sometimes wonder, the son of Indian parents and a British citizen who spends much of his time in Japan (and is therefore—what else?— an American permanent resident)?

Pico Iyer, "The Global Village Finally Arrives"

Useful Procedure for Writing with Examples

Asking yourself the following questions will help you write effective paragraphs using exemplification.

1. What am I trying to say?

2. What examples might support that idea? (Use listing.)

3. How many examples and what order should I use?

4. Are my examples specific, vivid, and representative?

5. Have I made a connection between my examples and my topic sentence or thesis?

Connecting Reading and Writing: Living in the Age of Irritations

If it is true that anger is a normal human emotion, then perhaps we are becoming more and more normal. Of course, anger has no pure form. It ranges from mild discontent to uncontrollable rage. Its sources are just as varied. What sets off one person may go unnoticed by another. Or what sets off one person at a particular time may not bother that same person at another time, depending on any number of circumstances. Some argue that we live in the Age of Irritations. The population density, the cultural (in the broadest sense) differences, the competitive grabbing for "the golden ring," the decline in civility, and the simultaneous demands from home, work, school, and associates are all sources of stress-producing irritations.

How often do you become irritated? What does it take to move your irritation down the fast track to anger? The reading selections that follow give you a sampling of what sets off some people. In "The Mean Season," Roy Rivenburg discusses the various forms of rudeness we all know and love to hate. He gives us contemporary examples, a bit of history, and even some speculation about where we're headed.

As a newspaper reporter, Jennifer Oldham has done research for her article "Amid Backlash, Calls for Cell Phone Etiquette." What she has found may bother those of you who love your cell phones. The message waiting is that most people who are not using cell phones hate to be around them.

In the first selection, "Sweet and Sour Workplace," student Sarah Betrue recounts her experience on the job (the conventional hothouse of all irritations), which in this case is a Chinese restaurant. You can follow her writing process by studying her Writing Process Worksheet.

You will find a full-size, blank Writing Process Worksheet on page 6. It can be photocopied, filled in, and submitted with each assignment if your instructor directs you to do so.

THE QUIGMANS   by Buddy Hickerson

"Stop me if I'm off-base here . . . but you could use a good massage."

B. Hickerson, copyright 1998. Los Angeles Times Syndicate. Reprinted by permission.

Writing Process Worksheet

TITLE Sweet and Sour Workplace

NAME Sarah Betrue   **DUE DATE** Friday, October 15, 11 a.m.

ASSIGNMENT   In the space below, write whatever you need to know about your assignment, including information about the topic, audience, pattern of writing, length, whether to include a rough draft or revised drafts, and whether your paper must be typed.

Paragraph of about 300 words on irritations that produce stress and anger. Use specific examples for support. Take the examples from experiences at work, home, school, or any place in my life. Audience: people similar to me, who will be familiar with stress, although maybe not with my examples. Submit this completed sheet, a rough draft, marked for revision, and a typed final draft.

STAGE ONE   **Explore**   Freewrite, brainstorm (list), cluster, or take notes as directed by your instructor. Use the back of this page or separate paper if you need more space.

School
—Parking
—Registration
   for classes
—Confusing,
   difficult
   assignments
—Annoying students
—Food

Home + personal
—Keeping
   balance
—Boyfriend
—Shopping

Work
—Complaining boss
—Fellow employees
   —immature
   —self-centered
   —lazy
—Customers
   —freeloaders
   —name callers

STAGE TWO   **Organize**   Write a topic sentence or thesis; label the subject and the treatment parts.

<u>Stressful and frustrating situations</u> <u>occur daily behind the scenes at</u>
                     subject   treatment
<u>my workplace, making it almost impossible for me to maintain a positive</u>
<u>attitude.</u>

Write an outline or an outline alternative.

  I. Boss
      A. Strict
      B. Unappreciative
         1. Usually
         2. This morning
 II. Fellow employees
      A. Cooks
      B. Cashiers
      C. Waitresses

      1. Self-centered

      2. Behaving typically yesterday

III. Customers

    A. Complaining generally

    B. One in particular

      1. Demanding

      2. Insulting

STAGE THREE   **Write**   On separate paper, write and then revise your paper as many times as necessary for <u>c</u>oherence, <u>l</u>anguage (usage, tone, and diction), <u>u</u>nity, <u>e</u>mphasis, <u>s</u>upport, and <u>s</u>entences (CLUESS). Read your paper aloud to hear and correct any grammatical errors or awkward-sounding sentences.

Edit any problems in fundamentals, such as <u>c</u>apitalization, <u>o</u>missions, <u>p</u>unctuation, and <u>s</u>pelling (COPS).

Sweet and Sour Workplace

Sarah Betrue

A full-time student and a full-time worker, Sarah Betrue has a very busy life, which would go more smoothly if she did not have so many irritations. We are likely to identify with her experiences and to admire her for beginning and ending her work day in tranquility.

Every morning as I enter my workplace, I admire the vibrant colors of both the tropical fish in the aquarium and the ancient silk Chinese robes hung from the wall. But as I take the dreaded step from the dining area to the kitchen, the scenery drastically changes. <u>Stressful and frustrating situations occur daily behind the scenes at the restaurant, making it almost impossible for me to maintain a positive attitude.</u> Yesterday is a typical shift. <u>The first voices I hear are the owners complaining about how filthy the restaurant looks,</u> although the night before the other employees and I worked with Ajax for three hours scrubbing shelves and floor sinks. As the day progresses, I try to squeeze in some extra cleaning between busy times, but I find myself doing all the extra work myself. The young girls I work with think having this job is just an extension of their social lives. During lunch hour, the dining area is packed, the line for takeout has reached a ridiculous length, and two phone calls are on hold. <u>That's when Morgan decides to call her boyfriend on her cell phone.</u> Naturally I become frustrated and proceed to speak with her. She glares at me with fire in her eyes and screams, "I've got more important things to deal with at this time!" Getting nowhere with politeness, I grab the phone from her hand and turn it off. No sooner has this crisis ended than the house phone rings again. <u>On the line is a very unhappy woman.</u> After listening to a few colorfully disparaging descriptions of a meal she ordered, I tell her I cannot give refunds or food exchanges if her order is not returned first. She threatens to report our restaurant to newspapers and authorities, and then tells me to do something I am physically incapable of doing and hangs up in my ear. At the end of the day I am so angry and frustrated with having to put

Topic sentence

Example

Example

Example

up with such occurrences that I want to grab hold of one of the woks and hit someone upside the head. But just as I reach for the handle, I get a vision, an image of my paycheck, and I begin to relax. <u>I leave the restaurant with no blood on my hands, wishing everyone a wonderful evening</u>.

Concluding sentence

Exercise 1   **DISCUSSION AND CRITICAL THINKING**

1. What evidence is there that Betrue is not essentially a negative thinker?

2. What kind of order does Betrue use for her three specific supporting examples?

3. If you were one of the owners of the restaurant, how would you react to Betrue's paragraph?

The Mean Season

Roy Rivenburg

In this article, Roy Rivenburg, a veteran reporter for the *Los Angeles Times*, covers all the bases of rudeness. After giving the particulars, he looks for historical patterns and trends, and he explores a bit of the psychology and philosophy behind the current lack of civility. At the same time he acknowledges those who maintain that instances of incivility are overstated.

1   Read this story, dirt bag! Yeah, we're talking to you. And no, we don't care if it offends your precious sensibilities. In case you're too stupid to have noticed—and you probably are—this country seems to have turned a lot meaner and ruder lately.

2   To get a clue, try stepping into a crosswalk. As humorist Henry Beard notes: Once upon a time, for a New Yorker visiting Los Angeles, that was an unnerving experience. "Cars would always stop for you," he marvels. "You'd hear the brakes screech and you'd assume, being from Manhattan, that the only possible explanation was the driver planned to get out and kill you." Today, the once-venerated California pedestrian must dodge traffic like a matador. And Beard sees the change as part of a much larger shift: a meltdown of courtesy, a wave of in-your-face aggressiveness and a collective mean streak that has snaked into schools, churches, the media—everything.

3   The kinder, gentler nation has fallen and it can't get up:

• Television commercials used to compare the sponsor's produce to an anonymous "Brand X." Now, advertisers such as MCI and AT&T openly refer to each other as corporate scum.

• Greeting card companies have added "Drop dead" and "You're an [expletive]" messages to their product lines. Other entrepreneurs deliver bouquets of dead flowers and revenge-o-grams of rotting fish.

- High school sports leagues have started banning postgame handshakes to avoid fistfights.
- News reports are laced with stories of fatal duels over parking spaces, loud stereos, and subway seats.

4   "We're playing tag with hate," says Dr. Mark Goulston, a Santa Monica psychiatrist. Then again, who even wants to be nice when the chief apostles of it are Barney the Dinosaur and Mr. Rogers?

5   Still, things could be worse. Go back to almost any period in history—the Old West, eighteenth-century London, ancient Rome—and it's hard to conclude, despite the absence of Howard Stern, that previous generations were somehow more civil than this one. "It's easy to idealize the past," says historian William McNeill, "but human beings have been very nasty to each other for a very long time." People in the Middle Ages didn't carry swords as a fashion statement, he notes. And frontier America was a far cry from "Little House on the Prairie."

6   Indeed, when anthropologists dug up one Old West graveyard a few years ago, they found that two-thirds of the men under age 45 had died violently. Among the victims: William Johnson, whose head was blown off by his father-in-law's shotgun after he made the faux pas of mentioning at the dinner table that he had fought for the Union in the Civil War. But others argue that the current decline of civility is unprecedented. And they blame everything from microwave ovens to Jack in the Box hamburger ads.

7   Lauren Burton has had a ringside seat on the passage from We Decade to Me Decade to Up Yours Decade. As director of the L.A. County Bar Association's dispute resolution office, she has noticed a surge in neighbor-to-neighbor combat lately. In Encino, it was a two-year jihad of lawsuits, countersuits, and water-hose fights over the noise of a bouncing basketball. In the San Gabriel Valley, it was spitting, more water squirting, and an outdoor light aimed through a bedroom window because of a shedding pecan tree. In Long Beach, it was a double homicide sparked by a longstanding argument over the volume of a stereo. Each year, thousands of such feuds erupt in the cities and suburbs of Southern California, Burton says. It's the 1990s sequel to the Hatfields and McCoys, whose infamous battle supposedly began with an 1860 dispute over a hog and ultimately claimed twenty lives.

8   "People think of two things now when they have a conflict," she says. "One is revenge, the other is, 'Sue the bastard.'" Part of the trouble, she suggests, is a clash of cultures. As neighborhoods become more diverse, the differing backgrounds and desires can create a social powder keg. Throw in a little overcrowding, take away some religion, add a dose of hippie wisdom and things can get completely out of hand, experts say, especially in the United States.

9   Unlike Japan, for instance, which crams citizens closer together but counters possible side effects with "a culture that has historically chosen rules and conformity over freedom, we took the crowding but didn't suppress our [liberties]," says Rex Julian Beaber, a psychologist and attorney. And there's a price to pay. "It's a function of anonymity," he says. "In a small town, everyone knows everyone and your reputation is changed for life if you do something bad. [In a big city], you can kill in a crowd and walk away." Or, as psychiatrist Goulston puts it: "One reason more people are

jerks is because they know they can get away with it. Years ago, we thought someone would stop us or punish us or our conscience would bother us."

10   On February 5, 1994, gentility officially qualified as deviant behavior. That's when Oprah did a show on people who commit random acts of senseless kindness. Suddenly, on national TV, an ominous truth set in: Nice people had become the freaks.

11   The rest of the country seemed to be moving down the trail blazed by New York, which for years had been pioneering new and innovative alternatives to politeness. It's gotten so bad, according to the *New York Times,* that the city "appears to be the most foul-mouthed [place] in the nation, rivaling only prison and the armed forces." Close behind in the need-to-have-their-mouths-washed-out-with-soap department are movies and music. Films for adults now average seventy to eighty expletives each, the profanity article notes.

12   Still, civility supporters do see rays of hope. Beaber says a resurrection of manners is already under way among America's "most savage humans: lawyers." The L.A. County court system has "promulgated new rules of courtesy" to halt "increasingly volatile, vicious and demonic attacks" between attorneys, Beaber says.

13   And there's more to come as society scrambles to deal with phenomena that previous generations couldn't even have imagined. "We'll see increasing attempts to formalize what was before an unspoken social norm," he says. "For example, it used to be that a manufacturer of children's games wouldn't dream of creating a game where you cut off a person's head and it squirts blood." Now, with grisly video games like Mortal Kombat on the market, "The Senate is holding hearings and [might create] rules to stop this," Beaber says.

14   Even if such efforts draw fire from civil libertarians, he predicts that "the middle class is sufficiently tired of the effects of the breakdown of [decency] that they're going to be willing to give up [some freedoms]." He likens it to gun-control laws. "The Brady bill wasn't passed because of liberals, who always supported [such regulations]. It was passed because conservatives had seen [so much] carnage in schools and on the streets that they deserted the conservative ship."

15   Others contend "niceness laws" won't work. But their alternatives sound hokey, impractical, or both. Dispute-fixer Burton, for example, says, "We should divide the city into 365 areas and hold a 'Get to Know Your Neighbors Day' for each of the neighborhoods over the next year. It's harder to be inappropriate and confrontational with someone you really know," she explains. Goulston's advice is merely "count to ten" before reacting to someone else's behavior. He admits it might sound naive, but says small-scale efforts can pay off: "That's why some Neighborhood Watch programs are more effective than police." Even the federal government has gone altruistic. In February, it announced National Random Acts of Kindness Day, which advised putting coins into someone else's parking meter, anonymously buying ice cream cones for kids or mailing greeting cards to strangers.

16   Meanwhile, in New York, satirist Beard—who co-founded the National Lampoon—says what the country really needs is a dose of humor. With political correctness at an apex, he observes, too many Americans are ready

to blow up at the slightest provocation. "It's an unfortunate combination of events. We're getting nastier and oversensitive at the same time. People oughta lighten up."

17   And then there's Timothy Miller. A psychologist and author from Stockton, he insists that the whole meanness thing is an illusion: "People are reacting primarily to what they see on TV news and too little to what's really going on." In truth, he says, crime rates are flat, manners just seem to be in decline because there are more older people and they always think youngsters are beasts, and "events like freeway shootings—although appalling and emotionally gripping—are extremely rare."

18   Most other observers, however, suggest oblivion could be just around the corner. The so-called era of gentility, they say, which began in the 1850s and lingered into [the twentieth] century, was an aberration, a fluke.

19   Ultimately, discussions of this sort come back to a question of human nature. Call it Original Sin, call it a biological inclination to violence, call it a reaction to improper toilet training, but the story is still the same: The human heart is clouded by darkness. "If you could read the mind of Joe Blow Civilized Driver after he gets cut off on the freeway, it is as bestial, vicious, and rapacious as a tiger," Beaber says. "He may not act it out by beating the [other driver] with a tire iron, but that's his impulse and his fantasy."

20   In a 1994 pastoral letter, America's Catholic bishops sounded a similar theme, saying, "It is futile to suggest we can end all violence . . . merely by our own efforts. . . . We must realize that peace is most fundamentally a gift from God." Any solution that doesn't include prayer, they wrote, will inevitably fall short.

21   Goulston suspects another element is needed. "Americans never act until there's some sort of a wake-up call," he says. Could that be the Oklahoma City bombing? Goulston doesn't know. "But if that isn't it," he wonders, "then what kind of wake-up call will it take?"

Exercise 2   **VOCABULARY HIGHLIGHTS**

Write a short definition of each word as it is used in the essay. (Paragraph numbers are given in parentheses.) Be prepared to use the words in your own sentences.

entrepreneurs (3)	volatile (12)
apostles (4)	oblivion (18)
unprecedented (6)	aberration (18)
random (10)	inclination (19)
innovative (11)	rapacious (19)

Exercise 3   **DISCUSSION AND CRITICAL THINKING**

1. Is Rivenburg objective or subjective in his discussion of meanness and rudeness?

2. Which sentence in the first paragraph is the thesis?

3. What ideas do the examples in paragraph 3 support?

4. List three examples of the causes of recent neighbor-to-neighbor combat.

5. How did Japan deal with the problem of population density?

6. Why are there fewer interpersonal disputes in small towns?

7. What does psychologist Timothy Miller argue?

8. Do you agree with Beaber, who maintains that human beings are inclined toward meanness? Why or why not?

Amid Backlash, Calls for Cell Phone Etiquette

Jennifer Oldham

A staff writer with the *Los Angeles Times,* Jennifer Oldham wrote this article as one in a series on the effects of technology on society. The article attracted a lot of attention from those who use cell phones and those who do not. A poll by NBC (in 1999) found that 28 percent of the survey group owned cell phones and 59 percent of that same group did not want to sit next to anyone using a cell phone. The members of the latter group were irritated by cell phone use only as it invaded their cone of sound, which is Oldham's chief concern in this selection.

1   Secondhand cell phone conversations are fast replacing secondhand smoke as public enemy No. 1 in crowded venues nationwide. Once a status symbol, mobile phones have become a necessity for about 76 million Americans—in grocery stores, commuter trains, public restrooms, even at weddings. But while cell phone use in such venues has become commonplace, public acceptance has not.

2   As is the case with many new technologies that move into the mainstream, there are no social norms dictating how and where to use a mobile phone. And it shows.

3   Fed up with customers who have phones attached to their ears, restaurants, theaters, colleges, and churches have taken steps to ban mobile phone use. Those who ignore the policies face the wrath of other patrons and often are forced to conduct their conversations outside. "Whenever someone's cell phone would ring, eighteen sets of eyes would roll in their sockets," said restaurateur Danny Meyer, who has asked patrons to turn off their mobile phones in the four eateries he co-owns in New York. "A lot of people were being downright rude and showy and talking way over the crowd." Patrons at New York's popular Union Square Cafe are greeted with signs that read, "Please 86 all cell phone use in the dining room."

4   It should hardly come as a surprise that mobile phones have become as common as day planners for busy Americans. The 76 million mobile phone users in the United States represent a 300-percent increase from the 19 million in 1994, according to the Cellular Telephone Industry Association. And the number is expected to grow 25 percent annually as more people take advantage of offers for free phones and free calling time.

5   But with the influx of any time–anywhere communication comes the inevitable backlash. Call them the mobile phone etiquette pioneers, the brave souls who have dared to suggest that being tethered to the world twenty-four hours a day might not be such a good idea. At UCLA's new law library, officials took action to silence mobile phones after conversations created a ruckus in the first-floor reading room. "During finals in May, we had so many complaints from students about cell phones that we put up a laminated sign with a big phone with a slash through it," said Karen Nikos, director of communications at the UCLA School of Law. At the Stephen S. Wise Temple in Los Angeles, rabbis decided to print an announcement at the bottom of a weekly bulletin asking worshipers not to use their phones at the synagogue.

6   But intrusive cell phone use may not be the result of cheaper technology so much as the overall demise of common courtesy in the United States. "This is one part of a larger patchwork of behavior that shows disrespect for the value of public space and public discourse and sense of community in favor of celebration of oneself," said Jim Katz, a professor of communications at Rutgers University in New Jersey and author of "Connections: Social and Cultural Studies of the Telephone in American Life."

7   Once purchased for use only in emergencies, mobile phones today are wielded in such a freewheeling manner that it's no wonder that stabs at imposing mobile phone etiquette have taken users by surprise. Whittier resident Doris Riley didn't think twice recently when she dialed her boss during breakfast at one of her favorite eateries. But she considered boycotting its rich coffee after she was kicked out of the dining room during a call. "The owner came running at me very loud and said: 'You can't use a cell phone here. We have people eating and they want to eat in peace,'" she said. "I was really embarrassed because it's so small there. Everything went dead silent." Millie's, a hip Silver Lake hangout that Riley often visits with friends, is among a growing number of Southland restaurants that ask diners to yak outside. Owner Patti Peck says that when someone makes a call in the dining room, it's not unusual for the staff to start chanting, "No phones, no phones" and for customers to join in.

8   Ron Riddle, a resident of Dayton, Ohio, doesn't own a cell phone. But he does eat out often and is all in favor of restaurants controlling the atmosphere in their dining rooms—within limits. "Which seating preference would you like this evening, sir?" Riddle said, "Smoking or nonsmoking? Cell phone or non–cell phone? Crying babies or non–crying babies? Loudmouth drunks or non–loudmouth drunks?" Those on etiquette's front lines say they have received positive feedback about their policies. Roberto Aguilar, who manages the French restaurant Aubergine in Newport Beach, said a request on the menu—"Please no cell phones, thank you"—has prompted customers to tell him they were amazed to not hear one ring during their meal.

9   For New York restaurateur Meyer, the freshly imposed restrictions at his establishments haven't hurt business. "I have a file full of letters from people saying, 'Thank you for taking a stand.' Most people are happy to know what you expect of them," he said. "This technology has grown up so quickly that most people have not stopped to think what the etiquette should be."

| **Exercise 4** | **DISCUSSION AND CRITICAL THINKING** |

1. Is the author objective or subjective?

2. Which is the topic sentence, the first or the second sentence of the essay? Notice that the third sentence echoes the topic sentence.

3. How many examples are used in paragraph 3?

4. How does Jim Katz, professor of communications at Rutgers University, explain the use of the cell phone?

5. Does a restriction on cell phone use seem to affect business negatively?

6. How many specific examples (by name or time) are included? Give paragraph numbers of their location.

7. Is this topic presented fairly? Explain.

Practicing Patterns of Exemplification

A well-designed outline can help you make clear connections between your topic sentence and your examples. Remember that in some instances you can support your point with a single example extended in detail, and in other cases you may need several examples. In Exercise 5, the topic sentences are developed by multiple examples.

| **Exercise 5** | **COMPLETING PATTERNS OF EXEMPLIFICATION** |

Fill in the blanks to add more examples that support the topic sentence.

1. Topic sentence: Just walking through my favorite mall (or shopping center) shows me that the world is smaller than it used to be.

    I. People of different cultures (with specific examples)

    II. Foods of different cultures (with specific examples)

    III. _____

    IV. _____

2. Topic sentence: Driving to work (or school) this month and observing the behavior of other drivers have convinced me that road rage has invaded my community.

    I. A man honking his horn impatiently at an elderly driver

    II. _____

    III. _____

✎ **Topics for Writing with Examples**

Reading-Related Topics

1. Discuss at least three examples from the reading selections that show how a reaction to irritation can easily turn into anger or even violence.

"Sweet and Sour Workplace"

2. With this selection as a model, use examples to develop your ideas on how you have experienced and dealt with irritation at school, home, or work.

3. With this selection as a model, use examples to write about irritations in a neighborhood; in theaters during a movie; on airplanes, buses, or trains; on streets, highways, and freeways; or in restaurants.

"The Mean Season"

4. Use your own examples to support your discussion of one of the following statements (modify it a bit if you like):

We're playing tag with hate.

Civility supporters see rays of hope.

Manners just seem to be in decline because there are more older people and they think youngsters are beasts.

The human heart is clouded by darkness.

The human heart is lit by sunshine.

Recent events have started to waken Americans to a real problem with meanness (and they're getting madder than hell).

5. Keep track of acts of kindness and goodness versus acts of rudeness and meanness for a certain time period. Your study can cover many aspects of life, or it can be focused on work, school, streets, or home. You might station yourself at some location (a doorway, a crosswalk) where people have the opportunity to choose between being considerate or not being considerate. Use examples and give simple statistics. This could be an opportunity for you to work collaboratively with classmates in a candid-camera activity.

"Amid Backlash, Calls for Cell Phone Etiquette"

6. If you are bothered by the use of cell phones in public places such as restaurants, stadiums, classrooms, or places of worship, develop a paper with examples taken from what you have observed.

7. Use this selection as a model for writing a paragraph or essay of exemplification based on the idea that driving and using a cell phone are not a good com-

bination. If you do not have an abundance of examples, consider doing research in a library or on the Internet.

8. If you believe that the benefits of cell phones outweigh the problems, write a paragraph or essay of exemplification in which you explain how people depend on the cell phone for work, family, or school.

Career-Related Topics

Use specific examples to support one of the following statements as applied to business or work:

9. It's not what you know; it's who you know.

10. Don't burn your bridges.

11. Like Lego, business is a matter of connections.

12. Tact is the lubricant that oils the wheels of industry.

13. The customer is always right.

14. Money is honey, my little sonny, and the rich man's joke is always funny.

15. If you take care of the pennies, the dollars will take care of themselves.

16. A kind word turns away wrath.

General Topics

Make a judgmental statement about an issue you believe in strongly and then use an example or examples to illustrate your point. These are some possible topics:

17. The price of groceries is too high.

18. Professional athletes are paid too much.

19. A person buying a new car may get a lemon.

20. Drivers sometimes openly ignore the laws on a selective basis.

21. Politicians should be watched.

22. Working and going to school is tough.

23. Working, parenting, and going to school is tough.

24. All computer viruses have common features.

25. Many people under the age of eighteen spend too much time playing computer games.

26. Some computer games teach children useful skills.

Writer's Guidelines: Exemplification

1. Use examples to explain, convince, or amuse.

2. Use examples that are vivid, specific, and representative.

   • Vivid examples attract attention.

   • Specific examples are identifiable.

   • Representative examples are typical and therefore the basis for generalizations.

3. Tie your examples clearly to your topic sentence.

4. Draw your examples from what you have read, heard, and experienced.

5. Brainstorm a list of possible examples before you write.

6. Order your examples by time, space, or level of importance.

7. Ask yourself the following questions as you proceed:

   • What am I trying to say?

   • What examples might support that idea? (Use listing.)

   • How many examples and what order should I use?

   • Are my examples specific, vivid, and representative?

   • Have I made a connection between my examples and my topic sentence or thesis?

19

Process Analysis: Writing About Doing

"All jobs have procedures. While we are learning, the procedures may seem extremely complicated, perhaps almost impossible. . . . Most of us remember our struggles with routines that we now perform without conscious thought."

—"The Joy and Grief of Work"

Writing Paragraphs of Process Analysis

I f you have any doubt about how frequently we use process analysis, just think about how many times you have heard people say, "How do you do it?" or "How is [was] it done?" Even when you are not hearing those questions, you are posing them yourself when you need to make something, cook a meal, assemble an item, take some medicine, repair something, or figure out what happened. In your college classes, you may have to discover how osmosis occurs, how a rock changes form, how a mountain was formed, how a battle was won, or how a bill goes through the legislature.

If you need to explain how to do something or how something was (is) done, you will write a paper of *process analysis*. You will break down your topic into stages, explaining each so that your reader can duplicate or understand the process.

Two Types of Process Analysis: Directive and Informative

The questions How do I do it? and How is [was] it done? will lead you into two different types of process analysis—directive and informative.

Directive process analysis explains how to do something. As the name suggests, it gives directions and tells the reader how to do something. It says, for example,

315

"Read me, and you can bake a pie (tune up your car, analyze a book, write an essay, take some medicine)." Because it is presented directly to the reader, it usually addresses the reader as "you," or it implies the "you" by saying something such as "First [you] purchase a large turnip, and then [you] . . ." In the same way, this textbook addresses you or implies "you" because it is a long how-to-do-it (directive process analysis) statement.

Informative process analysis explains how something was (is) done by giving data (information). Whereas the directive process analysis tells you what to do in the future, the informative process analysis tells you what has occurred or what is occurring. If it is something in nature, such as the formation of a mountain, you can read and understand the process by which it emerged. In this type of process analysis, you do not tell the reader what to do; therefore, you usually do not use the words *you* or *your.*

Working with Stages

Preparation or Background

In the first stage of the directive type of process analysis, list the materials or equipment needed for the process and discuss the necessary setup arrangements. For some topics, this stage will also provide technical terms and definitions. The degree to which this stage is detailed will depend on both the subject itself and the expected knowledge and experience of the projected audience.

The informative type of process analysis may begin with background or context rather than with preparation. For example, a statement explaining how mountains form might begin with a description of a flat portion of the earth made up of plates that are arranged like a jigsaw puzzle.

Steps or Sequence

The actual process will be presented here. Each step or sequence must be explained clearly and directly and phrased to accommodate the audience. The language, especially in directive process analysis, is likely to be simple and concise; however, avoid dropping words such as *and, a, an, the,* and *of* and thereby lapsing into "recipe language." The steps may be accompanied by explanations about why certain procedures are necessary and how not following directions carefully can lead to trouble.

Time Order

The order will usually be chronological (time based) in some sense. Certain transitional words are commonly used to promote coherence: *first, second, third, then, soon, now, next, finally, at last, therefore, consequently,* and—especially for informative process analysis—words used to show the passage of time such as hours, days of the week, and so on.

Basic Forms

Consider using this form for the directive process (with topics such as how to cook something or how to fix something).

How to Fry Green Tomatoes

   I. Preparation

      A. Stove and utensils

      B. Cast-iron skillet

      C. Ingredients

         1. Sliced green tomatoes

         2. Cornmeal

         3. Buttermilk

         4. Bacon grease (or oil)

         5. Seasoning (salt, pepper, and so on)

  II. Steps

      A. Heat skillet on high flame

      B. Add bacon grease to coat skillet

      C. Dip sliced green tomatoes in buttermilk

      D. Dip sliced green tomatoes in cornmeal

      E. Drop sliced green tomatoes into hot skillet

      F. Reduce flame under skillet

      G. Brown and turn sliced green tomatoes once

      H. Drain golden brown green tomatoes on paper towel

      I. Serve

Consider using this form for the informative process (with topics such as how a volcano functions or how a battle was won).

How a Tornado Occurs

   I. Background

      A. Cool, dry air from the north

      B. Warm, humid air from the south

      C. Usually afternoon or early evening

  II. Sequence

      A. Narrow zone of thunderstorms forms

      B. Warm, humid air rises

      C. More warm air rushes in to replace it

      D. In-rushing air rotates

      E. Pressure drops

      F. Wind velocity increases

      G. Twisting, snaking funnel-shaped cloud extends down from larger cloud formation

Combined Forms

Combination process analysis occurs when directive process analysis and informative process analysis are blended, usually when the writer personalizes the account. Take this scenario:

Two people with the log-on names Captain Ahab and Ishmael are e-mailing.

> Ishmael: "I'm really intrigued with your idea of raising your own catfish, but I don't know how to make a pond."

> Captain Ahab: "Let me tell you how I made mine. First I shoveled out a 20' × 5' × 5' hole in my back lawn. Then I turned on the hose and . . ."

This process analysis begins as if it is only informative, but the main intent and the main need are clearly directive.

Often the personalized account is more interesting, and many assignments are done in that fashion. A paper about making a pecan pie may be informative—but uninspiring. A paper about the time you helped your grandmother make a pecan pie (giving all the details) may be informative, directive, and entertaining. It is often the cultural framework provided by personal experience that transforms a pedestrian directive account into something memorable.

Consider this student paragraph about something that has occurred, which tells us how to do something if we choose to do so.

Pupusas, Salvadoran Delight

Patty Serrano

We all have at least one kind of food that reminds us of childhood, something that has filled our bellies in times of hunger and perhaps comforted our minds in times of stress. For Patty Serrano, a community college student living at home, that special dish is *pupusas.* In El Salvador these are a favorite item in homes and restaurants and at roadside stands. In Southern California, they're available in little restaurants called *pupusarias.*

Topic sentence | Every time my mom decides to make pupusas, we jump for joy. <u>A pupusa contains only a few ingredients, and it may sound easy to make, but really good ones must be made by experienced hands</u>. My mom is an expert, having

Preparation | learned as a child from her mother. All the <u>ingredients</u> are <u>chosen fresh.</u> The <u>meat,</u> either pork or beef, can be bought prepared, but my <u>mom chooses to

Steps
1 | <u>prepare it herself.</u> The <u>meat</u>, which is called "carnitas," <u>is ground and cooked with tomatoes and spices.</u> The cheese—she uses a white Jalisco—has to be stringy because that kind gives pupusas a very good taste, appearance, and
2 | texture. Then comes the <u>preparation of the "masa," or cornmeal</u>. It has to be soft but not so soft that it falls apart in the making and handling. All of this is
3 | done while the "comal," or skillet, is being heated. She then grabs a chunk of <u>masa</u> and <u>forms it into a tortilla</u> like a magician turning a ball into a thin pan-
4 | cake. Next she grabs small chunks of <u>meat</u> and <u>cheese</u> and <u>places them in the
5 | middle of the tortilla</u>. The <u>tortilla</u> is <u>folded in half and formed again.</u> After <u>plac-
6 | ing the pupusa into the sizzling skillet</u> with one hand, she is already starting another pupusa. It's amazing how she does two things at the same time. She
7 | <u>turns</u> the <u>pupusas over and over</u> again <u>until</u> she is sure that <u>they are done.</u> We watch, mouths open, plates empty. In my family it is a tradition that I get the

first pupusa because I like them so much. I love opening the hot pupusas, smelling the aroma, and seeing the stringy cheese stretching in the middle. I'm as discriminating as a wine taster. But I never eat a pupusa without "curtido," chopped cabbage with jalapeño. Those items balance the richness of

Concluding sentences   the other ingredients. <u>I could eat Mom's pupusas forever. I guess it has something to do with the way my mom makes them, with experienced, magical, loving hands.</u>

Useful Prewriting Procedure

All the strategies of freewriting, brainstorming, and clustering can be useful in writing a process analysis. However, if you already know your subject well, you can simply make two lists, one headed "Preparation" or "Background" and the other "Steps" or "Sequence." Then jot down ideas for each. After you have finished with your listing, you can delete parts, combine parts, and rearrange parts for better order. That editing of your lists will lead directly to a formal outline you can use in Stage Two of the writing process.

Patty Serrano used the following lists as her initial prewriting activity for "*Pupusas,* Salvadoran Delight."

Preparation	Steps
—get vegetables	—cook meat
—meat, fresh	—cook tomatoes and spices
—cheese, stringy white Jalisco	—shape tortilla
—spices	—put meat, cheese, vegetables
—~~masa~~	into tortilla
—skillet	—fold and seal tortilla
—hot stove	—place pupusa into skillet
	—make more pupusas
	—turn pupusas
	—remove pupusas
	—eat pupusas

Connecting Reading and Writing: The Joy and Grief of Work

Work is inseparable from life. There is a German saying—"You are what you eat." There should be another saying—"You are what you do for a living." After all, one reason we change jobs is that we say the work is adversely affecting other parts of our lives. The effects are not just a matter of stress. Whatever procedures, attitudes, and thought processes we develop at work are likely to find their way into our everyday lives. For instance, a professor's teacherish behavior at times emerges even when he or she is relating to loved ones.

Work can also be full of repetition, a necessary condition of almost any job, but more so in some. If we are involved in repetition, we may perceive it as tedium and

THE QUIGMANS by Buddy Hickerson

"Hold still, it's my first day!"

B. Hickerson, copyright Los Angeles Times Syndicate. Reprinted by permission.

imagine that out there somewhere are exciting careers teeming with intellectual stimulation and creativity. Regardless of the job, if a person does it long enough, it will probably become to an important extent a "been-there, done-that" activity. Once I talked to a heart specialist, telling him of my gratitude for his doing just the right thing in saving the life of my relative. "It's all a matter of procedures," he said, with a dismissive wave of his hand. "I respond to each symptom and choose a procedure. It's as automatic and predictable as fixing a car. I don't have much choice."

All jobs have procedures. While we are learning, the procedures may seem extremely complicated, perhaps almost impossible. Virtually every workplace has a collection of legends about mistakes made by new employees, and most of us remember our struggles with routines that we now perform without conscious thought.

All three reading selections in this section relate to what people do at work. In "The Skinny on Working for a Dermatologist," J. Kim Birdine writes about her preparation and steps in assisting a dermatologist in the operating room. Barbara Garson takes us through the golden arches via "McDonald's—We Do It All for You," a process analysis included in an interview with a long-time fast-food worker. "Making Faces" is a paragraph by student Seham Hemmat. She gives make-overs in a mall beauty shop. Her Writing Process Worksheet shows you how her writing project evolved from idea to final draft.

You will find a full-size blank worksheet on page 6. It can be photocopied, filled in, and submitted with each assignment if your instructor directs you to do so.

Writing Process Worksheet

TITLE Making Faces

NAME Seham Hemmat   **DUE DATE** Thursday, November 18, 8 a.m.

ASSIGNMENT In the space below, write whatever you need to know about your assignment, including information about the topic, audience, pattern of writing, length, whether to include a rough draft or revised drafts, and whether your paper must be typed.

Write a directive process analysis. Personalize it by using a narrative framework. If possible, write about one procedure you do at work. Audience: general readers outside the field of work. One paragraph of about 250 words. Include this sheet completed, one or more rough drafts, and a typed final.

STAGE ONE **Explore** Freewrite, brainstorm (list), cluster, or take notes as directed by your instructor. Use the back of this page or separate paper if you need more space.

Preparation
—Check out customer
—Get right products
—Discuss price
—Discuss time

Steps
—Take off old makeup
—Wash face
—Toner on
—Moisturizer
—Foundation
—Powder
—Fix eyebrows
—Fix lashes
—Put on blush
—Add liner and lipstick

STAGE TWO **Organize** Write a topic sentence or thesis; label the subject and the treatment parts.

<u>If you'd like to do what I do,</u> <u>just follow these directions.</u>
              subject   treatment

Write an outline or an outline alternative.

I. Preparation
   A. Evaluate client
   B. Select supplies
      1. Cleanser
      2. Toner
      3. Others
   C. Check tray of tools

II. Steps

    A. Strip off old makeup

    B. Scrub face

    C. Put on toner

    D. Add moisturizer

    E. Rub on foundation

    F. Dust on powder

    G. Gel eyebrows

        1. Trim

        2. Shape

        3. Pencil

    H. Curl lashes

    I. Dab on blush

    J. Paint lips

STAGE THREE   **Write**   On separate paper, write and then revise your paper as many times as necessary for <u>c</u>oherence, <u>l</u>anguage (usage, tone, and diction), <u>u</u>nity, <u>e</u>mphasis, <u>s</u>upport, and <u>s</u>entences (CLUESS). Read your paper aloud to hear and correct any grammatical errors or awkward-sounding sentences.

Edit any problems in fundamentals, such as <u>c</u>apitalization, <u>o</u>missions, <u>p</u>unctuation, and <u>s</u>pelling (COPS).

Making Faces

Seham Hemmat

By evening Seham Hemmat is a community college student. By day she is an employee of a mall specialty store where, to use her words, she does "face detail work." She rewrote this paragraph of process analysis six times, twice reading it aloud to her peer group and listening to their suggestions (especially those from the two male members) before she was satisfied with the content and tone. Her word choice suggests a somewhat humorous view of work she takes seriously, but not too seriously.

The Face Place, a trendy mall store, is where I work. Making faces is what I do. I don't mean sticking out my tongue; I mean reworking the faces of women who want a new or fresh look. When I get through, if I've done a good job, you can't tell if my subject is wearing makeup or not. <u>If you'd like to do what I do, just follow these directions.</u> Imagine you have a client. Her name is Donna. <u>Check her out</u> for skin complexion, skin condition, size of eyes, kind of eyebrows, and lip shape. Then <u>go to the supply room and select</u> the <u>items</u> you need for the faceover, including a cleanser and toner with added moisturizers. <u>Put them on a tray by your brushes and other tools and basic supplies.</u> <u>Begin by stripping off her old makeup</u> with a few cotton balls and cleanser. Donna's skin is a combination of conditions. Her forehead, nose, and chin are oily, and her cheeks are dry. <u>Scrub her down</u> with Tea Tree, my favorite facial cleanser from a product line that is not tested on animals. Scour

Topic sentence

Preparation

Steps 1

2

3 the oil slicks extra. Then <u>slather on</u> some <u>Tea Tree toner</u> to close her pores so
4 the dirt doesn't go back in. <u>Add</u> a <u>very light moisturizer</u> such as one called
5 Elderflower Gel. Donna has a pale complexion. <u>Put on a coat of 01 foundation,</u>
   the fairest in the shop, which evens out her skin tone. Next, with a big face
6 brush, <u>dust on a layer of 01 powder</u> to give her a smooth, dry look. Now
   Donna, who's watching in a mirror, speaks up to say she wants her eyebrows brushed and lightened just a bit. She has dark eyebrows and eyelashes
7 that won't require much mascara or eyebrow pencil. <u>So use gel to fix the</u>
   <u>eyebrows</u> in place while you <u>trim, shape, and pencil them.</u> Move downward
8 on the face, going next to her eyes. Use brown mascara to <u>curl her already</u>
9 <u>dark lashes</u>. With your blusher brush, <u>dab</u> some peach rose <u>blush on</u> her
10 <u>cheeks</u> and <u>blend it in.</u> <u>Line her lips</u> with bronze sand lip liner pencil and <u>fill in</u>
   <u>the rest</u> with rouge mauve lipstick. Swing Donna around to the big lighted
   mirror. Watch her pucker her lips, squint her eyes, flirt with herself. See her

Concluding sentences   smile. Now you pocket the tip. Feel good. <u>You've just given a woman a new</u>
   <u>face, and she's out to conquer the world.</u>

| Exercise 1 | DISCUSSION AND CRITICAL THINKING |

1. Is this paragraph of process analysis mainly directive or informative?

2. How does Hemmat take her paragraph beyond a list of mechanical directions?

3. In addition to using chronological order (time), what other order does she use briefly?

4. What word choice may have come from suggestions offered by the males in her discussion group?

The Skinny on Working for a Dermatologist

J. Kim Birdine

After having traveled a long way, from a Korean orphanage to the United States, J. Kim Birdine is still on the move. In writing this essay of process analysis, she demonstrates the same intellectual quali- ties she uses so well in her role as an assistant to a doctor, both in the office and in the operating room.

As a medical assistant for a dermatologist, I am actively involved in every aspect of the practice, recommending products, doing laser treatments for veins, and administering skin peels. The younger patients generally see the doctor to correct their skin problems, whether they're suffering from a persistent dry patch, uneven skin tone, or a bout with acne. A good number of the patients come in for cosmetic reasons, wanting their wrinkles smoothed out or their dark blotches lasered off. The most important part of my job, though, is to prepare surgical trays for the patients with skin cancer and to assist the doctor through the procedure.

My initial concern when setting up a surgical tray is that everything is sterile. This means that all the metal instruments, gauze, and applicators (Q-Tips) are put through an Autoclave (steam sterilizer), to ensure sterilization. Once everything is sterile, I begin setting up my surgical tray by placing a sterile field on a tray, which has long legs and wheels at the base so it can be rolled. The tray should stand about waist high so the physician can reach the instruments easily. The sterile field is a large white tissue that I carefully take out of a sealed pack, touching it only at the corners to unfold it to its full size. It serves as a base on which to place all the instruments.

Next all of the metal instruments are placed on the tray with a long-handled "pick-up." The necessary instruments are a scalpel, a skin hook, large forceps, small forceps, straight scissors, curved scissors, a large needle holder, and a small needle holder. All are placed with handles facing toward me, except the small needle holder and the straight scissors. These two should be positioned at a corner away from me with the handles facing out. The position of all of the instruments is important so that the doctor can reach them with ease. The ones placed in the corner are for me to use while assisting with suturing. A surgical tray is not complete without a small stack of gauze (large) and about twenty applicators. The entire tray is covered with another sterile field exactly like the one placed initially on the tray.

Just prior to surgery, I set up extras. I place on the counter anesthesia—a 3cc syringe of lidocaine with epinephrine—and a disinfectant skin cleanser, along with two pair of surgical gloves, one for the doctor and one for me. I turn on the hyfrecator, which is a cauterizer used to stop bleeding by burning the tissue. I prepare a specimen bottle indicating on its label the patient's name, the date, the doctor's name, and the area of the body from which the specimen is taken. I remove the sterile field on top of the instruments and place the sutures requested by the doctor and a different kind of sterile field, which has a hole in the middle of it, on the tray. This field enables the doctor to place the hole directly over the surgery site, exposing only the area to be worked on and covering the surrounding areas.

During surgery, once the doctor removes the section that needs to be tested, I place it in the specimen jar, seal the lid on it, and place it on the counter. I have to be attentive to the surgery at this point to assist in reducing the bleeding. My job is to apply gauze or applicators wherever bleeding occurs and to ready the hyfrecator in case the doctor needs it. When bleeding is minimized, the doctor begins suturing. At this point I have the small needle holder in hand as well as the straight scissors. I use the small needle holder to grab the tip of the needle after the doctor inserts it through the skin, to pull it through for her. This makes her job easier. I use the straight scissors to cut the suture once she is finished with knotting. Sometimes she does some internal suturing for the tissue under the skin, with dissolvable thread, and knots each turn. This is when I cut directly on top of the knot. The surface suturing is usually knotted at the beginning and at the end of the line of sutures and needs cutting down to one-quarter of an inch.

After surgery, I use peroxide to clean the patient's surgical site. I apply either a pressure bandage or a plain Band-Aid with antibiotic ointment. The pressure bandage is applied usually when there is a concern of more bleeding post surgery. I explain to the patient how to take care of the surgical area and when to come back to have the sutures removed. This makes my job complete, until it is time for another set-up, when I will repeat the same process of ensuring a sterile environment for the patient.

Exercise 2   **DISCUSSION AND CRITICAL THINKING**

1. Underline and label the thesis (in the first paragraph).

2. Annotate the essay for the preparation and the steps of this process analysis. Number the parts of each stage. Underline key words corresponding with your annotations.

3. Why is the preparation stage longer than the steps stage for Birdine?

4. On what principle is Birdine's order of presentation based—time or space?

McDonald's—We Do It All for You

Barbara Garson

In this essay from *The Electronic Sweatshop*, Barbara Garson interviews a former McDonald's griddleman, who explains why he quit and will never return. It's an inside look at the workplace that produces that burger the same way every time, no matter where you are. A well-established and highly regarded playwright and journalist, Garson has recently focused her attention on workers in a computerized society of service-oriented jobs.

1   "They called us the Green Machine," says Jason Pratt, recently retired McDonald's griddleman, "'cause the crew had green uniforms then. And that's what it is, a machine. You don't have to know how to cook, you don't have to know how to think. There's a procedure for everything and you just follow the procedures."

2   "Like?" I asked. I was interviewing Jason in the Pizza Hut across from his old McDonald's.

3   "Like, uh," the wiry teenager searched for a way to describe the all-encompassing procedures. "O.K., we'll start you off on something simple. You're on the ten-in-one grill, ten patties in a pound. Your basic burger. The guy on the bin calls, 'Six hamburgers,' so you lay your six pieces of meat on the grill and set the timer." Before my eyes Jason conjures up the gleaming, mechanized McDonald's kitchen. "Beep-beep, beep-beep, beep-beep. That's the beeper to sear 'em. It goes off in twenty seconds. Sup, sup, sup, sup, sup, sup." He presses each of the six patties down on the sizzling grill with an imaginary silver disk. "Now you turn off the sear beeper, put the buns in the oven, set the oven timer and then the next beeper is to turn the meat. This one goes beep-beep-beep, beep-beep-beep. So you turn your patties and then you drop your re-cons on the meat, t-con, t-con, t-con." Here Jason takes two imaginary handfuls of reconstituted onions out of water and sets them out, two blops at a time, on top of the six patties he's arranged in two neat rows on the grill. "Now the bun oven buzzes [there are more than a half dozen different timers with distinct beeps and buzzes in a McDonald's kitchen]. This one turns itself off when you open the oven door so you just take out your crowns, line 'em up and give 'em each a squirt of mustard and a squirt of ketchup." With mustard in his right hand and ketchup in his left, Jason wields the dispensers like a pair of six-shooters up and down the lines of buns. Each dispenser has two triggers. One fires the premeasured squirt for ten-in-ones—the second is set for quarter-pounders.

4   "Now," says Jason, slowing down, "now you get to put on the pickles. Two if they're regular, three if they're small. That's the creative part. Then the lettuce, then you ask for a cheese count ('cheese on four please'). Finally the last beep goes off and you lay your burger on the crowns."

5   "On the *crown* of the buns?" I ask, unable to visualize. "On top?"

6   "Yeah, you dress 'em upside down. Put 'em in the box upside down too. They flip 'em over when they serve 'em."

7   "Oh, I think I see."

8   "Then scoop up the heels [the bun bottoms] which are on top of the bun warmer, rake the heels with one hand and push the tray out from underneath and they land (plip) one on each burger, right on top of the re-cons, neat and perfect. [The official time allotted by Hamburger Central, the McDonald's headquarters in Oak Brook, Illinois, is ninety seconds to prepare and serve a burger.] It's like I told you. The procedures make the burgers. You don't have to know a thing."

9   McDonald's employs 500,000 teenagers at any one time. Most don't stay long. About 8 million Americans—7 percent of our labor force—have worked at McDonald's and moved on.[1] Jason is not a typical ex-employee. In fact, Jason is a legend among the teenagers at the three McDonald's outlets in his suburban area. It seems he was so fast at the griddle (or maybe just fast talking) that he'd been taken back three times by two different managers after quitting.

10   But Jason became a real legend in his last stint at McDonald's. He'd been sent out the back door with the garbage, but instead of coming back in he got into a car with two friends and just drove away. That's the part the

---

[1] These statistics come from John F. Love, *McDonald's Behind the Golden Arches.* Additional background information in this chapter comes from Ray Kroc and Robert Anderson, *Grinding It Out,* and Max Boas and Steve Chain, *Big Mac.*

local teenagers love to tell. "No fight with the manager or anything . . . just drove away and never came back. . . . I don't think they'd give him a job again."

11   "I would never go back to McDonald's," says Jason. "Not even as a manager." Jason is enrolled at the local junior college. "I'd like to run a real restaurant someday, but I'm taking data processing to fall back on." He's had many part-time jobs, the highest-paid at a hospital ($4.00 an hour), but that didn't last, and now dishwashing (at the $3.35 minimum). "Same as McDonald's. But I would never go back there. You're a complete robot."

12   "It seems like you can improvise a little with the onions," I suggested. "They're not premeasured." Indeed, the reconstituted onion shreds grabbed out of a container by the unscientific-looking wet handful struck me as oddly out of character in the McDonald's kitchen.

13   "There's supposed to be twelve onion bits per patty," Jason informed me. "They spot check."

14   "Oh come on."

15   "You think I'm kiddin'. They lift your heels and they say, 'You got too many onions.' It's portion control."

16   "Is there any freedom anywhere in the process?" I asked.

17   "Lettuce. They'll leave you alone as long as it's neat."

18   "So lettuce is freedom; pickles is judgment?"

19   "Yeah but you don't have time to play around with your pickles. They're never gonna say just six pickles except on the disk. [Each store has video disks to train the crew for each of about twenty work stations, like fries, register, lobby, quarter-pounder grill.] What you'll hear in real life is 'twelve and six on a turn-lay.' The first number is your hamburgers, the second is your Big Macs. On a turn-lay means you lay the first twelve, then you put down the second batch after you turn the first. So you got twenty-four burgers on the grill, in shifts. It's what they call a production mode. And remember you also got your fillets, your McNuggets. . . ."

20   "Wait, slow down." By then I was losing track of the patties on our imaginary grill. "I don't understand this turn-lay thing."

21   "Don't worry, you don't have to understand. You follow the beepers, you follow the buzzers, and you turn your meat as fast as you can. It's like I told you, to work at McDonald's you don't need a face, you don't need a brain. You need to have two hands and two legs and move 'em as fast as you can. That's the whole system. I wouldn't go back there again for anything."

Exercise 3	**DISCUSSION AND CRITICAL THINKING**

1. Number the steps in the procedure given in paragraphs 3 through 8. Underline some key words and put the numbers in the left margin.

2. Jason Pratt says, "The procedures make the burgers." Is that bad for the burger customers or bad for the burger makers? Or both? Explain.

3. Is Pratt a typical McDonald's employee? What positive things might be said about the company?

4. How are the procedures followed by McDonald's different from other procedures you have encountered in similar jobs?

5. How do you account for the fact that some people work at McDonald's, even doing grill duty, for a long time? Do they like to work there? Do some people thrive on the repetition? Have some people learned to deal creatively with the repetition?

Practicing Patterns of Process Analysis

Underlying a process analysis is a definite pattern. In some presentations, such as directions with merchandise to be assembled, the content reads as mechanically as an outline, and no reader objects. The same can be said of most recipes. In other presentations, such as your typical college assignments, the pattern is submerged in flowing discussion. The directions or information must be included, but the writing should be well developed and interesting. Regardless of the form you use or the audience you anticipate, keep in mind that in process analysis the pattern provides a foundation for the content.

| **Exercise 4** | **COMPLETING PATTERNS OF PROCESS ANALYSIS** |

Directive Process Analysis: Complete this pattern for replacing a flat tire with a spare. Work in a group if possible.

I. Preparation

   1. Park car.

   2. _____

   3. Obtain car jack.

   4. _____

   5. _____

II. Steps

   1. Remove hub cap (if applicable).

   2. Loosen lug nuts a bit.

   3. _____

   4. _____

   5. Remove wheel with flat tire.

   6. _____

   7. _____

   8. Release jack pressure.

   9. _____

Informative Process Analysis: Complete this pattern for an explanation of how a watermelon seed grows into a plant and produces a watermelon. Work in a group if possible.

 I. Background (what happens before the sprouting)

  1. Seed planted in cultivated land

  2. _____

  3. Receives heat (from sun)

 II. Sequence (becomes plant and produces fruit)

  1. Sprouts

  2. _____

  3. Responds to sunlight and air

  4. _____

  5. _____

  6. Flower pollinated

  7. _____

✎ Topics for Writing Process Analysis

Reading-Related Topics

"*Pupusas:* Salvadoran Delight"

1. Write about a special food prepared in your family now or in your childhood. The food could be your favorite dish, or it might be a treat prepared for a special holiday. Personalize your process analysis.

"Making Faces"

2. Using this paragraph as a model (omit the hypothetical customer if you like), write about any other grooming or personal service that you either perform for hire or understand very well and can perform. Suggestions: hair, nails, facials, skin art (tattooing or painting), skin alteration (piercing).

"The Skinny on Working for a Dermatologist"

3. Write about a job that required you to play an important supporting role. Explain both how you helped and what the other person did.

"McDonald's—We Do It All for You"

4. Write about procedures you either use at a job you have now or used in a previous job.

5. If procedures you worked with at a job were not written down, write them in concise, numbered parts.

6. Using some of the same terminology used by Jason Pratt, write a procedural statement of how to eat a McDonald's burger. Refer to the parts of the burger as it is to be consumed. Include sound effects. Use buzzers if you like. Time each stage. Title of something like "Eating a Burger in Ninety Seconds."

Career-Related Topics

7. Explain how to display, package, sell, or demonstrate a product.

8. Explain how to perform a service or to repair or install a product.

9. Explain the procedure for operating a machine, computer, piece of equipment, or other device.

10. Explain how to manufacture, construct, or cook something.

General Topics

Most of the following topics are directive as they are phrased. However, each can be transformed into a "how-it-was-done" informative topic by personalizing it and explaining stage by stage how you, someone else, or a group did something. For example, you could write either a directive process analysis about how to deal with an obnoxious person or an informative process analysis about how you or someone else dealt with an obnoxious person. Keep in mind that the two types of process analysis are often blended, especially in the personal approach. Many of the following topics will be more interesting to you and your readers if the process is personalized.

Most of the topics require some narrowing to be treated in a paragraph. For example, writing about playing baseball is too broad; writing about how to throw a curve ball may be manageable.

11. How to end a relationship without hurting someone's feelings

12. How to pass a test for a driver's license

13. How to get a job at _____

14. How to eat _____

15. How to perform a magic trick

16. How to repair _____

17. How to assemble _____

18. How to learn about another culture

19. How to approach someone you would like to know better

Writer's Guidelines: Process Analysis

1. Decide whether your process analysis is mainly directive or informative, and be appropriately consistent in using pronouns and other designations.

   • For the directive analysis, use the second person, addressing the reader as *you*. The *you* may be understood, even if it is not written.

   • For the informative analysis, use

     a. the first person, speaking as *I* or *we,* or

     b. the third person, speaking about the subject as *he, she, it,* or *they,* or by name.

2. Consider using these basic forms.

Directive	**Informative**
I. Preparation	I. Background
A.	A.
B.	B.
II. Steps	II. Steps
A.	A.
B.	B.
C.	C.

3. Listing is a useful prewriting activity for process analysis. Begin with the Roman numeral headings indicated in guideline 2.

4. The order of a process analysis will usually be chronological (time based) in some sense. Certain transitional words are commonly used to promote coherence: *first, second, third, then, soon, now, next, finally, at last, therefore,* and *consequently.*

20

Cause and Effect: Determining Reasons and Outcomes

"Many people walk a fine line between being passionate about something and being obsessed about it. The first is productive; the second is destructive."

—"Compulsions and Addictions"

Writing Paragraphs of Cause and Effect

ause-and-effect relationships are common in our daily lives. A single situation may raise questions about both causes and effects:

> My computer crashed. Why? (cause)
>
> What now? (effect)

In a paragraph, you will probably concentrate on either causes or effects, although you may mention both of them. Because you cannot write about all causes or all effects, you should try to identify and develop the most important ones. Consider that some causes are immediate, others remote; some visible, others hidden. Any one or a group of causes can be the most important. The effects of an event can also be complicated. Some may be immediate, others long-range. The sequence of events is not necessarily related to causation. For example, *B* (inflation) may follow *A* (the election of a president), but that sequence does not mean that *A* caused *B*.

Exploring

One useful approach in exploring a cause-and-effect analysis is *listing*. Write down the event, situation, or trend you are concerned about. Then on the left side list the causes and on the right side list the effects. Looking at the two lists, determine the best side (causes or effects) for your study.

Here is a pair of lists on the topic of alcoholism.

Causes	Event, Situation, or Trend	Effects
inherited		fights
work	my dad's	arguments
social drinking out of	alcoholism	bad driving
control		embarrassed us
lack of self-control		looked bad
worry about money		stomach problems
		lost job
		broke
		robbed piggy bank
		DUI
		accidents
		died

Organizing

After you have evaluated the items on your lists, choose three or so of the most important causes or effects and proceed.

The causes could be incorporated into a *topic sentence* and then developed in an *outline*.

Topic Sentence: <u>Drinking</u> <u>took its toll in many ways.</u>
                       subject   **treatment**

I. Social

   A. Neighborhood

      1. Argued

      2. Embarrassed us

   B. Home

      1. With Mom

      2. With us

II. Physical

   A. Appearance

   B. Health

III. Work

   A. Absences

   B. Fired

IV. Loses control

   A. Piggy-bank theft

   B. Accident

Your paragraph will derive its structure from either causes or effects, although both causes and effects may be mentioned. Give emphasis and continuity to your writing by repeating key words, such as *cause, reason, effect, result, consequence,* and *outcome.*

If your pattern of causes or effects occurred in a sequence, then maintain that chronological order. Otherwise, arrange your points according to emphasis, from least to most important or from most to least important. The basic structure of your paragraph will look like this:

Topic sentence

  I.   Cause or Effect 1

  II. Cause or Effect 2

  III. Cause or Effect 3

Concluding sentence

Connecting Reading and Writing: Compulsions and Addictions

We are probably all compulsive at times, and we may obsess about something so that our life gets out of balance. Compulsion, which may be addiction if prolonged or severe, occurs when something seems so compelling that we shove aside or ignore more important matters such as families, obligations, even cherished values. The causes of this condition vary according to the obsession. The dependency may be chemical, as with alcoholism or drug abuse. It may be mainly psychological, reinforced by months or years of practice until the behavior becomes ingrained. For example, a workaholic may labor from early morning to late at night, from Monday through Sunday. The workaholic takes work to vacations, ball games, the dinner table, and the marriage bed. People become obsessed with other activities as well—playing golf, watching television, fixing cars, cooking, or even writing. It's a matter of a person pursuing something until it becomes that person and that person becomes it. That pursuit then takes over and transforms the multidimensional person into a one-dimensional person. Many people walk a fine line between being passionate about something and being obsessed about it. The first is productive; the second is destructive.

THE QUIGMANS   by Buddy Hickerson

Evening with a flight attendant.

B. Hickerson, copyright 1997. Los Angeles Times Syndicate. Reprinted by permission.

In this section, three writers introduce us to lives ruled by compulsion. In "Television Changed My Family Forever," Linda Ellerbee explains how her family became obsessed with television and how their relationships were forever altered. In "Work, Work, Work: For Workaholics, the Job Can Be a Disease," journalist Bob Walter provides insights into one of our most common compulsions.

"My Dad, the Bank Robber" by student Louis Crissman takes us to the clearly addictive level of compulsion—alcoholism, as his father's social drinking becomes antisocial and then harmful with far-ranging effects. Crissman's prewriting lists and outline introduced you to his topic in the beginning of this chapter. Now you can see how he proceeded with a cause-and-effect assignment, beginning with the Writing Process Worksheet, omitting his two rough drafts here, and concluding with the final draft.

You will find a full-size blank worksheet on page 6. It can be photocopied, filled in, and submitted with each assignment if your instructor directs you to do so.

. . . .

Writing Process Worksheet

TITLE My Dad, the Bank Robber

NAME Louis Crissman   **DUE DATE** Friday, April 20, 1 p.m.

ASSIGNMENT In the space below, write whatever you need to know about your assignment, including information about the topic, audience, pattern of writing, length, whether to include a rough draft or revised drafts, and whether your paper must be typed.

Write a paragraph of 200 to 300 words about someone you know or know of who has an addiction. It can be chemical, or it can be an extreme preoccupation that has caused him or her to lose a sense of balance in relation to values and to others. Submit this completed worksheet, a rough draft, and a final typed draft. Audience: general.

STAGE ONE **Explore**   Freewrite, brainstorm (list), cluster, or take notes as directed by your instructor. Use the back of this page or separate paper if you need more space.

Causes		Situation		Effects
inherited		my dad's		fights
work	}	alcoholism	}	arguments
social drinking				bad driving
out of control				embarrassed us
lack of self-control				looked bad
worry about money				stomach problems
				lost job
				broke
				robbed piggy bank
				DUI
				accidents
				died

STAGE TWO   **Organize**   Write a topic sentence or thesis; label the subject and the treatment parts.

Drinking took its toll in many ways.
<u>subject</u>   <u>treatment</u>

Write an outline or an outline alternative.

- I. Social
    - A. Neighborhood
        1. Argued
        2. Embarrassed us.
    - B. Home
        1. With Mom
        2. With us
- II. Physical
    - A. Appearance
    - B. Health
- III. Work
    - A. Absences
    - B. Fired
- IV. Loses control
    - A. Piggy-bank theft
    - B. Accident

STAGE THREE   **Write**   On separate paper, write and then revise your paper as many times as necessary for coherence, language (usage, tone, and diction), unity, emphasis, support, and sentences (CLUESS). Read your paper aloud to hear and correct any grammatical errors or awkward-sounding sentences.

Edit any problems in fundamentals, such as capitalization, omissions, punctuation, and spelling (COPS).

My Dad, the Bank Robber

Louis Crissman

Student Louis Crissman writes from the dark side of compulsions. His father was an alcoholic, and eventually all aspects of his father's life were affected by his disease.

Kids of alcoholics almost never think of drunks as funny. Actually I did when my father first became an alcoholic, back when he didn't know he was one, and we didn't either. Because he could go to work and he could dance without falling down and he could hold conversations without getting angry, he was just a guy who drank too much at times. Then when we learned he was an alcoholic, we kept his secret. At least we thought it was a secret because we didn't talk about it. <u>But drinking overtook his life in stages.</u> <u>His dignity went first.</u> He'd embarrass us by being drunk at night when he came home and parked crooked on the driveway, fought with neighbors about little things, and argued with Mom about everything. He wanted to help coach my

Topic sentence
Effect (social)

Effect (physical)	Little League baseball team, but I told him I didn't want him to because I knew he would show up drunk and yell at everyone. <u>Then his sickness took over his body.</u> He lost weight, his nose got red with little veins, and his flesh
Effect (work)	turned puffy. <u>Next he "got laid off" as he put it, but we all knew he was fired</u>
Effect (personal to author)	<u>for drinking on the job.</u> <u>Finally there was *the* night.</u> I was lying in my bed about midnight when Dad came in. He was carrying a knife, just a kitchen butter knife. I pretended I wasn't peeking at him. He went to my piggy bank that was loaded mostly with quarters and picked it up as quietly as he could and turned it upside down. Then he stuck the knife in the slot in the piggy's back and shook the bank so quarters slid down the knife blade. He extracted maybe half of them, more than twenty dollars' worth, and heaped them on my baseball glove lying there on the dresser. Then he crammed them into his pocket and slipped away in the night. That was a week before <u>the accident.</u>
Effect (on himself)	He <u>killed himself in a smashed car.</u> He hit a tree, not someone else. Mom said it was a blessing. At the funeral we all tried to remember how he was before his compulsion took over. We knew when it started. It started when his drinks became more important than we were or even he was. <u>To kids of alcoholics,</u>
Concluding sentence	<u>even those funny little amphibians in the commercials about beer aren't really funny</u>.

Exercise 1	**DISCUSSION AND CRITICAL THINKING**

1. Does Crissman refer at all to causes?

2. What examples does he use?

3. What is the order of presentation?

4. How do you judge the title? Would it have been better or worse if Crissman's father had robbed a commercial bank instead of a piggy bank?

Television Changed My Family Forever

Linda Ellerbee

Television producer and writer Linda Ellerbee remembers her first experiences with television as a child. She had two lives, BTV and ATV, <u>b</u>efore television and <u>a</u>fter television. Her recollections are of a family transformed by a preoccupation with an object not much larger than a breadbox. The transformation was simple: Activities gave way to TV watching. Ellerbee's recollections come from her book *Move On.*

1   Santa Claus brought us a television for Christmas. See, said my parents, television doesn't eat people. Maybe not. But television changed people. Television changed my family forever. We stopped eating dinner at the dining-room table after my mother found out about TV trays. We kept the TV trays behind the kitchen door and served ourselves from pots on the stove. Setting and clearing the dining-room table used to be my job; now, setting and clearing meant unfolding and wiping out TV trays, then, when we'd finished, wiping and folding our TV trays. Dinner was served in time for one program and finished in time for another. During dinner we used to talk to one another. Now television talked to us. If you had something you absolutely had to say, you waited until the commercial, which is, I suspect, where I learned to speak in thirty-second bursts. As a future writer, it was good practice in editing my thoughts. As a little girl, it was lonely as hell. Once in a while, I'd pass our dining-room table and stop, thinking I heard our ghosts sitting around talking to one another, saying stuff.

2   Before television, I would lie in bed at night listening to my parents come upstairs, enter their bedroom and say things to one another that I couldn't hear, but it didn't matter, their voices rocked me to sleep. My first memory, the first one ever, was of my parents and their friends talking me to sleep when we were living in Bryan and my bedroom was right next to the kitchen. I was still in my crib then. From the kitchen I could hear them, hear the rolling cadence of their speech, the rising and falling of their voices and the sound of chips.

3   "Two pair showing."

4   "Call?"

5   "Check."

6   "Call?"

7   "Call." *Clink.*

8   "I raise." *Clink Clink.*

9   "See your raise and raise you back." *Clink clink clink.*

10   "Call." *Clink Clink.*

11   "I'm in." *Clink.*

12   "I'm out."

13   "Let's see 'em."

14   It was a song to me, a lullaby. Now Daddy went to bed right after the weather and Mama stayed up to see Jack Paar (later she stayed up to see Steve Allen and Johnny Carson and even Joey Bishop, but not David Letterman). I went to sleep alone, listening to voices in my memory.

15   Daddy stopped buying Perry Mason books. Perry was on television and that was so much easier for him, Daddy said, because he could never remember which Perry Mason books he'd read and was always buying the wrong ones by mistake, then reading them all the way to the end before he realized he'd already read them. Television fixed that, he said, because although the stories weren't as good as the stories in the books, at least he knew he hadn't already read them. But it had been Daddy and Perry who'd taught me how fine it could be to read something you liked twice, especially if you didn't know the second time wasn't the first time. My mother used to laugh at Daddy. She would never buy or read the same book again and again. She had her own library card. She subscribed to magazines and belonged to the Book-of-the-Month Club. Also, she hated mystery stories. Her favorite books were about doctors who found God and women who

found doctors. Her most favorite book ever was *Gone with the Wind,* which she'd read before I was born. Read it while she vacuumed the floor, she said. Read it while she'd ironed shirts. Read it while she'd fixed dinner and read it while she'd washed up. Mama sure loved that book. She dropped Book-of-the-Month after she discovered *As the World Turns.* Later, she stopped her magazine subscriptions. Except for *TV Guide.* I don't know what she did with her library card. I know what she didn't do with it.

16   Mom quit taking me to the movies about this time, not that she'd ever take me to the movies very often after Mr. Disney let Bambi's mother get killed, which she said showed a lack of imagination. She and Daddy stopped going to movies, period. Daddy claimed it was because movies weren't as much fun after Martin broke up with Lewis, but that wasn't it. Most movies he cared about seeing would one day show up on television, he said. Maybe even Martin & Lewis movies. All you had to do was wait. And watch.

17   After a while, we didn't play baseball anymore, my daddy and me. We didn't go to baseball games together, either, but we watched more baseball than ever. That's how Daddy perfected The Art of Dozing to Baseball. He would sit down in his big chair, turn on the game and fall asleep within five minutes. That is, he appeared to be asleep. His eyes were shut. He snored. But if you shook him and said, Daddy, you're asleep, he'd open his eyes and tell you what the score was, who was up and what the pitcher ought to throw next. The Art of Dozing to Baseball. I've worked at it myself, but have never been able to get beyond waking up in time to see the instant replay. Daddy never needed instant replay and, no, I don't know how he did it; he was a talented man and he had his secrets.

18   Our lives began to seem centered around, and somehow measured by, television. My family believed in television. If it was on TV, it must be so. Calendars were tricky and church bells might fool you, but if you heard Ed Sullivan's[1] voice you knew it was Sunday night. When four men in uniforms sang that they were the men from Texaco who worked from Maine to Mexico, you knew it was Tuesday night. Depending on which verse they were singing, you knew whether it was seven o'clock or eight o'clock on Tuesday night. It was the only night of the week I got to stay up until eight o'clock. My parents allowed this for purely patriotic reasons. If you didn't watch Uncle Milty[2] on Tuesday nights, on Wednesday mornings you might have trouble persuading people you were a real American and not some commie pinko[3] foreigner from Dallas. I wasn't crazy about Milton Berle, but I pretended I was; an extra hour is an extra hour, and if the best way to get your daddy's attention is to watch TV with him, then it was worth every joke Berle could steal.

19   Television was taking my parents away from me, not all the time, but enough, I believed. When it was on, they didn't see me, I thought. Take holidays. Although I was an only child, there were always grandparents, aunts, uncles, and cousins enough to fill the biggest holiday. They were the best times. White linen and old silver and pretty china. Platters of turkey and ham, bowls of cornbread dressing and sweet potatoes and ambrosia. Homemade rolls. Glass cake stands holding pineapple, coconut, angel food

---

[1]Host of *The Ed Sullivan Show,* broadcast on CBS Sunday evenings from 1948 to 1971.
[2]Milton Berle, popular TV comedian of the same era.
[3]Communist.

and devil's food cakes, all with good boiled icing. There was apple pie with cheese. There were little silver dishes with dividers for watermelon pickles, black olives and sliced cranberry jelly. There was all the iced tea you'd ever want. Lord, it was grand. We kids always finished first (we weren't one of those families where they make the kids eat last and you never get a drumstick). After we ate, we'd be excused to go outside, where we'd play. When we decided the grown-ups had spent enough time sitting around the table after they'd already finished eating, which was real boring, we'd go back in and make as much noise as we could, until finally four or five grown-ups would come outside and play with us because it was just easier, that's all. We played hide-and-seek or baseball or football or dodge ball. Sometimes we just played *ball.* Sometimes we just played. Once in a while, there would be fireworks, which were always exciting ever since the Christmas Uncle Buck shot off a Roman candle and set the neighbor's yard on fire, but that was before we had a television.

20   Now, holiday dinners began to be timed to accommodate the kickoff, or once in a while the halftime, depending on how many games there were to watch; but on Thanksgiving or New Year's there were always games so important they absolutely could not be missed under any circumstances, certainly not for something as inconsequential as being "it" and counting to ten while you pretended not to see six children climb into the back seat of your car.

21   "Ssshhh, not now, Linda Jane. The Aggies have the ball."

22   "But you said . . . you promised. . . ."

23   "Linda Jane, didn't your daddy just tell you to hush up? We can't hear the television for you talking."

Exercise 2   DISCUSSION AND CRITICAL THINKING

1. Is Ellerbee concerned more with causes or effects?

2. What are some of the effects of television in her home? Mark them in the margins by writing the word *effect,* and briefly list them here.

3. Why did Ellerbee pretend she liked Milton Berle?

4. What did the family do during holidays before TV entered their lives and afterward?

5. Ellerbee recalls the arrival of the television set in her house with sadness. Do most people now, children and parents, watch television too much and become addicted to television? Are most people aware of the extent to which their lives are centered on television? How does television viewing affect your life?

6. How valuable to families is the shared experience of watching certain TV shows? Are there shows that everyone in your family watches, which give you cultural experiences in common?

Work, Work, Work: For Workaholics, the Job Can Be a Disease

Bob Walter

Today, more people are aware of alcohol and drug abuse; what may not be as apparent is that some people abuse work in much the same way. Through the use of case studies and interviews with experts, newspaper reporter Bob Walter explores this problem and one of its solutions: Workaholics Anonymous. This article first appeared in *The Sacramento Bee.*

1   They are out here among us. Heck, they probably are passing us. Heads down, arms flailing, walking purposefully. They are the cornerstones of many a workplace and many a home. Until they die or burn out, disintegrating into nonproducers despite their obsessions for the job. They are workaholics. Or "busyholics."

2   In these sensitive, politically correct days, they seem to be the last of the compulsives who we laugh about. Alcoholics aren't funny anymore, if they ever were. Neither are drug abusers or compulsive overeaters. But workaholics are different. And they are everywhere.

3   "What's the problem? It's not like an alcoholic or a drug addict," said a spokeswoman for a major Northern California employer. She was only half joking. Harry, a Sacramento vocational trainer and former college professor, is a workaholic. His last name will not be used here and neither will those of other workaholics. But Harry has a special reason for preferring anonymity. "If you put my name in the paper and say 'Harry So-and-so is a workaholic, he spends 80 hours a week on the job,' you would have people calling up and saying that we want this guy to come work for us," Harry said. He also was only half joking. "They give the gold medals to workaholics," said Theo, 52, a Sacramento physician and workaholic. "Some organizations will promote you based on the degree of your workaholism," he said. "They don't care if you stay at the office until 10 every night, because they have a different bottom line than your health."

4   Theo and Harry are members of Workaholics Anonymous, a support group based on the twelve-step recovery program used by Alcoholics Anonymous and others. Workaholics Anonymous is an eleven-year-old, worldwide group, but not exactly a huge one. The Sacramento chapter meets once a week and rarely draws more than six or eight people. There are just three groups in the greater Los Angeles area and a handful in the Bay Area. "That's the problem . . . we workaholics tend to have a hard time squeezing stuff into our schedule," Harry said.

5   Dave, 48, is secretary of the Sacramento chapter. He was trained, more or less, by working for two workaholic parents in the family's graphic service and supply business. "I learned very young that work activity got the praise," Dave said. "I didn't have to think about other things. I didn't feel any pain. And I never had an intimate relationship in my life. Work became my drug of choice."

6   Through childhood and the Air Force, where he worked in the laundry for extra money during his "off-duty" hours, Dave honed his skill at substi-

tuting work for feelings. He eventually became president of the $3 million-a-year family business. Dave worked 10 hours a day, seven days a week—officially. That didn't count the work he took home or on purported vacations. He even took work to bed. "I don't know how much . . . I just worked all the time," he said. "I became less and less involved with my family . . . I was only comfortable at work or in my own home. I had no self-confidence, no self-esteem and no self-worth."

7   At the suggestion of an old friend, Dave started attending WA meetings in 1990. "The first thing I learned was . . . what I was going through was not unique to me," he said. "I never learned how to deal with feelings or emotions. I knew that there was something wrong, but I thought it was with me." Dave is one of the lucky ones. His family stayed together. He survived bouts of compulsive eating and exercising that he briefly substituted for work. And the group has helped him find some balance and make room for emotions in his life.

8   Dr. Jan Krupp, a Bay Area physician who specializes in executive health, said some companies encourage workers and executives to lead balanced lives. But far more firms tend to "sponsor workaholics," he said. They are looking for people to skip lunch and put in monster hours. "In a lot of companies, the people who are not workaholics eventually get fired." Krupp also said the problem is not limited to companies. The legal and medical profession are overpopulated with workaholics, he said. It takes that kind of mind-set for most people just to qualify for medical or law school and then survive it.

9   Krupp said at least half the workaholics that he sees already recognize their problem. "Some say it's OK, they love what they are doing. They don't have any other interests and that's fine," he said. "Some say it's necessary to work that hard to stay where they are and others are just insecure. They don't realize that . . . if they don't take some time for their bodies and their families, they will lose their life, socially or otherwise. It's a debilitating disease in itself and it leads to lots of other problems . . . ulcers, hypertension, alcoholism, obesity."

10   Dr. Robert Diamond, a Sacramento psychiatrist who treats mostly children, said it often takes a major problem with a child to jar workaholics into treatment. Because they are so rigid, he said, many workaholics tend to "schedule things . . . including time with their children." But they usually are so adept at avoiding feelings that they miss the impact of their behavior on the child's emotional state. Sometimes those effects simply are passed along.

11   Harry learned his compulsion from a busyholic mother who actually didn't spend much time on her job as a schoolteacher. "People think to be a workaholic means you work huge hours on your main job . . . but that's not necessarily true," Harry said. In fact, some busyholics are not employed at all. Harry's mother was always selling something—encyclopedias on the weekends, for example—and couldn't sit still for a minute.

12   Harry's compulsion was to become a college professor to please his mother and win the love of his professor grandfather—who had been dead for thirty years. And he did become one, giving up a secure job, a wife and two small children in the process. Harry always worked part time in addition to his regular job. He spent all his time either working or obsessing about it, which was easier than feeling emotions.

13   These days, Harry is working less than forty hours a week and says his life has genuine balance. He can relax and enjoy a new romantic relationship, as well as becoming closer to his children from that earlier marriage. He credits Workaholics Anonymous for much of his progress. His message to other candidates is not to be dissuaded by the religious aspect of twelve-step programs. Spirituality is important, he says, "but you can be atheist or agnostic."

14   According to Dave, the program is "a lifetime quest. But that's OK, it takes as long as it takes." And he'll keep working until he gets it right.

*   *   *

15   ## Are You a Workaholic?

1. Do you often feel the need to get a few more tasks done—and then a few more—before you can relax?

2. Does this uncomfortable desire result in frantic, compulsive working?

3. Are you so busy that you often don't even know what you really want to do?

4. Is your sense of self-esteem based mostly on how others judge your performance at work and elsewhere?

5. Do you resent being expected to complete tasks and then procrastinate, unable to concentrate on the task at hand and yet too scared to stop?

6. Do you often think of yourself as either the most intelligent, capable person around or the most incapable and worthless?

7. Do you frequently operate out of the mini-crisis mode?

8. Do you judge yourself based on accomplishments? Must you always be accomplishing something to feel OK about yourself?

9. Do you go on intense work binges to get the praise of co-workers or bosses?

10. Do you believe people will not respect or like you just the way you are?

11. Do you tend to overschedule yourself, believing that people will like you more if you can do more and do it faster?

12. When others praise you, do you discount yourself as unworthy of the praise?

13. Do you take work with you to bed? On weekends? On vacation?

14. Have your long work hours hurt your family or other relationships?

15. Do you think about work while driving, while falling asleep, or when others are talking?

If you answered yes to three or more of these questions, there is a chance you are a workaholic or are well on your way to becoming one.

Exercise 3	**DISCUSSION AND CRITICAL THINKING**

1. Why does Walter believe we can still laugh at workaholics?

2. How are employers' attitudes a cause of workaholism?

3. What early training did Dave get about work? (paragraph 5)

4. What did Dave substitute for work, and why were the substitutions not good choices?

5. How do most companies react to workaholism as a problem?

6. What are some of the possible physiological effects of workaholism? (paragraph 9)

7. How do many workaholics commonly deal with the needs of family members?

8. To what extent is workaholism related to work?

Practicing Patterns of Cause and Effect

A detailed outline and your subsequent writing may include a mixture of causes and effects, but almost always one of these, either causes or effects, will be emphasized and will provide the main structure of your paper. Whether you are writing a basic outline for an assignment outside of class without a significant time restraint or you are writing in class under the pressure of time, you will always have a chance to jot down prewriting lists in the following form.

Exercise 4	**COMPLETING PATTERNS OF CAUSE AND EFFECT**

Fill in the blanks to complete the list of causes and the list of effects.

1. Causes

   Topic sentence: Reasons for emigrating to the United States are varied.

   I. Desire for a better education.

   II. _____

   III. _____

   IV. _____

2. Effects

   Topic sentence: Getting adequate exercise will yield several benefits.

   I. Muscle tone

   II. _____

III. _____

IV. _____

✎ Topics for Writing Cause and Effect

Reading-Related Topics

1. Write about the effects of addictive behavior on a family or on an individual who is addicted. Use *addiction* in a broad sense to mean preoccupation that has resulted in a loss of balance and the harmful neglect of values and human relationships. The addiction may be chemical (for example, drugs), psychological (for example, gambling), or social or personal (for example, golf, housekeeping, car maintenance)—any pursuit that has become a fixation.

"My Dad, the Bank Robber"

2. Using this paragraph as a model, write a paragraph of effects about someone you know who is (or was) addicted to alcohol; nicotine; or drugs such as marijuana, cocaine, crack, and so on. You may have known the person for a long time and witnessed the transformation from nonaddiction to addiction. Consider working with the following headings for prewriting lists: family, work, personal (physical and psychological), and social. You may choose instead to concentrate only on the physical, psychological, and social effects on the individual.

"Television Changed My Family Forever"

3. Write about the effects of television watching on your family. Unlike Ellerbee, you may conclude that there are more good effects than bad.

4. If you are from an immigrant family, write about what happened when your family learned about American culture by watching television soon after you arrived in this country.

5. Write about the effects television watching has had on you. How has your life changed by the amount of TV viewing you do and by your choice of programs? This topic will be especially revealing if you have a television-free segment (a time when you did not watch television) to compare with a television-watching segment.

6. In a discussion of effects, concentrate on one kind of programming, such as the news; for example, how does the content of the news affect the way you see society and behave (less or more fearfully, less or more aggressively, less or more generously, and so on)?

"Work, Work, Work: For Workaholics, the Job Can Be a Disease"

7. Write about why someone you know has become a workaholic. How have such factors as the individual's personality, the individual's financial needs, and society's competitive values influenced the person?

8. Write about a workaholic you know. Either broadly consider the effects on the person and his or her family, or concentrate on the effects on the person alone.

9. Emphasizing either causes or effects, write about a workaholic who is a student or an unemployed busyholic who compulsively works, perhaps on a car, around the house, or in the yard.

Career-Related Topics

10. Discuss the effects (benefits) of computers on the business community, family life, society generally, specific groups (age, income, activities), or an individual.

11. Discuss the needs of individuals, families, or institutions for (and thus the causes of development of) a particular product or type of product.

12. Discuss the effects of using a certain approach, system, or philosophy in sales, personnel management, or customer service.

General Topics

13. Write a paragraph about the causes of crime (for one individual involved in crime), unemployment (one person who is out of work), leaving home (one person who has left home), emigrating (one person or family), poverty (one person who is poor), school dropout (one person), going to college (one who did), or the success of a product or program on television.

14. Write a paragraph about the effects of disease (a particular disease, perhaps on just one person), fighting (one or two people involved in a dispute), fire (a particular one), alcoholism (a certain alcoholic), getting a job (a person with a particular job), early marriage (a person who married very young), teenage parenthood (one person or a couple), or dressing a certain way (one person and his or her style).

Writer's Guidelines: Cause and Effect

1. Have your purpose clearly in mind.

2. Be sure that you have sufficient knowledge of the subject to develop it.

3. Distinguish clearly between causes and effects by using three columns. From your lists select only the most relevant causes or effects.

Causes	Event, Situation, or Trend	Effects

4. The basic structure of your paragraph will probably look like this:

   Topic sentence

   I.   Cause or Effect 1

   II. Cause or Effect 2

   III. Cause or Effect 3

   Concluding sentence

5. For order, arrange your causes or effects according to time or emphasis.

21

Comparison and Contrast: Showing Similarities and Differences

"$\mathcal{E}$*ach of us, especially in a culturally diverse society, reflects the experiences we have had and the persons we have met, and, consequently, we come away being a combination of many cultural groups."*

—"Cultural Blends and Clashes"

Writing Paragraphs of Comparison and Contrast

Comparison and contrast is a method of showing similarities and dissimilarities between subjects. *Comparison* is concerned with organizing and development points of similarity; *contrast* has the same function for dissimilarity. Sometimes a writing assignment may require that you cover only similarities or only dissimilarities. Occasionally, an instructor may ask you to separate one from the other. Usually, you will combine them in a paragraph or essay. For convenience, the term *comparison* is often applied to both comparison and contrast because both use the same techniques and are usually combined into one operation.

Generating Topics and Working with the 4 *P*'s

Comparison and contrast is basic to your thinking. In your daily activities, you consider similarities and dissimilarities among persons, things, concepts, political leaders, doctors, friends, instructors, schools, nations, classes, movies, and so on. You naturally turn to comparison and contrast to solve problems and to make decisions in your affairs and in your writing. Because you have had so many comparative experiences, finding a topic to write about is likely to be only a matter of choosing from a great number of appealing ideas. Freewriting, brainstorming, and clustering will help you generate topics that are especially workable and appropriate for particular assignments.

Many college writing assignments will specify a topic or ask you to choose one from a list. Regardless of the source of your topic, this procedure for developing your ideas by comparison and contrast is the same as the procedure for developing topics of your own choosing. That procedure can be appropriately called the "4 P's": *purpose, points, patterns,* and *presentation.*

Purpose

Are you trying to show relationships (how things are similar and dissimilar) or to show that one side is better (ranking)? If you want to show that one actor, one movie, one writer, one president, one product, or one idea is better than another, your purpose is to persuade. You will emphasize the superiority of one side over the other in your topic sentence and in your support.

If you want to explain something about a topic by showing each subject in relationship with others, then your purpose is informative. For example, you might be comparing two composers, Beethoven and Mozart. Both were musical geniuses, so you then decide it would be senseless to argue that one is superior to the other. Instead, you choose to reveal interesting information about both by showing them in relation to each other.

Suppose that you are an immigrant from Vietnam and you want to compare the lives of women in Vietnam and women in America. To narrow your topic, you might decide to focus on women who marry and have children. Your intention is to inform: to show how the women in the two cultures are similar and dissimilar, not to show that one is better than the other. Here is a way in which you might proceed.

Points

First, you would come up with a list of ideas, or points, to apply somewhat equally to the two sides. Next, you would select two or three related items and circle them. You might soon discover that some of the items on your list could be combined. You might decide to order your points by time (chronological order, as shown here), space, or emphasis (importance).

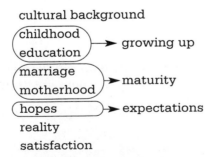

cultural background

childhood
education → growing up

marriage
motherhood → maturity

hopes → expectations

reality

satisfaction

Patterns

Then you would organize your material. There are two basic comparison and contrast patterns: **subject-by-subject** and **point-by-point.**

The **subject-by-subject** pattern presents all of one side and then all of the other.

Topic sentence
I. Vietnam
   A. Growing up

   B. Maturity

   C. Expectations

II. America
   A. Growing up

   B. Maturity

   C. Expectations

Concluding Sentence(s)

The **point-by-point** pattern shows the points in relation to the sides (subjects) one at a time. This is the more common pattern.

Topic sentence
I. Growing up
   A. Vietnam

   B. America

II. Maturity
   A. Vietnam

   B. America

III. Expectations
   A. Vietnam

   B. America

Concluding Sentence(s)

Presentation

Both patterns of organizing your points can be very effective. The subject-by-subject pattern is strong in that it presents one side completely and then the other, in clear blocks of information. (You can help your reader by occasionally referring to the other side, in phrases such as "Unlike her Vietnamese counterpart," and so on.) The point-by-point pattern groups points closer together and, therefore, establishes connections directly. It is important that each point be developed; otherwise, this pattern can read like an outline, mechanical and predictable. Some writers believe that the subject-by-subject pattern works best for shorter assignments such as the paragraph and that the point-by-point pattern works best for longer pieces such as the essay.

Some assignments may require only comparisons or only contrasts and some a separation of the two, but most assignments require a blending of similarities and dissimilarities in relation to points. Regardless of the pattern you select, you would use your outline (or cluster or list) to begin writing your paragraph. You would use appropriate explanations, details, and examples for support.

Connecting Reading and Writing: Cultural Blends and Clashes

Culture here is used in the broad sense to indicate groups of people with recognizable identities. That means generation, ethnic, gender, sexual preference, physical and mental condition, age, and region. As we meet those who are different from us, we may discover up close the considerable range of dissimilarities and at the same time recognize the far greater degree of commonality in human beings. Of course, we can't put an individual into one slot. Each of us, especially in a culturally diverse society, reflects the experiences we have had and the persons we have met, and, consequently, we come away being a combination of many cultural groups. A person could be an older, female, Asian-American, slightly deaf, Southern, heterosexual individual and thereby take part in six different cultures on the basis of those characteristics alone.

THE QUIGMANS   by Buddy Hickerson

B. Hickerson, copyright Los Angeles Times Syndicate. Reprinted by permission.

The cultural encounters that we are most aware of concern those we know and those we identify with and, therefore, feel we know. In "Superman and Batman," by Judy Urbina, we travel the outer realm of diversity: two imaginary heroes who have become cultural icons. In "A Mixed Tex-Cal Marriage" José Antonio Burciaga discusses what happens when a Texas guy and a California gal get together and sort out differences.

Student Thung Tran takes us on an international journey to explore the different experiences of women in Vietnam and America. Her paragraph "Wives and Mothers in Vietnam and in America" immediately follows with a completed Writing Process Worksheet and her final draft.

You will find a full-size blank worksheet on page 6. It can be photocopied, filled in, and submitted with each assignment if your instructor directs you to do so.

Writing Process Worksheet

TITLE <u>Wives and Mothers in Vietnam and in America</u>

NAME <u>Thung Tran</u>   **DUE DATE** <u>Wednesday, February 16, 10 a.m.</u>

ASSIGNMENT

In the space below, write whatever you need to know about your assignment, including information about the topic, audience, pattern of writing, length, whether to include a rough draft or revised drafts, and whether your paper must be typed.

Write a paragraph of comparison and contrast about two people or two types of people who are culturally different. Use the subject-by-subject pattern. Assume that your readers do not know your subjects well. Turn in this completed worksheet, one or more rough drafts, and a typed final draft.

STAGE ONE

Explore   Freewrite, brainstorm (list), cluster, or take notes as directed by your instructor. Use the back of this page or separate paper if you need more space.

cultural background

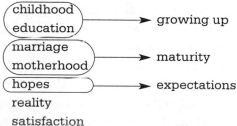

childhood
education ⟶ growing up

marriage
motherhood ⟶ maturity

hopes ⟶ expectations

reality

satisfaction

STAGE TWO

Organize   Write a topic sentence or thesis; label the subject and the treatment parts.

<u>Vietnamese immigrants discover just how American culture is different</u>
                              subject
<u>from Vietnamese culture, especially for the women who become wives</u>
                                              treatment
<u>and mothers.</u>

Write an outline or an outline alternative.

I. Vietnam
    A. Growing up
    B. Maturity
    C. Expectations

II. America
    A. Growing up
    B. Maturity
    C. Expectations

STAGE THREE

Write On separate paper, write and then revise your paper as many times as necessary for coherence, language (usage, tone, and diction), unity, emphasis, support, and sentences (CLUESS). Read your paper aloud to hear and correct any grammatical errors or awkward-sounding sentences.

Edit any problems in fundamentals, such as capitalization, omissions, punctuation, and spelling (COPS).

Wives and Mothers in Vietnam and in America

Thung Tran

Born in Vietnam, Thung Tran emigrated to America as a young girl. After observing her mother make the unsteady transition from Vietnamese woman to American woman, Tran was well qualified to write this comparison and contrast paragraph.

Topic sentence

I.

A.

B.

C.

II.

A.

B.

C.

Concluding sentences

Fleeing from communism, many Vietnamese left their country to resettle with their families in the United States. Here they discovered just how American culture is different from Vietnamese culture, especially for the women who become wives and mothers. In Vietnam, a young girl is educated in Confucian theories: "Obey your father as a child, and your husband when you get married." Living with her in-laws after marriage, her role is that of child bearer and housekeeper. She has to be a good wife, a good mother, and a good daughter-in-law if she wants to be happy. She is the first to rise and the last to go to bed in a household that includes her husband and his parents. She will seldom make decisions and will always be obedient. She expects her husband to support the family financially, protect her, and help his relatives direct the family. In American society the female has a different pattern of experiences. As a girl she learns to think for herself and develop her talents. After she marries, unlike her Vietnamese counterpart, she is likely to work outside the home. Because she provides a part of the financial support, she expects her husband to share some of the work of raising the children, keeping the house, and maintaining a relationship with the in-laws on both sides, who probably live in a separate house. In America, ideally, the wife and mother will probably have more independence in the home and more responsibilities outside the home. In Vietnam the wife may be left with a secure position but few options.

Exercise 1

DISCUSSION AND CRITICAL THINKING

1. Has Tran organized her paragraph using a point-by-point or subject-by-subject pattern?

2. List any references to the other side that Tran uses to emphasize her comparison.

3. Does Tran shade the evidence to favor one side?

4. In ideal circumstances what advantages does each woman experience?

Superman and Batman

Judy Urbina

Displaying a keen knowledge of the private lives of Superman and Batman, Judy Urbina compares these two foremost cultural icons of the comic-book world. We know these crime busters. One leaps over tall buildings, and the other climbs all over the Gotham skyline with his trusty bat hooks. Unfortunately, they never meet face to face, for, despite their many cultural differences, they have much in common. But, Urbina says, we naturally identify more with one than the other. Holy Rhetoric,_____! Which one is it?

During the Depression in the 1930s, Superman and Batman were created as the first big comic-book heroes. More than two thousand similar but lesser characters were to follow. Both Superman and Batman have been enormously successful, but one seems to have more personality and is probably closer to most of us emotionally. Which hero wins out in this struggle for our hearts and minds? Taking into account their upbringing, motives, and criminal targets, one can argue that it is Batman who is more credible.

Neither came originally from a home environment we are likely to identify with completely. Superman was conceived on the planet Krypton by a highly intelligent couple. His life was threatened because Krypton was going to destruct. Superman's parents bundled him up in a kiddie spacecraft and launched him on a long journey to Earth to save his life. He was raised on a farm by Jonathan and Martha Kent, who adopted him and grew to love him as their own. Batman, however, had an upbringing to which we can more easily imagine as a complete pattern. Really Bruce Wayne in disguise, Batman was left an orphan by his parents, who were killed in a mugging right in front of him. Fortunately for Bruce Wayne, his parents were rich, and he inherited millions when they died. He was raised by his butler, unlike Superman, who was nurtured by a conventional adoptive mom and dad. Obviously the upbringing of these two heroes had a lot to do with the kind of heroes they grew up to be.

Both comic book heroes had different motives for confronting killers and spoilers. Superman instinctively knew he was sent to Earth to fight crime. When his birth parents shipped him off to Earth as an infant, they programmed the spacecraft to educate him on the ways of the Earthlings. Superman's adoptive parents reinforced those lessons by teaching him that he had to hide his powers and use them for the well-being of the human race. On the contrary, Batman soon became a revenge-driven vigilante after his parents were killed in the mugging, so he decided to devote his life to fighting crime, with his butler as a domestic accomplice. To Batman no criminal is a good criminal. Although all of us citizens know we should not take the law into our own hands, nevertheless, we celebrate Superman and Batman as heroes, all the time identifying more with the guy in the fancy bat car.

Like all superheroes, each of these two has an arch enemy. Superman's arch enemy is Lex Luther, who has a brilliant criminal mind. Lex Luther is always trying to destroy Superman. He knows everything about Superman, right down to his weakness—the mineral Kryptonite. Batman's main enemy is the Joker. As a teen the Joker killed Batman's parents. Then Batman "accidentally" dropped the Joker into acid and permanently disfigured his face, so they are constantly getting into battles. More people are able to relate to Batman because most of us at least think about vengeance if someone has done us wrong. Superman just wants to fight for "truth, justice, and the American way," all worthwhile values, but they're abstract.

Superman does not offer love or self-knowledge as keys to a perfect world. He offers only physical strength. Displaying more cunning and base passion, Batman preys on fears and insecurities of criminals as keys to a perfect world. He wants to keep the bad men and women intimidated and on the run. His presence in Gotham strikes fear in the hearts of the wicked. Neither crime fighter is much concerned about rehabilitation. Mainly they knock heads. But Batman seems to enjoy his work more than Superman because Batman's getting even. The fact that we are in touch with that source of satisfaction says as much about us as it does about Batman.

Exercise 2   DISCUSSION AND CRITICAL THINKING

1. Does Urbina use a point-by-point or subject-by-subject pattern in this essay?

2. Make a simple point-by-point outline of this essay, using *upbringing, motives,* and *enemies* as Roman numeral headings.

   I. _____

      A. _____

      B. _____

   II. _____

      A. _____

      B. _____

   III. _____

      A. _____

      B. _____

3. Underline and label the thesis of the essay (in the first paragraph).

4. Underline and label the topic sentences of paragraphs 2, 3, and 4.

5. Why does Superman lose out to Batman, according to the writer, in the battle for credibility?

6. Which character is your favorite? Why?

7. Do these characters resemble your other heroes? Explain.

A Mixed Tex-Cal Marriage

José Antonio Burciaga

A distinguished publisher and writer, José Antonio Burciaga died in 1996, leaving a rich legacy of poems, short stories, and essays. He was a Chicano cultural activist, muralist, humorist, and founding member of the comedy group Culture Clash. His *Undocumented Love* won the Before Columbus American Book Award for poetry in 1992. This essay, about him and his wife, is included in his book *Drink Cultura* (1993).

1 According to Cecilia, my wife, we have a mixed marriage. She's from California, I'm from Texas. Though we have no regrets, this truly proves that love is blind.

2 When Cecilia and I first met, we thought we had a lot in common. As young, professional Chicanos in Washington, D.C., we both supported the United Farm Workers' grape and lettuce boycotts, the Coors boycott, the Gallo Wine boycott, the Farah Pants boycott, and the Frito Bandido boycott. We still boycott some of those items, for many reasons; health, habit, nostalgia or plain, ordinary guilt if we indulged in any of these.

3 As first-generation Mexican-Americans, we both spoke *Español*, graduated from Catholic schools, and had similar politics.

4 But, as we were soon to discover, the vast desert that separates Texas and California also differentiates the culture and style of Chicanos. Because we met far from Texas and California, we had no idea at first of the severity of our differences.

5 We both liked enchiladas—the same enchiladas, I thought, until the first time Cecilia prepared them. They looked like enchiladas, and they smelled like enchiladas. And then I bit into one.

6 "These are good, *corazón*," I said. "But these are *entomatadas*. They have more tomato than chile. *Mí Mamá* used to make them all the time."

7 She threw me a piquant stare as I chewed away. "Hmmm, they're great!" I stressed through a mouthful.

8   Californians, like her parents who immigrated from the coastal state of Jalisco, Mexico, use more tomatoes than Texans like my parents, who came from the central states of Durango and Zacatecas and use more chiles.

9   Cecilia grew up with white *menudo,* tripe soup. White menudo? How could anyone eat colorless menudo? And not put hominy in it? Ours was red-hot and loaded with hominy. In Texas, we ate our menudo with bread. In California, it's with tortillas. Texas flour tortillas are thick and tasty, California flour tortillas are so thin you can see through them.

10   She didn't particularly like my Tony Lama boots or my country-western and Tex-Mex musical taste. I wasn't that crazy about Beach Boys music or her progressive, California-style country-western.

11   In California, the beach was relatively close for Cecilia. On our first date she asked how often I went to the beach from El Paso. Apparently, geography has never been a hot subject in California schools. That's understandable considering the sad state of education, especially geography, in this country. But in Texas, at one time the biggest state in the union, sizes and distances are most important.

12   In answer to Cecilia's question, I explained that to get to the closest beach from El Paso, I had to cross New Mexico, Arizona and California to reach San Diego. That's 791 freeway miles. The closest Texas beach is 841 freeway miles to the Gulf of Mexico.

13   Back when we were courting, California Chicanos saw *Texanos* as a little too *Mexicano,* still wet behind the ears, not assimilated enough, and speaking with either thick Spanish accents or "Taxes acksaints."

14   Generally speaking, Texanos saw their *Califas* counterparts as too weird, knowing too little if any Spanish and with speech that was too Anglicized.

15   After our marriage we settled in neutral Alexandria, Virginia, right across the Potomac from the nation's capital. We lived there a couple of years, and when our firstborn came, we decided to settle closer to home. But which home, Califas or Texas? In El Paso we wouldn't be close to the beach, but I thought there was an ocean of opportunity in that desert town. There was some Texas pride and machismo, to be sure. It was a tug-of-war that escalated to the point of seeking advice, and eventually I had to be realistic and agree that California had better opportunities. In EPT, the opportunities in my field were nonexistent.

16   The rest is relative bliss. Married since 1972, I'm totally spoiled and laid-back in Northern Califas, but I still miss many of those things we took for granted in Texas, or Washington, D.C.—the seasonal changes, the snow, the heat, heating systems, autumn colors, and monsoon rains; the smell of the desert after a rain, the silence and serenity of the desert, the magnified sounds of a fly or cricket, distant horizons uncluttered by trees, and the ability to find the four directions without any problem. I do miss the desert and, even more, the food. El Paso *is* the Mexican-food capital of this country.

17   Today, I like artichokes and appreciate a wide variety of vegetables and fruits. I even like white, colorless menudo and hardly ever drink beer. I drink wine, but it has to be a dry Chardonnay or Fume Blanc although a Pinot Noir or Cabernet Sauvignon goes great with meals. Although I still yearn for an ice cold Perla or Lone Star beer from Texas once in a while, Califas is my home now—mixed marriage and all.

| Exercise 3 | DISCUSSION AND CRITICAL THINKING |

1. Which sentence states the thesis most emphatically (see paragraph 1)? Copy it here.

2. In paragraphs 6 through 15, what are the three points used for comparison and contrast?

3. In paragraphs 16 and 17 Bruciaga discusses how he has changed. In what ways does that imply comparison and contrast?

4. Because all of us are culturally complex, being the products of many cultures, we frequently blend and clash with others in matters of age, ethnicity, gender, sexual preferences, religion, and so on. As for the broad concept of "mixed marriage," are Cecilia and José fairly typical compared with other marriage partners you know? Do you have some examples of those more extreme and less extreme? You might also discuss this topic in connection with friendships you have or know about.

Practicing Patterns of Comparison and Contrast

Shorter compositions such as paragraphs are likely to be arranged subject by subject, and longer compositions such as essays are likely to be arranged point by point, although either pattern can work in either length. In longer works, especially in published writing, the two patterns may be mixed. Being able to organize your material quickly and effectively according to the pattern that is best for your material is important to your success as a writer. Even in a timed assignment, make a simple scratch outline that will guide you in writing a piece that is unified and coherent.

| Exercise 4 | COMPLETING PATTERNS OF COMPARISON AND CONTRAST |

Fill in the blanks to complete the comparison and contrast items in the following outlines.

1. Friends: Marla and Justine

   I. Marla

      A. Appearance

      B. _____

      C. _____

  II. Justine

      A. _____

      B. Personality

      C. _____

2. Two Bosses: Mr. Santo and Ms. Elliott

   I. Disposition

      A. Mr. Santo

      B. Ms. Elliott

  II. Knowledge of _____

      A. _____

      B. Ms. Elliott

 III. _____

      A. Mr. Santo

      B. _____

✎ Topics for Writing Comparison and Contrast

Reading-Related Topics

"Wives and Mothers in Vietnam and in America"

1. Using this paragraph as a model, write about men or women in different societies. Begin with whatever they have in common and then discuss how their experiences are different. You might want instead to consider different aspects of one society: city and suburb, male and female, straight and gay, young and old, and so on. As you compare and contrast, keep in mind that you are generalizing and that individuals differ within groups—avoid stereotyping.

"Superman and Batman"

2. Select two other pop culture icons and compare and contrast them: Rambo and Tarzan, the Terminator and Ghostbusters, two well-known athletes such as McGwire and Sosa or Coleman and Bryant, two other comic-book characters, two characters from sitcom or a cop drama, one character from a television series and a real person (either a well-known person—perhaps a celebrity—or just someone you know, such as a family member or friend).

"A Mixed Tex-Cal Marriage"

3. Using this essay as inspiration, write about a marriage or relationship between two individuals who are significantly different. Consider making a list about their possible differences (such as religion; education; country, city, or suburban background; politics; ethnicity; preferences for food, activities, behavior). In your discussion don't overlook the common characteristics that brought and keep them together, and briefly mention how each person has compromised.

Career-Related Topics

4. Compare and contrast two products or services, with the purpose of showing that one is better.

5. Compare and contrast two management styles or two working styles.

6. Compare and contrast two career fields to show that one is better for you.

7. Compare and contrast a public school and a business.

8. Compare and contrast an athletic team and a business.

9. Compare and contrast two computers.

10. Compare and contrast two computer games or two software programs for word processing or for a business procedure.

General Topics   11. The following topics refer to general subjects. Provide specific names and other detailed information as you develop your ideas by using the 4 *P*'s.

Two diets

Two fast-food restaurants

Two textbooks

Two gymnasiums

Two careers

Two people who play the same sport

Two generations

Two motorcycles, cars, or snowmobiles

Two actors, singers, or musicians

Two ways of learning

Two ways of exercising

Two kinds of child care

Two mothers: one who stays at home and one who works outside the home

12. Use the Internet to research the price, quality, style, and durability of two items that are for sale. Make copies of your data. Write a comparison and contrast paper explaining that one item is better than the other. Submit the computer printout along with the materials required by your instructor.

Writer's Guidelines: Comparison and Contrast

1. Work with the 4 *P*'s:

   • *Purpose:* Decide whether you want to inform (show relationships) or persuade (show that one side is better).

   • *Points:* Decide which ideas you will apply to each side. Consider beginning by making a list to select from. Order can be based on time, space, or emphasis.

   • *Patterns:* Decide whether to use subject-by-subject or point-by-point organization.

   • *Presentation:* Decide to what extent you should develop your ideas. Use references to the other side to make connections and use examples and details to support your views.

2. Your basic subject-by-subject outline will probably look like this:

   I. Subject 1

      A. Point 1

      B. Point 2

      C. Point 3

    II. Subject 2

        A. Point 1

        B. Point 2

        C. Point 3

3. Your basic point-by-point outline will probably look like this:

    I. Point 1

        A. Subject 1

        B. Subject 2

    II. Point 2

        A. Subject 1

        B. Subject 2

    III. Point 3

        A. Subject 1

        B. Subject 2

Argument: Writing to Persuade

"Often one side is shouting freedom, and the other is yelling public good. . . . Ideally, they come to express their views calmly and logically, moderating the heat of their passion with the coolness of reason."

—"To Regulate or Not"

Writing Paragraphs of Argument

Persuasion and Argument Defined

Persuasion is a broad term. When we persuade, we try to influence people to think in a certain way or to do something. *Argument* is persuasion on a topic about which reasonable people disagree. Argument involves controversy. Whereas exercising appropriately is probably not controversial because reasonable people do not dispute the idea, an issue such as gun control is. In this chapter we will be concerned mainly with the kind of persuasion that involves argument.

Components of a Paragraph of Argument

Statements of argument are informal or formal in design. An opinion column in a newspaper is likely to have little set structure, whereas an argument in college writing is likely to be tightly organized. Nevertheless, the opinion column and the college paper have much in common. Both provide a proposition, which is the main point of the argument, and both provide support, which is the evidence or the reasons that back up the proposition.

For a well-structured paragraph, an organizational plan is desirable. Consider these elements when you write a paragraph of argument, and ask yourself the following questions as you develop your ideas.

Background: What is the historical or social context for this controversial issue?

Proposition (the *topic sentence* of a paragraph of argument and the thesis of an essay): What do I want my audience to believe or do?

Qualification of proposition: Can I limit my proposition so that those who disagree cannot easily challenge me with exceptions? If, for example, I am in favor of using animals for scientific experimentation, am I concerned only with medical experiments or with any use, including that pertaining to the cosmetic industry?

Refutation (taking the opposing view into account, mainly to point out its fundamental weakness): What is the view on the other side, and why is it flawed in reasoning or evidence?

Support: In addition to sound reasoning, can I use appropriate facts, examples, statistics, and opinions of authorities?

The basic form for a paragraph of argument includes the proposition (the topic sentence) and support. The support sentences are, in effect, *because* statements; that is, the proposition is valid *because* of the support. Your organization should look something like this.

Proposition (topic sentence): It is time to pass a national law restricting smoking in public places.

   I. Discomfort of the nonsmoker (support 1)

  II. Health of the nonsmoker (support 2)

 III. Cost to the nation (support 3)

Kinds of Evidence

In addition to sound reasoning generally, you can use these kinds of evidence: facts, examples, statistics, and authorities.

First, you can offer facts. Martin Luther King, Jr., was killed in Memphis, Tennessee, on April 4, 1968. Because an event that has happened is true and can be verified, this statement about King is a fact. But that James Earl Ray acted alone in killing King is to some a questionable fact. That King was the greatest of all civil rights leaders is opinion because it cannot be verified.

Some facts are readily accepted because they are general knowledge—you and your reader know them to be true because they can be or have been verified. Other "facts" are based on personal observation and are reported in various publications but may be false or questionable. You should always be concerned about the reliability of the source for both the information you use and the information used by those with other viewpoints. Still other "facts" are genuinely debatable because of their complexity or the incompleteness of the knowledge available.

Second, you can cite examples. If you use examples, you must present a sufficient number, and the examples must be relevant.

Third, you can present statistics. Statistics are facts and data of a numerical kind that are classified and tabulated to present significant information about a given subject.

Avoid presenting a long list of figures; select statistics carefully and relate them to things familiar to your reader. The millions of dollars spent on a war in a single week, for example, become more comprehensible when expressed in terms of what the money would purchase in education, highways, or urban renewal.

To test the validity of statistics, either yours or your opponent's, ask: Who gathered them? Under what conditions? For what purpose? How are they used?

Fourth, you can cite evidence from, and opinions of, authorities. Most readers accept facts from recognized, reliable sources—governmental publications, standard reference works, and books and periodicals published by established firms. In addition, they will accept evidence and opinions from individuals who, because of their knowledge and experience, are recognized as experts.

In using authoritative sources as proof, keep these points in mind:

- Select authorities who are generally recognized as experts in their field.

- Use authorities who qualify in the field pertinent to your argument.

- Select authorities whose views are not biased.

- Try to use several authorities.

- Identify an authority's credentials clearly in your paragraph or essay.

Exercise 1	FACT OR OPINION

Identify the italicized statements as fact (F) or opinion (O). (See Answer Key for answers.)

*Elvis deserves to be called the King of Rock and Roll. Born in 1935 in Tupelo, Mississippi,*¹ he went on to become *the greatest entertainer of the mid-twentieth century.*² *Eighteen of his songs were No. 1.*³ His movie musicals are still seen and loved by television viewers. Who can watch *Viva Las Vegas* and not admire his versatility? His fans are still enthusiastic. *More than 500,000 people go to Graceland each year*⁴ to visit his grave and see his former home, and *every month over fifty letters arrive there,*⁵ all addressed to Elvis Presley. *That kind of attention is appropriate for the King.*⁶

1. _____   5. _____

2. _____   6. _____

3. _____   7. _____

4. _____

Exercise 2	FACT OR OPINION

Identify each sentence as one based on fact (F) or opinion (O).

_____   1. Blue jeans were first worn by miners in the 1849 Gold Rush.

_____   2. They were made of canvas that originally had been ordered to use in constructing tents.

———— 3. They became the best pants the miners ever wore.

———— 4. Later, jeans were sold to American farmers.

———— 5. By the 1960s, blue jeans caught on with several prominent fashion designers.

———— 6. Europeans adopted blue jeans as the natural clothes style for rock-and-roll music.

———— 7. Blue jeans are still scarce in Eastern Europe.

———— 8. They were once smuggled in and sold there on the black market.

———— 9. Some people apparently regarded blue jeans as a symbol of rebellion.

———— 10. The love of blue jeans will never end.

Logical Fallacies

Certain flawed patterns in thought, commonly called *logical fallacies,* are of primary concern in critical thinking.

These are among the most common logical fallacies:

1. *Post hoc, ergo, propter hoc* (After this, therefore, because of this): When one event precedes another in time, the first is assumed to cause the other.

   Examples: "I knew I'd have a day like this when I saw that black cat run across the driveway this morning."

   "See what I told you. We elected him president, and now we have high inflation."

2. *False analogy:* False analogies ignore differences and stress similarities, often in an attempt to prove something.

   Examples: "A person has to get a driver's license because unqualified drivers could have bad effects on society. Therefore, couples should also have to get a license to bear children because unqualified parents can produce delinquent children."

   "The leader of that country is a mad dog dictator, and you know what you do with a mad dog. You get a club and kill it."

3. *Hasty generalization:* This is a conclusion based on too few reliable instances.

   Example: "Everyone I've met this morning is going to vote for the incumbent. The incumbent is going to win."
   "How many people did you meet?"
   "Three."

4. *False dilemma:* This fallacy presents the reader with only two alternatives from which to choose. The solution may lie elsewhere.

   Examples: "Now, only two things can be done with the school district. You either shut it down now or let it go bankrupt."

"The way I see it, you either bomb them back into the Stone Age or let them keep on pushing us around."

5. *Argumentation ad hominem* (Arguing against the person): This is the practice of abusing and discrediting your opponent instead of keeping to the main issues of the argument.

Examples: "Who cares what he has to say? After all, he's a wild-eyed liberal who has been divorced twice."

"Let's put aside the legislative issue for one moment and talk about the person who proposed it. For one thing he's a southerner. For another he's Catholic. Enough said."

Exercise 3   **CRITICAL THINKING**

Each of the following sentences is based on a logical fallacy. Identify the logical fallacies with these labels: post hoc (PH), false analogy (FA), hasty generalization (HG), false dilemma (FD), or ad hominem (AH). (See Answer Key for answers.)

_____ 1. It's no wonder she had a terrible honeymoon. She didn't wear something blue during the wedding ceremony.

_____ 2. My kids' loud music is driving me crazy. There are only two possible solutions: either the boom boxes go or the kids go.

_____ 3. After reading two Harlequin romances, I can say that the French are the most romantic people in the world.

_____ 4. I'm not surprised. You elect a liberal mayor, and now taxes have gone up.

_____ 5. Larry Brown says that practice makes perfect. So I plan to get married lots of times before I settle down.

_____ 6. I can't recommend the fiction of F. Scott Fitzgerald. What could an admitted alcoholic have to say that would be of value?

_____ 7. I'm not surprised. I knew I'd win the Pillsbury bake-off when I found that lucky penny this morning.

_____ 8. Today I met a group of ten Russian tourists. Now I can see why people say the Russians are friendly.

_____ 9. Joe DiMaggio has always liked his coffee, and now he's in the Hall of Fame. Obviously the secret to becoming a great baseball player is in your coffee maker.

_____ 10. How can you take heavy metal music seriously? The musicians who play that stuff are druggies with long hair and tattoos.

Exercise 4   **CRITICAL THINKING**

Each of the following sentences is based on a logical fallacy. Identify the logical fallacies with these labels: post hoc (PH), false analogy (FA), hasty generalization (HG), false dilemma (FD), or ad hominem (AH).

_____ 1. I trained my dog not to wet on the carpet by rubbing his nose in the "mess" he created; therefore, I will potty train my children by rubbing their noses in the "messes" they make.

_____ 2. The continued use of nuclear energy will lead to either nuclear war or catastrophic nuclear accidents.

_____ 3. Everyone in the front office is dipping Lippy Snuff. I figure it's the hottest item on the market.

_____ 4. Our dog eats only once a day, and look how healthy he is. I don't know why you kids keep yellin' for three meals a day.

_____ 5. No wonder she's been going around crying all day. Yesterday the government slapped a tax on Lippy Snuff.

_____ 6. I refuse to listen to his musical interpretation of the Yalta Conference because he's a card-carrying member of the ACLU.

_____ 7. Either we cave in to the terrorist demands, or we strike back with nuclear weapons.

_____ 8. After watching the high school kids on the bus today, I would say that the whole education system could use a required course in manners.

_____ 9. It's no wonder my Winnebago exploded today. Yesterday I bought a tank of cheap gasoline.

_____ 10. I wouldn't trust him as far as I can throw a heifer. He rides a Harley and drinks Rebel Yell.

Connecting Reading and Writing: To Regulate or Not

Automobile speed, drinking, skateboarding, taxes, benefits, bicycling, concerts, the price of milk, imports, immigration, HMOs, housing density, interest rates, voting, seat belts, helmets for cyclists, insecticides, wetlands, airport noise—what do those words make you think of? Probably laws and regulations—and people arguing. Often one side is shouting freedom, and the other is yelling public good. Or perhaps there are formal debates, and thoughtful people argue on either side of a hot issue. Ideally, they come to express their views calmly and logically, moderating the heat of their passion with the coolness of reason.

That is the tone we seek in argumentation, and it's the tone we find in our reading selections. In "How About Low-Cost Drugs for Addicts?" Louis Nizer suggests that we legalize drugs, sell them or dispense them free in state-run shops, and reg-

THE QUIGMANS   by Buddy Hickerson

B. Hickerson, copyright 1994. Los Angeles Times Syndicate. Reprinted by permission.

ulate the whole process. Keith A. King's scholarly study presents arguments both for and against school uniforms.

In the two student works, Eric Miller writes both a paragraph and an essay version of "A New Wind Blowing," arguing that in certain circumstances restrictions should be imposed on smokers. With the Writing Process Worksheet, we can trace his exploration of the topic through the writing of his papers. His rough drafts are not included here.

You will find a full-size blank worksheet on page 6. It can be photocopied, filled in, and submitted with each assignment if your instructor directs you to do so.

Writing Process Worksheet

TITLE A New Wind Blowing

NAME Eric Miller   **DUE DATE** Monday, September 5, 10 a.m.

ASSIGNMENT   In the space below, write whatever you need to know about your assignment, including information about the topic, audience, pattern of writing, length, whether to include a rough draft or revised drafts, and whether your paper must be typed.

Write a paragraph of argumentation on an approved topic. Length: about 250 to 300 words. Audience: general, some who disagree with your view. Research your topic. Include different kinds of evidence. Submit this completed worksheet, one or more rough drafts, and a typed final draft.

STAGE ONE   **Explore**   Freewrite, brainstorm (list), cluster, or take notes as directed by your instructor. Use the back of this page or separate paper if you need more space.

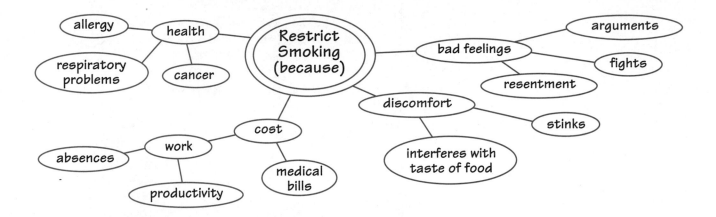

STAGE TWO   **Organize**   Write a topic sentence or thesis; label the subject and the treatment parts.

<u>Smoking in public places</u> <u>should be restricted by a national law.</u>
          subject   treatment

Write an outline or an outline alternative.

   I. Smokers unhappy if restricted
       A. Belief of violation of their rights
       B. But could benefit

  II. Main reason to restrict smoking: health
       A. Illness and death from secondhand smoke
          1. Many people with respiratory illness
          2. Califano estimates 5,000 deaths a year
       B. Cancer from secondhand smoke
          1. Secondary smoke listed as a carcinogen
          2. Nonsmokers with smokers, 80 percent more likely to get cancer

 III. Second reason: discomfort
       A. Disagreeable odor
       B. Must be seen in relation to whole problem

  IV. Third reason: cost
       A. Medical bills
       B. Lost productivity

STAGE THREE   **Write**   On separate paper, write and then revise your paper as many times as necessary for <u>c</u>oherence, <u>l</u>anguage (usage, tone, and diction), <u>u</u>nity, <u>e</u>mphasis, <u>s</u>upport, and <u>s</u>entences (CLUESS). Read your paper aloud to hear and correct any grammatical errors or awkward-sounding sentences.
Edit any problems in fundamentals, such as <u>c</u>apitalization, <u>o</u>missions, <u>p</u>unctuation, and <u>s</u>pelling (COPS).

A New Wind Blowing
(paragraph)

Eric Miller

Eric Miller isn't asking people to stop smoking, he's asking them only to stop smoking in public places.

	One of the most common complaints heard in restaurants and work places pertains to smoking. In all crowded public places, when a smoker lights up,
Proposition (topic sentence)	people get upset for reasons they believe are valid. Along with them, I say <u>it is time to pass a national law restricting smoking in public places.</u> <u>Reasonable</u>
Qualification	<u>exceptions can be worked out.</u> Three reasons make this proposition right.
Support 1	<u>One is discomfort.</u> Most people don't like to breathe secondhand smoke. It
Support 2	smells bad. <u>That reason is coupled with the health reason.</u> Studies indicate (as reported by <u>Joseph Califano</u>, former Secretary of Health, Education, and Wel-
Authoritative statement with statistics	fare) <u>that more than 5,000 Americans die each year from secondhand smoke and that people living with smokers are 80 percent more likely to get lung</u>
Authoritative statement	<u>cancer than those who do not live with smokers.</u> In 1993 t<u>he Environmental Protection Agency formally classified secondhand smoke as a potent carcino-</u>
Support 3	<u>gen</u>—in a class with asbestos. <u>Connected with this health problem is the mat-ter of cost.</u> The last five surgeons general have agreed that secondhand smoke is a significant health problem, with a huge cost to society in medical bills and lost job productivity. Although many smokers concur with the pro-
Refutation	posal for restriction, <u>others feel that they would lose their rights. They shouldn't.</u> They can continue to smoke, but only if they do not jeopardize the
Concluding sentence	health of others in public places. <u>Discomfort, bad health, and bills for taxpay-ers are too much for society to pay to live without restriction.</u>

Exercise 5	**DISCUSSION AND CRITICAL THINKING**

1. Why does Miller qualify his proposition?

2. What are the different kinds of evidence offered by Miller?

3. Assume the position of those who take the other view. How would you argue against Miller?

A New Wind Blowing
(essay)

Eric Miller

This is a demonstration written by the same student (later in the semester) to show how a paragraph can be expanded to become an essay.

Confusion prevails on the issue of smoking in public places. Both smokers and nonsmokers are confused and would like the problem solved. On one side are many who, because of preference or addiction, desire to smoke. On the other side are primarily those who do not smoke and do not want to breathe the smoke of those who do. Laws vary from community to community; businesspersons wonder what is morally right and what price they may eventually have to pay in relation to this issue. For all the right reasons, the solution has become quite clear. It is time to pass a national law restricting smoking in public places.

Smokers may be disturbed by this proposition. They may feel that their rights would be violated both at work and elsewhere. They shouldn't, because a national law restricting them can benefit them also. This law would eliminate the hostility felt by a large percentage of the nonsmokers and, therefore, improve relationships between smokers and nonsmokers. Moreover, no one will be fired, and no one will be deprived of the privilege of visiting public places; the only restriction is on smoking. The smokers can continue to puff away—as long as they do not imperil the health of others.

The main reason that smoking should be restricted is the issue of health, the health of those who breathe secondhand smoke. Joseph Califano, former Secretary of Health, Education, and Welfare, reports that more than 5,000 Americans die each year because of secondhand smoke, and that nonsmokers who live with smokers are 80 percent more likely to get lung cancer than those who are married to nonsmokers. Moreover, some people are allergic to tobacco smoke, and some have respiratory illnesses that are made worse by the tobacco smoke. In 1993, the Environmental Protection Agency classified tobacco smoke as a carcinogen and placed it in a group with asbestos. The study by the EPA discovered that all people tested—and many were nonsmokers—had nicotine in their blood.

A second reason is the discomfort factor. Tobacco smoke has a disagreeable odor to most nonsmokers. In a restaurant, the pleasing aroma of food is altered if not destroyed by tobacco smoke, and because the senses of smell and taste are so closely related, tobacco smoke interferes with the pleasure of eating. The smell also clings to the clothes and hair of nonsmokers. There are, of course, other unpleasant clinging odors created by human beings, and were it not for the fact that secondhand smoke is a health issue the discomfort factor might not be enough to warrant the proposed restriction.

Another factor is the cost involved. The last five surgeons general have agreed that secondhand smoke is a significant problem with huge costs to the entire nation. Nonsmokers and all taxpayers pay large sums to take care of problems caused by secondhand smoke. People who are made ill by secondhand tobacco smoke miss work, losing time and money, and their employers lose productivity. Some may argue that creating nonsmoking areas, installing signs, and enforcing the rules would cost money, but the bill for these adjustments is nowhere close to what we are paying in the absence of a national law.

Powerful lobbies for tobacco companies are on the other side. But on the side of restriction are logic, honesty, and an abundance of scientific information. On the side of restriction is also a large group of smokers who are unable

Margin labels:

Fact

Thesis/proposition

Refutation

Support
Authoritative statement
Statistics
Statistics
Examples

Fact

Support

Support
Authoritative statement

Fact

or unwilling to quit smoking and see the rightness of such a proposal. <u>A new wind is blowing across the nation—and it is smoke free, at least in public places</u>.

Concluding sentence

How About Low-Cost Drugs for Addicts?

Louis Nizer

According to Louis Nizer in this article, first published in the *New York Times,* if we want to win the war against drugs, we should change the strategy and, instead, sell drugs to addicts.

1   We are losing the war against drug addiction. Our strategy is wrong. I propose a different approach.

2   The government should create clinics, manned by psychiatrists, that would provide drugs for nominal charges or even free to addicts under controlled regulations. It would cost the government only 20 cents for a heroin shot, for which the addicts must now pay the mob more than $100, and there are similar price discrepancies in cocaine, crack, and other such substances.

3   Such a service, which would also include the staff support of psychiatrists and doctors, would cost a fraction of what the nation now spends to maintain the land, sea, and air apparatus necessary to interdict illegal imports of drugs. There would also be a savings of hundreds of millions of dollars from the elimination of the prosecutorial procedures that stifle our courts and overcrowd our prisons.

4   We see in our newspapers the triumphant announcements by government agent that they have intercepted huge caches of cocaine, the street prices of which are in the tens of millions of dollars. Should we be gratified? Will this achievement reduce the number of addicts by one? All it will do is increase the cost to the addict of his illegal supply.

5   Many addicts who are caught committing a crime admit that they have mugged or stolen as many as six or seven times a day to accumulate the $100 needed for a fix. Since many of them need two or three fixes a day, particularly for crack, one can understand the terror in our streets and homes. It is estimated that there are in New York City alone 200,000 addicts, and this is typical of cities across the nation. Even if we were to assume that only a modest percentage of a city's addicts engage in criminal conduct to obtain the money for the habit, requiring multiple muggings and thefts each day, we could nevertheless account for many of the tens of thousands of crimes each day in New York City alone.

6   Not long ago, a Justice Department division issued a report stating that more than half the perpetrators of murder and other serious crimes were under the influence of drugs. This symbolizes the new domestic terror in our nation. This is why our citizens are unsafe in broad daylight on the most traveled thoroughfares. This is why computers and television sets are stolen from offices and homes and sold for a pittance. This is why parks are closed to the public and why murders are committed. This is why homes

need multiple locks and burglary systems, and why store windows, even in the most fashionable areas, require iron gates.

7 The benefits of the new strategy to control this terrorism would be immediate and profound.

8 First, the job would lose the main source of its income. It could not compete against a free supply for which previously it exacted tribute estimated to be hundreds of millions of dollars, perhaps billions, from hopeless victims.

9 Second, pushers would be out of business. There would be no purpose in creating addicts who would be driven by desperate compulsion to steal and kill for the money necessary to maintain their habit. Children would not be enticed. The mob's macabre public-relations program is to tempt children with free drugs in order to create customers for the future. The wave of street crimes in broad daylight would diminish to a trickle. Homes and stores would not have to be fortresses. Our recreational areas could again be used. Neighborhoods would not be scandalized by sordid street centers where addicts gather to obtain their supply from slimy merchants.

10 Third, police and other law-enforcement authorities, domestic or foreign, would be freed to deal with traditional nondrug crimes.

11 There are several objections that might be raised against such a salutary solution.

12 First, it could be argued that by providing free drugs to the addict we would consign him to permanent addiction. The answer is that medical and psychiatric help at the source would be more effective in controlling the addict's descent than the extremely limited remedies available to the victim today. I am not arguing that the new strategy will cure everything. But I do not see many addicts being freed from their bonds under the present system.

13 In addition, as between the addict's predicament and the safety of our innocent citizens, which deserves our primary concern? Drug-induced crime has become so common that almost every citizen knows someone in his immediate family or among his friends who has been mugged. It is these citizens who should be our chief concern.

14 Another possible objection is that addicts will cheat the system by obtaining more than the allowable free shot. Without discounting the resourcefulness of the bedeviled addict, it should be possible to have government cards issued that would be punched so as to limit the free supply in accord with medical authorization.

15 Yet all objections become trivial when matched against the crisis itself. What we are witnessing is the demoralization of a great society: the ruination of its school children, athletes, and executives, the corrosion of the workforce in general.

16 Many thoughtful sociologists consider the rapidly spreading drug use the greatest problem that our nation faces—greater and more real and urgent than nuclear bombs or economic reversal. In China, a similar crisis drove the authorities to apply capital punishment to those who trafficked in opium—an extreme solution that arose from the deepest reaches of frustration.

17 Free drugs will win the war against the domestic terrorism caused by illicit drugs. As a strategy, it is at once resourceful, sensible, and simple. We are getting nowhere in our efforts to hold back the ocean of supply. The answer is to dry up demand.

Exercise 6	DISCUSSION AND CRITICAL THINKING

1. What is Nizer's proposition?

2. Which paragraphs (by number) contain the main support?

3. Which paragraphs (by number) contain the refutation?

4. What kinds of evidence (facts, examples, statistics, authoritative statement) does Nizer offer? Give specific examples.

Should School Uniforms Be Mandated?

Keith A. King

Published in the *Journal of School Health,* the arguments for and against school uniforms, which you will read in two different essays, are parts of a longer scholarly study. The following paragraph, also excerpted from King's essay, gives some background:

> Violence among today's young people, especially at school, has been labeled by many health professionals as a potential threat to the overall health and academic success of children. Approximately one in four students reports worrying about becoming a victim of crime or threats at school, and one in eight reports having been victimized at school. In the light of such reports, schools have implemented violence-prevention programs, which have shown moderate success.

Because the two positions discussed in the following essays are both written by the same author, they are not traditional arguments. However, the main components of the argument are presented and will provide you with information so that you can reflect and write.

The Case for School Uniforms

1 The school should provide a safe and disciplined learning environment for students. Violence in schools destroys such an environment and can negatively affect student motivation for learning. Everett and Price found that due to increased prevalence of school violence, one in five public school

students feels less eager to go to school every day, one in seven feels less inclined to pay attention to learning in school, and one in ten stays home from school or cuts class. In unsafe school environments, teachers cannot teach to their maximum potential, and students cannot learn to their full capability.

2   Youths who feel safe, secure, and free from threats of violence perform better academically. Those who fear for their safety in school or on the way to school may not learn effectively, and they may turn to truancy as a viable alternative to facing the daily threats of violence. One of every ten to twelve youths who stays away from school does so because of fear. In their response to increasing school violence, several teachers, principals, parents, and students believe uniforms could help reduce violence.

3   Many people believe adoption of school-uniform policies will lead to increased school safety, student discipline, and student learning. More specifically, many have argued that school uniforms assist in reducing school violence and theft; preventing gang activity, such as students wearing gang colors and gang insignia; providing discipline in students; helping students to concentrate on their school work; helping students to resist peer pressure; and helping school officials easily recognize school intruders.

4   In a survey of the United Teachers of Dade County, Florida, approximately 60 percent of the group's members supported mandatory uniforms for school children. Similarly, of the 5,500 principals surveyed as attendees of the National Association of Secondary School Principals' annual conference in February 1996, more than 70 percent believed that requiring students to wear uniforms to school would reduce violent incidents and discipline problems. Morever, greater than 80 percent of Long Beach Press-Telegram readers supported school uniforms.

5   Some school personnel believe students and teachers tend to behave the way they are allowed to dress. Instead of adopting a policy for mandatory school uniforms, several schools have adopted a mandatory dress code policy for teachers as well as students, which aims to establish clear appearance and behavioral standards for all.

6   Long Beach Unified School District was the first large urban school district in the United States to require school uniforms for all students in grades kindergarten through eight, and it subsequently experienced great decreases in school violence, crime, and negativity. Despite allowing parents the option to request exemption from school uniforms, fewer than 500 parents—less than 1 percent of all parents—requested exemption in the first year of implementation. Fewer than 400 parents—again, less than 1 percent of all parents requested exemption during the 1995–96 academic year.

7   Other schools have followed the Long Beach example. To date, twelve states (California, Indiana, Iowa, Louisiana, Massachusetts, Minnesota, New Jersey, Tennessee, Texas, Utah, Virginia, and Washington) have state policies that permit individual schools or districts to adopt school-uniform policies or dress codes. Nonetheless, Long Beach Unified and Oakland are the only two school districts to have adopted mandatory uniform policies at the district level. Most school-uniform policies are determined at the individual school level. The White House Manual on School Uniforms revealed that several schools with mandatory uniform policies have shown

subsequent decreases in school violence and truancy and increases in positive student demeanor.

Exercise 7	**DISCUSSION AND CRITICAL THINKING**

1. Which paragraphs give the background?

2. Which paragraph states and then details the proposition?

3. What two kinds of evidence are presented in paragraph 4?

4. What kind of evidence is given in paragraph 5?

5. What are the two points of support in paragraph 6?

The Case Against School Uniforms

1 While most parents and teachers seek to ensure the safety and security of their school children, some believe adopting a mandatory school-uniform policy is not the appropriate method for ensuring such safety. Two groups opposing mandatory school uniforms are civil libertarians and older students. Loren Siegel, who is director of the ACLU Public Education Department, has stated no one knows for certain whether school uniforms are actually beneficial. While Long Beach Unified School District claims that mandatory school uniforms resulted in decreased school crime and violence, other steps to improve student behavior—such as more teachers patrolling hallways during class changes—were implemented at the same time as the school-uniform policy. Due to these possible confounding variables, the ACLU has stated that it is currently impossible to determine whether uniforms were responsible for the results. In addition, no empirical studies show that uniforms consistently produce positive changes in student behavior over time.

2 The ACLU has also labeled mandatory school-uniform policy as not constructive, since such a policy only serves as a "band aid" to a set of serious problems that require multifaceted, multidisciplinary actions. The ACLU stresses that, instead of being directed toward uniforms, resources should be directed toward creating more attractive, clean, and safe school buildings; smaller classes; well-stocked libraries; easily accessed computers; and more elective courses, such as music, drama, and art. Such measures could help schools foster long-lasting, positive changes among school children.

3 Some individuals feel that mandatory school uniforms may teach students a negative lesson about conformity. Some believe that students should base life choices on their own internal values, rather than on rules and regulations arbitrarily set for them, and that this is vitally important to

their future health and discipline. Such an argument touches directly upon the rights of freedom of expression for all U.S. citizens. In turn, the ACLU has argued that mandatory uniforms violate students' free expression rights.

4   Although most younger children seem to be amenable to uniforms and even like them, many older students, especially adolescents, respond very negatively to school uniforms. One Long Beach seventh grader stated, "It's like we're all in jail." Adolescence is a period when youths attempt to find their own uniqueness and individuality in various ways. One way is through fashion. While many political cartoonists joke that today's youths already wear uniforms of baggy pants, T-shirts, and baseball caps worn backward, these uniforms are acquired by free choice, not enforced by authority figures.

5   The ACLU conducted a series of focus groups and discussions with high school students to identify what students believed to be solutions to the problem of school violence. School uniforms were not among the solutions students mentioned. Their suggestions did include schools seriously confronting and discussing issues of racial and cultural conflict; providing "safe corridor" programs, which protect student safety to and from school; securing their entrances; providing them more extracurricular activities and clubs; establishing open forums to give them opportunities for self-expression; helping them find part-time jobs; and teaching them conflict-resolution skills.

6   In October 1995, working on behalf of low-income families, the ACLU of Southern California filed a lawsuit against the Long Beach Unified School District. The lawsuit claimed that the district fails to help low-income students purchase uniforms and has punished students who do not wear them. It also claimed the district does not adequately inform parents about their rights to request exemption from the program. ACLU attorneys assert that low socioeconomic families are going without food, utilities, and rental payments in order to purchase mandatory school uniforms. In response to these claims, Long Beach Unified School officials state that the district has spent more than $100 thousand in donations from individuals and organizations to purchase uniforms and other supplies for financially burdened students. The officials quickly point out that typically, a set of three school uniforms for the year costs between $70 and $90, an amount far less than many students spend for one item of designer clothing.

7   Another argument against implementing school uniforms involves using student clothing as a barometer for possible personal problems, such as drug use, gang involvement, or sexual abuse. Students' school uniforms may cover up such problems that their clothing might otherwise reveal. In addition, some argue that a mandatory uniform policy tends to penalize everyone as opposed to addressing the children who cause the majority of problems.

Exercise 8	DISCUSSION AND CRITICAL THINKING

1. Copy the proposition of the opposing view (from paragraph 1) here.

2. What countermeasure does the ACLU propose?

3. What are the main points in paragraphs 2 through 7?

Practicing Patterns of Argument

The pattern of argument mimics the pattern of the typical paragraph of development: main idea followed by support. With the argument, the main idea is called the proposition and the points of support are developed by presentation of evidence. Refutation should be included if it can be used effectively.

Exercise 9	COMPLETING PATTERNS OF ARGUMENT

Fill in the blanks with supporting statements for each proposition. Each outline uses the following pattern:

Proposition

   I. Support 1

  II. Support 2

 III. Support 3

1. Proposition: College athletes should be paid.

   I. _____

  II. They work long hours in practice and competition.

 III. They have less time than many other students for study.

2. Proposition: Zoos are beneficial institutions.

   I. _____

  II. They preserve endangered species by captive breeding.

 III. They study animal diseases and find cures.

✎ Topics for Writing Argument

Reading-Related Topics

"A New Wind Blowing"

1. Using either the paragraph or the essay as a model, write from the other side of the issue.

"How About Low-Cost Drugs for Addicts?"

2. Write an argument on the other side of this issue. The author provides some of the opposing views in the refutation toward the end of the essay.

3. Write a summary of Nizer's argument. Then, using clear, specific references to that summary, agree or disagree with him.

4. Imagine that you are an addict. Write a letter to Nizer, explaining why you think his plan will or will not work. Alternatively, from the same perspective write your explanation to the general public.

"Should School Uniforms Be Mandated?"

5. Using King's arguments as resource material and points of reference, write your own review. To what extent are you for or against school uniforms? If you use statistics, give credit to the source by using a phrase such as "according to" or "so and so says." If you have relevant experiences, include them. Give your own opinions, but state them as such.

Career-Related Topics

6. Write a paragraph of argument to convince people that workers at a particular company should or should not be laid off.

7. Write a paragraph of argument to convince people that workers in a particular service industry should or should not go on strike.

General Topics

Write a paragraph of argument on one of the following broad subject areas. You will have to limit your focus. You may also modify the topic to fit specific situations.

8. School drug tests

9. School metal detectors

10. Sex education

11. Defining sexual harassment

12. Changing the juvenile justice system

13. Endangered species legislation

14. Advertising tobacco

15. Combatting homelessness

16. State-run lotteries

17. Jury reform

18. Legalizing prostitution

19. Censoring rap or rock music

20. Cost of illegal immigration

21. Installation of local traffic signs

22. Foot patrols by local police

23. Change in (your) college registration procedure

24. Local public transportation

25. Surveillance by video (on campus, in neighborhoods, or in shopping areas)

26. Zone changes for stores selling liquor

27. Curfew for teenagers

28. Laws keeping known gang members out of parks

Writer's Guidelines: Argument

1. Consider which aspects of the formal argument you need for your paper:

   - *Background:* What is the historical or social context for this controversial issue?

   - *Proposition* (the *topic sentence* or *thesis*): What do I want my audience to believe or do?

   - *Qualification of proposition:* Have I limited my proposition so that I cannot be easily challenged with exceptions?

   - *Refutation* (taking the opposing view into account, mainly to point out its weaknesses): What is the view on the other side, and why is it flawed in reasoning or evidence?

   - *Support:* In addition to sound reasoning, have I used appropriate facts, examples, statistics, and opinions of authorities?

2. The basic pattern of a paragraph or argument is likely to be in this form:

   Proposition (the topic sentence)

   I. Support 1

   II. Support 2

   III. Support 3

Mixed Bag

"*You have not only altered, declawed, and malformed your winged and four-legged cousins; you have done it to yourselves.*"

John (Fire) Lame Deer

"*To cook soul food you must use all of your senses. You cook by instinct, but you also use smell, taste, touch, sight, and, particularly, sound.*"

Sheila Ferguson

"*A study that provided the basis for the definition found that compulsive Internet use was related not to finding information, but to social support, sexual fulfillment, and the ability to create a persona.*"

Jonathan Gaw

"*I seized the opportunity to say, 'I don't want an arranged marriage,' but she sang on ever louder, singing a song of a distant home.*"

Chantra Shastri

"*Every day, hundreds of gay youths hide in their rooms and cry from pain caused by the mean and careless behavior of those who claim to love them.*"

Michael Holguin

—"from The Mix in the Bag"

The Mix in the Bag

hese readings represent a variety of perceptions, experiences, and tastes. With each reading incorporating several forms, they are intended to stimulate thought, serve as models, and be subjects for analysis and comparative studies.

Listening to the Air

John (Fire) Lame Deer and Richard Erdoes

John Lame Deer's message for us is to withdraw from the "conveniences" that have made us "civilized" and "advanced" and contemplate nature and our place in it. He says human beings have set up barriers that have diminished us as people and have altered and destroyed much of our natural world. He wants us to rethink our roles and our responsibilities and to spend more time "listening to the air." His message comes through journalist Richard Erdoes.

1   Let's sit down here, all of us, on the open prairie, where we can't see a highway or a fence. Let's have no blankets to sit on, but feel the ground with our bodies, the earth, the yielding shrubs. Let's have the grass for a mattress, experiencing its sharpness and its softness. Let us become like stones, plants, and trees. Let us be animals, think and feel like animals.

2   Listen to the air. You can hear it, feel it, smell it, taste it. *Woniya waken*—the holy air—which renews all by its breath. *Woniya, woniya waken*—spirit, life, breath, renewal—it means all that. *Woniya*—we sit together, don't touch, but something is there; we feel it between us, as a presence. A good way to start thinking about nature, talk about it. Rather talk to it, talk to the rivers, to the lakes, to the winds as to our relatives.

3   You have made it hard for us to experience nature in the good way by being part of it. Even here we are conscious that somewhere out in those hills there are missile silos and radar stations. White men always pick the few unspoiled, beautiful, awesome spots for the sites of these abominations. You have raped and violated these lands, always saying, "Gimme, gimme, gimme," and never giving anything back. You have taken 200,000 acres of our Pine Ridge reservation and made them into a bombing range. This land is so beautiful and strange that now some of you want to make it into a national park. The only use you have made of this land since you took it from us was to blow it up. You have not only despoiled the earth, the rocks, the minerals, all of which you call "dead" but which are very much alive; you have even changed the animals, which are part of us, part of the Great Spirit, changed them in a horrible way, so no one can recognize them. There is power in a buffalo—spiritual, magic power—but there is no power in an Angus, in a Hereford.

4   There is power in an antelope, but not in a goat or in a sheep, which holds still while you butcher it, which will eat your newspaper if you let it. There was a great power in a wolf, even in a coyote. You have made him into a freak—a toy poodle, a Pekingese, a lap dog. You can't do much with a cat, which is like an Indian, unchangeable. So you fix it, alter it, declaw it, even

cut its vocal cords so you can experiment on it in a laboratory without being disturbed by its cries.

5   A partridge, a grouse, a quail, a pheasant, you have made them into chickens, creatures that can't fly, that wear a kind of sunglasses so that they won't peck each other's eyes out, "birds" with a "pecking order." There are some farms where they breed chickens for breast meat. Those birds are kept in low cages, forced to be hunched over all the time, which makes the breast muscles very big. Soothing sounds, Muzak, are piped into these chicken hutches. One loud noise and the chickens go haywire, killing themselves by flying against the mesh of their cages. Having to spend all their lives stooped over makes an unnatural, crazy, no-good bird. It also makes unnatural, no-good human beings.

6   That's where you fooled yourselves. You have not only altered, declawed, and malformed your winged and four-legged cousins; you have done it to yourselves. You have changed men into chairmen of boards, into office workers, into time-clock punchers. You have changed women into housewives, truly fearful creatures. I was once invited into the home of such a one.

7   "Watch the ashes, don't smoke, you stain the curtains. Watch the goldfish bowl, don't breathe on the parakeet, don't lean your head against the wallpaper; your hair may be greasy. Don't spill liquor on that table: It has a delicate finish. You should have wiped your boots; the floor was just varnished. Don't, don't, don't . . ." That is crazy. We weren't made to endure this. You live in prisons which you have built for yourselves, calling them "homes," offices, factories. We have a new joke on the reservation: "What is cultural deprivation?" Answer: "Being an upper-middle-class white kid living in a split-level suburban home with a color TV."

8   Sometimes I think that even our pitiful tar-paper shacks are better than your luxury homes. Walking a hundred feet to the outhouse on a clear wintry night, through mud or snow, that's one small link with nature. Or in the summer, in the back country, leaving the door of the privy open, taking your time, listening to the humming of the insects, the sun warming your bones through the thin planks of wood; you don't even have that pleasure anymore.

9   Americans want to have everything sanitized. No smells! Not even the good, natural man and woman smell. Take away the smell from under the armpits, from your skin. Rub it out, and then spray or dab some nonhuman odor on yourself, stuff you can spend a lot of money on, ten dollars an ounce, so you know this has to smell good. "B.O.," bad breath, "Intimate Female Odor Spray"—I see it all on TV. Soon you'll breed people without body openings.

10   I think white people are so afraid of the world they created that they don't want to see, feel, smell, or hear it. The feeling of rain and snow on your face, being numbed by an icy wind and thawing out before a smoking fire, coming out of a hot sweat bath and plunging into a cold stream, these things make you feel alive, but you don't want them anymore. Living in boxes which shut out the heat of the summer and the chill of winter, living inside a body that no longer has a scent, hearing the noise from the hi-fi instead of listening to the sounds of nature, watching some actor on TV having a make-believe experience when you no longer experience anything for yourself, eating food without taste—that's your way. It's no good.

11   The food you eat, you treat it like your bodies, take out all the nature part, the taste, the smell, the roughness, then put the artificial color, the

artificial flavor in. Raw liver, raw kidney—that's what we old-fashioned full-bloods like to get our teeth into. In the old days we used to eat the guts of the buffalo, making a contest of it, two fellows getting hold of a long piece of intestines from opposite ends, starting chewing toward the middle, seeing who can get there first; that's eating. Those buffalo guts, full of half-fermented, half-digested grass and herbs, you didn't need any pills and vitamins when you swallowed those. Use the bitterness of gall for flavoring, not refined salt or sugar. *Wasna*—meat, kidney fat, and berries all pounded together—a lump of that sweet *wasna* kept a man going for a whole day. That was food, that had the power. Not the stuff you give us today: powdered milk, dehydrated eggs, pasteurized butter, chickens that are all drumsticks or all breast; there's no bird left there.

12   You don't want the bird. You don't have the courage to kill honestly—cut off the chicken's head, pluck it and gut it—no, you don't want this anymore. So it all comes in a neat plastic bag, all cut up, ready to eat, with no taste and no guilt. Your mink and seal coats, you don't want to know about the blood and pain which went into making them. Your idea of war—sit in an airplane, way above the clouds, press a button, drop the bombs, and never look below the clouds—that's the odorless, guiltless, sanitized way.

13   When we killed a buffalo, we knew what we were doing. We apologized to his spirit, tried to make him understand why we did it, honoring with a prayer the bones of those who gave their flesh to keep us alive, praying for their return, praying for the life of our brothers, the buffalo nation, as well as for our own people. You wouldn't understand this and that's why we had the Washita Massacre, the Sand Creek Massacre, the dead women and babies at Wounded Knee. That's why we have Song My and My Lai now.

14   To us life, all life, is sacred. The state of South Dakota has pest-control officers. They go up in a plane and shoot coyotes from the air. They keep track of their kills, put them all down in their little books. The stockmen and sheepowners pay them. Coyotes eat mostly rodents, field mice and such. Only once in a while will they go after a stray lamb. They are our natural garbage men cleaning up the rotten and stinking things. They make good pets if you give them a chance. But their living could lose some man a few cents, and so the coyotes are killed from the air. They were here before the sheep, but they are in the way; you can't make a profit out of them. More and more animals are dying out. The animals which the Great Spirit put here, they must go. The man-made animals are allowed to stay—at least until they are shipped out to be butchered. That terrible arrogance of the white man, making himself something more than God, more than nature, saying, "I will let this animal live, because it makes money"; saying, "This animal must go, it brings no income, the space it occupies can be used in a better way. The only good coyote is a dead coyote." They are treating coyotes almost as badly as they used to treat Indians.

Exercise 1   DISCUSSION AND CRITICAL THINKING

1. How should we begin to start thinking about nature, according to Lame Deer?

2. How have we made it hard to experience nature in the good way by being part of it?

3. Lame Deer says, "You have not only altered, declawed, and malformed your winged and four-legged cousins; you have done it to yourselves." Explain that statement.

4. In what ways are Native American primitive home conditions better than those of urban people in Lame Deer's view?

5. How do Native Americans, according to Lame Deer, regard killing and life?

Exercise 2	**READING-RELATED WRITING**

1. Summarize what Lame Deer said. Be sure to emphasize the main points of his concern.

2. Write a two-part response. In the first part, summarize Lame Deer's message. In the second part evaluate his ideas.

3. Select one of Lame Deer's main ideas and explain how it relates to one of society's problems.

4. Lame Deer makes some statements about domesticated animals (paragraph 4). Agree or disagree in a brief written statement.

5. Discuss what part(s) of Lame Deer's message can and should be applied in a practical sense.

Soul Food at a Black American Family Reunion

Sheila Ferguson

Sheila Ferguson is the author of *Soul Food: Classic Cuisine from the Deep South.* Let her tell you about soul food in the proper setting, the Black American family reunion.

1   Soul food . . . is a legacy clearly steeped in tradition; a way of life that has been handed down from generation to generation, from one black family to another, by word of mouth and sleight of hand. It is rich in both history and variety of flavor.

2   To cook soul food you must use all of your senses. You cook by instinct, but you also use smell, taste, touch, sight, and, particularly, sound. You learn to hear by the crackling sound when it's time to turn over the fried chicken, to smell when a pan of biscuits is just about to finish baking, and to feel when a pastry's just right to the touch. You taste, rather than measure, the seasonings you treasure; and you use your eyes, not a clock, to judge when that cherry pie has bubbled sweet and nice. These skills are

hard to teach quickly. They must be felt, loving, and come straight from the heart.

3   Ah, but when you taste good soul food then it'll take ahold of your soul and hang your unsuspecting innards out to dry. It's that shur-'nuf everlovin' down-home stick-to-your-ribs kinda food that keeps you glued to your seat long after the meal is over and done with, enabling you to sit back, relax, and savor the gentle purrings of a well satisfied stomach, feeling that all's right with the world. . .

4   It was down South . . . that I went to my first family reunion. Now, I know I should be telling you that the highlight of this affair was the prayers that one member was chosen to deliver. But if I were to tell the gospel truth, and I think I'm a-gonna, it was definitely the dishes that everybody turned out. Oh, dear, I'm making myself sound like some kinda pagan, but all that food, spread out majestically, on a long banquet-sized picnic table, sure was one sight for a small girl to behold. The table at the farm on Blanton Street in Charlotte kinda sloped with the terrain, but that didn't stop us from keeping the food well-balanced and from swatting the flies away from the pecan pies, stacked a mile high, I might add. With one long and narrow slice you had a hunk of pie big enough to last you for quite a spell.

5   I should explain, though, that a black American family reunion stands for a great deal more than just the sharing of a really fine meal. It is a testimonial both to the past and to what the future holds in store for the entire family. We gather to share all that is most precious to us, especially with those family members we don't get to see that often. We eat, we drink, and we pray, but also we encourage each other and lift our heads in praise of what our offspring have accomplished. We share in each other's joys and good fortunes and offer solace when the chips are down. We comfort each other and this enables us to retain a special kind of closeness, even when we're hundreds of miles apart.

6   Every time our family gets together we try to pay some humble tribute to the accomplishments of our race in one way or another. My family, for example, after discovering the existence of my great-great-grandfather Dennison Harrell, now meets annually for a grand family reunion expressly in his honor. We come together from all over the States and in my case from across the Atlantic each time—tracing new family members we have never met before, as we continue to pay homage to the man who founded our family in America. Everyone who attends gives in the best of spirit and puts all of their personality into the dishes they concoct. At the same time, we are remembering all of our forebears and all that they gave, often against apparently insurmountable odds.

7   This is precisely why we feel we must get down to some real serious cookin' at the time of a family reunion. It represents sharing the very best with those we love the very most and that love is best conveyed in the pride we take in preparing our food. By now, it has become a family tradition. And believe you me, can we burn when we cook. Everyone is asked to bring a dish, usually their specialty, and each cook has to maintain an exceedingly high standard of cooking, baking, and innovation. One dish just walks all over and surpasses another, and we always delight in sharing and comparing recipes. Once Aunt Peacie brought along her "Jesse Jackson Sweet Potato Pie." Well, it was gone before you had a chance to take a good look.

Man, that pie was "the T"—the talk of the day. But another thing is for dang sure: if your cooking isn't quite up to scratch, you sure as shootin' won't be asked to bring a dish next time round! You'll be nicely passed over with, "Oh, honey, that's OK, why don't you just sit this one out."

8   Even if it's not a big family reunion, it is still considered an extreme insult if you don't put yourself out and cook a fine and exquisite meal. I wouldn't dream of presenting my family and friends with a meal consisting of frozen fried chicken, frozen collard greens, store-bought cartons of butter-milk sausage biscuits and gravy made out of some sorry old box of granules. Oh, they'd eat it all right. But they would just feel so put down and outright insulted that they would commence telling me off, royally, right on the spot. Then, they would continue to talk about me for fifteen more years! My folks pull no punches when it comes to telling you off and they don't necessarily wait until they're politely out of earshot either. I can just hear them signifying now: "Well, she sure didn't sweat long over that sad plate of stuff." "Do you call that food? Sure was pathetic." "I don't care how busy the girl is, she could certainly take a little time to think about her family once in a while, humph!" That is the spirit through which soul food traditions continually evolve—*pressure!*

| Exercise 3 | DISCUSSION AND CRITICAL THINKING |

1. How does one use all five senses to prepare soul food?

2. According to Ferguson, why is soul food, soul food?

3. What does a black American family reunion stand for?

4. What have Ferguson and her family done on a personal level?

5. What are the standards of cooking?

| Exercise 4 | READING-RELATED WRITING |

1. Write about the tradition of reunions or the celebration of a certain holiday in your family. Explain how people work together and what they take pride in.

2. Write about a particular reunion you have gone to.

3. Write about the equivalent of soul food in another culture. Use Ferguson's description as a framework for your discussion.

4. Write about the significance of particular foods at a specific cultural holiday.

Are Kids Too Tangled in the Web?

Jonathan Gaw

The American Psychological Association has identified an emerging area of concern: adolescents' obsession with the Internet. Presenting a definition of Internet dependency along with causes and effects, journalist Jonathan Gaw explores the extent to which a hobby for some becomes an obsession for others. His examples include both those who have problems handling the Internet, an integral part of society, and those who cope with the Internet very well.

1   Recent events have raised parents' concerns that the hours teens spend online can lead to danger or addiction. Others say the Net fetish is just a phase. A 14-year-old Coon Rapids girl runs away from home with an Internet acquaintance. Two Bloomington teenagers are arrested for allegedly using their computers to intercept credit card numbers. A 15-year-old Bemidji boy tries to board a bus bound for Denver to meet two women he befriended on the Net.

2   While the incidents leave some parents worried that their children's interest in computers could lead to obsession or dangerous behavior, psychologists draw similarities between computer use and innocuous behavior typically engaged in and grown out of by teens.

3   Much like memorizing the statistics on baseball cards, tinkering with cars in the driveway, and talking on the telephone for hours on end, chatting on the Internet and playing computer games can provide both a hobby and an escape. In some cases, such infatuation goes too far. The extent to which the hobby becomes obsessive, where the person disconnects from other parts of life, can reflect avoidance of painful experiences. "Any compulsive behavior is about people learning to avoid something else," said Lynn John Rambeck, a clinical psychologist in Edina. "It might be a lot easier to deal with life to get on the computer and in a chat room where you can act out a comfortable role."

4   Adolescents are only just developing skills to cope with life's ups and downs, and they might be more susceptible to obsessive behaviors as a form of escape. "The longer we live, the more we know that we do come out on the other end," said Elizabeth George, executive director of the Minnesota Council on Compulsive Gambling Inc. The Internet, gambling, and other activities do not in and of themselves produce a compulsive behavior, psychiatrists said. "Some people just charge their problems head on and don't avoid them," Rambeck said. "You need both a personality predisposition to addictions and exposure to the opportunity to be addicted at a vulnerable time." Children's obsessive behavior concerning the Internet, however, has produced anecdotes that have frightened parents.

5   Last week, a 15-year-old Bemidji boy packed up a few changes of clothes, a heavy, metal baton for protection, and his baseball and basketball card collections and left home planning to travel to Denver to visit two women he met over the Internet. A distraught mother, who dug through discarded computer files to find out where he went, called the bus station in

time to prevent him from boarding a Greyhound. "He tells me that he didn't want to leave us, that he didn't want to run away," said Charlene Gove, who raises two sons by herself while attending Bemidji State University. "He felt like he was in love with this person, even though he's never seen [her]. . . . There needs to be some law drawn up pertaining to the enticing and luring of children away from their homes via the Internet."

6   Two weeks ago, a 14-year-old Coon Rapids girl left town with a New Jersey man she had met on the Internet. Richard Crandon was later charged in federal court with possessing sexually explicit photographs of the girl and himself. He was also charged in Anoka County District Court with third-degree criminal sexual conduct and soliciting a minor to engage in sex. Crandon and the girl had gotten as far as Pennsylvania when he told police that he heard authorities were looking for them. He then put the girl on a bus back to Minneapolis.

7   Also last month, two Bloomington teenagers were arrested for allegedly using their computers to intercept credit card numbers and then ordering hundreds of dollars' worth of computer equipment and home electronics. It's unclear whether the boys went through the Internet in getting the credit card numbers or if they hacked a stand-alone computer system.

Growing Up

8   While stories of computer obsession grab headlines, John Rockwell may be a more typical example of a young Internet user. At one time, the 19-year-old University of St. Thomas student spent almost as much time on the Internet as most people do at work. He enjoyed the anonymity of the medium, the opportunity to "meet" new people around the world, and the role-playing.

9   Then his interests changed. Now phone conversations with his girlfriend and his job assembling customized golf clubs keep him busy—and off the Net. His preoccupation with the online world was similar to his golfing at least once a day, which he has since dropped, and, before that, playing video games for four hours at a time. "I don't use it nearly as much as before," said Rockwell, who used to log 140 hours a month online, most of it in chat rooms where people from all over the world can gather electronically.

10   Rockwell, who remembers first typing on a computer keyboard when he was 4 years old, met a woman in a Web-based chat room last year. Last January, he flew down to meet her and her parents for the first time in Orlando. "We had our parents talk and everything before we met," Rockwell said. A few months later, she and her parents visited Rockwell and his family in Minnesota. Now, Rockwell, a computer science student, is considering transferring to Florida State University. "I don't know if I really had Internet addiction," he said. "I was more obsessed about this girl."

A New Medium

11   The psychiatric world is still coming to terms with the new communications phenomenon. Recently, a University of Pittsburgh at Bradford (Pennsylvania) researcher presented a paper at the American Psychological Association's national conference outlining ten criteria for identifying pathological Internet use. A study that provided the basis for the definition found that

compulsive Internet use was related not to finding information, but to social support, sexual fulfillment, and the ability to create a persona.

12   In the study, the 396 participants classified as "Internet dependent" said that chat rooms and multi-user dungeons (MUDs—areas featuring fantasy role-playing games) were the parts of the Internet they used the most, while electronic mail and the World Wide Web were among the least used. The nondependents in the study, on the other hand, said they used chat rooms and MUDs the least, while the Web and e-mail were the most popular features.

13   Many experts studying compulsions hesitate to label excessive computer use with the term "addiction," preferring to reserve that word for chemical dependencies. "While you might have excessive or obsessive use of the computer, these are things that people can grow out of or they can change or modify their behavior," said Douglas Noverr, chair of the Department of American Thought and Language at Michigan State University. "There may be analogies to addiction, but it's not the same thing."

14   Others argue that a "high" can be induced both physiologically and psychologically. "The definition of addiction just keeps expanding," said Donald E. Maypole, professor of social work at the University of Minnesota–Duluth. "In the 1960s, certain foods were labeled as addictive, in the 1970s it was sex, and gambling came in the 1970s and 1980s." During adolescence, people are learning to take social risks, and an Internet chat room could be an easy way to do that, Rambeck said. Just as teenagers grow out of chatting on the phone for hours on end, eventually children with healthy self-esteem learn to branch out from computers.

Self-Expression

15   Aaron Brethorst, a 15-year-old from Minneapolis, said he was an awkward adolescent when he first got into computers nearly three years ago after his mother, an elementary school teacher, brought home a Macintosh. A friend introduced him to Bitstream Underground, a Minneapolis electronic bulletin board system that has become one of the area's largest Internet providers, and Brethorst got into the social aspects of electronic communication.

16   "It allowed me to express myself, and people judged me on how I behaved and who I was instead of what I looked like," he said. "That's one of the most important parts about computing and the Internet. People take you for how you act and carry yourself [online] instead of what you look like, your age, gender, or race."

17   Brethorst spends four or five hours a day catching up on the latest computer trends, repairing and selling computers, and reading computer magazines—only now, it's as a professional. He runs a one-man computer consulting firm, Atlas Heavy Industries, and is a third-party representative for another computer firm.

18   While he no longer frequents chat rooms, he feels that they play a valuable role in social development and that their dangers have been overblown. "If the Internet were not there, people would be obsessed in other ways with other things," Brethorst said. "They obviously have problems, and they just found a focus in the Internet. The Net is filling the role in parents' eyes that used to be filled by rock 'n' roll and television."

What Constitutes Pathological Internet Use?

19 Individuals who met four or more of these criteria over a year were classified as dependent in a study presented last month to the American Psychological Association by Kimberly Young, an assistant professor of psychology at the University of Pittsburgh. Do you

- Feel preoccupied with the Internet (i.e., think about it when off-line)?

- Feel a need to use the Internet longer to achieve satisfaction?

- Have an inability to control your Internet use?

- Feel restless or irritable when attempting to cut down or stop Internet use?

- Use the Internet as a way of escaping from problems or of relieving a poor mood (i.e., feelings of helplessness, guilt, anxiety, or depression)?

- Lie to family members or friends to conceal the extent of involvement with the Internet?

- Jeopardize significant relationship, job, or educational or career opportunity because of the Internet?

- After spending an excessive amount of money on online fees, often return another day?

- Go through withdrawal when off-line (e.g., increased depression, anxiety)?

- Stay online longer than intended?

Exercise 5   **VOCABULARY HIGHLIGHTS**

Write a short definition of each word as it is used in the essay. (Paragraph numbers are given in parentheses.) Be prepared to use the words in your own sentences.

innocuous (2)	pertaining (5)
susceptible (4)	explicit (6)
predisposition (4)	anonymity (8)
vulnerable (4)	pathological (11)
distraught (5)	persona (11)

Exercise 6   **DISCUSSION AND CRITICAL THINKING**

1. What are some examples of typical innocuous behavior that teens engage in and outgrow?

2. What two factors must be present for compulsive behavior to develop?

3. According to the University of Pittsburgh researcher (paragraph 11), compulsive Internet use is related not to finding information but to what?

4. How does Douglas Noverr (paragraph 13) distinguish between addiction and compulsion?

5. Why do others disagree with Noverr?

6. This essay is concerned mainly with teens. To what extent could the ideas also be applied to adults?

7. How would you rank the characteristics of the Internet-dependent person presented at the end of the article?

Exercise 7   **READING-RELATED WRITING**

1. Write about someone you know who meets several of the criteria in the list of questions under "What Constitutes Pathological Internet Use?" (page 390).

2. Write a response to one of the following statements from the article. You should make clear what the statement means, whether you agree with it, and how it relates to any experiences you have had (people and situations you are familiar with, what you have observed).

    a. "The extent to which the hobby becomes obsessive, where the person disconnects from other parts of life, can reflect avoidance of painful experiences." (paragraph 3)

    b. "While stories of computer obsession grab headlines, John Rockwell may be a more typical example of a young Internet user." (paragraph 8)

    c. "Adolescents are only just developing skills to cope with life's ups and downs, and they might be more susceptible to obsessive behaviors as a form of escape." (paragraph 4)

    d. "There needs to be some law drawn up pertaining to the enticing and luring of children away from their homes via the Internet." (Mother of a would-be runaway, paragraph 5)

    e. "It might be a lot easier to deal with life to get on the computer and in a chat room where you can act out a comfortable role." (Lynn John Rambeck, a clinical psychologist, paragraph 3)

    f. "Psychologists draw similarities between computer use and innocuous behavior typically engaged in and grown out of by teens." (paragraph 2)

    g. "In the study, the 396 participants classified as 'Internet dependent' said that chat rooms and multi-user dungeons (MUDs—areas featuring fantasy role-playing games) were the parts of the Internet they used the most." (paragraph 12)

Yearning for Love

Chantra Shastri

Having lived in America for five years, Chantra Shastri asks for freedom—freedom to make a choice in marriage, a choice based on love.

I need not go beyond myself to find examples of love, at least the yearning for love. My home is now America, but I have not left India far behind. There, in ways still cherished by my traditional family, freedom is based on gender, and I am a female. My parents expect women to cook, clean, and nurture. My parents expect me to marry the man of their choice, although my brother will have the freedom to choose his own mate. If I disobey, I will no longer be recognized by my parents. It is easy to give in to such a custom; it is difficult to disobey. My parents have always believed as they do. I cannot change them, nor do I want to, but I wish they would accept my difference in this different country. I think my mother understands. Last week, I saw her crying while she ironed our clothes. When I asked her why she was crying, she wiped the warm tears off her thin, soft cheeks and pretended not to hear me as she sang. Her singing made me sad because I knew why she had cried, and she knew I knew. I seized the opportunity to say, "I don't want an arranged marriage," but she sang on even louder, singing a song of a distant home. In times such as these, like my father, she too covers her ears with the thick dried mud of tradition. She doesn't want to hear me. It is easier that way.

Exercise 8	**DISCUSSION AND CRITICAL THINKING**

1. Why did Shastri's mother cry?

2. What chance does Shastri have to make her own choice?

3. What would you advise her to do?

Exercise 9	**READING-RELATED WRITING**

1. Using an example or examples, write about similar marriage customs of a culture other than Indian. What about the custom of obtaining a parent's or the parents' permission?

2. Assume the role of a counselor or a close friend; summarize what you believe Shastri is saying, then give her advice.

3. Write about parental restrictions or controls you are aware of. Concentrate on a specific family.

Someone Is Listening

Michael Holguin

Student Michael Holguin grew up with shame and guilt because he believed he was wicked. His belief was implanted and reinforced by all institutions he encountered—family, church, school, and government. It was wrong in every sense to be sexually attracted to people of the same gender. Therefore, he knew he must keep his mortal sin a secret.

In today's society there is a form of child abuse that not even Oprah talks about. Unlike some other forms of abuse, it knows no limitations—no ethnic, no religious, no educational, and no socioeconomic boundaries. Lives are destroyed by parents who act in fear and ignorance. Dreams are shattered by the cruel and hurtful words of friends. Every day, hundreds of gay youths hide in their rooms and cry from pain caused by the mean and careless behavior of those who claim to love them.

In a Judeo-Christian society it is common for families to attend church with their children. The pastor in many of these churches stands at the podium and announces, "Homosexuals are an abomination unto the Lord." The church walls shake from the resounding "Amen" from the congregation. The pastor continues, "Homosexuals are sick. Perverted. They are a danger to our children." In agreement the congregation once more says, "Amen." I know how this feels. As a gay person, I recall the pain of many Sundays during my childhood. I prayed extra hard for God's cure before someone would find out my secret and embarrass me and my family, because I remembered what had happened to Jason the year before. So I kept answering the altar call every Sunday when the unwanted feeling wouldn't go away. The fear of rejection and eternal damnation made me too terrified to confide in anyone or to ask for help. After all, my parents seemed to tell me I deserved such a fate every time they said, "Amen."

Every day at school became more difficult to endure. I faced the jokes in the locker room. Even my best friend told some, and sometimes, to keep from being discovered, I told some. At this point, how much self-esteem could I have had? I cringed when my coach urged us to "kick those faggots' asses" but I still kicked. Yet every day my feelings were denied. My health teacher told us, "Someday you will all grow up and get married and have children." I couldn't understand why I had no such desire. I would turn on the television, and there would be a cop show on. This week's criminal was a gay child molester . . . again. I think "Baretta" had the same story the week before. I changed the station to "Barney Miller," where there was an old man wearing a polyester jumpsuit and a silk scarf around his neck, and talking with a lisp. Couldn't they drop the lisp just once. I wonder. I cringe, thinking this is my inevitable fate, my curse.

By the time I reached my teen years, I'd heard and seen so much negativity toward my "condition" that my life at home became plagued with constant fears.

I became afraid of rejection. I knew my Christian family would think I was sick, perverted, and dangerous to children. Dad would be disappointed, even though I had six brothers to carry on the family name. Mom would not want me around because she'd worry about what to tell Grandma and Grandpa. My brother would pretend he didn't know me at school.

My fears were reinforced by close-up examples. Once I had a friend named Daniel, who was the son of a local preacher. I don't know where Daniel got the nerve at the age of twelve to tell his parents he was gay, but that's what he did. It was also at the age of twelve that his father put him out on the street after all the beatings failed to cure him. Daniel managed to stay alive on the streets as a prostitute. He's in prison now, dying of AIDS. The fear of rejection was real.

I learned how to fit in out of fear of humiliation but especially out of fear of physical abuse. I had seen Daniel's father and brothers beat him up almost daily. An even earlier memory from when I was very young involved a boy named Terry, who everyone knew was different. Some kids had figured Terry out. One day behind the school, way out in the field, four kids beat Terry up. Kicking and slugging him as he fell to the ground, they called out "Sissy" and "Queer" as they swung at him. We had only heard the word *queer* from the older boys, and no one was sure what it meant exactly. We hadn't encountered the word *faggot* yet. I suppose I didn't like Terry much either, but I felt bad as I watched in terror, knowing that the next time it could be me that they considered "different."

After years of living with low self-esteem, a battered self-image, and a secret life, one's psyche tends to give out. The highest rate of teen suicide is among gay youths. In a recent five-year study, it was determined that fear of rejection was the number one cause of suicide among gay teenagers. After losing the loving environment of friends and families, many gays turn to other means for comfort. Drug and alcohol abuse is high among gays. Many turn to multiple lovers, looking for acceptance and emotional support. The result of this has been the devastating spread of AIDS. With nowhere to go, suicide often seems to be the only option. My friend Billy, when visiting his younger sister at his mother's home, would have to stay on the front porch and talk through the screen door at his mother's request. Last February, at the age of 19, Billy drove up to the mountains and there took his own life. Before he died he wrote on the hood of his car, "God, help me." I recall my own suicide attempt, which was the result of my inability to deal with a life-style everyone close to me was unable to accept. It was only my self-acceptance that eventually saved me from being a statistic.

When planning a family, people should ask themselves, "Will I love my children for who they are, or will I love them only if they're what I want them to be?" If people answer the latter, they shouldn't be parents. The same kind of thing might be said for others who are responsible for helping children develop. Abuse comes in many forms, and ignorance and self-centeredness are usually its foundation. Parents, preachers, teachers, clergy, friends— please be cautious of what you say. The children are listening.

Exercise 10	CRITICAL THINKING AND DISCUSSION

1. What are the sources of abuse of gay youth?

2. Why does this kind of abuse go largely unreported?

3. What is Holguin's main support? Underline and annotate the thesis (proposition) and the supporting points.

4. How did Holguin survive?

Exercise 11	READING-RELATED WRITING

1. Write a paragraph or essay in which you advocate some specific kind of education that would alleviate this problem in schools.

2. Pretend that you are a sympathetic parent of a gay child and explain how you would help your child to cope with attitudes in society.

3. Discuss this problem from a lesbian perspective. Is it essentially the same or different in significant respects?

4. Write about why some people have such strong negative reactions to homosexuality.

5. Write an argument in which you are the advocate for another type of "outsider" such as a minority in terms of race, religion, political or philosophical beliefs, or medical condition.

Appendixes

Appendix A: Parts of Speech

To classify a word as a part of speech, we observe two simple principles:

- The word must be in the context of communication, usually in a sentence.

- We must be able to identify the word with others that have similar characteristics—the eight parts of speech: nouns, pronouns, adjectives, verbs, adverbs, prepositions, conjunctions, or interjections.

The first principle is important because some words can be any of several parts of speech. The word *round,* for example, can function as five:

1. I watched the potter *round* the block of clay. (verb)

2. I saw her go *round* the corner. (preposition)

3. She has a *round* head. (adjective)

4. The astronauts watched the world go *round.* (adverb)

5. The champ knocked him out in one *round.* (noun)

Nouns

- **Nouns are naming words.** Nouns may name persons, animals, plants, places, things, substances, qualities, or ideas—for example, *Bart, armadillo, Mayberry, tree, rock, cloud, love, ghost, music, virtue.*

- **Nouns are often pointed out by noun indicators.** These noun indicators—*the, a, an*—signal that a noun is ahead, although there may be words between the indicator and the noun itself.

    the slime   *a* werewolf   *an* aardvark

    the green slime   *a* hungry werewolf   *an* angry aardvark

Pronouns

A **pronoun** is a word that is used in place of a noun.

- Some pronouns may represent specific persons or things:

I	me	myself	it
itself	that	she	her
herself	he	him	himself
they	them	themselves	we
us	ourselves	you	yourself
yourselves	who	whom	

- Indefinite pronouns refer to nouns (persons, places, things) in a general way:

    each   everyone   nobody   somebody

- Other pronouns point out particular things:

Singular	**Plural**
this, that	*these, those*
This is my treasure.	*These* are my jewels.
That is your junk	*Those* are your trinkets.

- Still other pronouns introduce questions.

    Which is the best CD player?

    What are the main ingredients of a Twinkie?

Verbs

Verbs show action or express being in relation to the subject of a sentence. They customarily occur in set positions in sentences.

- **Action verbs** are usually easy to identify.

    The aardvark *ate* the crisp, tasty ants. (action verb)

    The aardvark *washed* them down with a snoutful of water. (action verb)

- The **being verbs** are few in number and are also easy to identify. The most common *being* verbs are *is, was, were, are,* and *am.*

Gilligan *is* on an island in the South Pacific. (being verb)

I *am* his enthusiastic fan. (being verb)

- The form of a verb expresses its tense, that is, the time of the action or being. The time may be in the present or past.

Roseanne *sings* "The Star-Spangled Banner." (present)

Roseanne *sang* "The Star-Spangled Banner." (past)

- One or more **helping verbs** may be used with the main verb to form other tenses. The combination is called a *verb phrase.*

She *had sung* the songs many times in the shower. (helping verb and main verb indicate a time in the past)

She *will be singing* the song no more in San Diego. (helping verbs and main verbs indicate a time in the future)

- Some helping verbs can be used alone as main verbs; *has, have, had, is, was, were, are, am.* Certain other helping verbs function only as helpers: *will, shall, should, could.*

The most common position for the verb is directly after the subject or after the subject and its modifiers.

At high noon only two men (subject) *were* on Main Street.

The man with a faster draw (subject and modifiers) *walked* away alone.

Adjectives

Adjectives modify nouns and pronouns. Most adjectives answer the questions *What kind? Which one?* and *How many?*

- Adjectives answering the **What kind?** question are descriptive. They tell the quality, kind, or condition of the nouns or pronouns they modify.

red convertible	*dirty* fork
noisy muffler	*wild* roses
The rain is *gentle.*	Bob was *tired.*

- Adjectives answering the **Which one?** question narrow or restrict the meaning of a noun. Some of these are pronouns that become adjectives by function.

my money	*our* ideas	the *other* house
this reason	*these* apples	

- Adjectives answering the **How many?** question are, of course, numbering words.

some people	*each* pet	*few* goals
three dollars	*one* glove	

- The words *a, an,* and *the* are adjectives called *articles.* As "noun indicators," they point out persons, places, and things.

Adverbs

Adverbs modify verbs, adjectives, and other adverbs. Adverbs answer the questions *How? Where? When?* and *To what degree?*

Modifying Verbs: They <u>did</u> their work <u>quickly</u>.
                        v   adv

He <u>replied</u> <u>angrily</u>.
   v   adv

Modifying Adjectives: They were <u>somewhat</u> <u>happy</u>.
                            adv   adj

- Adverbs that answer the **How?** question are concerned with manner or way.

  She ate the snails *hungrily.*

  He snored *noisily.*

- Adverbs that answer the **Where?** question show location.

  They drove *downtown.*

  He stayed *behind.*

  She climbed *upstairs.*

- Adverbs that answer the **When?** question indicate time.

  The ship sailed *yesterday.*

  I expect an answer *soon.*

- Adverbs that answer the **To what degree?** question express extent.

  She is *entirely* correct.

  He was *somewhat* annoyed.

Most words ending in *-ly* are adverbs.

He completed the task <u>skillfully</u>.
                      adv

She answered him <u>courteously</u>.
                 adv

However, there are a few exceptions.

The house provided a <u>lovely</u> view of the valley.
                     adj

Your goblin mask is <u>ugly</u>.
                    adj

Prepositions

A **preposition** is a word or words that function as a connective. The preposition connects its object(s) to some other word(s) in the sentence. A preposition and its object(s)—usually a noun or pronoun—with modifiers make up a **prepositional phrase.**

Bart worked <u>against</u> great <u>odds</u>.

    prep   **object**

    prepositional phrase

Everyone <u>in</u> his <u>household</u> cheered his effort.

    prep   **object**

    prepositional phrase

Some of the most common prepositions are the following:

about	before	but	into	past
above	behind	by	like	to
across	below	despite	near	toward
after	beneath	down	of	under
against	beside	for	off	until
among	between	from	on	upon
around	beyond	in	over	with

Some prepositions are composed of more than one word and are made up from other parts of speech:

according to	as far as	because of	in spite of
ahead of	as well as	in back of	instead of
along wtih	aside from	in front of	together with

Caution: Do not confuse adverbs with prepositions

I went *across* slowly. (without an object—adverb)

I went *across* the field. (with an object—preposition)

We walked *behind* silently. (without an object—adverb)

We walked *behind* the mall. (with an object—preposition)

Conjunctions

A **conjunction** connects and shows a relationship between words, phrases, or clauses. A phrase is two or more words acting as a part of speech. A clause is a group of words with a subject and a verb. An independent clause can stand by itself: *She plays bass guitar.* A dependent clause cannot stand by itself: *when she plays bass guitar.*

There are two kinds of conjunctions: coordinating and subordinating.

Coordinating conjunctions connect words, phrases, and clauses of equal rank: noun with noun, adjective with adjective, verb with verb, phrase with phrase, main clause with main clause, and subordinate clause with subordinate clause. The seven common coordinating conjunctions are *for, and, nor, but, or, yet,* and *so.* (They form the acronym FANBOYS.)

Two Nouns: Bring a <u>pencil</u> <u>and</u> some <u>paper</u>.

               noun **conj**   **noun**

Two Phrases: Did she go <u>to the store</u> <u>or</u> <u>to the game</u>?

             prep phrase **conj** **prep phrase**

Paired conjunctions such as *either/or, neither/nor,* or *both/and* are usually classed as coordinating conjunctions.

<u>Neither</u> the coach <u>nor</u> the manager was at fault.
    conj   **conj**

Subordinating conjunctions connect dependent clauses with main clauses. The most common subordinating conjunctions include the following:

after	because	provided	whenever
although	before	since	where
as	but that	so that	whereas
as if	if	till	wherever
as long as	in order that	until	
as soon as	notwithstanding	when	

Sometimes the dependent clause comes *before* the main clause, where it is set off by a comma.

<u>Although she was</u> in pain, she stayed in the game.
  conj **sub** **v**

    dependent clause

Sometimes the dependent clause comes *after* the main clause, where it usually is *not* set off by a comma.

She stayed in the game <u>because she was needed</u>.
       conj **sub**   **v**

      dependent clause

Caution: Certain words can function as either conjunctions or prepositions. It is necessary to look ahead to see if the word introduces a clause with a subject and verb—conjunction function—or takes an object—preposition function. Some of the words with two functions are these: *after, for, since, until.*

After the concert was over, we went home. (clause follows—conjunction)

After the concert, we went home. (object follows—preposition)

Interjections

An **interjection** conveys strong emotion or surprise. When an interjection appears alone, it is usually punctuated with an exclamation mark.

Wow!   Curses!   Cowabunga!   Yabba dabba doo!

When it appears as part of a sentence, an interjection is usually followed by a comma.

Oh, I did not consider that problem.

The interjection may sound exciting, but it is seldom appropriate for college writing.

| Exercise 1 | **IDENTIFYING PARTS OF SPEECH** |

Identify the part of speech of each italicized word or group of words by placing the appropriate abbreviations in the blanks. (See Answer Key for answers.)

n	*noun*	*pro*	*pronoun*
v	*verb*	*adj*	*adjective*
adv	*adverb*	*conj*	*conjunction*
prep	*preposition*		

_____ _____ 1. The *turtle* can be defined as a reptile *with* a shell.

_____ _____ 2. It is a *toothless* creature that *can smell* and see well.

_____ _____ 3. Some live *mostly* in the water, whereas others live mostly *in* places as dry as the desert.

_____ _____ 4. Both sea *and land* turtles will burrow and hibernate.

_____ _____ 5. Turtles are well known *for their* longevity.

_____ _____ 6. *Some live* to be more than a hundred years old.

_____ _____ 7. *Many* people purchase turtles for *pets*.

_____ _____ 8. Young turtles *eat chopped* raw meat, greens, fish, and worms.

_____ _____ 9. *They* need both sunlight *and* shade.

_____ _____ 10. *Some* people paint their *pet* turtles, a practice that can damage the turtles' shells.

_____ _____ 11. *Most* turtles are not *suitable* for pets.

_____ _____ 12. The snapping turtle *is* one such *species*.

_____ _____ 13. *It* can be *vicious* when cornered.

_____ _____ 14. The *common* snapper weighs up to sixty pounds and can snap off a set of fingers *with* one bite.

_____ _____ 15. Folklore holds that *when* a snapping turtle bites someone, it will not let go *until* it hears thunder.

_____ _____ 16. Stories *circulate* about a farmer who cut off the head of a snapping turtle that was biting someone, *yet* even without its body, the snapper would not let go.

_____ _____ 17. The box turtle is a *gentle creature* and makes a good pet.

_____ _____ 18. It has a *hooked* beak, red eyes, and a splotchy *yellow* and brown shell.

_____ _____ 19. It eats worms, snails, berries, *and* other *fruit*.

_____ _____ 20. In the summer in the Midwest, one *can find* many box turtles crawling about, their solemn beaks red from a *meal* of blackberries.

Exercise 2   **IDENTIFYING PARTS OF SPEECH**

Identify the part of speech of each italicized word or group of words by placing the appropriate abbreviations in the blanks.

n	noun		pro	pronoun
v	verb		adj	adjective
adv	adverb		conj	conjunction
prep	preposition			

_____ _____ 1. *Before* gunpowder was invented, soldiers *often* wore armor.

_____ _____ 2. The armor *protected* the soldiers against *sharp* blows.

_____ _____ 3. Early armor was designed *from* layers of animal *hide*.

_____ _____ 4. The *first* designs were in the form *of* shields.

_____ _____ 5. Other designs *covered* the *entire* body.

_____ _____ 6. Whole battles were *sometimes* won or *lost* because of armor.

_____ _____ 7. *Armor* craftsmen had *important* positions in society.

_____ _____ 8. Chain mail *armor* was made *of* small connected rings.

_____ _____ 9. *Japanese* armor of the 1500s was made *of* thousands of fishlike scales.

_____ _____ 10. Most European armor was made of *large* metal plates shaped to the *body*.

_____ _____ 11. *Some* of it was designed with precious metals and decorated with *artistic* patterns.

_____ _____ 12. The metal was *heavy, and* soldiers needed special assistance in mounting their horses.

_____ _____ 13. Because the metal was *so* strong, knights *often* tried to unseat their opponents instead of trying to pierce the armor.

_____ _____ 14. One famous soldier fell off his horse *and* into a stream *fifteen* inches deep.

_____ _____ 15. His armor *filled* with water *and* he drowned.

_____ _____ 16. *During* the crusades, European soldiers wore their *metal* armor into the deserts.

_____ _____ 17. The *armor* often became so hot the soldiers fell off their horses *in* exhaustion.

_____ _____ 18. With the development of the longbow *and* gunpowder, traditional armor *lost* its popularity.

_____ _____ 19. Lightweight *armor* has been used in *modern* warfare.

_____ _____ 20. The helmet is one *carryover* from earlier *designs*.

Exercise 3　　　IDENTIFYING PARTS OF SPEECH

Identify the part of speech of each italicized word or group of words by placing the appropriate abbreviations in the blanks.

n	*noun*	*pro*	*pronoun*
v	*verb*	*adj*	*adjective*
adv	*adverb*	*conj*	*conjunction*
prep	*preposition*		

_____ _____ 1. *For* about forty years, the Three Stooges were a popular *comedy* team.

_____ _____ 2. They were *often* accused of making films *in* bad taste, but no one accused them of being good actors.

_____ _____ 3. For decades they *made seven* or more pictures a year.

_____ _____ 4. Actually six *different* actors *played* the parts.

_____ _____ 5. The *most* famous threesome *was* Moe, Curley, and Larry.

_____ _____ 6. The Stooges specialized *in physical* comedy.

_____ _____ 7. They *took* special *delight* in hitting each other in the head and poking each other's eyes.

_____ _____ 8. Moe was the on-screen *leader* of this *zany* group.

_____ _____ 9. He assumed leadership in each film *because he* was more intelligent than the others, which isn't saying much.

_____ _____ 10. Curley was not bright, but he made up for his *dumbness* by having the *hardest* head in the world, at least in the world of Stooge movies.

_____ _____ 11. Larry *often got caught* between the flailing arms and kicking feet of Moe and Curley.

_____ _____ 12. The movies made *by* the Stooges *usually* came in two reels and were shown along with feature-length films.

_____ _____ 13. The Stooge movies *were given* such *titles* as *Half-Wits, Three Hams on Rye, Slap Happy Sleuths,* and *Matri Phony.*

_____ _____ 14. They made fun of *dignity* and physically abused each other with all kinds *of* lethal instruments, but they never got hurt.

_____ _____ 15. They received *little respect* from the filmmaking community.

_____ _____ 16. Only Moe saved *his* money *and* became wealthy.

_____ _____ 17. Apparently Curley *at* times lived his *movie* role off stage.

_____ _____ 18. After a *brief* marriage, Curley's wife *left* him, saying he punched, poked, pinched, and pushed her and left cigar butts in the sink.

_____ _____ 19. Moe tried to gain *respectability* as a character actor, but the audiences could never accept *him* in serious roles.

_____ _____ 20. A whole new television *audience has made* the Three Stooges the stars they never were in their lifetimes.

Appendix B: Taking Tests

Good test-taking begins with good study techniques. These techniques involve, among other things, how to read, think, and write effectively. Those skills have been covered in this book. Here we will discuss only a few principles that apply directly and immediately to the test situation.

At the beginning of the semester, you should discover how you will be tested in each course. Match your note-taking and underlining of texts to the kind or kinds of tests you will take. Objective tests will usually require somewhat more attention to details than will subjective or essay tests.

For both types of tests—and you will probably have a combination—you should carefully apportion your time, deciding how much to spend on each section or essay and allowing a few minutes for a quick review of answers. For both, you should also read the directions carefully, marking key words (if you are permitted to do so) as a reminder to you for concentration.

Objective Tests

Here are some tips on taking objective tests.

- Find out whether you will be graded on the basis of the number of correct answers or on the basis of right-minus-wrong. This is the difference: If you are graded on the basis of the number of correct answers, there is no penalty for guessing; therefore, if you want the highest possible score, you should leave no blanks. But if you are graded on the basis of right-minus-wrong (meaning one or a fraction of one is subtracted from your correct answers for every miss), then answer only if the odds of being right are in your favor. For example, if you know an answer is one of two possibilities, you have a 50 percent chance of getting it right; consequently, guess if the penalty is less than one because you could gain one by getting it right and lose less than one by getting it wrong. Ask your teacher to explain if there is a right-minus-wrong factor.

- If you are going to guess and you want to get some answers correct, you should pick one column and fill in the bubbles. By doing that, you will almost certainly get some correct.

- Studies show that in a typical four-part multiple choice test section, more answers are B and C than A and D.

- Statements with absolutes such as *always* and *never* are likely to be false, whereas statements with qualifications such as *usually* and *probably* are likely to be true.

- If you don't know an answer, instead of fixating on it and getting frustrated, mark it with what seems right, put a dot alongside your answer, and go back later for a second look if time permits.

- When (and if) you go back to check your work, do not make changes unless you discover that you obviously marked one incorrectly. Studies have shown that first hunches are usually more accurate.

Subjective or Essay Tests

Here are some tips on taking subjective tests.

- Consider the text, the approach taken by the instructor in lectures, and the overall approach in the course outline and try to anticipate essay questions. Then, in your preparation, jot down and memorize simple outlines that will jog your memory during the test if you have anticipated correctly.

- Remember to keep track of time. A time-consuming A+ essay that does not allow you to finish the second half of the exam will result in a failing grade.

- Study the essay questions carefully. Underline key words. Each essay question will have two parts: the subject part and the treatment part. It may also have a limiting part. If you are required, for example, to compare and contrast President Carter and President Bush on their environmental programs, you should be able to analyze the topic immediately in this fashion:

> The *subject* is President Carter and President Bush.
>
> The *limitation* is their environmental programs.
>
> The *treatment* is comparison and contrast.

Hence, you might mark it in this fashion:

treatment   limitation

(Compare and contrast) the (environmental programs) of

subject

(President Carter and President Bush)

The treatment part (here "compare and contrast") may very well be one of the forms of discourse such as definition, description, or analysis, or it may be something like "evaluate" or "discuss," in which a certain form or forms would be used. Regardless of what the treatment word is, the first step is to determine the natural points of division and to prepare a simple outline or outline alternative for organization.

- In writing the essay, be sure to include specific information as support for your generalizations.

Appendix C: Writing a Job Application Letter and a Résumé

Two forms of practical writing that you may need even before you finish your college work are the job application letter and the résumé. They will often go together as requirements by an employer. In some instances, the employer will suggest the form and content of the letter and résumé; in others, you will receive no directions and should adjust your letter and résumé to match the requirements and expectations as you perceive them. The models on pages 407 and 408 are typical of what job applicants commonly submit.

Job Application Letter

The following basic guidelines will serve you well:

- Use standard letter-size paper and type size and style.

- Do not apologize and do not brag.

- Do not go into tedious detail but do relate your education, work experience, and career goals relevant to the available job.
- Begin your letter with a statement indicating why you are writing the letter and how you heard about the job opening.
- End the letter by stating how you can be contacted for an interview.

Résumé

Employers are especially concerned about your most recent work experiences and education, so include them first, as indicated in the example on page 408. The heading "College Activities" can be replaced with "Interests and Activities." Your main concern is presenting relevant information in a highly readable form. Always end with a list of references.

---

203 Village Center Avenue
Glendora, CA 91740
July 11, 1999

Mr. Roy Ritter
Computers Unlimited
1849 N. Granada Avenue
Walnut, CA 91789

Dear Mr. Ritter:

I am responding to your advertisement in the Los Angeles *Times* for the position of salesperson for used computers. Please consider me as a candidate.

In one more semester I will have completed my Associate in Arts degree at Mt. San Antonio College with a major in business management and a minor in computer technology.

My experience relates directly to the job you offer. As a result of my part-time work for two years as lab technician at my college, I have come to know the operations of several different computers. I have also learned to explain the operations to people who have very little knowledge of computers. In my business classes, I have studied the practical approaches to advertising and sales while also learning theory. Each semester for the past two years, I have worked in the college bookstore, where I helped customers who were buying various products, including computers.

This job would coincide perfectly with my work at school, my work experience, and even my goal of being a salesperson with a large company.

Enclosed is my résumé with several references to people who know me well. Please contact them if you want information or if you would like a written evaluation. I am available for an interview at your request.

Sincerely yours,

Benjamin Johanson
Benjamin Johanson

Benjamin Johanson
203 Village Center Avenue
Glendora, CA 91740
(626) 987-5555

WORK EXPERIENCE

Lab Assistant in the Mt. San Antonio College Computer Lab	1997–99
Sales and Stock Technician in the Mount San Antonio College Bookstore	1997–99

EDUCATION

Full-time student at Mt. San Antonio College	1997–99
High school diploma from Glendora High School	1993–97

COLLEGE ACTIVITIES

Hackers' Club (1996–98)
Chess Club (1996–98)
Forensics Club (1997–99)—twice a regional debate champion

REFERENCES

Stewart Hamlen
Chairperson, Business Department
Mt. San Antonio College
Walnut, CA 91789
(909) 594-5611, ext. 4707

Bart Grassmont
Human Resources Director, Bookstore
Mt. San Antonio College
Walnut, CA 91789
(909) 594-5611, ext. 4706

Howard McGraw
Coach, Forensics Team
Mt. San Antonio College
Walnut, CA 91789
(909) 594-5611, ext. 4575

Appendix D: Brief Guide for ESL Students

If you came to this country knowing little English, you probably acquired vocabulary first. Then you began using that vocabulary within the basic patterns of your own language. If your native language had no articles, you probably used no articles; if your language had no verb tenses, you probably used no verb tenses, and so on. Using the grammar of your own language with your new vocabulary may initially have enabled you to make longer and more complex statements in English, but eventually you learned that your native grammar and your adopted grammar were different. You may even have learned that no two grammars are the same, and that English has a bewildering set of rules and an even longer set of exceptions to those rules. Part One of this book presents grammar (the way we put words together) and rhetoric (the way we use language effectively) that can be applied to your writing. The following are some definitions, rules, and references that are of special help to writers who are learning English as a second language (ESL).

Using Articles in Relation to Nouns
Articles

Articles are either indefinite (*an, a*) or definite (*the*). Because they point out nouns, they are often called *noun determiners.*

Nouns

Nouns can be either singular (*book*) or plural (*books*) and are either count nouns (things that can be counted, such as "book") or noncount nouns (things that cannot be counted, such as "homework"). If you are not certain whether a noun is a count noun or a noncount noun, try placing the word *much* before the word. You can say "much homework," so *homework* is a noncount noun.

Rules

- **Use an indefinite article (*a* or *an*) before singular count nouns and not before noncount nouns.** The indefinite article means "one," so you would not use it before plural count nouns.

Correct:	I saw a book. (count noun)
Correct:	I ate an apple. (count noun)
Incorrect:	I fell in a love. (noncount noun)
Correct:	I fell in love. (noncount noun)
Incorrect:	I was in a good health. (noncount noun)
Correct:	I was in good health. (noncount noun)

- **Use the definite article (*the*) before both singular and plural count nouns that have specific reference.**

Correct:	I read the book. (a specific one)
Correct:	I read the books. (specific ones)
Correct:	I like to read a good book. (nonspecific, therefore the indefinite article)
Correct:	A student who works hard will pass. (any student, therefore nonspecific)
Correct:	The student on my left is falling asleep. (a specific student)

- **Use the definite article with noncount nouns only when they are specifically identified.**

Correct:	Honesty (as an idea) is a rare commodity.
Correct:	The honesty of my friend has inspired me. (specifically identified)

> **Incorrect:** I was in trouble and needed the assistance. (not specifically identified)
>
> **Correct:** The assistance offered by the paramedics was appreciated. (specifically identified)

- **Place the definite article before proper nouns (names) of**

> oceans, rivers, and deserts (for example, *the* Pacific Ocean and *the* Red River).
>
> countries, if the first part of the name indicates a division (*the* United States of America).
>
> regions (*the* South).
>
> plural islands (*the* Hawaiian Islands).
>
> museums and libraries (*the* Los Angeles County Museum).
>
> colleges and universities when the word *college* or *university* comes before the name (*the* University of Oklahoma).

These are the main rules. For a more detailed account of rules for articles, see a comprehensive ESL book in your library.

Sentence Patterns

Chapter 2 of this book defines and illustrates the patterns of English sentences. Some languages include sentence patterns not used in standard English. The following principles are well worth remembering:

- **The conventional English sentence is based on one or more clauses, each of which must have a subject (sometimes the implied "you") and a verb.**

> **Incorrect:** Saw the book. (subject needed even if it is obvious)
>
> **Correct:** I saw the book.

- **English does not repeat a subject, even for emphasis.**

> **Incorrect:** The book that I read it was interesting.
>
> **Correct:** The book that I read was interesting.

Verb Endings

- **English indicates time through verbs.** Learn the different forms of verb tenses and the combinations of main verbs and helping verbs.

> **Incorrect:** He watching the game. (A verblike word ending in *-ing* cannot be a verb all by itself.)
>
> **Correct:** He is watching the game. (Note that a helping verb such as *is, has, has been, will,* or *will be* always occurs before a main verb ending in *-ing.*)

- **Take special care in maintaining consistency in tense.**

> **Incorrect:** I went to the mall. I watch a movie there. (verb tenses inconsistent)
>
> **Correct:** I went to the mall. I watched a movie there.

All twelve verb tenses are covered with explanations, examples, and exercises in the Verbs section of Chapter 5, pages 80–108.

Idioms

Some of your initial problems with writing English are likely to arise from trying to adjust to a different and difficult grammar. If the English language used an entirely systematic grammar, your learning would be easier, but English has patterns that are both complex and irregular. Among them are idioms, word groups that often defy grammatical rules and mean something other than what they appear to mean.

The expression "He kicked the bucket" does not mean that someone struck a cylindrical container with his foot; instead, it means that someone has died. That example is one kind of idiom. Because the expression suggests a certain irreverence, it would not be the choice of most people who want to make a statement about death; but if it is used, it must be used with its own precise wording, not "He struck the long cylindrical container with his foot," or "He did some bucket-kicking." Like other languages, the English language has thousands of these idioms. Expressions such as "the more the merrier" and "on the outs" are ungrammatical. They are also very informal expressions and therefore seldom used in college writing, although they are an indispensable part of a flexible, effective, all-purpose vocabulary. Because of their twisted meanings and illogic, idioms are likely to be among the last parts of language that a new speaker learns well. A speaker must know the culture thoroughly to understand when, where, and how to use slang and other idiomatic expressions.

If you listen carefully and read extensively you will learn English idioms. Your library will have dictionaries that explain them.

More Suggestions for ESL Writers

1. Read your material aloud and try to detect the inconsistencies and awkward phrasing.

2. Have others read your material aloud for the same purposes.

3. If you have severe problems with grammatical awkwardness, try composing shorter, more direct sentences until you become more proficient in phrasing.

4. On your Self-Evaluation Chart, list the problems you have (such as articles, verb endings, clause patterns), review revelant sections of Part One of this book, and concentrate on your own problem areas as you draft, revise, and edit.

| **Exercise 4** | **CORRECTING A FIRST DRAFT** |

Make corrections in the use of articles, verbs, and phrasing. (See Answer Key for answers.)

George Washington at Trenton

One of most famous battles during the War of Independence occur at Trenton, New Jersey, on Christmas Eve of the 1776. The colonists outmatched in supplies and finances and were outnumbered in troop strength. Most observers in other countries think rebellion would be put down soon. British overconfident and believe there would be no more battles until spring. But George Washington decide to fight one more time. That Christmas, while large army of Britishers having party and thinking about the holiday season, Americans set out for surprise raid. They loaded onto boats used for carrying ore and rowed across Delaware River. George Washington stood tall in lead boat. According to legend, drummer boy floated across river on his drum, pulled by rope tied to boat. Because British did not feel threatened by the ragtag colonist forces, they unprepared to do battle. The colonists stormed living quarters and the general assembly hall and achieved victory. It was good for the colonists' morale, something they needed, for they would endure long, hard winter before fighting again.

Answer Key

Chapter 1
Exercise 1

1. Mahatma Gandhi
2. he
3. You (understood)
4. good
5. fasts, writings, speeches
6. He
7. Gandhi
8. British
9. leaders, agitators
10. Gandhi

Exercise 3

1. live, travel
2. varies
3. is
4. spend
5. make
6. will beat
7. are, live
8. hoots, shakes
9. hear, go
10. are

Exercise 5

Verbs are underlined.

1. You (understood) <u>Read</u>, <u>learn</u>
2. cities <u>were</u>
3. Government, religion <u>were</u>
4. <u>was</u> difference
5. They <u>built,</u> <u>sacrificed</u>
6. ceremonies <u>related</u>
7. society <u>had</u>
8. family <u>included</u>

Chapter 1, continued

9. boys <u>went</u>; girls <u>went</u>, <u>learned</u>

10. Aztecs <u>wore</u>; they <u>lived</u>; they <u>ate</u>

11. Scholars <u>developed</u>

12. calendars <u>are</u>

13. language <u>was</u>

14. language <u>was</u>, <u>represented</u>

15. religion, government <u>required</u>

16. soldiers <u>could caputre</u>, <u>enlarge</u>

17. Hernando Cortez <u>landed</u>

18. He <u>was joined</u>

19. Aztecs <u>rebelled</u>

20. Spaniards <u>killed</u>; they <u>defeated</u>

Review 1

Verbs are underlined.

1. You (understood) <u>Read</u>

2. What <u>causes</u>

3. <u>can</u> they <u>do</u>

4. Earthquakes <u>shake</u>

5. <u>is</u> answer

6. earth <u>is covered</u>

7. they <u>are</u>

8. plates <u>bump</u>, <u>pass</u>

9. rocks <u>are squeezed</u>, <u>stretched</u>

10. They <u>pull</u>, <u>pile</u>, <u>cause</u>

11. breaks <u>are called</u>

12. formation <u>is</u>

13. wave <u>travels</u>

14. vibrations <u>are</u>

15. force <u>is</u>

16. scientists <u>have tried</u>

17. <u>has been</u> success

18. Earthquakes <u>are identified</u>

19. states <u>experience</u>

20. quake <u>is</u> <u>occurring</u>

Chapter 2

Exercise 6

_____S_____ 1. The most popular (sport) in the world <u>is</u> soccer.

_____CC_____ 2. (People) in ancient China and Japan <u>had</u> a form of soccer, and even (Rome) <u>had</u> a game (that) <u>resembled</u> soccer.

_____CX_____ 3. The (game) as (it) <u>is played</u> today <u>got</u> its start in England.

_____S_____ 4. In the Middle Ages, whole (towns) <u>played</u> soccer on Shrove Tuesday.

_____CC_____ 5. (Goals) <u>were built</u> at opposite ends of town, and (hundreds) of people (who) <u>lived</u> in those towns <u>would play</u> on each side.

_____S_____ 6. Such (games) <u>resembled</u> full-scale brawls.

_____S_____ 7. The first (side) to score a goal <u>won</u> and <u>was declared</u> village champion.

_____CP_____ 8. Then both (sides) <u>tended</u> to the wounded, and (they) <u>didn't play</u> again for a whole year.

_____S_____ 9. The (rules) of the game <u>were written</u> in the late 1800s at British boarding schools.

_____CP_____ 10. Now nearly every European (country) <u>has</u> a national soccer team, and the (teams) <u>participate</u> in international tournaments.

Exercise 8

_____S_____ 1. In ancient Egypt 3,000 years ago, both (men) and (women) <u>used</u> cosmetics.

_____CP_____ 2. One (concern) <u>was</u> the matter of using beauty aids, but (another) <u>was</u> protection against the brilliant desert sun.

_____S_____ 3. The three main (colors) of their makeup <u>were</u> green, black, and red.

_____CX_____ 4. These (colors) <u>came</u> from crushed rocks (that) <u>were mixed</u> with water or oil.

_____CC_____ 5. (Lipstick) <u>was made</u> from crushed iron ore and oil; (it) <u>was applied</u> with a brush (that) <u>was made</u> of animal hair and bristles.

_____S_____ 6. (They) <u>applied</u> dark green and black makeup around their eyes by using small sticks.

Chapter 2, continued

___S___ 7. (They) made perfume by crushing flowers and fragrant woods, and by mixing that substance with oil.

___CX___ 8. (They) put cones of this perfume into their hair where (it) melted slowly and gave off a fragrance.

___CX___ 9. Although (they) were apparently concerned about making themselves attractive to others, (they) quite effectively protected their skin, lips, and hair from the dry desert air.

___S___ 10. Many (containers) of these cosmetics have been preserved in the pyramids.

Review 1

___CP___ 1. (Bastille Day) is a holiday in France, for the (French) love freedom.

___CP___ 2. The (Bastille) was a famous prison in Paris, and the French (people) know its history.

___S___ 3. The (Bastille) will not be forgotten as a symbol in France and in other French-speaking countries.

___CC___ 4. For hundreds of years, the (Bastille) was used to imprison those (who) offended the royalty, but on July 14, 1789, the common (people) stormed the gates.

___CC___ 5. The (police) guarding the Bastille decided to surrender; if (they) did not, (they) would lose their lives.

___CX___ 6. During the French Revolution (that) followed, the common (people) became fierce fighters for freedom.

___CX___ 7. After the war, (some) of the common people showed that (they) too were capable of cruelty.

___S___ 8. Nevertheless, the (French) remember the Bastille as a symbol of political repression.

Chapter 2, continued

<u>CP</u> 9. On July 14 of each year, (businesses) in France <u>close,</u> and (people) gather

in the cities.

<u>S</u> 10. (Bastille Day) is among the most famous of all national holidays any-

where.

Chapter 3

Exercise 1

1. Jim Thorpe, a Sac and Fox Indian, was born near Prague, Oklahoma, **, but** At the age

of sixteen, he left home to enroll in the Carlisle Indian School in Pennsylvania.

2. He had had little experience playing football, **, yet** He led his small college to victo-

ries against championship teams.

3. He had scarcely heard of other sports, **, but** He golfed in the 70s, bowled above 200,

and played varsity basketball and lacrosse.

4. In the 1912 Olympic Games for amateur athletes at Stockholm, Jim Thorpe

entered the two most rigorous events, the decathlon and the pentathlon, **, yet** He

won both.

5. King Gustav V of Sweden told him, "You, Sir, are the greatest athlete in the

world, **; and** " Jim Thorpe said, "Thanks, King."

6. Later it was said he had once been paid fifteen dollars a week to play baseball,

making him a professional athlete, **, so** The Olympic medals were taken from him.

7. Soon a major league baseball scout did offer Thorpe a respectable contract, **, and** He

played in the National League for six seasons.

8. Not content to play only one sport, he also earned a good salary for that time in

professional football, **, yet** After competing for fifteen years, he said he had never

played for the money.

9. Many regard Jim Thorpe as the greatest athlete of the twentieth century, **, for** He

excelled in numerous sports at the highest levels of athletic competition.

Chapter 3, continued

10. Off the playing fields, he was known by his friends as mostly a modest, quiet

    man, On the fields, he was a person of joyful combat.
        ^ , but

Exercise 3

1. The legendary island of Atlantis has fascinated people for centuries, It probably
                                                             ^ ; however

   never existed.

2. According to the Greek writer Plato, the people of Atlantis were very ambitious

   and warlike, They planned to conquer all of the Mediterranean.
              ^ ; in fact,

3. Initially, they were successful in subduing areas to the west, They became
                                                              ^ ; therefore,

   wealthy.

4. Then the people of Atlantis became proud, They became corrupt and wicked.
                                           ^ ; moreover,

5. They were confident and attacked Athens, Athens and its allies defeated the
                                          ^ ; however,

   invaders.

6. The story of Atlantis is probably just a tale, Many people have believed it.
                                                ^ ; however,

7. Some writers have tried to link the legend with such real places as America and

   the Canary Islands, No link has been found.
                     ^ ; nevertheless,

8. The Minoan civilization on Crete was destroyed by tidal waves, A similar fate
                                                               ^ ;

   may have befallen Atlantis.

9. Some people speculate about a volcanic explosion on Atlantis, A volcanic erup-
                                                              ^ ; in fact,

   tion did destroy part of the island Thira in the Eastern Mediterranean in 1500

   B.C.E.

10. Some writers have conjectured that American Indians migrated to the New

    World by way of Atlantis, Archaeologists dispute that idea.
                           ^ ; however,

Exercise 5

1. The freeway congestion was under study. ~~The problem~~ that occurred every

   Friday at noon,

2. The vacationers had a good time, The bears destroyed a few tents and ate
                                  ^ , even though

   people's food.

Chapter 3, continued

3. The teenagers loved their senior prom, ~~,~~ *, although,* The band played badly.

4. Farmers gathered for miles around, *because,* Jeff had grown a fifty-pound cucumber.

5. *If* Backseat drivers make unwanted suggestions in the nag-proof model, They

   can be ejected from the vehicle.

6. The marriage counselor gave bad advice, *who* ~~He~~ charged only half price.

7. The robots would not do their work. *Because* ~~They~~ needed fresh batteries. | *that* |

8. The hurricane was expected to hit during the night, The residents checked

   their flashlights.

9. *When* The ice sculptor displayed his work in the dining hall, The customers applauded.

10. *After* Someone stole the artwork of ice, No evidence was found.

Exercise 7

1. *Although* A grumpy bear had stalked the grounds, Summer camp had been a great expe-

   rience for the campers, *, and* They vowed to return.

2. *After* The stuffed cabbage ran out, The party ended, *, and* The guests went home.

3. *Because* It was a costume party, All the guests dressed as movie legends, *the* *, and* Ten were Elvis

   impersonators.

4. *When* A new Elvis theme park opened in our town, I attended, *, and* I think I saw the King.

5. *Because* My father encouraged me to take up a hobby, I began collecting stamps, *, and* Now

   my hobby has become a business.

6. They were in a wilderness camp, *, and* They were not allowed to bring pets, *, although* They

   were allowed to bring toys.

7. *Because* He had no leather shoes to wear, Young Stu could not go to the prom, *, but* He hoped

   there would be a prom next year.

8. People were hungry, *, and* They ate massive quantities of hot dogs at the game, *, though* They

   knew the dogs were made of mystery meat.

9. *While* The ambulance drivers were taking a break, A man had a choking fit, *, and* The drivers

   came to his rescue.

Chapter 3, continued

Even though

10. The film was filled with scenes of violence. It included a charming love story. The public liked it.

Exercise 9

1. Ernest Hemingway won the Nobel Prize for literature in 1954. ~~He was mainly~~ an American writer of fiction.

3. After high school he became a reporter. ~~He worked~~ for the Kansas City *Star.*

5. In 1920 he returned to journalism with the Toronto *Star.* ~~He~~ *and* met his future first wife, Hadley Richardson.

7. ~~Hemingway~~ work*ing* conscientiously on his writing. He soon became a leader of the so-called Lost Generation.

9. During World War II Hemingway armed his fishing boat and hunted for German submarines. ~~He patrolled~~ *in* the waters of the Caribbean.

Review 1

1. The Mercury Comet was judged the winner. ~~It had~~ *with* imitation zebra-skin seat covers. ~~It had~~ *and* an eight-ball shift knob.

2. Koko had a great plan to make some money. *, but* She had financial problems. *and* could not develop her plan.

3. The mixture could not be discussed openly. *because* Competitors were curious. *, and* Corporate spies were everywhere.

4. Babette's bowling ball is special. It is red and green. *, and* It is decorated with her phone number in metal-flake.

5. *Although* The young bagpiper liked Scottish food. ~~He~~ *and* enjoyed doing Scottish dances. Wearing a kilt in winter left him cold.

6. Ruby missed the alligator farm. She fondly remembered the hissing and snapping of the beasts as they scrambled for raw meat. *, but* Her neighbors were indifferent to the loss.

Chapter 3, continued

7. *Although*
   Many people are pleased to purchase items with food preservatives, Øthers are
   because
   fearful, They think these chemicals may also preserve consumers.

8. Leewan loves her new in-line roller skates, *because* They look and perform much like ice
   , but
   skates, They are not as safe as her conventional roller skates.

9. Fish sold at Discount Fish Market were not of the highest quality, *because* Some of them
   and
   had been dead for days without refrigeration, ~~They~~ were suitable only for bait.

10. Cliff wanted to impress his date, *, so* He splashed on six ounces of He-Man cologne,
    and
    ~~He~~ put on his motorcycle leathers and a flying scarf.

Chapter 4

Exercise 1

1. When Leroy Robert Paige was seven years old, Þe was carrying luggage at a
   railroad station in Mobile, Alabama.

2. He was a clever young fellow, Who invented a contraption for carrying four
   satchels (small suitcases) at a time.

3. After he did that, Þe was always known as Satchel Paige.

4. His fame rests on his being arguably the best baseball pitcher, Who ever played
   the game.

5. Because of the so-called Jim Crow laws, Þe, as an African American, was not
   allowed to play in the major leagues, Until 1948 after the Major League color
   barrier was broken.

6. By that time he was already forty-two, Although he was in excellent condition.

7. He had pitched, Wherever he could, mainly touring around the country.

8. When he faced Major Leaguers in exhibition games, Þe almost always won.

9. Because people liked to see him pitch, Þe pitched almost every day, While he
   was on tour.

10. One year he won 104 games. During his career he pitched 55 no-hitters and
    won more than 2,000 games.

Chapter 4, continued

11. He pitched his last game in the majors at the age of fifty-nine.

12. In 1971 he was the first African-American player, <u>Who was voted into the Base-ball Hall of Fame in a special category for those</u>, <u>Who played in the old Negro Leagues.</u>

Exercise 3

1. <u>As a subject of historical record</u>, <u>D</u>ancing seems to be a natural human act.

2. Even prehistoric cave paintings depict dancing figures, <u>Scrawled outlines of people in motion.</u>

3. Dancing takes many forms, but mainly it is a matter of moving rhythmically, <u>In time to music.</u>

4. Most children jump up and down when they are excited. They sway back and forth when they are contented.

5. <u>Having studied the behavior of many ethnic groups</u>, <u>A</u>nthropologists confirm that dancing reveals much, <u>A</u>bout a group's culture.

6. People dance for various reasons, <u>Such as to entertain others, to relax, to inspire others, and to celebrate life.</u>

7. One stylized form of dancing is the ballet, <u>A</u> <u>story told with graceful, rhythmic movement and music.</u>

8. Folk dances often relate stories, <u>Of the dancers' culture.</u>

9. Young people can get to know each other at social dances, <u>While enjoying themselves.</u>

10. Each generation of social dancers seems to have its own style, <u>Sometimes a modified revival, such as swing.</u>

Exercise 5

Answers will vary.

1. Harry polished his vehicle, a Ford Ranger truck with fine Corinthian leather seats.

2. He drove to pick up Jane for their date.

Chapter 4, continued

3. Jane wanted to go to the opening-day baseball game at Dodger Stadium.

4. She hoped for a new memory, a never-to-be-forgotten experience.

5. Jane dreamed of being seen on big-screen Diamond Vision in the stadium.

6. They arrived with the first sound of the bat on ball.

7. Harry bought peanuts and Crackerjacks for Jane.

8. Jane had brought a baseball glove so that she might catch a well-hit ball.

9. She brought her portable television set so she could hear and see her heroes up close.

10. Seeing the rain clouds, they feared that the game might be canceled.

Exercise 7

(1) Fleas *are* remarkable animals. (2) Although they do not have wings, *they* jump more than twelve inches. (3) Fleas *live* on many kinds of animals. (4) *They* Suck blood from their victims. (5) They often move from pets to human beings. (6) They do not discriminate. (7) They land on poets, politicians, physicians, and anyone else in close proximity. (8) *They* Carry germ-ridden blood and spread diseases. (9) Fleas *were and continue to be* the main spreader of bubonic plague. (10) Rodents, including those infected with diseases, *provide* providing fleas with transportation and food. (11) Nowadays one attacker is called the human flea. (12) This creature *lives* in houses, where it lays eggs on the carpet. (13) *It* Often bites human beings. (14) Another kind of flea is the chigoe. (15) *It* Burrows under the skin and lays its eggs. (16) For flea control, cleanliness and insecticide are important. (17) Our pets, mainly our cats and dogs, *are* among the main carriers of fleas in the typical household.

Exercise 9

1. Delete "which"
2. People go
3. Delete "who"
4. Tourists regard the
5. St. Augustine has the
6. teams go to
7. Tourists can
8. displays are available at

Chapter 4, continued

9. Delete "who"

10. Delete "which"

Exercise 12

1. CS; optimism, but a

2. RO; winter, and they

3. OK

4. RO; winter, yet they

5. CS; branches, and some

6. RO; managing, for they

7. CS; food, so they

8. CS; winter, and the

9. RO; depressed, but they

10. RO; help, and seven

Exercise 14

1. CS; Although Chris

2. CS; Because she

3. RO; While she . . . teens, she

4. RO; 1974, when she

5. CS; When she

6. RO; Although Evonne . . . first, Martina

7. RO; notable because she

8. CS; Because Chris

9. RO; "ice princess" because she

10. OK

Exercise 16

1. CS; 1980s; however, she

2. RO; dance; moreover, she

3. CS; school; therefore, with

4. OK

5. OK

6. CS; singer; moreover, she

7. RO; *Susan;* she

8. CS; media; consequently, she

9. CS; prospered; however, she

10. RO; herself; similarly, other

Chapter 4, continued

Exercise 18

1. CS; coat. They

2. RO; parades. The

3. OK

4. RO; distance. Enemies

5. OK

6. RO; uniform. The

7. CS; hand. The

8. CS; India. They

9. OK

10. RO; color. They

Review 1

Dinosaurs were giant lizardlike animals; *T* they lived more than a hundred million years ago. Some had legs like lizards and turtles, *and* some had legs more like birds. The ones with legs like birds, ~~C~~ould walk easily with raised bodies. They varied in size, *and* many were huge. The largest, the diplodocus, *was* about ninety feet long, equal to the distance between the bases in baseball. ~~Weighing~~ *It weighed* more than ten elephants. The smallest weighed no more than two pounds and was no bigger than a chicken. Some dinosaurs ate meat, *and* almost certainly some dinosaurs ate other dinosaurs. ~~U~~*They* sed their strong claws and fierce teeth to tear at their victims.

Dinosaurs were different, ~~I~~n design as well as size. They had horns, spikes, bills, armorlike plates, clublike tails, bony crests, and teeth in many sizes and shapes; *T* their heads were proportionately tiny or absurdly large, *, and* ~~T~~heir mouths varied, *Depending* on their eating habits.

Chapter 5

Exercise 1

1. saw

2. paused, grew

3. knew

4. extracted

5. jumped, ate

Chapter 5, continued

6. forced, accepted

7. nodded, dragged

8. thrust, flung

9. lifted, displayed

10. didn't

Exercise 3

1. lost

2. laid

3. did, won

4. became, ran

5. eaten, served

6. ruined, put

7. cost, raise

8. sit, liked

9. rose, headed

10. knew, lusted

Exercise 6

1. had received

2. had worked

3. walked

4. had

5. could have gone

6. will have completed

7. are considering

8. has had

9. had built

10. will go

Exercise 8

1. is

2. are

3. is

4. is

5. is

6. is

Chapter 5, continued

7. are

8. is

9. are

10. are

Exercise 10

Judy had a weird hobby. A few years ago, she ~~start to~~ *started* collect shreds of automobile tires in the street. She ~~goes~~ *went* home and put them into interesting patterns on her
mother's carpet. Then she ~~takes~~ *took* a big can of industrial-strength glue and glued
them together. Her mother ~~is~~ *was* not amused by this tire-shred mosaic. Sometimes the
glue stuck to the carpet. On those occasions, Judy's mother shook her fists and
~~chases~~ *chased* Judy around the house. Then one day, an art critic ~~walks~~ *walked* through the neighborhood in search of folk art. The critic saw Judy's tire-shred mosaic and ~~buys~~ *bought* it
for a thousand dollars. Judy's mother ~~smiles~~ *smiled*. She was very proud of her artistic
daughter.

Exercise 12

1. A

2. P

3. P; A police officer questioned the victim at the scene of the accident.

4. P; The solemn judge sentenced the noisy rappers to listen to a hundred waltz CDs.

5. P; Hungry bears interrupted the picnic.

6. P; During the confusion, the bears grabbed the food.

7. P; I have given you your last warning.

8. P

9. A

10. P; You may post book reviews on many different online sites.

Exercise 14

1. My watch runs slowly.

2. My computer costs little.

3. The horse ran swiftly.

4. They wrote well.

Chapter 5, continued

5. The dog sleeps on the bed.

6. Mr. Hawkins sells real estate.

7. José attends Santa Ana College.

8. I like this assignment.

9. We students have succeeded here.

10. She combs her hair.

Exercise 16

1. were

2. were

3. were

4. were

5. be

Review 1

	From	*To*
1.	is	was
2.	is	was
	begins	began
3.	runs	ran
4.	works	worked
5.	gives	gave

Review 2

1. was

2. were

3. was

4. was

5. were

Review 4

1. Whitney is rebuilding her desktop.

2. Anika can lead our group.

3. Matthew scored the last touchdown.

4. Maria works at the department store.

5. Jonathan attracts favorable attention.

Chapter 6
Exercise 1
1. her
2. She, I
3. he
4. them, us
5. me, us
6. We
7. We, him
8. who
9. whomever
10. me

Exercise 3
1. Whom
2. whom
3. whom, I
4. whom
5. who
6. who
7. who
8. Whom
9. who
10. Who

Exercise 5
1. me
2. me
3. who
4. I
5. who
6. who
7. whom
8. me
9. who
10. who, who

Chapter 6, continued

Exercise 8

	From	*To*
1.	you	they
	you	they
2.	you	she
3.	you	I
4.	you	they
5.	you	they
6.	you	we
	you were	we are
7.	you	they
8.	you	they
9.	you	she
10.	you	he

Exercise 10

1. its
2. he or she
3. his or her
4. it
5. his
6. their
7. his or her
8. their
9. their
10. its

Exercise 12

1. they, us
2. they
3. their
4. their
5. their
6. they
7. his or her
8. they

Chapter 6, continued

9. his

10. his or her

Exercise 14

1. (a) V

   (b) OK

2. (a) OK

   (b) V

3. (a) V

   (b) OK

4. (a) V

   (b) OK

5. (a) V

   (b) OK

6. (a) V

   (b) OK

7. (a) OK

   (b) V

8. (a) V

   (b) OK

9. (a) V

   (b) OK

10. (a) OK

    (b) V

Review 1

1. me

2. who

3. me

4. me

5. We

Review 2

	From	*To*
1.	you	one
2.	you go	he goes

Chapter 6, continued

3. one   you
4. you   I
5. you   him

Review 3

	From	*To*
1.	C	
2.	their	its
3.	his	their
4.	their	his
5.	his	their

Review 4

	From	*To*
1.	their	his or her
2.	they	he or she
3.	his or her	their
4.	their	his
5.	he or she	they

Review 5

1. that kind of control made
2. Joanne said to Mabel, "I want my paycheck."
3. According to a well-known saying, we
4. Jim's coworkers say
5. Louanne, "I bought . . . price."

Chapter 7

Exercise 3

1. most
2. real
3. bad
4. hardly
5. most
6. badly
7. most
8. hardly
9. really
10. best, best

Chapter 7, continued

Exercise 4

	From	*To*
1.	real	really
2.	no	any
3.	good	well
4.	no	any
5.	well	good
6.	real	really
7.	more	more nearly
8.	never	ever
9.	real	really
	horribler	more horrible
10.	most nastiest	nastiest

Exercise 5

1. really, well
2. most
3. greatest
4. any
5. worse
6. friendlier
7. well
8. most
9. most
10. well

Exercise 7

1. D; As we drove through the field, the wild jackrabbits were excited.

2. M; Carrying fresh meat, the delivery truck drove past the library.

3. D; Walking through the meadow, we observed that the satisfied wolverines slept deeply after gorging on the road kill.

4. M; Hoping to meet an available female, he went for a walk with his cute puppy.

5. M; Watching a television program, I saw a slimy monster.

6. M; Nursing a head wound inflicted by crazed weasels, the lass ran home to her parents.

7. M; I fearfully began to unwrap the ticking package from my loved one.

8. M; I watched the plane trailing smoke and flames.

Chapter 7, continued

9. M; I saw the men, soaked to the bone, remove their boots at the front door.

10. D; To avoid the construction, the driver took a detour.

Review 1

Old-time cowboys are among the ~~better~~ ^{best-}known figures in American folklore. Of course, they were ~~versatiler~~ ^{more versatile} than the word *cowboy* suggests. They did whatever work was needed on ranches, and they were able to do it ~~real good~~ ^{really well}. They mended fences, built sheds, took care of ranch equipment, and branded calves. They rounded up cattle, riding on their horses. Many times the roundups, as they were called, took in hundreds of square miles of range. After the cattle were rounded up, some were taken as trail herds to places such as Dodge City, Kansas, to be sold.

Chapter 8

Exercise 1

1. vicious, relentless, (and) inexplicable
2. family moves (and) it finds
3. to make (and) to ignore
4. invited (but) neglected
5. has inherited (and) has caused
6. physician separates (and) they hate
7. twin is (and) other is
8. embittered (and) vindictive
9. unreasoning, angry, (and) brutal
10. crashes (and) devours

Exercise 3

1. X; change eating to eat
2. X; change escaping to escapes
3. X; delete he finds
4. X; delete having
5. P
6. X; change dish, to dish and
7. X; change upsetting to upset
8. X; delete who had

Chapter 8, continued

9. P

10. X; change <u>becoming</u> to <u>become</u>

Exercise 5

1. color, amazement

2. action-packed

3. how to save them

4. to live

5. joys, sorrows

6. truth, justice, freedom

7. survives, triumphs

8. love, care

9. fly, float

10. loves, sends

Exercise 6

1. hulking, unrelenting

2. to destroy

3. life, woman

4. survive

5. humans are the slaves

6. begins

7. attack

8. to destroy

9. ugly, harmless

10. arrogant, obnoxious

Exercise 7

1. (not only) robbed . . . (but also) gave

2. (Both) Humphrey Bogart (and) Katharine Hepburn

3. (either) himself (or) Mr. Hyde

4. (neither) . . . jobs (nor) compassion

5. (either) die . . . (or) go

6. (either) develop . . . (or) go

7. (not only) gets . . . (but also) goes

8. (both) who framed (and) who is playing

Chapter 8, continued

9. (not only) heartaches (but also) . . . joy
10. (either) his dignity (or) his life

Review 1

   Ken Kesey wrote *One Flew over the Cuckoo's Nest* as a novel. It was later made into a stage play and a film. The title was taken from a children's folk rhyme: "One flew east, one flew west, / One flew over the cuckoo's nest."

   The narrator in the novel is Chief Bromden, the central character is Randle McMurphy, and Nurse Ratched ~~is the villain.~~ the villian is Bromden sees and ~~can~~ hear but does not speak. He is a camera with a conscience. McMurphy is both an outcast and ~~serves as~~ a leader, and he speaks out for freedom and ~~as an individual.~~ individuality Nurse Ratched is the voice of repression. She is the main representative of what Bromdon calls the "Combine." She organizes, directs, controls, and, if necessary to her purposes, ~~will~~ destroy.

Chapter 9
Exercise 1

   1. .
   2. !
   3. .
   4. !
   5. !
   6. .
   7. .
   8. .
   9. ?
   10. .

Exercise 3

   1. consideration,
   2. cowpokes, . . . hungry,
   3. belief, . . . thick,
   4. Barstow, California, . . . Mojave, . . . Las Vegas,

Chapter 9, continued

5. decided, therefore, . . . open,

6. Winthrop, . . . match, . . . Cleveland,

7. marshmallows, Pies,

8. small,

9. gang, . . . bored,

10. knew, of course,

11. kit, . . . sixties,

12. young, . . . harried,

13. responded, of course,

14. kind,

15. gum, talk,

16. I, however,

17. You, sir, . . . Fullerton,

18. Dumas, . . . *Musketeers,*

19. was, however,

20. 19, 1961,

Exercise 5

1. monster, . . . desperate,

2. house,

3. simple,

4. however,

5. monster, . . . dejected,

6. innocent, . . . brother,

7. horror,

8. demands,

9. him,

10. away, . . . parts,

11. anticipation,

12. project,

13. say, . . . unexpected,

14. away,

15. married, . . . fully, . . . enraged,

16. wedding, . . . horrified,

17. killing the monster,

Chapter 9, continued

18. desolate, . . . North,

19. visit,

20. friend, love, . . . soul, and, therefore,

Exercise 7

1. society,

2. horses;

3. farm;

4. horses;

5. honest;

6. careful; otherwise,

7. age,

8. condition;

9. problem;

10. older,

11. traders;

12. horses;

13. horses,

14. men,

15. OK

16. pulling; therefore,

17. horses; after all,

18. animals; therefore, . . . Liberal, Kansas; Waco, Texas; and Seminole, Oklahoma.

19. riding,

20. people;

Exercise 9

1. Professor Jones said, "Now we will read from The Complete Works of Edgar Allan Poe."

2. The enthusiastic students shouted, "We like Poe! We like Poe!"

3. The professor lectured for fifty-seven minutes before he finally said, "In conclusion, I say that Poe was an unappreciated writer during his lifetime."

4. The next speaker said, "I believe that Poe said, 'A short story should be short enough so that a person can read it in one sitting.'"

Chapter 9, continued

5. Then, while students squirmed, he read The "Fall of the House of Usher" in sixty-eight minutes.

6. "Now we will do some reading in unison," said Professor Jones.

7. Each student opened a copy of <u>The Complete Works of Edgar Allan Poe</u>.

8. "Turn to page 72," said Professor Jones.

9. "What parts do we read?" asked a student.

10. "You read the words, or maybe I should say word, of the raven," said the professor.

Exercise 11

1. Ben Johnson (1572–1637) wrote these poems: "On My First Son" and "Though I Am Young and Cannot Tell."

2. William Blake (1757–1827)—he is my favorite poet—wrote "The Tyger."

3. In that famous poem, he included the following words: "Tyger, Tyger, [the spelling of his time] burning bright / In the forests of the night."

4. Rudyard Kipling (1865–1936) wrote in several forms: short stories, poems, and novels.

5. Robert Frost (1874–1963)—he is probably America's best-loved poet—lived in New England for most of his life.

6. He wrote about many subjects in his environment: trees, walls, spiders, and ants.

7. Poet, philosopher, speaker—Frost had many talents.

8. Dylan Thomas (1914–1953) was a great poet and a flamboyant individual.

9. Thomas acquired a reputation—some day he didn't deserve it—for being a drunk.

10. One of Thomas's most moving poems, "Fern Hill," begins with this line: "Now as I was young and easy under the apple boughs."

Exercise 13

1. "I've heard that you intend to move to El Paso, Texas," my brother-in-law said.

2. "My date of departure on United Airlines is July 11," I answered.

3. "Then you've only thirty-three days remaining in California," he said.

4. My mother gave me some Samsonite luggage, and Dad gave me a Ronson razor.

5. Jennifer does not know I am leaving for the University of Texas.

6. Jennifer, my mother's dog, is one-quarter poodle and three-quarters cocker spaniel.

7. That dog's immediate concern is almost always food rather than sentimentality.

Chapter 9, continued

8. I wouldn't have received my scholarship without the straight <u>A</u>'s from my elective classes.

9. I am quite indebted to Professor Jackson, a first-rate teacher of English and several courses in speech.

10. I wasn't surprised when Grandma gave me a box of stationery and a note asking me to write Mother each Friday.

Review 1

1. There's the question of defining a healthy or well-functioning family.

2. What measure is appropriate to make that judgment?

3. "You can't really talk about 'good' families unless you're talking about good for what," said Marian Yarrow, a psychologist at the National Institute of Mental Health.

4. Some believe that even the definition of <u>family</u> is ambiguous.

5. The Census Bureau considers a family to be "two or more persons related through birth, marriage, or adoption living under one roof."

6. Until recently, popular image dictated that a family consisted of a mother, a father, and two children.

7. But the reality is that families come in all shapes and sizes: traditional families, stepfamilies, blended families, single-parent families, childless couples, and extended families.

Chapter 10

Exercise 1

1. hear

2. than

3. their

4. through

5. piece

6. all right

7. passed

8. too

9. advice

10. a lot

11. already

12. chose

13. receive

14. quite

15. could have

16. lose

Chapter 10, continued

17. it's

18. accept

19. know

20. paid

Review 1

1. famous

2. location

3. noticeable

4. dropped

5. likely

6. hopeless

7. management

8. hottest

9. robbed

10. stopped

11. safely

12. argument

13. judgment

14. courageous

15. swimming

16. committed

17. occurrence

18. omitted

19. beginning

20. preferred

Chapter 13

Exercise 1

    Young voters are not voting ~~the way~~ *as often as* they should. The latest figures show

that only 20 percent are going to the ~~poles~~ *polls*. The next-older generation ~~is,~~ the

so-called baby boomers, ~~they~~ are going to the ~~poles~~ *polls* at about twice that rate.

Because I'm part of the young group, I'm concerned, but the answers to why

we usually don't bother to vote are ~~as~~ obvious ~~as the nose on your face. For~~ *One factor is that*

~~one thing the~~ *many* younger people don't think voting changes anything. The politi-

Chapter 13, continued

cal parties are all about the same, and the candidates look and talk alike, even

though they seem angry with each other. ~~For another~~ ^{A factor is that many} ~~a lot of~~ young voters

don't have parents ~~that~~ ^{who} voted or even talked about politics when they were

growing up, they don't either. ^{so} Still another ~~thing~~ ^{point} is that the issues ~~going~~ ^{current}

~~around~~ don't ~~more~~ ^{inspire} young people that much. The politicians talk about the

national debt and social security and health care ~~and~~ ^{but} we're concerned about

jobs and the high cost of education. If ~~they could get people we~~ ^{political parties would offer candidates we} could believe

in and ~~they~~ ^{those candidates} would talk about issue^s that matter to us, then maybe ~~they'd see~~

^{we'd vote.} ~~more of us at the polls.~~

Chapter 15

Exercise 1

The Leadership of Martin Luther King, Jr.

1   On December 1, 1955, in Montgomery, Alabama, a <u>black woman</u> named <u>Rosa Parks</u> was <u>arrested</u> for <u>refusing to give up</u> her <u>bus seat</u> to a <u>white man</u>. In <u>protest</u>, <u>Montgomery blacks</u> organized a <u>year-long bus boycott</u>. The boycott <u>forced white city leaders</u> to <u>recognize</u> the <u>blacks' determination and economic power</u>.

2   <u>One of</u> the <u>organizers</u> of the bus boycott was a Baptist minister, the Reverend <u>Martin Luther King, Jr</u>. King <u>soon</u> became a <u>national leader</u> in the growing <u>civil rights movment</u>. With stirring speeches and personal courage, he <u>urged blacks</u> to <u>demand their rights</u>. At the same time, he was completely <u>committed to nonviolence</u>. Like Gandhi, . . . he believed that justice could triumph through moral force.

3   In April 1963, <u>King began</u> a <u>drive</u> to <u>end segregation</u> in <u>Birmingham, Alabama</u>. <u>He</u> and his <u>followers boycotted segregated business</u> and <u>held peaceful marches</u> and <u>demonstrations.</u> Against them, the Birmingham <u>police used electric cattle prods, attack dogs, clubs</u>, and <u>fire hoses</u> to break up marches.

4   <u>Television cameras</u> brought those <u>scenes</u> into the <u>living rooms of millions of Americans</u>, who were <u>shocked</u> by what they saw. On <u>May 10</u>, Birmingham's <u>city leaders gave in</u>. A <u>committee</u> of <u>blacks</u>

Chapter 15, continued

<u>and whites oversaw</u> the gradual <u>desegregation of the city</u> and <u>tried</u> to <u>open</u> more <u>jobs</u> for <u>blacks</u>. The <u>victory</u> was later <u>marred</u> by grief, however, when a <u>bomb exploded</u> at a Birmingham <u>church, killing four black children</u>.

Chapter 22
Exercise 1
1. O
2. F
3. O
4. F
5. F
6. F
7. O

Exercise 3
1. PH
2. FD
3. HG
4. PH/AH
5. FA
6. AH
7. PH
8. HG
9. PH
10. AH

Appendix A
Exercise 1
1. n, prep
2. adj, v
3. adv, prep
4. conj, adj
5. prep, adj
6. pro, v
7. adj, n
8. v, adj

Appendix A, continued

9. pro,   conj

10. adj,   adj

11. adj,   adj

12. v,   n

13. pro,   adj

14. adj,   prep

15. conj,   conj

16. v,   conj

17. adj,   n

18. adj,   adj

19. conj,   n

20. v,   n

Appendix D

Exercise

George Washington at Trenton

One of *the* most famous battles during the War of Independence ~~occur~~ *occurred* at Trenton, New Jersey, on Christmas Eve of ~~the~~ 1776. The colonists *were* outmatched in supplies and finances and ~~were~~ outnumbered in troop strength. Most observers in other countries ~~think~~ *thought the* rebellion would be put down soon. *The* British *were* overconfident and ~~believe~~ *believed* there would be no more battles until spring. But George Washington ~~decide~~ *decided* to fight one more time. That Christmas, while *a* large army of Britishers *were having a* party and thinking about the holiday season, *the* Americans set out for *a* surprise raid. They loaded onto boats used for carrying ore and rowed across *the* Delaware River. George Washington stood tall in *the* lead boat. According to legend, *the* drummer boy floated across *the* river on his drum, pulled by *a* rope tied to *a* boat. Because *the* British did not feel threatened by the ragtag colonist forces, they *were* unprepared to do battle. The colonists stormed *the* living quarters and the general assembly hall and achieved victory. It was good for the colonists' morale, something they needed, for they would endure *a* long, hard winter before they fighting again.

Text Credits

Maya Angelou, "Liked for Myself," from *I Know Why the Caged Bird Sings* by Maya Angelou. Copyright © 1969 by Maya Angelou. Reprinted by permission of Random House, Inc.

José Antonio Burciaga, "A Mixed Tex-Cal Marriage," from *Drink Cultura* by José Antonio Burciaga, Joshua Odell Editions, Santa Barbara, 1993. Reprinted with permission of Cecilia P. Burciaga.

Linda Ellerbee, "Television Changed My Family Forever," from *Move On*, copyright © 1991 by Linda Ellerbee. Used by permission of Putnam Berkley, a division of Penguin Putnam, Inc.

Sheila Ferguson, from *Soul Food* by Sheila Ferguson. Copyright © 1989 by Sheila Ferguson. Used by permission of Grove/Atlantic, Inc.

John Fire/Lame Deer, "Listening to the Air." Reprinted with permission of Simon & Schuster from *Lame Deer, Seeker of Visions* by John Fire/Lame Deer and Richard Erdoes. Copyright © 1972 by John Fire/Lame Deer and Richard Erdoes.

Barbara Garson, "McDonald's—We Do It All for You." Reprinted with the permission of Simon & Schuster from *The Electronic Sweatshop*, by Barbara Garson. Copyright © 1988 by Barbara Garson.

Jonathan Gaw, "Are Kids Too Tangled in the Web?" from the *Minneapolis St. Paul Star Tribune*, September 7, 1997, p. B1. Reprinted with permission.

Keith A. King, "Should School Uniforms Be Mandated in Elementary Schools?" Reprinted with permission from *Journal of School Health*. American School Health Association, Kent, OH.

N. Scott Momaday, "The Story of the Well-Made Shield." Copyright © 1992 by N. Scott Momaday, from *In the Presence of the Sun: Stories and Poems*, by N. Scott Momaday. Reprinted by permission of St. Martin's Press, LLC.

Louis Nizer, "How About Low-Cost Drugs for Addicts" from the *New York Times*, 1986. Copyright © 1986 by The New York Times Co. Reprinted by permission.

Jennifer Oldham, "Amid Backlash, Calls for Cell Phone Etiquette," by Jennifer Oldham, staff writer for the *Los Angeles Times* from July 15, 1999. Copyright Los Angeles Times. Reprinted by permission.

Rou Rivenburg, "The Mean Season," by Roy Rivenburg, staff writer for the *Los Angeles Times* from July 14, 1995, p. E-1. Copyright Los Angeles Times. Reprinted by permission.

Gary Soto, "The Jacket," from *A Summer Life*. Copyright © 1990 by University Press of New England. Reprinted by permission.

Bob Walter, "Work, Work, Work: For Workaholics, the Job Can Be a Disease . . ." from The *Sacramento Bee*, April 17, 1994. Copyright, The Sacramento Bee, reprinted with permission.

Yi-Fu Tuan, "American Space, Chinese Place," by Yi-Fu Tuan. Copyright © 1974 by *Harper's Magazine*. All rights reserved. Reproduced from the July issue by special permission.

Author and Title Index

Subject Index

verb tenses
consistency in, 97, 104, 268
and irregular verbs, 82–85
kinds of, 89–92
in narratives, 268, 280
perfect, 90, 91
perfect progressive, 90, 92
points for ESL students, 410
progressive, 90, 91
and regular verbs, 80–82
simple, 89, 90
vocabulary, self-evaluation of, 4. *See also*
diction; words

weather, whether, 203
whether/or, 156, 159
which, 44
who, whom, 44, 112, 127

whoever, whomever, 44
word choice. *See* diction
words
abstract and concrete, 282
combination, 156
compound, 184, 190
confusing, 200–203
filler, 11, 94
frequently misspelled, 199–200
general and specific, 282
hyphenated, 184
quotation marks for special, 176
repetition of key, 232
sequence, 231, 241
signal, in parallel structure, 150–151,
156
transitional, 231 (*see also* transitional
words)

write, writen, written, 203
writing process
defined, 214
editing, 232–233, 238
organizing support, 224–226
prewriting strategies, 215–220
revising, 231–232, 238
strategies for self-improvement in,
2–5
writing effective topic sentences,
221–222
writing first draft, 230–231,
238
See also prewriting strategies
Writing Process Worksheet, 4, 6, 214,
233–234, 238, 269

you're, your, 203

Writing Process Worksheet

TITLE _____

NAME _____ DUE DATE _____

ASSIGNMENT

In the space below, write whatever you need to know about your assignment, including information about the topic, audience, pattern of writing, length, whether to include a rough draft or revised drafts, and whether your paper must be typed.

STAGE ONE

Explore   Freewrite, brainstorm (list), cluster, or take notes as directed by your instructor. Use the back of this page or separate paper if you need more space.

STAGE TWO

Organize   Write a topic sentence or thesis; label the subject and the treatment parts.

Write an outline or an outline alternative.

STAGE THREE

Write   On separate paper, write and then revise your paper as many times as necessary for coherence, language (usage, tone, and diction), unity, emphasis, support, and sentences (CLUESS). Read your paper aloud to hear and correct any grammatical errors or awkward-sounding sentences.

Edit any problems in fundamentals, such as capitalization, omissions, punctuation, and spelling (COPS).

Writing Process Worksheet

TITLE _____

NAME _____ DUE DATE _____

ASSIGNMENT In the space below, write whatever you need to know about your assignment, including information about the topic, audience, pattern of writing, length, whether to include a rough draft or revised drafts, and whether your paper must be typed.

STAGE ONE **Explore** Freewrite, brainstorm (list), cluster, or take notes as directed by your instructor. Use the back of this page or separate paper if you need more space.

STAGE TWO **Organize** Write a topic sentence or thesis; label the subject and the treatment parts.

Write an outline or an outline alternative.

STAGE THREE **Write** On separate paper, write and then revise your paper as many times as necessary for coherence, language (usage, tone, and diction), unity, emphasis, support, and sentences (CLUESS). Read your paper aloud to hear and correct any grammatical errors or awkward-sounding sentences.

Edit any problems in fundamentals, such as capitalization, omissions, punctuation, and spelling (COPS).

Writing Process Worksheet

TITLE _____

NAME _____ DUE DATE _____

ASSIGNMENT In the space below, write whatever you need to know about your assignment, including information about the topic, audience, pattern of writing, length, whether to include a rough draft or revised drafts, and whether your paper must be typed.

STAGE ONE **Explore** Freewrite, brainstorm (list), cluster, or take notes as directed by your instructor. Use the back of this page or separate paper if you need more space.

STAGE TWO **Organize** Write a topic sentence or thesis; label the subject and the treatment parts.

Write an outline or an outline alternative.

STAGE THREE **Write** On separate paper, write and then revise your paper as many times as necessary for coherence, language (usage, tone, and diction), unity, emphasis, support, and sentences (CLUESS). Read your paper aloud to hear and correct any grammatical errors or awkward-sounding sentences.

Edit any problems in fundamentals, such as capitalization, omissions, punctuation, and spelling (COPS).

Writing Process Worksheet

TITLE _____

NAME _____ DUE DATE _____

ASSIGNMENT   In the space below, write whatever you need to know about your assignment, including information about the topic, audience, pattern of writing, length, whether to include a rough draft or revised drafts, and whether your paper must be typed.

STAGE ONE   **Explore**   Freewrite, brainstorm (list), cluster, or take notes as directed by your instructor. Use the back of this page or separate paper if you need more space.

STAGE TWO   **Organize**   Write a topic sentence or thesis; label the subject and the treatment parts.

Write an outline or an outline alternative.

STAGE THREE   **Write**   On separate paper, write and then revise your paper as many times as necessary for coherence, language (usage, tone, and diction), unity, emphasis, support, and sentences (CLUESS). Read your paper aloud to hear and correct any grammatical errors or awkward-sounding sentences.

Edit any problems in fundamentals, such as capitalization, omissions, punctuation, and spelling (COPS).

Writing Process Worksheet

TITLE _____

NAME _____ DUE DATE _____

ASSIGNMENT In the space below, write whatever you need to know about your assignment, including information about the topic, audience, pattern of writing, length, whether to include a rough draft or revised drafts, and whether your paper must be typed.

STAGE ONE **Explore** Freewrite, brainstorm (list), cluster, or take notes as directed by your instructor. Use the back of this page or separate paper if you need more space.

STAGE TWO **Organize** Write a topic sentence or thesis; label the subject and the treatment parts.

Write an outline or an outline alternative.

STAGE THREE **Write** On separate paper, write and then revise your paper as many times as necessary for coherence, language (usage, tone, and diction), unity, emphasis, support, and sentences (CLUESS). Read your paper aloud to hear and correct any grammatical errors or awkward-sounding sentences.

Edit any problems in fundamentals, such as capitalization, omissions, punctuation, and spelling (COPS).

Writing Process Worksheet

TITLE _____

NAME _____ DUE DATE _____

ASSIGNMENT In the space below, write whatever you need to know about your assignment, including information about the topic, audience, pattern of writing, length, whether to include a rough draft or revised drafts, and whether your paper must be typed.

STAGE ONE **Explore** Freewrite, brainstorm (list), cluster, or take notes as directed by your instructor. Use the back of this page or separate paper if you need more space.

STAGE TWO **Organize** Write a topic sentence or thesis; label the subject and the treatment parts.

Write an outline or an outline alternative.

STAGE THREE **Write** On separate paper, write and then revise your paper as many times as necessary for coherence, language (usage, tone, and diction), unity, emphasis, support, and sentences (CLUESS). Read your paper aloud to hear and correct any grammatical errors or awkward-sounding sentences.

Edit any problems in fundamentals, such as capitalization, omissions, punctuation, and spelling (COPS).